THE COMPLETE GUIDE TO
RUTAN AIRCRAFT
THIRD EDITION
DON & JULIA DOWNIE

TAB BOOKS Inc.
Blue Ridge Summit, PA

To the hard-working homebuilders reaching for affordable flying through innovative concepts; may they continue to build fine airframes with new designs, leading the way to aviation's future.

THIRD EDITION
SECOND PRINTING

Printed in the United States of America

Library of Congress Cataloging in Publication Data

Downie, Don.
The complete guide to Rutan aircraft.

Includes index.
1. Airplanes, Home-built. I. Downie, Julia.
II. Title.
TL671.2.D63   1987   629.133′340422   87-7107
ISBN 0-8306-2420-1 (pbk.)

Cover photographs courtesy of Downie and Associates.

Questions regarding the content of this book
should be addressed to:

Reader Inquiry Branch
Editorial Department
TAB BOOKS Inc.
P.O. Box 40
Blue Ridge Summit, PA 17214

Contents

Foreword

In every field of creative activity the influence of one person will, at some point, change the course of that activity dramatically for all time.

Burt Rutan's influence on aviation is profound, and it is interesting to take a look at this phenomenon.

Burt's productivity is legendary. His energy and drive have made it possible for him to complete projects in weeks that others might expect to require in years.

Originality is, of course, the hallmark of Burt Rutan. This is true in operating procedures as well as airplane design. His car-top test rig used to measure stability and control characteristics of design configurations has been used by others—but by no one more effectively than Burt.

Canard airplane configurations go back to the Wright Brothers, but none have been as successful as Burt's. Many new designs are now showing up as canards, and it is easy to speculate that Burt will be remembered as the man who re-introduced them.

Most designers create only one airplane design, and the rest of their efforts are variations on that theme. It has been said that Burt doesn't even copy himself.

Integrity is another of Burt's attributes. This is manifested in his reluctance to release designs without adequate testing.

There is no doubt of Burt's influence on the future homebuilt aircraft, and it is very likely that his innovations will point the way for improved general aviation aircraft as well. All aviation is his beneficiary.

John Thorp

John Thorp is one of the most respected aircraft designers in the United States—or any other country. The developer of many innovative designs, from the pre-WWII Lockheed Little Dipper to his popular T-18 homebuilt, Thorp has earned the respect of the entire aviation community.—Don Downie

Introduction

We first met Burt Rutan at a mini-symposium of the Society of Experimental Test Pilots in San Diego, California. The next time we saw him was at Brackett Field near Los Angeles, California, where he was just beginning to demonstrate his new twin-engine Defiant to the aviation press. At that time, the eminently successful "push-pull" had only 30 hours flight time and was barely permitted into the Los Angeles area.

We approached Burt about doing this book on several occasions before he found enough time in his schedule to give us the green light. At that time, he supplied copies of his voluminous quarterly builders publication, *Canard Pusher*, a detailed package of how-to-do-it instructions he had prepared to educate new builders in the fine art of foam and fiberglass structures. We waded through a great many magazine articles—some accurate and some very "blue sky"—about Rutan, who is a designer unique in homebuilt aircraft circles.

We flew with Burt in his other designs. We flew with his brother Dick in the popular Long-EZ

prototype and then went on to fly the ship solo. We flew in the No. 2 VariViggen with builder Mike Melvill. We took Rutan's parents, George and Irene Rutan, in the back of our Cessna to a VariEze fly-in at Bullhead City, Arizona, and absorbed the flavor and enthusiasm of the growing family of builders who share both flying and fabrication experiences with each other. We "kicked tires" and admired the meticulous detail many homebuilders who have vested unending hours in work and rework to come out with a product of which they are truly proud—as they should be.

It is certainly fitting that Rutan's developments have been made in the Mojave Desert, "over the hill" from the Southern California hub of aerospace activity. This is where many aviation and space breakthroughs have been made. And one of the more enjoyable parts of the preparation of this material has been the many flights up over the Sierra Madre Mountains to Mojave, where Rutan's RAF (Rutan Aircraft Factory) is located.

Once you top the mountains, usually at 8500 or

9000 feet, you make a radio call to Edwards Approach to find out if Restricted Area 2515 is "hot." If the famed Edwards Air Force Flight Test Center is working, you must deviate over Palmdale and on up the highway and railroad to Mojave, a WWII Marine test center. On most weekends, however, the air is free and "Eddie Approach" will supply traffic advisories and let you fly directly over this great base. At the time of the development of the first supersonic aircraft, the broad dry lake at Edwards AFB was perhaps the most valuable piece of real estate in the free world. It provided isolated security plus a broad table-top airfield where very high-speed aircraft could be landed safely "gear-up." The sonic barrier was first broken here by the X-1. Even the first flight of the NASA space shuttle landed here.

Some of these flying visits to Mojave have been a bit stimulating. Winds swirling over the Sierra Madres can cause their own special brand of turbulence where you have the camera cases and yourselves well tied down in flight. Midday summer dust devils and blossoming cumuli over the desert make for excellent sailplane flying, but do produce a rough ride in a light powered aircraft. When you sit in the air-conditioned sanctity of Rutan's back office and design room, you frequently hear the wind pick up, bang doors, rattle the roof, blow sand, and generally make its presence known. You never leave your airplane parked in front of Mojave's RAF without having it securely tied down. On more than one occasion, our departure takeoff has been made right from Rutan's tiedowns, facing down the taxi ramp into a 30 to 35-knot wind that would beep the stall warner even before the plane was untied. Under these conditions, one or more of Rutan's staff would hold the wing struts until we had completed our run-up and were pointed directly into the wind. These are just some of the interesting things that happen at Mojave.

The three years since the first edition of this book was written have been exciting, not only to Burt Rutan, his family and associates, but to the aviation community in general. And the two of us

have continued to fly over the hills to meet with new builders and keep an eye on developments. We have seen Rutan's procedures streamlined with videotaped builder aids and regularly scheduled miniseminars and flight demonstrations. We have journeyed each year to Oshkosh and watched the new canards expand "EZ Street" to a four-lane freeway. We've joined a banquet room filled with Rutan's builders from all over the United States and several foreign countries.

We've flown Rutan's do-it-yourself soaring design, the self-launching Solitaire. We've also launched off in the one-of-a-kind AMS/OIL racing biplane and the STOL bush plane, The Grizzly.

Above and beyond the homebuilt scene has been prototype development of the Fairchild NGT (New Generation Trainer) and the formation of SCALED (Scaled Composites: the Advance Link to Efficient Development) in a plush new 30,000-square foot facility adjoining the original RAF hangar and office at Mojave.

In the fall of 1983, the 85 percent prototype Starship I, the twin pusher canard for Beechcraft, came out of Rutan's new development company, SCALED Composites, Inc. The company also developed a one-of-a-kind microlight for the late Colin Chapman, director of the Lotus Company in England. Who knows what is now brewing behind the closely guarded doors at SCALED? (Even the Shadow may not know!)

Perhaps the most intriguing activity at Mojave, however, is the very hush-hush Voyager project. Voyager's crew hopes to fly around the world, nonstop, non-refueled. The audacity of this small group of pioneers, working only with their own talent and their own money in planning to conquer one of the few remaining aviation challenges on our planet, seems more exciting than any of the plots on today's soaps.

In the past, aviation's pioneering activity has come from Wichita and Kerrville, Lock Haven and Vero Beach, or Seattle and Fort Worth. Today, much of this action originates at Mojave.

The eight years since the first edition of this book was written have been exciting, not only to Burt Rutan, his family and associates, but to the aviation community in general. And the two of us have continued to fly over the hills to meet with new builders and keep an eye on developments. We have seen Rutan's procedures streamlined with videotaped builder aids and regularly scheduled mini-seminars and flight demonstrations. We have journeyed each year to Oshkosh and watched the new canards expand "EZ Street" to a four-lane freeway.

We've flown Rutan's do-it-yourself soaring design, the self-launching Solitaire. We've also launched off in the one-of-a-kind AMS/OIL racing biplane and the STOL bush plane, the Grizzly.

Above and beyond the homebuilt scene has been prototype development of the Fairchild NGT (New Generation Trainer) and the formation of SCALED (Scaled Composites: the Advance Link to Efficient Development) in a plush new 30,000-square-foot facility adjoining the original RAF hangar and office at Mojave.

In the fall of 1983, the 85 percent prototype Starship I, the twin pusher canard for Beechcraft, came out of Rutan's new development company, SCALED Composites, Inc. The company also developed a one-of-a-kind microlight for the late Colin Chapman, director of the Lotus Company in England. SCALED became a subsidiary of Beech Aircraft and Burt joined Beech as a Vice President, Engineering. RAF was closed as Burt went out of the kitplane business except for token builder aid.

Voyager, the very hush-hush round-the-world, nonstop, nonrefuel project, took shape and against overwhelming odds became the aviation success story of the decade. It has been a fascinating story to cover over these past six years. In this edition, you will find a condensed report on Voyager: how it was built, how it flew, who were the volunteers who helped, and the dramatic ending.

Burt Rutan is in the prime of life. He is continuing to develop new and successful designs. Who knows what will occur to make yet another chapter for a future edition of this book?

Chapter 1

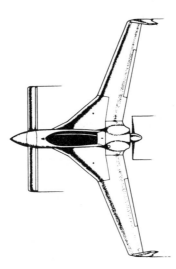

The Rutan Revolution

A wild and wonderful thing happened to aviation in 1975. That's the year that the first canard pusher VariEze was introduced at the EAA's mammoth fly-in at Oshkosh, Wisconsin. Little did any of us covering the aviation scene visualize what might follow.

With little exaggeration, what happened then might be called "The Rutan Revolution." Following the first public exposure to this unique, novel, weird, spectacular, completely unconventional little airplane, the whole picture of homebuilding changed. The aerodynamics and construction procedures perfected on the VariEze went right down the line to the Quickie design, the Long-EZ, push-pull Defiant, experimental STOL Grizzly, and the prize-winning self-launching sailplane, Solitaire.

The majority of really popular homebuilt designs to come along since that time have had Rutan's influence to a greater or lesser degree. Among the non-Rutan designs are the Q2, Dragonfly, and Glasair.

The crowning glory to date, both in size and market potential, is Starship I, presently the

world's largest composite aircraft (see Chapter 14). Developed by Rutan's SCALED Composite, Inc., for the Beechcraft Corporation, Starship was the hit of the 1983 NBAA (National Business Aircraft Association) Convention and points the way to a whole new line of licensed composite production aircraft.

The start of it all was Rutan's prototype VariEze, now enshrined in the EAA's sparkling museum at Oshkosh. This was the opening of perhaps the most exciting chapter in modern aviation. It breathed new life into a humdrum production of conventional all-metal aircraft where annual improvements are usually slightly more power, more accessories, and more price at the expense of performance.

OUTSTANDING NEW DESIGNS

The largest aviation meeting in the world takes place in Oshkosh, Wisconsin each August (see *The Oshkosh Fly-In*, TAB Book No. 2315, for history and details). During the conclave, the EAA presents many awards. One of the most coveted is the "Outstanding New Design" trophy. In 1974, this award went to Burt Rutan for the VariViggen. The 1975 award was also Burt's; this time for the VariEze. And again in 1978 a Rutan design was the recipient as the Quickie was honored. Each of these designs is detailed in subsequent chapters.

THE HOMEBUILT SCENE

The homebuilt scene in aviation is a careful melding of innovative designs and a pioneering of new materials, systems and structures to produce some of the finest airplanes in the air. It's the builder and the pilot (not always the same person) who explore the flight test envelope on each new product, and there are many of them. It's the pilot-owner who takes his new pride and joy cross-country, spreading the gospel of his new design throughout the land. It's the FAA, in part, who watches like a fitful parent as these offspring leap off into a world of flight sometimes larger and more challenging than that visualized in the designer's eye.

The homebuilt scene also encompasses the Experimental Aircraft Association (EAA), the veteran organization of homebuilders who share experiences, attend regional chapter meetings, and plan local fly-ins that proliferate during good flying weather—culminating in the annual Oshkosh Fly-in (airshow, symposiums and hardware displays) where attendance figures are in the hundreds of thousands each August.

The homebuilt scene is a change of life for the neophyte. How about sharing your bedroom with a growing fuselage or wing section? Condo dwellers build in the living room, while those blessed with a private garage or carport have autos that have never seen the protection of shade. Chicken coops and overgrown packing crates serve as building or storage areas. There are new friends and a whole new vocabulary. Hardware is now pop rivets, epoxy and steel tubing. The wish book comes from Aircraft Spruce & Specialty Co., Ken Brock Manufacturing, Stolp Starduster, or some other supplier of materials and parts. Sweaty palms come from awaiting the next newsletter with its list of mandatory changes or suggested improvements in construction.

The homebuilt scene can also be highly competitive. Take the case of retired fighter pilot, Don Taylor, of Hemet, California, who was the first homebuilder to fly around the world. He loaded his Thorp T-18 with 151.2 gallons of fuel for a non-stop flight from Hemet to Nassau with a return to land in Florida. Taylor flew 16 hours and 40 minutes because "he wanted to rack up one more record for my generation before Dick Rutan lays waste to the record books with the Long-EZ."

The homebuilt scene is a challenge and an opportunity to build new things and explore new horizons. It's a whole new ballgame!

AS THE FAA SEES IT

In order to qualify as a homebuilt airplane, the

Fig. 1-1. The Rutan VariEze is one homebuilt aircraft for which kits are sold. The FAA has determined that these kits meet its criteria for homebuilt aircraft.

Fig. 1-2. Crowds gather to inspect new homebuilt designs at every fly-in. Here a VariEze is on display at Chino. Note the variety of homebuilt designs and classic aircraft in the background.

builder must do 51 percent of the work. This can be handled in two ways, generally. The FAA has sent an evaluation team out to visit the designer/kit producer of some of the really high-volume designs—Bensen Gyrocopter, Scorpion Helicopter, BD-5, KR-1 and 2, VariEze (Fig. 1-1), Bryan Aircraft's HP series of sailplanes, and a few others—to determine if the kit, as it is shipped to the customer, qualifies under the current homebuilt regulations. Those that did were included on a list sent to all FAA field offices, stamped "approved." All the rest of the homebuilts are evaluated on a one-by-one basis by the local GADO or EMDO inspector . . . and, yes, there are some problems. In some areas a kit can be built, but in others the builder gets a hassle out of his inspector. It boils down to the opinions of individuals. The builder usually contacts the EAA, which in turn contacts the FAA at the Washington level. In many in-

stances, the dispute is resolved in favor of the builder.

Regarding insurance on homebuilts, some companies won't touch them; others will. Some designs with a record of numerous claims are hard to insure. Generally, premiums are rather high—a fudge factor thrown in by insurance companies to offset the many unknowns of homebuilt aircraft.

FAA and NTSB (National Transportation Safety Board) statistics on homebuilt accidents reveal some interesting facts about today's homebuilt pilot. His average age is 43.3 and his average flying time is a high 2,103 hours, with 67.7 hours in the type of aircraft he was flying when he came to the attention of these groups. While 10.4 percent of all general aviation "store-bought" accidents are caused by continued flight into deteriorating weather, the homebuilder's average is down to 1.4 percent.

So today's homebuilder is a mature person; he or she has both dedication and good judgment in varying amounts.

THE EAA, TODAY AND YESTERDAY

Almost without exception, the builders and aficionados of Rutan's designs are members of the Experimental Aircraft Association.

Today the Experimental Aircraft Association (EAA) ranks as the world's largest sport aviation organization. Originally, the EAA came from modest beginnings by a small group of men in January, 1953 in Milwaukee, Wisconsin, Several aviation enthusiasts—who liked to build airplanes—got to-gether and decided to form an organization of members with like interests. That group was led by Paul H. Poberezny, founder and current President of EAA.

When it was initially a local organization, publicity in *Mechanix Illustrated* magazine in 1955 caused a flood of inquiries from airplane lovers from all over the world asking to join. In a few years, the EAA grew from a membership of eight to a roster in the thousands. EAA's theme became the answer to the average man's desire to fly. If he couldn't afford to buy an airplane, he'd just build his own.

In the subsequent years, EAA became a strong international organization, issuing over 145,000

Fig. 1-3. EAA President Paul Poberezny feels that the name "Experimental" should be changed to either "Sport or "Custom." The Experimental sign is displayed prominently on the inside of the canopy of the original VariEze.

Fig. 1-4. Rutan's skew-wing design on the flight line at Oshkosh. NASA pilot talks with EAA security staff. Note long probe on the front of the tiny research plane.

membership cards to people in 91 countries. Current active, paid-up membership is 100,000. EAA has also created a system of local chapters which are considered the heart of the organization. Over 600 groups now hold regular meetings, and many schedule their own fly-ins (Fig. 1-2), providing a cohesive, active force at the local level.

EAA is involved in all facets of aviation from the "grass roots" activities which bind the organization together to the complexities of Washington representation of sport aviation interests. Today, there is hardly an event in aviation in which EAA is not involved some way.

Since its formative years, EAA has held an annual Fly-In Convention. The first was staged in Milwaukee in 1953. Today they are co-sponsored with the EAA Air Museum Foundation and are held in Oshkosh, Wisconsin. The EAA Sport aviation Convention and exhibition constitutes the world's largest aviation event, attracting over 14,000 aircraft and 800,000 people. Between the last

weekend in July and the first weekend in August air traffic at Oshkosh is three times as busy as Chicago's O'Hare Field.

No longer limited to people who build their own airplanes, EAA now represents and appeals to all sport aviation interests, including general aviation, builders of powered hang gliders, racing and rotary-wing enthusiasts (Fig. 1-3).

Rutan's influence on the homebuilt scene over the years has been a wonder to watch. At Oshkosh '82, there was an impressive display of his designs and their derivatives: 16 Long-EZs, 64 VariEzes, 2 VariViggens, 1 Defiant, 1 Grizzly, 1 Cozy, 1 Gemini, and 1 AMS/OIL Racer. And this year for the first time the AD-1 skew wing, designed by Burt in 1977, was also at the EAA show and flown every evening by NASA test pilot Tom McMurtry (Fig. 1-4).

HOMEBASE FOR THE DESIGNER

Burt Rutan (Fig. 1-5) is one of a small group of

Fig. 1-5. Burt Rutan talks with veteran airshow pilot Art Scholl (in checkered shirt) of Rialto, California, during the EAA's Chino Fly-in. Scholl is a veteran motion picture pilot and aerobatic flight school operator.

pioneers essential to the homebuilt scene. He formed the RAF (Rutan Aircraft Factory) in 1969 as a part-time, one-man effort to develop nonconventional research aircraft. In 1974, RAF became a full-time business, and Burt moved into a rented WWII barracks building on the Mojave, California, Airport.

Rutan's move to the desert area of Mojave, California (Fig. 1-6), was dictated by several factors. First, he was familiar with the Mojave Desert after spending seven years as a flight-test project engineer at nearby Edwards Air Force Base. The 9600 × 300-foot runways at Mojave, a former U. S. Navy and Marine Base at the end of WW II, have 360 days of VFR weather each year. It is far enough away from the Los Angeles megalopolis so that hangar space and housing are relatively reasonable. The 100-miles-by-road distance from Los Angeles discourages casual "tire-kickers," yet is within a short flight of all of the Southland's aviation organizations. Daily United Parcel Service helps materially.

The two VariEze prototypes (Fig. 1-7) were developed in the WWII barracks. Three years later,

Rutan leased 5,550 square feet of steel hangar and air-conditioned shop and office space on the flight line.

Specialty of the house at the RAF is efficient prototype development from initial concept definition to completed flight test at minimum cost and time schedule. RAF has been entirely self-supporting—current development costs always being paid by profits from previously completed projects. The company has never accepted deposits or payments for items during the development cycle.

Over the years, there has been a regular Saturday morning briefing and tape presentation at 10 A.M. with flight demonstrations at noon at the Mojave base. This open house is popular with both homebuilders and those who have not yet started building. Visitors will congregate from all over the country, sometimes scheduling Mojave in their vacation plans.

Fig. 1-6. The flight line at Mojave as seen from the back seat of the VariEze. Rutan's desert facility is located at the top center of the photo.

Fig. 1-7. Original VariEze and No. 1 Long-EZ are parked in front of Rutan Aircraft Factory at Mojave, California. Dick Rutan lifts the nose of the Long-EZ before locking down the nose gear for flight.

Some irreverent visitors to Rutan's regular weekly gathering comment that these mini-seminars are just like going to church with "Reverend Rutan" in the pulpit. These same people suggest that when an Eze is parked nose down, it should be pointed toward Mojave.

SPEED RECORDS FOR THE LONG-EZ

Dick Rutan and Jeana Yeager (Fig. 1-8) have set new world class speed records. These closed course records are categorized by weight and by distance flown. Separate records are recognized for female pilots. The weight category for Class lb. (Clb) is for lightplanes under 1000 kg (2205 lbs.). Speed records are recognized at distances of 3 km, 15/20 km, 100 km, 500 km, 1000 km and 2000 km. Since the Long-EZ can go long distances at high speed, Dick and Jeana attempted to break the following records:

Speed Clb Absolute Closed Course

500 km	USA	G. Mock	Aero Commander 200	1965	206.7 mph
1000 km	USA	H. Fishman	Waco Meteor	1969	200.4 mph
2000 km	CZECH	L. Stastny	Sokol CK-CLE	1956	173.7 mph

Speed Clb Female Closed Course

500 km	(none set)				
1000 km	CZECH	V. Touzimska	Sokol L-40	1980	131.4 mph
2000 km	CZECH	V. Touzimska	Sokol L-40	1980	128.9 mph

To put things in perspective, the 2000 km speed record requires a full-throttle low-altitude dash a distance equal to a trip from Los Angeles to Dallas! The aircraft used was a modified Long-EZ (N169SH) built by Dick and Jeana. It was powered by a Lycoming 0-320 D2G (160 hp) engine. With a special "speed prop" the aircraft attains a true airspeed of 223 mph clean (without bugs or rain on the wings). It was found that when the wing leading edges got clobbered with bugs or wet with rain (loss of laminar flow), the speed would drop to around 212 mph. Speed records are set by block speeds, however, resulting in losses due to wind and turns at each end of the course.

The attempts were not as easy and straightforward as one might have hoped. On Dick's first attempt, he experienced a broken aluminum fitting in the fuel system that dumped about five gallons per hour through the engine compartment—luckily, no fire, but it did result in inadequate fuel to go the distance. Two of Dick's record runs were done in rain showers, resulting in extensive prop damage at the 3000 rpm condition he was using. In all the attempts, the 0-320 logged over 25 hours of time at 108 percent of rated power, at 11 percent over rated rpm, without problems. The Microlon manufacturer sponsored the attempts. The engine was treated with Microlon oil treatment.

Attempts in all record categories were successful. The new world class speed records are listed below.

Fig. 1-8. Dick Rutan and his partner Jeana Yeager with their record-breaking Long-EZ at Mojave. Note auxiliary tank in the back seat.

During the 1983 CAFE flights, Jeana lost a good portion of her propeller and landed safely on Interstate Highway 5 under an overpass. There was minor damage as the blue racer slid into a Datsun, but Jeana was not injured.

FUEL RECORDS: MORE MPG

In efficiency races, Rutan's designs have been most successful. Competing in the annual California CAFE (Competition for Aircraft Fuel Efficiency) 400 in 1983, Gary Hertzler, Phoenix, Arizona, re-

		Speed Clb Absolute Closed Course			
500 km	USA	R. Rutan	Long-EZ	1982	211.51 mph
1000 km	USA	R. Rutan	Long-EZ	1982	207.84 mph
2000 km	USA	J. Yeager*	Long-EZ	1982	204.58 mph

		Speed Clb Female Closed Course			
500 km	USA	J. Yeager	Long-EZ	1982	207.10 mph
1000 km	USA	J. Yeager	Long-EZ	1982	205.00 mph
2000 km	USA	J. Yeager*	Long-EZ	1982	204.58 mph

* Jeana Yeager holds the Absolute and the Female 2000 km records. She topped Dick's earlier 1982 2000 km record by over 5 mph.

peated his earlier 1982 victory, piloting his VariEze at 145.2 mph and an average 44.63 mpg. This competition formula is *speed × mpg × cabin payload* to rate the fundamental fuel efficiency. After winning the 1982 CAFE 400, Gary Hertzler completely redesigned his cowling, cut 20 pounds off the empty weight, and recontoured the wing and canard to cut down on trim drag. His improvements put the Arizona pilot some 12 mpg ahead of the two other VariEzes participating in the five-pylon climb and descent course.

CLOSED COURSE DISTANCE RECORDS

Two closed course distance records have been established by Dick Rutan in canards. The first was with the VariEze in 1975. The record books show a distance of 1638 statute miles in 13.3 hours in Cla category. (See Chapter 4 for a detailed report.)

Four years later in December (1979), Dick flew the prototype Long-EZ in a closed course from Mojave to Bishop, California, and return 15 laps, setting a world class closed course distance record of 4800.28 statute miles in 33.7 hours. (See Chapter 7 for a step-by-step description.)

STRAIGHT LINE DISTANCE RECORDS

Straight line distance records are something else again. First, let's cover a record attempt that didn't quite make it. Builder W. A. "Rodie" Rodewald, a retired USAF fighter pilot, spent a year and a half on his Long-EZ in Hawaii. During construction, he read about Dick Rutan's Long-EZ distance record from Alaska to Grand Turk Island and began looking closely at the Long-EZ's performance—particularly its long-range capability. It was immediately apparent that equipped with suitable navigation gear, he had within his grasp some very economical transportation back to the mainland . . . and beyond! Thus, from very early in the project, emphasis was placed on optimizing the airplane as a very long-range cruiser (Fig. 1-9).

Rodewald is a very experienced homebuilder, having built a Breezy, Baby Ace, VariEze, and a Quickie. And he is also a very experienced aviator, having been a fighter pilot throughout his 32-year career, flying everything from the P-61 Black Widow to the F-4 Phantom.

Rodie decided to attempt to break Dick Rutan's straight-line distance record by flying from Hawaii to the east coast of the United States, with a fly-by at Oshkosh '82. Rodewald detailed the preparation for the flight in the *Canard Pusher* as well as the following description of the actual flight. (The complete report was also printed in *Sport Aviation*,

Fig. 1-9. W. A. "Rodie" Rodewald during preparation for his trans-Pacific flight to Sacramento and on to Oshkosh. Note two fiberglass auxiliary tanks in the back seat.

January 1983 issue, under the title "Lucky You Fly The Long-EZ."):

From Oahu Eastward

I told my wife Rosemary (the night before the flight) to plug in the seven-knot tailwind forecast over the Pacific and that I would work out the winds over the mainland when I got there. I went to bed at 1500 hours. Launch was scheduled for 0430 and I slept until 0400.

A last check of wind and weather showed no change, so I started the last-minute countdown. It didn't go too smoothly and I was an hour fifteen late on launch.

The LORAN gave good track information and I split the Golden Gate; however because of the ground station layout and the fact that I went station to station (Honolulu to Fallon), crosstrack was sketchy and primarily DR. I had a couple of big shocks over the water. The first was at 15 + 48, which was the overwater planned flight time. There was no West Coast. Obviously, the wind wasn't as planned. There was no VOR and no ADF information. Only the LORAN said I was on course, so all I could do was keep on trucking. Two hours later the shock sort of wore off. The moon had come up and gone down. Wow! It was dark and lonely out there by myself. Then the engine quit! I changed from auxiliary to wing tanks very quickly and it started right up. I was two hours overdue on the flight plan to the West Coast and "only" 12 hours of fuel left. How lucky I really was would not be realized for another two hours . . . for I was almost four hours over flight plan before the overwater portion ended! Almost any other airplane in the class would have gone down in the water. "Lucky you fly the Long-EZ," I thought to myself.

I had picked up a 14-knot headwind versus the 7-knot tailwind forecast. It didn't take a lot of calculating to figure out what to do. It was quite obvious the flight wouldn't go to Oshkosh as planned, so rather than cross the Rockies at night and then have to land in Nebraska, I stopped in Sacramento.

The next morning I went to prop the Long-EZ to depart for Oshkosh and discovered a piece

missing from the prop. I called Bruce Tifft at Oshkosh for consultation. He said to take a like piece from the other blade and try it for balance. I filed the piece out (3″ × 3 3/8″) and gave both blade tips a little varnish. It ran up okay, so I launched for Oshkosh. The winds from Reno to Salt Lake City were the first tailwinds I'd had, but they shut off at Salt Lake City. The LORAN was working like a charm, giving me lat and long, steering info, miles off course, miles and time to go, mag heading, and ground speed. I was going from waypoint to waypoint. It sounded the horn at each waypoint, where I would punch the next and away I would go. This was living! The West Coast LORAN stations stayed on until Nebraska then the Great Lakes chain came on. I had LORAN coverage all the way!

It was 12 hours from Sacramento to Oshkosh. On arrival I found the field was closed for a thunderstorm. I diverted to Fond du Lac and arrived after dark, meeting hordes of people in the same boat ergo, no place to stay. After three hours, I finally slept in the airplane. It wasn't easy sleeping. The worst part was that the airplane wouldn't hold a heading and I kept banking and turning for a long time even after I'd fallen asleep. I kept having a recurring nightmare: The engine would be droning away and suddenly go silent. I would wake up with real fear, open the canopy, and let in more of those damn Wisconsin mosquitoes.

The numbers for Honolulu to Oshkosh were 4,497 statute miles, 32 hours, 125 gallons, 140 mph, 3.9 gph and 36 mpg.

As I was planning and getting ready for this trip, I was often asked "Why?" It's not why! It's "Why not?" Mountain climbers are for the most part forced to climb mountains others have already climbed. In a Long-EZ, you have countless originals to climb.

Lucky you fly the Long-EZ.

(The foregoing was reprinted with permission from W. A. Rodewald, Waialua, Hawaii, who subsequently joined the Voyager project detailed in Chapter 15).

From Tundra to the Tropics

The most spectacular straight line world class

distance record to date was flown by Dick Rutan. When he lifted off from the Anchorage International Airport early on the morning of June 5, 1981, Dick had hopes of hanging up a world distance record for the Clb (1000 kg) class of 5,000 statute miles. He didn't quite make it, but he did establish a mark that will take some real effort to better. Thirty hours and eight minutes later, he landed at Grand Turk Island in the British West Indies. Great circle distance was 4563.35 sm. The old NAA/F.A.I. record was 2794 sm from Bremerton, Washington, to Homestead, Florida, in 1976 by Rodney Nixon in a Cessna 170A.

Only the long-range performance from the new technology of the Rutans makes such records possible. Dick could have actually carried another 171 pounds of fuel and tank and still been under the maximum takeoff weight of 2,204 pounds.

The airplane that Dick and Jeana Yeager had built was anything but a stock Long-EZ. The engine is a 160-hp Lycoming rather than the stock 115-hp powerplant. There's a remote-controlled oil cooler door, Compucruise computer, and full IFR equipment, both vacuum and electric. For the record attempt, Dick installed a 65-gallon collapsible fuel bladder similar in design but not material to a waterbed. Then a 24-gallon fiberglass conformal tank was fitted under the rear of the canopy. With full fuel in the two normal 30-gallon tanks, the airplane carried 150 gallons, 13 gallons more than "Rodie" Rodewald's Pacific Ocean crossing.

Jeana flew to Anchorage with Dick before the start of the record attempt. The collapsible bladder tank was empty and Jeana held the conformal tank, which had been cut in half, right in her lap. It was a very tight fit as far as Santa Clara, California, where a friend arranged to have the bisected fiberglass tank taken aboard an Air Guard C-130. It arrived before the Long-EZ did.

The couple cleared out of the U.S. at Sand Point, Idaho, with full standard tanks. They completely overflew Canada and cleared into Alaska with a very skeptical U.S. Customs Inspector at Northway, Alaska, after a mere 9.5 hours in the air. Then it was on to Anchorage with a twelve-day wait for acceptable weather.

Fred Keller, prizewinning EZ and Defiant builder (see Chapter 12), was NAA/F.A.I. observer when the weather prognosticators finally called for 30 to 40-knot tailwinds over northern Canada. To counter cold weather on the first third of the trip, Dick dressed warmly and taped a plastic bag around each foot.

The barograph was sealed, fuel tanks were capped and sealed to preclude a clandestine landing for more fuel, and finally Keller sealed the canopy with a tiny breakaway wire. Dick needed only 2,800 feet to break ground and he climbed out at 600 fpm and 80 knots, leveling at 13,000 feet.

After the VariEze chase plane had peeled off, Dick was left with the simple navigating chore, but something more varied than the monotony of the closed course record detailed in Chapter 7. He crossed into British Columbia and had a stretch of dead reckoning navigation east of Fort Nelson. Would you believe he carried a set of Green Hornet tapes to combat boredom!

The flight progressed according to plan throughout the long summer day of the northern latitudes. Dick crossed back into the U.S. near Minot, North Dakota, where the bladder tank ran dry. Then came Ottumwa and on toward Nashville when the rain began. It proved to be what Dick described as "the most harrowing night of my life." He hit a line of thunderstorms with their associated turbulence that stretched the full length of Tennessee. Rain poured in through cracks in the canopy that were never a problem in the bone-dry Mojave Desert.

Then things started going to pot in a handbasket. Dick lost his transponder and then his vacuum system and his attitude instruments. This left him at night in the middle of thunderstorm alley flying on his single remaining blind flight instrument, a electric turn-and-bank. Any instrument pilot will affirm that this isn't easy, not even in a Long-EZ.

With no transponder, the FAA centers gave him frequent vectors for radar identification. At times, he was too low to remain with the Center and was passed off to towers or flight service stations along the way. This meant frequency changes—just one more distraction while staying more-or-less right side up and traveling in a general direction toward the tip of Florida.

Eventually, he flew out of the weather northwest of Atlanta and enjoyed a most welcome dawn near Macon, Georgia, "I don't ever want to do that again!" explained Dick for what was later described as his "trial by whiskey compass."

Jeana had departed Anchorage for Orlando, Florida, by commercial jet where she was met by Johnny Murphy, the mayor of Cape Canaveral, and his Long-EZ. The plan was to rendezvous with Dick over the Vero Beach VOR, where the two planes would continue until a destination was picked. Murphy was also a designated NAA/F.A.I. observer and is the same homebuilder who flew nonstop from Florida to Oshkosh, meeting up with Dick who had flown in from San Francisco (see Chapter 7).

Dick with his pale blue Long-EZ and Murphy with Jeana in the back seat of his Long-EZ, *Sweet Music*, headed out the chain of islands that form the Bahamas. The Arctic clothing that Dick had blessed during the initial part of the flight soon became a chore as the temperature and humidity climbed. Within the confines of the Long-EZ cockpit, Dick found that he couldn't shed anything except perspiration.

Headwinds and storm delays had cut the flight envelope so that 5,000 miles and Puerto Rico were out of the question. Some 50 miles short of Nassau, the second wing tank went dry, leaving just 23.9 gallons of fuel in the conformal tank. Calculations indicated that the two Long-EZs would be abeam Grand Turk Island with six gallons of fuel remaining and 363 miles to Puerto Rico. Good as the Long-EZ was, there was no way to make it.

Johnny and Jeana landed first while Dick circled lazily over the island where years back many had watched early Mercury and Gemini launches. As soon as he had topped 30 hours in the air, Dick landed. Johnny checked and photographed the seals before breaking them. The barograph was still ticking so an official record was assured. Only then did Dick shoehorn himself out of the cockpit and begin shedding Arctic clothing.

Thanks to the Rutan revolution in design and construction, long-legged international flights by Long-EZs and their clones are becoming more and more common. When you can fly from Alaska to the Caribbean on just $285 (1981 dollars) for fuel, the once elusive corners of the world are now within a reasonable reach.

These records, spectacular though they may be, actually were only a prelude to the Voyager flight that became the Cinderella story of aviation in the 1980s. Each success with the Long-EZs made it just that much more possible even to contemplate the round-the-world, nonstop, nonrefuel effort that is covered in the last chapter of this book.

When the basic concept of Voyager was first discussed along the flight line at Mojave, skepticism was everywhere. Can you ever get off the ground with the required fuel? Are the engines sufficiently reliable? What about overflying the various countries in their present hostile moods? How can you communicate over that long a flight? Where do you find the funds, and how do you design and build the aircraft? How long can pilots operate efficiently in a limited cabin space?

However, success breeds on success, and Rutan's VariEzes and Long-EZs were traveling over significant areas of the globe with quiet, efficient performance. Based on what had already been done with the structural composites, the canard and increased aerodynamic performances, the last remaining record worth reaching for in suborbital flight became a viable goal. Rutan's design No. 76 grew slowly, painstakingly, hungrily into a spindly, scrawny, funny-looking "flexible flyer" with a unique profile that is probably familiar to more people in this world than any other single flying machine.

And it all started at Mojave, that wide, windswept spot on the map just outside the Edwards Air Force Base control zone, where civilian aircraft development has come of age.

But let's not get ahead of our story. First, we need to know the roots of Burt Rutan.

Chapter 2

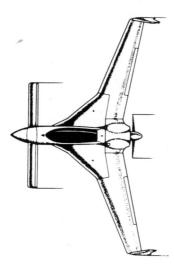

Rutan, The Designer

Just about all of Burt Rutan's life to date has been wrapped up in aviation (Fig. 2-1). He has become a pilot, an engineer, a pioneer. To learn what makes Burt Rutan tick, we explored resumes; we talked with family, friends and acquaintances; we talked with Burt. Here's what evolved.

MODEL BUILDER FIRST

Burt Rutan has never been a copier of anything. "I never knew Burt to build a model kit or work from someone else's plans," explained Burt's father, Dr. George Rutan, a dentist. "He always wanted to try something different. He worked on both free flight and radio-controlled models, but they were all original. Actually, his first efforts in the canard design were with gas-powered models."

Burt's parents, Dr. George and Irene Rutan (Fig. 2-2), live in Whittier, California, within a 2 ½-hour drive of Rutan's Aircraft Factory in Mojave. They attend many of the homebuilders' fly-ins and Irene is the avid historian for RAF. She is developing a scrapbook that she hopes will eventually con-

tain photos of all builders of Burt's designs and their finished aircraft. Dr. and Mrs. Rutan tell that Burt has been interested in airplanes—more in design and building than flying—for as long as they can remember.

Burt won his first model airplane contest in Dinuba, California, while still in grade school. Brother Dick, five years older, was also involved with model aircraft. At the same time, Dr. George was learning to fly and eventually purchased part of a Beech Bonanza. Thus, the two brothers and their sister Nellie, now an American Airlines stewardess, were exposed to a steady diet of aviation during their formative years.

In 1959, while attending the California Polytechnic University (Cal Poly) at San Luis Obispo, California, Burt won many model aircraft competitions including a U.S. Navy sponsored meet at Los Alamitos Naval Air Station near Los Angeles. He had a radio-controlled copy of his father's Bonanza along with several other entries. He brought back the first place trophy in the senior scale event. The

Fig. 2-1. Burt Rutan concentrates on his drawing board at Mojave. In this 1980 photo, he is detailing the last of the Long-EZ drawings.

following year, at age 16, Burt walked off with the Senior Control Line flying scale event with a large twin-engine model of the Fairchild F-27 Friendship. Rutan scaled up a three-view drawing of the F-27 from a magazine, copied colors from West Coast Airlines) and powered the ship with two K&B Allyn .35 cubic-inch glow plug engines. The F-27 had a complete interior hinged doors and workable flaps. The F-27 came to an untimely end

when another contestant backed into its line of flight. The contestant was injured and the gas model came out second best.

Rutan's thesis for Cal Poly's B. S. in Aeronautical Engineering degree also won $500 and that year's national award from the AIAA (American Institute of Aeronautics and Astronautics). Rutan built a radio-controlled model to study differential aileron yaw and proceeded to instrument the model

Fig. 2-2. Irene and George Rutan compare notes during a VariEze fly-in. Irene is the historian for the International Vari-Eze Hospitality Club. George, a dentist, is a Bonanza pilot. Both parents have flown with Burt and Dick in all the canard designs.

with on-board graph recorders. The subject of the paper prepared was *An Investigation of the Effect of Aileron Differential on Roll-Yaw Coupling During an Abrupt Aileron Roll.* Dr. Werner von Braun was honored by the AIAA at the same symposium.

Since Cal Poly's Aeronautics Department didn't have an operating wind tunnel with balanced inputs at the time, Burt designed and built a unit for the 12-inch diameter section that operated at speeds up to 150 mph.

When this wind tunnel wasn't big enough, Burt designed and built a novel car-top tunnel with precise data-collecting equipment (Figs. 2-3, 2-4). This was mounted atop his 1966 Dart station wagon where test data was obtained from medium-sized models driven at 80 mph—that's as fast as the Dart would go with the equipment on the roof. These data-collection runs were made at night when winds were low and traffic was light. It would take a 10- to 20-mile run for good data.

Fig. 2-3. Car-top wind tunnel mounted on 1966 Dart station wagon provided much early data that was not available from smaller school wind tunnels. Surprisingly, Rutan was never arrested for speeding during his 80-mph test runs. (courtesy Burt Rutan)

Fig. 2-4. Another view of car-top wind tunnel. (courtesy Burt Rutan)

No, Burt was never stopped for speeding by the San Luis Obispo police, but he was pulled over several times by curious patrolmen who wanted to know what he was doing. Some questioned the height of the unit, but Rutan had designed it to be just legal.

"That car-top wind tunnel brought back just beautiful data," beamed Rutan.

Burt first learned to fly in an old Aeronca 7AC Champ at Dinuba, California (Fig. 2-5). His instructor was Johnny Banks, perhaps better known as a country music disc jockey. Rutan soloed after five hours and fifteen minutes of dual instruction. At the time this material was prepared, Burt has logged more than 2,100 flying hours as pilot in command. He did all his own flight testing until his brother Dick joined the RAF in 1978.

After graduating from Cal Poly where he was third in his class with a 3.4 grade average, Burt had to make a decision—whether he wanted to work in space or in aircraft. Burt chose aircraft while many of his classmates went into space research, which was very big at the time—halfway between the first orbiting flights and the first moon landing. Burt was more interested in aircraft but didn't want to become buried in a big company like Boeing, Douglas or Lockheed. He applied at both Beech and Cessna,

Fig. 2-5. Rutan soloed in this Aeronca 7AC Champ at Dinuba, California in five hours and 15 minutes. (courtesy Burt Rutan)

but felt that he didn't want to get mired down in detail designing. He eventually chose civil service work in the flight test department at Edwards Air Force Base (Fig. 2-6). This was the lowest pay and highest risk job available, but Burt felt that it would be worthwhile.

Rutan stayed at Edwards and on temporary duty with the flight test center for nearly seven years. In a personal resume he prepared, Burt capsulized his work with the Air Force this way:

"June 1965 to March 1972—Flight Test Project Engineer at the Air Force flight test center, Edwards AFB, Grade GS 12, $18,400 P. A. Conducted fifteen

USAF flight test programs, ranging from large V/ STOL cargo aircraft to several types of fighters. Duties included planning, coordinating support agencies, research, test conduct (including flying), data analysis and reporting. Other functions included writing flight characteristics and emergency procedures sections of aircraft flight manuals, revision of specifications and accident investigations. Supervisory experience included employee training, evaluation, and consulting in both technical and personnel areas."

His flight time during this stint included USAF copilot time, mostly during hazardous tests, in the following aircraft: UH-IN; T-37; T-38; F-4B, C, E,

Fig. 2-6. Burt Rutan, lower right, with military flight test crew in front of a Lockheed C-130. The designer chose the lowest pay and highest risk job available in his military aircraft testing. (courtesy U.S. Navy)

Fig. 2-7. Parachute risers break as a 50,000-pound load is extracted from a C-130 at the El Centro, California Naval Air Station. If this load had jammed in the cabin, the C-130 would have crashed. (courtesy U.S. Navy)

and Agile Eagle; F-104A and B; F-106; C-130E; C-141A; and YA-26.

One of Burt's more interesting military assignments was as Project Director of a Low Altitude Parachute Extraction System (LAPES) where he really began earning his flight pay. "You are really sticking your neck out in flight test," he commented. "Within the first three weeks I was at Edwards on the XC-142A hovering machine, we had four people killed in the ten-man group I was with. One was in an auto wreck, two were in a Beech Baron and the other was hovering the XV5A."

One year after going to Edwards AFB, Rutan was in charge of the LAPES program that went to El Centro, California Naval Air Station, obstensibly for three weeks. The project lasted 14 months. Rutan thought it was a good assignment despite the hot desert location at El Centro because he was in charge of an eight-man test crew with "lots of responsibility and 150 miles away from the boss."

On at least one flight, Rutan earned his hazard pay. A 50,000-pound load was to be extracted at fifteen feet from the cargo hatch of a Lockheed C-130. The Engineer was aboard the Air Force C-130 during a LAPES in which the parachute deploy cables snapped as the 25-ton load was still

partially inside the cabin (Fig. 2-7). Under this condition, the aircraft pitched up uncontrollably even with full forward stick, pulling 2.8 Gs on a 3G airframe at an altitude of 15 feet. Fortunately, the palletized load continued out of the plane and crashed into the test site, completely ruining the cargo (Fig. 2-8). The transport aircraft zoomed sharply, but became controllable again just as soon as the cargo passed the rear of the hatch.

"If that load had jammed in the aft of the cabin, we'd have pitched up and promptly back into the ground, permanently," said Burt.

THINKING AHEAD

Many families have a habit of retaining correspondence and mementos of their offspring. George and Irene Rutan are no exception. Family communications give a singular insight into Burt Rutan at this point in his career. While Burt was working for the Air Force at Edwards AFB, he kept his family ties via tape cassettes. Dr. George and Irene came across one of these old tapes during the research on this project and shared these "thoughts from Burt to Pop," transcribed from one such cassette:

. . . as to what I want to do later—right now I

18

Fig. 2-8. C-130 pitches up as 50,000-pound payload just makes it out the cargo door. The pitch-up pulled 2.8 Gs on a 3-G airframe at 15 feet. Rutan was aboard on this test. (courtesy U.S. Navy)

kind of step back and say "What am I going to do now? What am I going to be doing five years from now?" And every time I ask myself that question, without exception, I come up with: I want to really make something of myself in aviation. I want to set a really good goal. I want to make it before I get too old. I want to get there quick. I do have patience, I think, but I do want to set a goal. I don't want to set an exact goal; I just want to reach out in this direction. I want to have a good position. I want to have my own airplane that I can get in and travel. I want to go places. I don't want to go places like New York and Chicago—I want to go to places like Muskogee, Oklahoma, and meet people. I want to do some sightseeing and have some fun. I want to fly low and see the country. I'd give a lot for the freedom I will need to do all this, I guess.

One of my first goals is to get that airplane[Viggen] done [Fig. 2-9] and refine it into a workable, buildable system and use what talents I have in management and marketing together with a good common sense approach to get good publicity and sell some plans for the thing. I'd like to make it well known; get the name Rutan in the magazines; get it into a certain segment of aviation.

You know, I used to be pretty well known with a small segment of people. That segment was the West Coast, even the National model airplane flyers. Actu-

Fig. 2-9. Burt Rutan sits in the half-finished cockpit of his prototype VariViggen in a garage at Mojave. He was working for the Air Force as a civilian engineer at the time. (courtesy Burt Rutan)

ally if one was very lucky, he could pick up a model magazine and page through it and find a picture of Burt Rutan. And it says he made an accomplishment; he won something. When I'd go to the meets, it was, "Burt Rutan? Oh yes, he was the guy that completely revolutionized the model aircraft carrier event by coming up with an airplane that he pulled the tail around on and it went real slow and got a lot of points even though it looked ugly." And shortly everyone copied me and were doing the same thing—flying airplanes that flew real slow. I kinda came up with it first and I won something at every meet, and I was able to do something in this small group of people. I thought it did me good; I thought it was really great. Something every kid should have.

I'll never forget that poster Mom and I saw when we were in Dallas. Remember, Mom? It said "Model Aviation Builds Better Boys." I think that kids nowadays that are getting into trouble in high school and grammar school, if they were as involved in any type of hobby—anything they'd like—anything that turns them on—skiing, fishing, anything—like I was involved in model aviation, you just wouldn't have . . . or rather you would have a better America. Anyway, right now I want to get back into something like that. It made me feel really good to be in that kind of segment. Right now, I'm not. Model airplane flyers no longer know about Burt Rutan—even the ones at Lancaster.

EAA is the next place that I want to become known. This is something that's just wide open! So many people in EAA just don't know what they're doing in areas where I really know it. I want to teach them. I want to give symposiums and speeches on how to design airplanes; how to build a better way; how to solve this problem or that. I think I have just the type of education and flight test experience that would be really valuable in this, and these guys would really be interested and I could feel really good in showing them a few things and getting back from them their knowledge that would help me. Sharing you know. Getting involved in a challenging segment of society. Travel around, go to their meets, show up and get in the magazines. Learn from it and improve myself.

Just working toward a relatively narrow goal, I guess it is, but with the chances of making a name and being able to expand into that. Maybe even later on

making a business out of it. Lots of people do. Like Hegy. [Ray Hegy is still making propellers in Marfa, Texas, at press time.] He made propellers for forty years. Goes to all these meets in his little airplane. He really enjoys himself, I think. I don't want to be quite that narrow; I kind of want to stretch out and reach a major goal, though. This is an area that I think I can move fast in. If I set myself a goal like to be President of McDonnell-Douglas, I think I would get bored before I got there. But I want to move up in the aviation area.

Gerry and I got the F-4E into a surprisingly vicious spin yesterday, but he popped out the drag chute and we recovered. There are rumors around the base as to what we did. I've been working on the data all day today . . ."

MILITARY FLIGHT TESTING

Later at Mojave, Rutan was project engineer on a series of spin test programs with the McDonnell-Douglas F-4. Following completion of this test program, Rutan made a presentation to the Aerospace profession at the 14th annual convention of the Society of Experimental Test Pilots. In this report he detailed some of the phases of the project which were to earn him, as a civilian, an Air Medal from the Government. Excerpts from his presentation which was entitled *Fighter Testing—Spin Test or Spin Prevention Test?* follow:

Let's look at what a contractor or other test agency is faced with when it comes to the spin program. He must satisfy specification requirements and will do so, of course, at minimum expense or with a minimum number of flights. Often he is required *only* to demonstrate recovery after a specified number of turns with several spin entry conditions and possibly one or more external store loadings. Thus, his test planning task is narrowed down to a safe progression of tests building up to the goal—"demonstrating five turns with a recovery within two additional turns." Once that goal is completed he's done. The general approach is to hold pro-spin controls for the required number of turns, then swap to the predicted optimum antispin controls.

I submit that the most important aspect of high

angle of attack handling qualities is too often being overlooked and that is *spin avoidance* or *spin resistance*. Maneuvers during the stall tests are generally terminated at adequate warning or maximum usable lift. Subsequent spin tests are conducted by doing intentional spins to meet specifications. Insufficient objective requirements are applied to guarantee testing will be accomplished for adequate spin resistance during tactical operations.

One might ask why a prompt spin recovery requirement is not sufficient. Several reasons are pertinent. Often the out-of-control maneuver or spin mode entered from a tactical entry with immediate recovery attempts is significantly different from the mode experienced following an intentional spin entry with pro-spin controls. Recovery characteristics (or success) from one mode cannot always be applied to another. Particularly with fighter/bombers, sufficient altitude is not always available for recovery from any spin; therefore, spin *susceptibility* and spin *prevention* information is far more important than spin recovery information. If a fighter is susceptible to departure or spins, the pilot will be reluctant to maneuver at maximum

performance. Thus, its operational effectiveness as well as safety is compromised. Ignoring spin susceptibility to concentrate on spin recovery is just as ridiculous as ignoring spin recovery to design the aircraft strong enough to survive the impending crash.

A test program was recently completed on the F-4E (Fig. 2-10) aimed primarily at determining departure and spin susceptibility and spin prevention methods. Classic spin tests had been conducted earlier by the contractor and the Navy on the F-4B, but no tests were flown with external stores or at aft cg positions.

For this F-4E program, Major Jerry Gentry was the project pilot. Lieutenant McElroy and myself shared engineering responsibilities and the back seat for the test missions.

The test aircraft was the second production F-4E. The E differs from the earlier F-4C and D by a longer nose housing an internal cannon, improved radar, slotted stabilator, more powerful engines, an additional fuselage fuel tank and fixed inboard leading edge flaps.

Special modifications included a mortar-de-

Fig. 2-10. Flight test crew with the U.S. Air Force F-4E at Edwards AFB before the aircraft was lost. Rutan is second from the right in this U.S. Air Force photo.

Fig. 2-11. U.S. Air Force F-4E in flight at Edwards AFB during spin test programs. Note spin chute parachute housing added at the tail of the airplane. Rutan flew many of the test missions in this aircraft. It was destroyed by a parachute malfunction during the program, but both pilot and observer escaped via parachute. (courtesy U.S. Air Force)

ployed 33½-foot diameter spin recovery parachute housed in additional structure built on the tail cone (Fig. 2-11). The production drag chute was located below the spin chute. Packed with the big spin recovery chute was enough riser to place its canopy 110 feet aft of the aircraft when deployed. This long riser length was determined from a McDonnell-Douglas development program after a shorter riser system failed to effect a recovery from a flat spin during the Navy spin program. External stiffeners were installed on the aft fuselage to absorb loads from the spin recovery parachute. Onboard cameras were mounted over the pilot's shoulders and on top of the fuselage to document the pilot's view of aircraft motions.

One of the more interesting findings of this program was that the F-4 will depart and spin without any aileron or rudder inputs. This is due to directional instability above 22 degrees angle of attack. Aileron inputs usually determine the departure direction (left departure with right aileron); but the susceptibility to depart and to spin is not significantly increased by aileron inputs if angle of attack is not increased. Control surface misrigging, stability augmentation malfunctions, and out-of-trim conditions also have no significant effect on departure or spin susceptibility.

Excluding the nose-high, low speed zoom or tail-slide type of stall entry, any severe out-of-control event was either a rolling departure or a spin.

The rolling departure was the most prevalent and was characterized by an initial divergency in yaw followed by a rapid roll. Most were only one roll but a few went two or three. They were easily distinguishable from spins by their lack of a sustained yawing motion. Stick smoothly full forward always effected recovery. Forward stick and the drag chute effected a more rapid recovery.

Of the many departures experienced in the test program, 101 resulted in spins. Let me emphasize that these were not intentional spins in the classical sense. The aircraft was forced to excessive angle of attack, often abruptly where it departed, but no lateral-directional inputs were applied with the intention of producing a spin. All spins developed shortly after departure without going through the rolling departure phase.

Two flat spins were experienced during the test program. The first developed during a high angle of attack, highly oscillatory spin with an asymmetric load when the stick-aft recovery control procedure was being investigated. Once the flat spin developed, the stick was returned to the forward stop but an aerodynamic recovery could not be attained. The aircraft was recovered with the spin recovery chute after 17½ turns. [Burt was aboard on this one.]

The second flat spin developed shortly after departure from a nose-low transonic entry with a clean loading. Again, an aerodynamic recovery could not be attained and the spin recovery chute was deployed. The spin chute separated from the aircraft before blossoming due to a failure of the attachment mechanism. The aircraft continued in the flat spin, the crew successfully ejected and the aircraft was destroyed.

In summary, this test program revealed that a new spin recovery control procedure was successful for all external store loadings, was easy for a pilot to apply and did not require critical recovery timing. New information was obtained for the Flight Characteristics section of F-4 Flight Manuals. A formal training film was prepared for F-4 aircrews reflecting the findings of the test program.

Later Rutan reported that he was "very happy" with the parachute system after the 17-turn recovery. "I thought that we'd never lose the plane after that. We had planned to be more conservative on the next few flights, but lost the aircraft on the very next trip that was not supposed to be very hazardous. Project pilot Major Jerry Gentry and Lt. McElroy bailed out safely."

At the conclusion of this program, Rutan was presented the Air Medal with the following commendation:

Mr. Elbert L. Rutan distinguished himself by

meritorious achievement while participating in sustained aerial flight as project engineer, Performance and Flying Qualities Branch, 6512 Test Group, at Edwards Air Force Base, California, from 1 October 1969 to 7 August 1970. During this period, Mr. Rutan demonstrated outstanding airmanship and professionalism in accomplishing his duties as a project engineer on the F-4E Stall/Near Stall Test Missions, exploring an unknown and hazardous portion of the flight envelope. The professional ability and outstanding aerial accomplishments of Mr. Rutan reflect great credit on himself and the United States Air Force.

WHY THE CANARD DESIGN?

Rutan designed and partially built the prototype canard VariViggen (Fig. 2-12) while working for the Air Force at Edwards AFB. Why the canard design?

Rutan had built his first radio-controlled canard design back in 1964 when he was just finishing his junior year at Cal Poly. At that time, the Swedish SAAB Model 37 canard fighter had not flown. The SAAB replacement for Sweden's "Draken" family of aircraft had began in 1962. The double-delta design combined STOL (short field takeoff and landing) with Mach 2 performance for

Fig. 2-12. Burt designed and began work on the VariViggen while still working for the Air Force at Mojave.

Sweden where ordinary roads served as landing strips under combat conditions (Fig. 2-13).

The designer liked what he saw in the initial Swedish Viggen and set about to design something in the same ballpark. Candidly, he explained (perhaps for the first time), "I wanted an aircraft for myself as close to a modern fighter as possible—something like the F-104 or F-4. I wanted a big stick, an array of buttons, high rate of roll—a real 'macho machine' where I'd really feel like I was flying a century-series fighter.

"I went ahead with the basic natural stall-limiting function of the canard configuration. The Viggen design gave me a test bed to explore the natural angle-of-attack-limiting, stallproof concept that we've followed throughout all subsequent designs."

The engineer admits that he really didn't plan

Fig. 2-13. SAAB JA-37 Viggen. This all-weather fighter was produced for the Swedish Air Force. A total of 329 were built. The new JA-37 carries a normal armament of six air-to-air missiles plus a formidable new 30-mm cannon. It was this design that inspired Rutan to proceed with his VariViggen. (courtesy SAAB-SCANIA Aerospace Division)

to leave his long tenure at Edwards AFB, but when he was approached by homebuilt designer-promoter Jim Bede to work for him, Rutan journeyed to Bede's Newton, Kansas facility twice before deciding to move—and even that decision was on a short-term basis.

Rutan had advanced rapidly to a GS-12 rating at Edwards. His next promotion would be to that of Section Chief where he would do no flying, but would attend many meetings and do program evaluations. "I liked my job better than those my bosses had. There were excellent benefits with 20 days of vacation a year, but I could take a leave and return to Edwards anytime within three years and retain all these benefits.

"When I finally decided to go with Bede, it was just like taking a sabbatical leave from my regular job. At that time I knew I couldn't quit the security of the civil service job, so when I visited Bede in Kansas for the second time, I planned to stay for only one year, and that was primarily because somebody wanted to pay me to work on homebuilt aircraft."

TEAMED WITH JIM BEDE

When Rutan moved to Valley Center, Kansas to work on the Bede project, his nearly-completed VariViggen was shipped right along with the household furniture.

Rutan's job at Bede was described as follows in his resume: *"Director of the Bede Test Center, Bede Aircraft, Newton, Kansas. Basic salary $18,500 P.A. Have directed development of three aircraft types including all flight and ground tests. Had total design and development responsibility for the jet BD-5J and trainer/simulator. Perform administrative and managerial duties for test department employees including four engineers, nine experimental mechanics, one buyer and one secretary. Assist marketing with demonstrations, seminars and technical presentations."*

Part of Rutan's agreement with Jim Bede was that he could continue to develop his VariViggen and sell plans to it without having a conflict of interest with his production job.

On a very cold Christmas week in Kansas,

Burt Rutan wrote this letter to his parents who, as some parents will do, kept it and supplied it to us. It makes interesting reading in that it foretells really what Rutan wanted to do with this portion of his life:

Dear Mom and Pop, Here I am again working on the plans. I realize I haven't written you in quite awhile. I've gotten about 100 orders for the plans now and still don't have them completed, so Carolyn and I have been really burning the midnight oil making out the final layout and inking, so we can satisfy the many people who have paid for their plans. They cost $51—nowadays. I don't think I'll have to worry about the IRS challenging the existence of RAF since it looks like we will show a couple thous. $ profit this year. Hope to sell more when we advertise! The plans are being done up first class with total of about 63 pages, completely detailed. I found I couldn't do them simple like I originally planned. Once I got started detailing things, I found I just couldn't leave things out. It's quite a job; about 400 hours total, but I'm having 500 copies printed, so if we can sell them it will be well worthwhile. I'm having them collated and mounted in plastic ring binders; printing and binding will cost about a thous. $. I'll send you a couple of copies as soon as we get them out of the printer—in about 3 weeks!!

We had our Christmas alone at home, just the family. Not a lot of hassle and just ended up being just a short break in drawing of the plans.

Things are about the same at work. Seem to keep busy with all the little projects and flying the jet a lot. Haven't touched the Viggen since I've been so busy on the plans.

It sure has been hectic lately; I would sure like to leave it for awhile and come on out and relax at the Hemet place, but I doubt if that's going to happen soon. Oh well, maybe some day RAF will be big enough so I won't have to report to someone and be my own boss; but guess I'm just dreaming there, too. Well, I guess I'm itching to get started on another airplane of my own. Got a lot of ideas but haven't decided yet whether it will be a little single place or a four-place made for cross-country. I'm confident I can build a 175 mph four-place with over 26 miles per gallon. What with the 55 mph speed limits that would

be an extremely attractive way to travel with the gas shortage. It would be considerably simpler to build than the VariViggen actually, but then I'm not too far along on the design.

Sure would be nice to be able to work on something like that full time. I guess I will someday since I believe like you do: that a guy should do what he enjoys as much as possible.

After just over two years with Jim Bede, Rutan decided to go to work on his own. Bede and Rutan parted on very good terms. "I was against the decision to try to certify the Bede aircraft, but at the time I felt that Jim might be able to pull it off. When I decided to leave, Jim and the factory threw a big party for me. It was all very interesting."

At this time, Rutan was already well into selling plans and developing support for the Viggen design. Originally Rutan had envisioned making a very simple, skimpy set of plans for experienced builders who liked the canard design to follow. "These were supposed to sell for $27 in those days," explained Burt. "However, it didn't work out that way. Every time I stopped drafting, there was something else to detail." The first sets of plans cost $51.

After six months of work on the Viggen, Rutan was making enough from the sales on plans, cowlings and machine parts to strike out on his own.

Rutan's original VariViggen, now in the EAA Museum, was painted to copy the Air Force Thunderbird's aerobatic display team (Fig. 2-14). Rutan had flown with them as an observer. The unique pusher canard configuration soon drew the nickname of "Thunder Chicken." This name was eventually painted on the side of the airplane.

The prototype VariViggen N27VV (Fig. 2-15) won the coveted EAA award for Outstanding New Design at the 1974 Oshkosh fly-in. This was but the first of a number of EAA honors for new design.

A HOME AT MOJAVE

Rutan returned to California and to the thing he really wanted to do: design his own airplanes and do consulting assignments for aerospace companies in advanced engineering. It was a gamble, one that

Fig. 2-14. Rutan's VariViggen in flight with a new paint job and engine cowling installed. Rutan reported, "An F-106 pilot who flew it said it handled more like a F-106 than any type he had flown, military included". (courtesy Don Dwiggins)

Fig. 2-15. The VariViggen in its configuration for initial test flights near Newton, Kansas. Notice tip fins and temporary cowling. After flight tests proved that the tip fins were unnecessary for stability, they were removed. (courtesy Burt Rutan)

many engineers have wanted to take all their lives.

Rutan picked Mojave, a windswept spot in California's Mojave Desert. The sprawling former military base has large runways, WWII Marine Corps barracks, a few aging hangars and is a boneyard for large outdated aircraft (Fig. 2-16). It is also a haven for sport aviation enthusiasts who are required to fly 25 or 50 hours over "unpopulated areas" before receiving FAA approval on their new homebuilt models.

Mojave qualifies as "unpopulated," despite claims of the Chamber of Commerce. When asked how many people lived in Mojave, Rutan quipped, "About half of them. The population is about the same as the altitude, 2,787."

Most of the residents of Mojave work on the railroad. The town is a staging area for freight trains going over the Tehachapi Pass between Los Angeles and Bakersfield, the high point on the west coast rail route.

In his second newsletter, then called the *VariViggen News*, Rutan advised his slowly growing number of builders that:

We are now conducting a full-time business primarily to support VariViggen builders. Our facility on the Mojave Airport (100 yards S.E. of tower building) consists of an office and shop sufficient to allow us to provide VariViggen components, related engineering support for VariViggen builders, technical and educational material (the car-top wind tunnel project is aimed primarily at highschools and colleges), and engineering analysis/test consulting.

We now see an important need for a periodic newsletter, complete enough to give all the information to builders that can assist them in their projects. Future newsletters will include essentially the same format information and photos as this one, with more builder-submitted information as it becomes available. All suggestions are considered. Remember this is your newsletter.

Even today, Rutan figures that he spends 15 percent of his time on his newsletter and technical reports. He writes the original material in longhand on a legal pad. Then Sally Melvill types up the copy and Burt does the layout and penned drawings.

The rented WWII barracks at the Mojave Airport lasted for almost three years before the pres-

Fig. 2-16. Mojave Airport as seen on final approach. Rutan's factory is located at the far right of the flight line just beyond the first large hangar.

ent 5,500-sq. ft. steel building was erected on the flight line (Fig. 2-17). This ramp-side air-conditioned structure provides immediate access to the 9,600-foot hard surface runways at Mojave. Rutan notes that the Mojave Desert provides an ideal atmosphere for flight tests—360 VFR days per year and a low population. He didn't mention it, but high desert habitues know that the winter mornings can be bitter cold and high winds will blow sand into every corner of a building or an airplane, but Southern California smog it has not.

Burt has assembled the essential hardware needed to do his engineering job. There is an Apple II computer, 48 byte with disk and tape storage using color video and Centronics printer output for engineering computations and the storage of mailing lists. A color video camera with portable video cassette recorder is used to document critical flight tests and display this data to visitors.

Since Burt lives within a couple of miles of the airport and the RAF has a Grumman Tiger as well as the twin-engine Defiant, the prototype Long-EZ and at least one VariEze, Burt really doesn't do a great deal of car driving. However, he did buy a nostalgia car—a 1950 Ford from a used car lot in Lancaster, similar to the car that his Dad owned while he was graduating from dental school. Burt paid $2,600 for the classic; that's $900 more than it cost new, but the two-door sedan had only 53,000 miles on it.

"I had my first date in high school with the Ford my Dad owned," reminisced Burt. "The family kept that car for all the years when I was growing up and I have some pleasant memories to go with it. That's why this new-to-me old Ford is something special."

In an RAF facility brochure, Rutan notes that his small company has four full-time employees.

Fig. 2-17. Rutan Aircraft Factory with the Mojave Airport in the background. Rutan's new building is the white-roofed structure in the center with a line of visiting VariEzes parked outside.

Burt lists himself as "owner, part-time airplane designer." In general RAF excels in efficient prototype development, from initial concept to completed flight testing at minimum cost and time schedule. RAF has been entirely self-supporting, current development costs always being paid by profits from previous completed projects. RAF has never accepted deposits nor payments for items during the development cycle.

WORLDWIDE SEMINARS

Burt has traveled over much of the free world giving talks and seminars on this country; he has journeyed to Canada to aid in approval of his novel design concepts. He has traveled to England, France and Germany for seminars. Most recently, he visited Australia and New Zealand at the invitation of the sport aviation enthusiasts down under. In a brief two-week trip, he was able to conduct seminars in Auckland and Wellington. Both Australian and New Zealand Governments provide a composite aircraft construction school to teach methods and inspections. Some of the class projects include building a VariEze, confidence samples and bookends.

Rutan is completely dedicated to the task of designing and refinement (Fig. 2-18). He would be the first to admit that he is not a "people person," but some of his critics have been a bit harsh. One British journalist commented, in print, "Some of the visitors are apt to find that Rutan, an intense 36-year-old (at that time), is too busy to talk to them. 'Look around but don't touch anything,' he says, scarcely glancing up from his drawing board . . ."

The British reporter continued to quote a VariEze builder who said, "We had come a very long way, about 6,000 miles, to see his project. We spent about an hour with him, then we pushed off; we couldn't stand it anymore. We didn't feel we got a very good response, quite honestly. In fact, we were steaming about it for 11 hours on the flight all the way home.

"An awful lot of people think that Rutan is God, but we altered our opinion of him. As far as we're concerned, his aeroplane flies absolutely beauti-

Fig. 2-18. Burt at the controls of the Long-EZ in front of the RAF hangar at Mojave prior to a demonstration flight. World War II aircraft in the background are but a few of the unusual aircraft to be found at Mojave.

fully. As a designer he may be great but as a public relations man he's pretty useless."

Rutan is frugal with the time he spends working with people vs. working at the drawing board. "We could spend all our time standing around and talking and never get any work done," he commented honestly. However, the designer appreciates that personal contacts are an essential part of a successful business, and he holds regular Saturday discussions on composite construction and demonstration flights of the various models available at Mojave. These Saturday sessions are scheduled except for the weekends when important fly-ins are listed far in advance (Fig. 2-19).

On a recent Saturday, all the other troops were out of town and Burt handled the program by himself. The front office was crowded with visitors who watched movies, viewed flight test video tapes, asked endless questions and then watched as Burt

Fig. 2-19. Rutan clowns it up with a balsa wood model glider modified with a penknife to a canard design. The Grand Canyon river raft poster in the background is a reminder for Burt of an exciting surface trip down the Colorado River.

builders' program, developed from one of the builders of the AMS/OIL Racer and once proprietor of "Revolutionary Propeller Manufacturing" to a smooth teacher and competent demonstration pilot. The two Michaels—Melvill and Dilley—relieve Burt of the repetitive Saturday briefings at Mojave. However, when he is at the airport, Burt now mingles and jokes with the visitors and shows a sincere concern for builder problems. Yes, on reaching age 40, Burt is maturing.

DICK RUTAN, TEST PILOT IN THE FAMILY

Dick Rutan (Fig. 2-20) is five years older than his brother Burt, has been involved in aviation all his life, and fits perfectly in the scheme of things at Mojave. Dick commented that their mother thought that both boys had been born with av/gas in their veins.

Dick took flying lessons while going to school

put on a flight demonstration in the Long-EZ. Normally these chores now fall on brother Dick or Mike Melvill, who is officially listed as Customer Relations man, but both were out of town.

Burt is essentially a shy person, belied by his 6′4″ frame and easygoing manner. When he puts lines on drafting paper and massages flight test data, his eyes glint and he really becomes alive. The people who build his products are delighted to have it work out this way.

During the busy three years following the foregoing assessment, Burt has worked hard at becoming more "people oriented." He is now able to talk before an Oshkosh forum of over 500 builders and not appear ill at ease. He has augmented his staff with professional people who have not only built his designs and understand the problems, but are truly interested in people and their difficulties. Michael Dilley, who is now handling the Solitaire

Fig. 2-20. Dick Rutan with a colorful hat, suited for all day in the sun at a fly-in at Chino, California.

in Dinuba, California, but couldn't solo because he was too young. Shortly thereafter, his father took lessons and went on to get his private pilot certificate.

When Dick was old enough, he applied to the Air Force for aviation cadet training. Since no pilot slots were open, Dick joined the Air Force and went on to become a commissioned navigator. He flew the back seat of fighters for seven years before an opening occurred to get into pilot training. He was a radar operator, a "scope dope," in F-89s and F-101s.

He flew the last actual F-89D scramble from Keflavik AFB as a radar observer. After years of trying, he was accepted for Air Force pilot training in 1966 and went through Class 67B.

Dick is a firm believer in parachutes and always watches the one he's going to ride during repack. He's been forced to bail out twice in his 20 years on active military duty. Once was over North Vietnam when his F-100 was shot up on a strafing run. He took a hit 20 miles inland from the water and the F-100 burned all the way to the shore. He ejected just off the coast in the Gulf of Tonkin and spent three hours in warm, clear water before being picked up by a Jolly Green heli-rescue team.

Dick volunteered for three special mission tours during the year he spent in Vietnam. He was flying a Commando Saber operation for pilots in that part of the war.

"After being shot down, I was eligible to return to the States," Dick remembers. "I had visions of taking my little girl to the zoo in a couple of weeks and all those good things you look forward to on return from overseas. I was so glad my tour was over, I even went to sleep in the helicopter on my way back to Da Nang Airbase. However, the front-line fighter operation was a challenge—that's where the action was, and that's where I wanted to be."

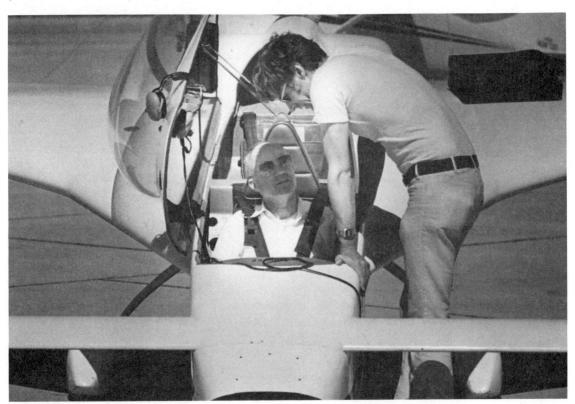

Fig. 2-21. Dick Rutan leans over the cockpit of the Long-EZ before going on a checkout flight with A.L. Letcher of Mojave.

Dick's other bailout was over England during a 3½-year tour with F-100s. He had been on an engineering test hop over the North Sea after taking off from the USAF base at Lakenheath Air Force Base. Weather at the time was typical of England in May 1970—900 feet with the tops at 35,000 feet. Dick made his routine list of checks on the engineering flight; routine that is until he made the prescribed −1 (negative) G maneuver. A mechanic had left an oil sample bottle loose and with the negative G maneuver the bottle stuck in the oil intake. Instantly there was no oil pressure, but the engine continued to run for 12½ minutes.

"I was halfway down the GCA approach at Lakenheath and just breaking out of the overcast when the engine literally blew up," he remembers. "I just had time to level out and eject. The 'chute opened and swung only twice before I was in trees. It was a nice, soft landing."

Dick has been a licensed flight instructor since 1969 (Fig. 2-21). For ten years before leaving the service, he taught in several USAF Aero Clubs in Cessnas and "whatever." He held the "E" (engine) part of his A&P before joining the service and completed the airframe section just before leaving the service.

At the time of this writing, Dick has a total of 6,000 flying hours in just about every type of aircraft ranging from the tiny 240-pound (empty weight) Quickie to the USAF C-124 transport with a gross weight of 185,000 pounds. Ask him what is his favorite fun flying machine he grins easily, "The company's first-line aircraft—the Long-EZ (Fig. 2-22)."

BURT LOOKS AHEAD IN AVIATION

In a completely different phase of aviation, Rutan has high hopes for the future of the Predator (Fig. 2-23) and feels that it will have a significant effect on feeding much of the world. The Predator is a large, turboprop agricultural aircraft. Its configuration is a unique joined-wing strutless biplane

Fig. 2-22. It gets hot in the desert, so Dick Rutan rides out in the air while taxiing to and from the flight line with the Long-EZ during a check ride with A.L. Letcher.

Fig. 2-23. Scale model of the Predator design shows several unique concepts in this large agricultural aircraft. (courtesy NASA)

nia, with his suggestion of joining the wings together.

Basic research is an area that Burt enjoys and does with aplomb. The AD-1 program is an intriguing example of this type of effort.

The AD-1 is a twin-engine jet research aircraft featuring an adjustable skew-wing (Fig. 2-24). It began as an RAF-submitted, unsolicited proposal to NASA for a feasibility study in December 1975. At the time, skeptics abounded within both NASA and the aircraft industry as to the possibility of building a manned, jet skew-wing research aircraft for less than several million dollars. The AD-1 design task, accomplished by RAF between May 1976 and February 1977, cost NASA only $15,000. Fabrication of the aircraft by Ames Industrial Corporation, including consulting, documentation, static load-testing, and delivery to the government in a completed, flight-ready condition was acomplished between November 1977 and February 1979, and cost NASA less than $240,000. It is interesting to note that the above work by RAF and AIC was done at a profit and at far less cost to the taxpayer than the NASA tasks of the wind-tunnel test, simulation and contractor monitoring. The AD-1 is all composite, using a glass-foam sandwich for all basic structure. It is powered by two TRS-18 microturbo turbojets. Its wing skews 60° actuated by redundant electric motors. NASA installed instrumentation and is currently test-flying the AD-1.

In the non-aviation field, Rutan has developed a solar water heating system that really thrives in the hot desert of Mojave. The RAF solar water heater is a system intended to be built by the hobbyist to provide a large percentage of his home water heating energy requirements. It was designed to minimize the cost-per-BTU ratio. It uses an east-west oriented parabolic collector and an all-composite storage tank. This system has continuously provided 100 percent of the hot water requirements at RAF since July 1977. Burt plans to market plans for this system.

By the end of 1983, Burt had watched general aviation and homebuilding in particular mature greatly. As to the future of the homebuilder, he feels that the best thing for the EAA to do is nothing

arrangement. It uses a PT-6A-34 engine and has a hopper payload of 6,700 pounds. It features the following performance improvements over current Ag aircraft: payload (59 percent), swath width (58 percent), speed (9 percent), climb (11 percent), stall speed (10 percent). It also promises major improvements in safety (stall-proof and crash protection). The Predator was designed during a RAF feasibility study conducted for an independent contractor. NASA has expressed an interest in the design and is currently building models for wind-tunnel tests. While Burt did the original design concept on the Predator, he is quick to credit inventor Dr. Julian Wolkovitch of Palo Alto, Califor-

Fig. 2-24. NASA composite photo of first flights by the AD-1 at Edwards AFB. This project began as an unsolicited design proposal by RAF to NASA. The flying testbed was constructed by Ames Industrial Corp, Bohemia, New York. (courtesy NASA)

at all. He feels that in the United States we have the best homebuilder rules in the world. He cites the report from an EZ builder in Japan who reports that he is restricted to takeoffs and landings within the pattern of the airport where he is based.

Burt continued with RAF until mid-1985, becoming by far the most successful homebuilt designer in the business. He developed SCALED Composites, Inc., a new company dedicated to proprietary development of flying aircraft, usually scaled down from the size of the final product. SCALED was then purchased by Beech Aircraft Corp., and Burt joined the company as a Vice President, Engineering. This expanding effort is covered in Chapter 14.

During this same timeframe, hush-hush work was being done on the round-the-world nonstop, nonrefueled aircraft, Voyager, which went on to become the aviation success story of the decade. (See Chapter 15.)

Chapter 3

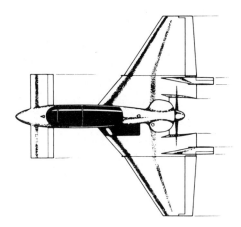

VariViggen: First of Rutan's Canards

Much of the early reporting on the VariViggen project was written first-person by Burt. However, an impersonal report on the roll-out of the original canard aircraft was penned by Art Stockel, Technical Editor of the Air Force Flight Test Center at Edwards Air Force Base and published in *Sport Aviation* magazine in May of 1972:

VARIVIGGEN COMPLETED

On February 27, 1972, Burt Rutan celebrated the rollout of his original canard aircraft, the Vari-Viggen (Fig. 3-1). This airplane is really something different. A lot of original thought and careful engineering were combined to result in such advanced features as these:

High lift at low angles of attack through the complementary vortex interaction of the forward canard surfaces and the rear-mounted wing with its reverse reflex.

Stall and spin-proof performance which retains safe flying qualities at the point of maximum attainable lift.

Elimination of adverse yaw effects by means of the fin-and-aileron geometric interface.

Minimal trim drag at high speed as a result of variable aft wing reflex.

Burt, who is a member of EAA Chapter 49 in Lancaster, California, began working on this aircraft design in 1963 while a student at Cal Poly. Being an aeronautical engineer at the Air Force Flight Test Center nowadays, he is not exactly a greenhorn amateur.

The actual construction of the VariViggen in the garage of his Lancaster home required nearly four years having begun in 1968 after extensive wind-tunnel tests and model experiments dating back to 1963.

"Model experiments" does not mean dropping a toy out of the bedroom window. It means building an aerodynamically true one-fifth scale model which was suspended on a specially built test rig atop a car. Quickly removable, the rig was clamped to the luggage carrier on the station wagon's roof. The rig allowed measurement of airspeed, angle of attack,

Fig. 3-1. VariViggen in flight with temporary 12-gallon auxiliary fuel tank mounted like a drop tank below the fuselage. Paint job is copied from the Air Force Thunderbird competition team and Rutan's version earned the name "Thunder Chicken." (courtesy Burt Rutan)

lift, drag, sideslip, side force, roll moment, elevator-aileron-rudder positions, and an extra data channel which permitted measurement of hinge moment (stick force) or structural load, etc.

Ailerons and rudders and elevators were controllable by the test engineer through an illuminated control box at the right front car seat.

Mounted on a spherical bearing, the model could be shifted fore and aft to test effects of varying CG's. A tape recorder was used to make verbal recordings of data during the test runs.

The "captive" model provided a wealth of information for design of the prototype. The original configuration was actually quite different from the design which was optimized during the car tests.

The visitor's first impression of the airplane when he comes through the door is that it really fills up that two-car garage! The rear wing outboard panels were mated to the fuselage after the plane was removed from the garage. The span, with outboard wing panels removed, is only 8 feet, allowing road towing.

In designing the prototype, Burt decided against going for optimum high speed. Instead, he wanted plenty of wing area for safe, docile, low speed flying qualities. This was considered a conservative approach to development of the configuration and, if it proves as successful as expected, a high performance version will be built to define the performance capabilities of the concept.

He settled for a slab-sided fuselage and flat-bottomed wings for ease of jigging and building (Fig. 3-2). All curved surfaces have a single curvature, except the nosecone, visor/glareshield, and aft fuselage top. These few pieces with compound curvature are all made of fiberglass and Burt has retained the female molds in case more parts are needed.

The main structure (plywood) was easy to build using normal techniques. Windshield and aft canopy have only single curvature, while a formed Plexiglas piece from an HP-11 glider was fitted to the front canopy. Spruce was used for spars and longerons, aircraft plywood for formers, ribs, and skin. The plywood skin was covered with lightweight Ceconite and finished with dope followed by polyurethane. Most of the building time (and this will surprise no one) was spent on fittings and systems such as the retractable gear, the trim and reflex electrical systems, and the controls.

As if things weren't hard enough to get done, Burt claims he used all metal, flush riveted construction for the outboard aft wing panels to get experience in metal construction.

To keep things convenient later on, the nosecone is hinged at the top, thus exposing master brake cylinders, nose gear retraction system, batteries, landing light, angle-of-attack transducer, and pitot-static system. A VOR antenna is installed inside the all wood canard surface.

The prototype VariViggen has a main wing span of 19 feet, a canard span of 8 feet, and a 19-foot length. There is a roomy cockpit for two pilots in tandem which incorporates modern fighter cockpit layout and affords really terrific visibility from both seats; that means both pilots can see well, not only forward but also directly up, down and rearward (both rudders and main landing gear wheels are visible from the seat).

The fully retractable tricycle landing gear is operated electrically, as are the trim bungee and wing reflex (more about this later).

A 150-hp four-cylinder Lycoming engine (which was bought used and then overhauled by Aronson Flying Service at Rosamond, California) powers the prototype. Burt had originally intended to build a single-place prototype with a 90-hp engine, but as many EAA builders can testify, things tend to grow, and a good deal on the larger engine turned up at just the crucial time.

Now a few words on the cockpit, which has separate opening canopy sections for pilot and passenger. The control stick has a gloriously functional handle with switches for electric reflex control, trim, and radio transmitting. Landing gear handle and landing light switch are just forward of the throttle—no need for fumbling around during approach to landing (Fig. 3-3). An angle-of-attack sensing system, used to select approach speed, also operates as back-up gear warning (besides the warning horn and light!) because it remains inoperative as long as the gear is retracted. An override switch permits the pilot to turn the angle-of-attack system on for gear-up maneuvering.

Upper and lower right-hand control consoles contain further items. The lower-right console carries the circuit breaker panel. Recording hourmeter, cockpit lighting switches, magneto switch, and engine starting controls are all on the upper-right console. This leaves the main instrument panel free for flight and engine instruments. The radio, when available, will be located on the left-side console.

The VariViggen weighs in empty at 900 lbs. and approximately 1500 lbs. when loaded. This results in a wing loading of 12.3 lbs./sq.ft. The ship has a power loading of 10.0 lbs./hp. (In case you're wondering, sweepback angle of the aft wing is 27° at the quarter chord.)

The rear-mounted engine drives a 70″ diameter, 70″ pitch wooden pusher propeller (Hegy) directly (no extension shaft). While it may appear that propeller ground clearance might be critical, this is

Fig. 3-2. VariViggen built and flown by Mike Melvill was the first aircraft to be completed from Burt Rutan's original plans.

Fig. 3-3. Instrument panel on Mike Melvill's VariViggen in flight. Note landing gear handle at the far left and complete IFR instrumentation.

definitely not the case, and Burt can show that when the airplane is fully rotated to take-off pitch, the propeller is nowhere near ground contact. The reason for this is that the prop blades track only 6″ below the wing's trailing edge. In fact, when the nose is lifted high enough to put the skids on the ground, the prop still has over 4″ of clearance.

An interesting safety feature should be pointed out here: the propeller is between the twin rudders, and anyone who wanted to blunder into the blades would have a hard time walking against the propwash!

In deciding on the unusual aircraft configuration, Burt felt that the canard feature had distinct advantages over the conventional as well as the delta-wing types. Obviously there is greater low speed lift available at low angles of attack because both surfaces contribute lift; there is more positive lift control with the canard approach, and at higher speeds trim drag and induced drag can be considerably reduced.

He was aware that many attempts had been made to reap these benefits, but most failed be-

cause of unacceptable stall characteristics, poor lateral directional stability, and "packaging" problems. However, one design has been very successful; the Swedish SAAB Viggen, a jet, is in production in two versions—attack and fighter. The Viggen has Mach-2 speed capability, excellent flying qualities without the need of electronic "black boxes' to augment stability, and it operates out of 1,500-foot dirt airstrips! Burt said his VariViggen was designed about the same time as the Viggen, the name having been added later. And, while it is not a copy, it shares some of the Viggen's design features, such as location of the canard surface high and in front of the main wing so the vortex from the canard will mix favorably with the main wing vortex to increase low speed lift. But Burt went one step further and used the front (canard) rather than rear control surfaces for elevator function. Consequently, a nose-up control input immediately increases lift—even before the angle of attack increases—and this extends overall maneuvering capability.

The most important reason for front elevator

control, however, was that the main wing control surfaces could now be employed in a very interesting manner as a controllable reflex (as well as the necessary aileron function) (Figs. 3-4 and 3-5). For increased lift at low angles of attack, the reflex surface is turned downward, causing more lift to be required of the canard (elevator) to balance out the resulting pitch-down tendency. Therefore, elevators and reflexes all act effectively as flaps. As a result, instead of the drastic nose-up approach to landing, the VariViggen's angle of attack is only three degrees at 70 mph (Fig. 3-6). This means that on a three-degree glidescope the fuselage is level!

The triple advantages of this low angle of attack are greatly improved visibility, improved roll and yaw flying qualities, and less power required for a go-around.

On the other hand, the controllable reflex is also used at high speed or cruise. It is set to minimize trim drag and fuselage drag regardless of CG, weight, or speed. As the aircraft is trimmed for cruise, the reflex is set to achieve a level fuselage attitude and minimum elevator drag (the Fowler-type surface is tucked into the slot).

Low speed characteristics are very safe. Wind tunnel and radio controlled model tests have shown

Fig. 3-4. Tufts on the left canard of the VariEze remain flush with the wing surface during a full stall.

Fig. 3-5. Only in a violent accelerated stall will the tufts break away from the surface of the VariViggen canard.

that the plane will not stall or spin. It just becomes "super stable" in pitch at angles of attack higher than about 15°. When full aft stick is applied the plane remains at a safe angle of attack. Sharp turns or banks can be made using only aileron, only rudder, or even with crossed controls, and the plane stays easily controllable. Burt says that a short field approach with minimum air speed (less than 50 mph) would be made with the stick trimmed and held full aft, using only the throttle for flightpath control! This may at first seem terrifying, but the data and radio controlled model test results indicate otherwise.

As it worked out, the VariViggen doesn't need differential aileron control to alleviate adverse yaw. The pressure difference on the wing's upper surface which is caused by aileron deflection acts directly on the vertical fins to turn the nose into the roll. Wind tunnel tests have shown that the plane should make coordinated turns even at approach speed while the pilot's feet are on the floor.

Cautious when it comes to predicting air speeds, Burt will only say that the VariViggen should cruise with a Thorp T-18 and land slower than a Cessna 150. He knows that all the theorizing, planning and building are now over and that actual flight testing is the next step.

Fig. 3-6. VariViggen coming across the numbers at Mojave. This Viggen is flown by Mike Melvill, who has put more time on the Viggen design than anyone else in the world to date.

THE VIGGEN FLIES

A year and a half later, Burt reported on his first flights in Kansas. First light of print on this memorable series of flights was in *Sport Aviation* in August 1973, entitled "VariViggen Designer Builder Report," by Burt Rutan, and the text follows:

About the time I had the airplane ready for taxi tests, I had decided to leave my job as project flight test engineer for the Air Force at Edwards Air Force Base in California and join Bede Aircraft, Inc., at Newton, Kansas. I found as I had suspected that developing and testing homebuilt airplanes is as much a challenge and a lot more fun than the supersonic jets! I was so anxious to get started at the Bede Test Center, I removed the wings from my newly completed VariViggen and packed it into

a moving van with my furniture and made the trip to Kansas without having made even the taxi tests.

The move was a good one; the aircraft arrived in excellent shape, and I was able to use the excellent shop facilities at the Bede Test Center and the expertise of Paul Griffin (Chief Designer) and Delmar Hostetler (Shop Foreman) to help me make the last minute adjustments to get on with taxi tests.

About the first of April '72, I got the engine running and started low speed taxi tests. I found the airplane to be very maneuverable on the ground. Its geometry is such that it can be nosed up to within three feet of a hangar, turned and taxied away without ground assist. I can easily see the wing tips and rudders from the cockpit and due to its short and low wings, it can be taxied between and around other airplanes much easier than conventional aircraft.

My original nose gear encountered shimmy while taxiing at only 25 mph. This was due to improper geometry and the use of a streamline type tire. Rather than spend a lot of time developing a suitable shimmy damper, I installed a BD-4 nose gear. This absolutely eliminated the shimmy, but since I had not provided any shock absorption, the gear gave a hard ride in bumps. Well, after all, this nose gear was just a temporary fix—who knew if this thing would even fly?

Another initial problem involved the engine. I had smooth operation up through about half throttle, then the engine would quit if the throttle were advanced further. I found I could get ⅔ throttle if I leaned the mixture, but that was all. I spent the next several weeks changing carburetors, air inlets, valve pushrods, ignition and just about everything I could think of.

I had the local FAA in for the final inspection and took care of their squawks: mark *Fuel* outside the fuel lid, *Fuel shut-off—pull* on the fuel shut-off handle, and safety the shoulder harness bolts.

After more tries to get the engine to operate properly, I convinced myself that it would run reliably up to ⅔ throttle and that's enough to fly. I set up a movie camera, run by Les Berven, our BD-5 Test Pilot, got the wife and kids out to the airport and started my first high speed taxi tests. I started at 35 knots and made successfully faster taxi runs in five-knot increments, checking controllability.

The nose gear left the ground on the 45 knot run and I found it very easy to hold the nose off in any attitude I wanted, and it fell through gently when decelerating through 30 knots. On the next run at 50 knots, I exercised the ailerons to see if it would rock while light on the main gear with the nose up. To my surprise, I found myself slightly off the ground rocking the tires on the runway! I decided the next run would be a brief flight down the runway at about 3 feet altitude. I accelerated to 55 knots, rotated and flew down about 4,000 feet of the 7,000-foot runway at Newton at about 10 ft. altitude. The feel of all three axes was solid and smooth—and I was one happy guy! The landing was a grease job but in my relief I let the nose down hard in one of the ruts in the runway and the nose gear

collapsed. A quick inspection revealed no major damage. The retraction link had buckled due to an impact load from the stiff gear, allowing the gear to partially retract. Faced with 90 minutes of daylight remaining and very still, no-wind conditions, I decided to make a quick repair and fly. Within a half hour I was on the end of the runway and setting my ⅔ throttle and lean mixture for takeoff.

As Dan Cooney (Chief Bede Chase Pilot) maneuvered the Cessna 172 chase plane into position, I started my take-off roll. Takeoff and climb were normal and a very strange feeling came over me as I cleared the end of the runway. The air was absolutely still and there I was climbing straight ahead. I had waited a long time for this moment, but somehow it felt like I was on my first solo.

I leveled off at 1,500' AGL and performed some stability checks—static and dynamic—and pleased with the results, I proceeded to do sideslips and maneuvering turns. I set the reflex at several positions and slowed up to full aft stick to check low speed handling. Again the aircraft felt solid, while still responsive—particularly in roll. So much for the work. I moved in to the Cessna for some pictures, then made a low pass down the runway and landed just at sunset after 50 enjoyable minutes of flying.

The next nine weeks were spent completing initial flight tests, improving engine operation, gathering stability and performance data to compare with wind tunnel results, getting my 50-hour restriction lifted, and adding a new cowling and spinner. I solved the engine problem by shifting the carburetor air inlet to the cooling air inlet location and replacing my Midas-special exhaust system with short stacks.

Tip fins on the wing tips were on for the first few flights for some extra directional stability just in case it would be needed. After tests showed that the amount of directional stability was more than adequate, the fins were removed.

By Oshkosh '72 (nine weeks after first flight), I had logged 75 hours and had taken the airplane cross country to Illinois and Oklahoma. Oshkosh was the highlight though, landing at the convention and taxiing to our parking place among the other homebuilts was the culmination of those years of designing and building. When my wife and I left Oshkosh loaded with 80 pounds of baggage (including the Stan Dzik trophy for design contribution), we agreed that those who have the opportunity to participate in sport aviation do have more fun.

The VariViggen spent the winter attending whatever fly-ins we could make, completing stall/ spin tests and getting a new paint job and interior. After more problems with the stiff nose gear, I built a new unit which uses an air-oleo strut, the lower end still being the BD-4 assembly. This one is giving excellent service with no problems, even on sod runways.

I have been unable to spin the aircraft during straight ahead stall entries or accelerated entries with all combinations of aileron and rudder controls. I haven't tried hammerhead entries (I'm chicken), but the radio-controlled model would not spin from hammerheads so I think I can safely say it is not spinnable.

The thing I like most about the airplane is its roll qualities. Its low adverse yaw, high roll rate, ability to stop the bank right where you want, combined with the fighter visibility and cockpit just make it fun to fly. An F-106 pilot who flew it said it handled more like the F-106 than any type he had flown, military included. The roll rate is surprisingly high even at 50 knots. This allows you to roll 120 degrees to level at the top of a steep wing over and fly away without dishing out.

Due to the position of the landing gear and thrust line, the nosewheel rotation speed is about ten knots above the minimum flying speed. Thus, on a full power takeoff, it is impossible to force the aircraft in the air at an unsafe speed. I generally make the takeoff roll holding full aft stick. At about 53 knots, the nose comes up slowly and is easy to control at just the position I want for initial climb. There is no tendency to bobble or hunt for the initial climb angle since pitch damping is high and the aircraft is not sensitive.

I generally fly final approach at 10 degrees angle of attack (all VariViggens have angle of attack indicators) which results in about 60 to 70 knots depending on gross weight. The speed bleed off at flare is fairly rapid without a great deal of tendency to float, even though there is a considerable ground effect. The ground effect is so great that if you want you can make a full stall type landing with touchdown as slow as 37 knots; that's right, 37 *calibrated*, not indicated. Full stop is easy within 300 feet.

VariViggens are less affected by winds during taxi than other types of similar wing loading. In fact, due to one rudder blanking the other, you can taxi in a 40-knot direct crosswind with no tendency to weathervane.

As I mentioned, rolls are fun. You can complete a 360° roll without altitude loss from a level flight speed as slow as 85 knots. But, the VariViggen is not an aerobatic airplane. It is strong enough, but due to its low aspect ratio (2.7), it slows down considerably during tight maneuvering. This makes vertical maneuvers such as loops very difficult. Also, of course, true snap rolls are impossible since you can't stall the main wing.

The climb and cruise speed of the VariViggen are not particularly good considering it is a two place retractable with 150 hp. It will cruise with a BD-4 or T-18 with equal power, but then, those are fixed gear aircraft. It may improve some when I get around to adding the 3 gear doors, but I doubt if it will be over 5 to 10 mph. Where the VariViggen performance really shines is at the low speed range.

RETURN TO THE DESERT

When Burt Rutan moved to Mojave in 1974, he brought the prototype VariViggen (N27VV) with him. In that year, his canard design won the Outstanding New Design trophy at the Oshkosh EAA meeting. In his second newsletter, then called *VariViggen News,* he wrote:

Even though the VariViggen had been to California twice before, we couldn't wait after arriving at Mojave for the first chance to really demonstrate her flying ability to the multitudes out West. The next weekend was the EAA Western Fly-in at Porterville, California. The following excerpt from the Bakersfield EAA Chapter 71 newsletter written by Denny McGlothlen tells it all:

"The star of the show was Burt Rutan with his VariViggen. Boy, this bird really turned me on. I was out on the runway when Burt flew in the airshow and saw the VariViggen make the low speed sharp turns right at liftoff—well, an airplane just isn't supposed to do such things but this one sure will. I can see that this is going to be a very much built airplane in the EAA ranks."

The VariViggen succeeded in awing the crowd there and also won the Most Popular trophy, the 2nd Monoplane trophy, and the 1st place cash prize for the spot landing contest. The VariViggen has won every spot landing contest it has entered. Due to the fantastic low speed maneuverability and visibility, you can use quick tight turns on short final to set up the correct height and speed for the accurate touchdown. The 2nd place winner at the Beatrice, Nebraska contest just shook his head and said, "That's not fair; that's not an airplane!"

We have two more airshows and a magazine article commitment within the next two weeks. After that we plan to remove the old cowling, give the aircraft a good inspection (she now has 400 flight hours) and install the new design cowling with prop extension. When testing is complete on the cowling we will begin cowling production.

In the early days of development, the unconventional landing gear arrangement raised many an eyebrow, particularly when the canard was parked on the ramp. Burt discussed this feature in his newsletter, along with the reasoning behind the selection of 180-hp engine and his ideas on modifications on the VariViggens:

Parking: Without pilot or copilot, the CG is very near (slightly aft of) the main wheel location. With weight on the main gear its reaction moves aft of the no-load position. Thus, when the pilot gets out, he lets the aircraft down on the aft skids. At first we were ashamed of this tail-sitting attitude and would immediately tie the nose gear to a tiedown or install an aluminum tube tripod under one skid whenever we parked. I don't do this anymore for the following reasons: 1) sitting on the skids, the center of pressure is well centered and the aircraft will take winds from *any* direction with little weathering or upsetting tendency common to the conventional parked aircraft; 2) when parked in a hangar, even a low wing aircraft will overlap all the way to the fuselage and thus a VariViggen will take up considerably less room than even smaller homebuilts; (I've put it in many hangars after the owner said "Sorry, we're full" without even moving other airplanes!) 3) this attitude allows more convenient pre-flight inspection of fuel, oil, landing gear and pulling the prop through; 4) baggage loading, fuel and oil loading is convenient while on the tail; 5) it is very easy to pull the nose down by the canard tip, step to the ladder and get in when ready for ingress; 6) we consider it a "status symbol"—just one other thing no other plane on the field can do! However, for an airshow, in order for people to more easily inspect the cockpit, we either tie the nose gear to a tail tiedown rope (VariViggens park backwards, too) or retract the nosewheel only (pull the main gear braker) and set it clear down on its nose. Thus, the canard is an excellent seat for four to watch the show!

Engine Selection: Since I mentioned that I would like to have 180 hp, many have thought it was for more speed. Not true, considering 75 percent power cruise, speed would only increase 10 mph with 180 hp. The main reason would be for better rate-of-climb, particularly at high altitude. Remember, low aspect ratio means lower climb performance. A VariViggen will not climb as well as a conventional aircraft with equal cruise speed and hp/weight ratio. Those that want better high altitude climb performance and want to use a heavier engine or constant-speed prop will find the airplane tail-heavy and for that reason I have not recommended them, due to the terrible requirement for lead in the nose. There is a better solution, however, that can eliminate this problem. I used this solution when I found my partially completed airplane to be tail-heavy. The original design had a shorter wingspan. I increased the span of the outboard wing panels. This moved the *allowable* CG range aft, thus solving the problem without lead. A disadvantage is a slightly reduced G-capability. If you are interested in using a constant-speed prop or heavier engine, send me the weight, length of engine and weight of the prop. I will then calculate for you the amount of extension to the wing tip, show how to make the extension and calculate the amount of reduction in allowable "G." This can only be done up to a point at which the control power of the canard is reduced and the overall CG range is too small. While this solution is better than lead nose weight, I still recommend 150 hp (180 hp for short airstrips or high density altitude flying) and a modern light weight wood prop.

Modifications: As you know, it has been our policy to not be adverse toward those who want to modify the VariViggen. We have had this policy mainly in the interest of promoting education and design progress. However, we have seen some examples of modifications, even some under construction, that will result in disappointing performance and in some cases unsafe flight characteristics. In all cases those individuals designed their modifications by aesthetics and by eyeball rather than by valid engineering calculation supported with appropriate tests. In most cases, when I was able to point out the disadvantages and calculate the effect on performance and stability, the author of the change decided to stick with the plans. One builder doubled the rudder area and didn't even know that that would reduce overall directional stability due to rudder float.

I must modify my policy to point out that I am not averse to anyone modifying the airplane that is qualified (or finds qualified help) and is willing to conduct the analysis and tests required to verify the modification before flying his aircraft. I am very averse to those who may give all the rest of us a bad image by building a "VariViggen" that either has poor performance or contributes to an accident statistic under the name VariViggen.

A plans-built aircraft has good utility and excellent flying qualities. Modifications that add weight, be they as subtle as extra heavy gussets everywhere or fiberglass over the wood skin—or more substantial—like 70 gallons fuel or four-place, etc., etc., can result in very disappointing climb performance at high altitudes. Our experience in flying N27VV over 400 hours in all kinds of flight conditions, runways, weather, density altitudes, etc., is very valuable, and we have found that due to the low aspect ratio (necessary for optimum low speed flying qualities) the airplane should have a lower weight-to-power ratio than conventional designs. You cannot expect to carry four people and more fuel adequately from Albuquerque in the summer unless you use at least 200 hp.

You cannot expect the same safe flying qualities if you stretch the nose several feet for "looks." This would decrease stability and actually slow down the aircraft! You cannot just assume that a beautiful flush inlet three inches from the top of the wing will provide adequate cooling. My measurements during development of an oil cooler system showed terrible pressure recovery during low speed.

I should point out that because with a canard aircraft both surfaces are lifting wings (the canard actually has a much greater wing loading than the main wing); their size, position, interference with each other, high lift devices, etc., have a very important effect on the CG range, the flying qualities and low speed performance. Their design is far more critical than with a conventional aircraft with one main lifting wing (sized for performance, etc.) and a tail sized merely to provide adequate static margin and sufficient CG range. For example, a formula-one racer has an extremely small tail—but it can be designed for one CG only and still provide adequate stability and sufficient control. But if it were a canard, the designer would have much less room for change, to provide a large flight envelope (speed, range and maneuverability) even for one CG.

Therefore, I am unable, without conducting the appropriate tests, to answer a question like "Is it okay to move the canard down eight inches to clear my extra radios in the instrument panel." I am not averse to you making the change, however, if you are willing to conduct the tests and verify satisfactory results. The car-top wind tunnel system is an excellent method; others are also valid.

Remember, this aircraft was not developed by guesswork, but by a very careful design-test program. Small changes can be full of surprises. If you modify an aircraft, when it is ready to fly you are an *experimental* test pilot, not a *production* test pilot—be prepared to accept the full responsibility to safely plan and conduct exploratory testing and critical flight envelope expansion, for there are no proven limits on your airplane.

I don't mean to inhibit progress, only to promote valid development. In this way we are also promoting education, which is what EAA is all about!

MIKE AND SALLY MELVILL BUILD FIRST VIGGEN

Mike Melvill (Fig. 3-7) and his wife Sally, both originally from Johannesburg, South Africa, have been an integral part of canard development since they first saw Burt Rutan's flight demonstration of the prototype VariViggen at Oshkosh. Mike was the first builder to complete his VariViggen and at the time this book was prepared, he had logged over 410 hours on N27MS (Rutan's Design #27 and Mike/Sally for MS).

Fig. 3-7. Mike Melvill, left, assists Burt Rutan during a Long-EZ checkout. Melvill was the first builder to complete a Viggen and, together with his wife Sally, has moved to the high desert of Southern California.

Before Mike Melvill purchased his VariViggen plans, he had joined the EAA and had a Cougar ⅔ built in his sitting room in Anderson, Indiana. The wings were in his bedroom. This was not acceptable, so he sold the parts and purchased a Cougar 90 percent finished, put it in the air and flew it for four years before he saw Rutan's Viggen.

Melvill (and it is spelled without an "e;" Mike says that his ancestors in Scotland had a violent argument four generations ago, dropped out of the clan, and also dropped the "e" from the family name) saw Rutan's Viggen demonstration and said, "That's the airplane for me. It's not as fast or as fuel efficient as some, but it'll carry two people with three suitcases in comfort."

To accommodate the new project, the Melvills purchased another house in Anderson—one with a 18′ × 32′ family room that was used for building. How long did it take? Mike rattles off the answer with a grin: "Three years, one month, twenty-two days. I don't know how many hours of work, but it was somewhere between three and four thousand. My out-of-pocket cost was $13,500 (in 1977 dollars), including a zero-time engine."

Mike learned to fly in Indiana when the tool and die shop where he was working needed a salesman who could fly to visit customers. During his Viggen project, he went directly by Rutan's plans until he got around to the landing gear retraction system. After breaking retraction cables during construction, he redesigned the entire system and built the complex parts on weekends at the tool and die shop where he was the foreman.

"The original design didn't work out for me and the one I designed was damn difficult for the average guy to build. I had the tools and the experience in the machine shop. I did all my own welding and machining. I made every part of the Viggen literally, except the fiberglass nosebowl and engine cowling. It was a tremendous education—better than college, I think.

"The Viggen has really been a part of our lives, Sally's and mine. We've flown it to Key West and Seattle; we've been in Oshkosh twice, and now we're both working for Burt in the California desert at Mojave with the Viggen, our No. 1 means of long-range transport (Fig. 3-8)."

While the Melvills were constructing their No. 1 Viggen in Indiana, Rutan was a visitor. He spent half a day crawling around looking at the project. Later Mike flew the airplane—the first one that Burt had ever seen fly except his own. Later they talked at Oshkosh and Mike was invited to come and work for Rutan. When he found out that Sally was a bookkeeper and the couple had always worked together for the same company, he said, "I need *her* worse than I do *you*."

So the Melvills moved west, VariViggen and all, and purchased a home in Tehachapi, 17 airmiles west and 1,200 feet higher than Mojave where you don't need air conditioning, even in the summer. The couple commute to work in a rare two-cylinder, 60-hp Aeronca 7ACA "Cheap Champ." The flight takes 15 minutes downhill and 20 minutes on the return. When they are forced to drive, it's 30 minutes each way (26 miles on a winding road) and nowhere near the fun!

Sally Melvill has a number of "firsts" in aviation. She's the first woman to solo the Viggen, and she has 40-50 hours in that ship as of this writing.

She was the first woman to solo the Long-EZ and does her economy practicing solo in the "Cheap Champ." Sally likes this little taildragger because it is sort of a challenge to fly, and Mike likes it for the miniscule fuel bills and because it is tandem (like his Viggen) and would be easy to land in the desert. Sally also has the glider rating in the family. "When I want to fly a glider, I go with her," grinned Mike.

Mike's mother Isobel visited the Mojave area recently and took her first lightplane ride ever with her son in his Viggen. Later she went along to tour most of Southern California, Arizona and Nevada in the back seat of the Viggen. Mike's father, who died before his son ever became involved with aviation, was in the South African Air Force in WWII flying Mosquitos on photo missions.

"I wish that my Dad had been able to see all this," said Mike.

The details of Mike Melvill's VariViggen construction, and particularly his contributions to the landing gear design, were well documented in early editions of the *VariViggen News* and in subsequent issues when the name of the quarterly publication changed to *Canard Pusher*.

Fig. 3-8. Mike Melvill pulls in close to the photo plane in the VariViggen as Dick Rutan follows with the Long-EZ.

In early newsletters, Burt Rutan described his own three gear-up landings in the prototype N27VV in this manner:

World's first VariViggen gear-up landing. It occurred during the airshow demonstrations on Saturday and Sunday for the fly-in. On Sunday, I had completed the airshow demo, all except the landing. When I moved the gear handle down, I heard a different noise and noted that although I had electrical power to the main gear (transit light on), the mains did not come down. The failure was later determined to be the spring that connects to the uplock arm.

The spring had apparently been nicked with pliers when forming the hook on one end in 1970 when the spring was installed. Five years later, during the airshow demo, the spring broke. Without this spring, the right main gear remained locked up. After several passes over the crowd, for inspection of gear position and some radio discussion with those on the ground on whether or not to land in an adjacent grass field, I decided to land on the main hard surface runway with the nose gear down. This was taking the risk that the nose gear would not fail and thus reduce the damage. I made a "full-stall"-type landing with engine and switches off, and after a short roll/slide, I got out to inspect the damage. Damage was limited to one skid (VS1 extension with small wheel), a small scrape on one wing tip (only one rivet damaged), and partial collapse of my centerline fuel tank. The tank remained attached firmly on its mount and did not leak. The nose gear took the "slap down" load well with no damage. About 20 volunteers lifted the aircraft up while I scampered underneath to manually free the uplock and to lock the gear down. I then taxied back to a hangar, inspected the aircraft, elected to pin the main gear down and locked for the flight home. Within 1½ hours of the gear-up landing, I took off and flew it back to Mojave where I was greeted by 60-knot surface winds. Landing and taxi-in were uneventful despite the fact that at the time two other aircraft were being jerked from their tie-downs and suffered wind damage much greater than my earlier gear-up landing!

I learned a bit from this experience:

1. Inspect uplocks during preflight and use appropriate quality control during their installation.

2. If faced with a main gear-up landing, pull the main gear circuit breaker, extend the nose gear and make a landing with the nose quite high (full flare) on a hard surface. This landing is really not more difficult than a conventional landing and you can expect very little damage.

3. Gear-up landings on VariViggens are far safer than on conventional aircraft where one of the first things to get damaged is the carb and fuel line and the possibility of a fire exists.

4. Note that the emergency extension free-fall system backs up an electrical failure and mechanical failure of the electrical motor and gear box, but does not extend the gear with a jammed uplock. I do not recommend a design change of any type since the gear has had nearly 1000 satisfactory cycles during all types of weather and flight conditions. Any change now would be starting at zero experience with a resulting increase in risk.

5. Gear-up landings have a very positive appeal from a marketing standpoint. It emphasizes how rugged the structure is to survive with only minor damage. We immediately received seven orders for plans from people who saw the landing!

VariViggen Gear-up Landing Sagas #2 & #3. We again were faced with having to land on our way to Oshkosh this year with the main gear retracted. We landed N27VV on a hard surface runway with the nose gear extended. We got the prop stopped before touchdown and slid out on the rear skids and nose gear. Again, the nose gear took the load with no damage; all damage was limited to the two aft skids and a non-critical scrape on the aileron control arms. Inspection revealed the problem to be the same uplock spring which caused the gear to remain locked up three months earlier at the Corona Fly-in. We were on our way that afternoon again after pinning the main gear down, and we flew the remainder of the trip to Oshkosh with the main gear down. The next day at Oshkosh we repaired the skids and rerigged the main gear to put it back in operation.

This time the uplock spring's loop had somehow slipped out of the bracket rather than failing like it had at Corona. The spring loop was returned to the bracket, this time twisting it backwards so its own torsion wouldn't tend to remove it.

I feel quite embarrassed by having this spring fail—twice! After all, a spring is something to trust—like gravity. I am recommending that you install a simple addition which consists of adding a branch to the existing emergency extension cable. The present emergency extension cable removes the electric motor from the system, allowing the uplock return springs to push the gear overcenter so it can freefall down. This only backs up a failure of the electrical motor and cannot extend the gear if the uplock springs fail or if the uplock would jam. By simply adding cables to the existing emergency cable and routing them to the top of the uplock bellcranks, the emergency handle would not only remove the motor, but would pull the uplocks out and force the gear overcenter and on its way down. Thus, the emergency handle overrides a spring failure *and* any jam of the gear.

Gear-up landing #3 is of no real concern to builders, since it does not involve a problem which can occur with your aircraft, since an obvious design improvement was incorporated into the plans before they were first released. The failure allowed the MG5 bolt to slip past the MG29 bolt during gear retraction. As such, the microswitch on MG29 was not activated and the gear motor continued to run, jamming the gear way over center and failing the cable. This failure occurred on the third flight of the day at the EAA Western Fly-in at Tulare, California, with Bob Eldridge in the back seat. I had taken off to compete in the spot landing contest. Since there was a lot of activity on the runway at Tulare, we decided to fly to another airport about 20 miles away to do our gear-up landing there. The landing on the nose gear and aft skids was uneventful (routine?); the gear was fixed, and we flew back to Tulare to compete in the spot landing contest.

Now—I don't expect to hear from any more of the VariEze fans about wanting to retract the main gear!

CHECKOUT BY THE DESIGNER

Since Melvills' VariViggen was the first to fly,

its progress was well documented in early issues of Rutan's quarterly *VariViggen News*. Taken in chronological sequence, some of these reports show how the new airplane evolved.

Prior to attempting his first flight, Mike prudently visited Rutan in California and flew with the designer in the prototype. These were Mike's comments as published in the newsletter:

Burt made the first takeoff and one of the lasting impressions was the sight of the shadow following along in the early morning sun.

Burt demonstrated level flight, slow flight, turns, steep turns, and most important, pitch trim changes with abrupt power changes. This is something that has been emphasized over and over and rightly so. It is an unusual condition, but to be perfectly honest, not a difficult thing to get used to. Personally, I had very little problem with it; however, I was thoroughly aware of the condition and I am very current in several different aircraft. This is a point that cannot be too strongly emphasized.

Any person thoroughly checked out and confident in say a Cessna 182, a Grumman Tiger and a taildragger, in my case a homebuilt Nesmith Cougar, will have no problem with the VariViggen.

After a little stick time in the back seat, we traded seats and I spent quite a while just taxiing the airplane all over the place and let me say this, there cannot be a more simple or manageable airplane anywhere. It is so easy to drive around on the ground and it goes right where you point it. Marvelous!

Then I did some high speed taxi runs; again just point it and go; no problem with keeping it on the centerline as it tracks perfectly straight, and the rudder becomes effective very early in the take-off run.

Next we tried some nosewheel liftoffs. This must be done in accordance with Burt's instructions in the owners manual. Get it stabilized at the speed you want, retard the throttle, then rotate. The nose will come up and is very easy to control. I want to emphasize, pitch control is excellent. Before I tried it, I was worried that pitch control may be marginal. However, this is not so at all. Pitch control is really great; you can put the nose anywhere you want to and maintain it there.

Then we did a couple of runway flights, liftoffs and flying in ground effect. Again, control is excellent, both pitch and roll, and I felt very happy in it. Full power takeoff was an anticlimax—it was very normal and flew just like any other high performance single engine. Handling qualities in the air are great. It flies perfectly in my opinion. In fact, I was very pleasantly surprised. It is all I had ever hoped for and more.

The landing, again was almost anticlimactic; with the correct airspeed and altitude, it will land itself. The only thing to remember when landing is *not* to try to full stall land it as you would a Cessna. It is much better to fly it on; the gear is very forgiving and takes care of most bumps. Don't try to hold the nose gear off right down to a virtual stop because it will stay up until the canard quits flying and then will fall through rather abruptly. This is no problem, but I personally think that you get a nicer landing by letting the nose down before the canard quits. Also, this gives you better braking, as all the weight will be on the wheels instead of some of the weight being carried on the wings, which it would at the high angles of attack possible by holding the nose off.

If you try to stall it on, it is possible to hit the tail skids on the runway, so until you get really familiar with the airplane, listen to Burt and fly it on!

To recap: make sure you read and fully understand the owners manual on test flights. Then go out and enjoy your Viggen, it is a super airplane.

Burt's comments: Mike is a very proficient pilot. He handled the airplane in the first few seconds like he had 100 hours in it. I particularly noticed how well he flew the rudders—must be his Cougar experience. Mike should feel right at home and confident on his first flight in his Viggen.

The very next issue had this enthusiastic reply from Mike:

Well, we finally got there! At 11:30 A.M., 9-22-77, I took off from the Anderson Municipal Airport, and everything behaved as it should. It stayed up for about 45 minutes, did *not* retract the gear and made a perfect landing. I cannot describe the feeling, it was absolutely fantastic. Thank you so much for a fabulous flying machine! Later the same day I climbed to 5,500 and retracted the gear and checked it out generally.

As of today, I have 13.2 hours on it with no problems. At 7,500' in level flight, she trues out at 170 mph at 2700 rpm. I have a 70 × 70 "Ted" prop, but for an 0-360 even that is not enough, as it will over-rev at low altitude. At 3,500 feet she will indicate 165 mph at 2700 rpm, but this is not full throttle. Initial climb solo is 1,500 f./min. At 5,000' solo she makes a steady 1,000 ft./min. All systems operate perfectly, reflex, electric trim, and gear are really first class and I am very satisfied.

My radios (TERRA 360 com & 200 NAV) are really outstanding, and the tower at Anderson says I have the best transmission of any radio in the area. I cannot say enough about the airplane. She really is a hell of a fine craft. I love it.

Empty weight, 1,252 lbs.
Empty cg 132.78
Main tank holds 24.7 gals.
Wings hold 6.5 each - 13 gals. total

So far I have flown it at 125"cg, 124, 123, & 122. It handles well in all planes so far.

Yesterday I loaded 170 lbs. in the passenger seat and could hardly tell any difference.

It takes 16 minutes to transfer 13 gals. from the wings to the mains. Cyl head temps run between 375 & 425, oil temp 165°, ground handling is excellent, brakes are very good. Rotation with full throttle occurs with full aft stick at 70 mph indicated. Initial climb at 85 mph indicated for gear retraction, then trimmed down to 120 mph for good cooling gives 1,000 ft./min. R. O. C. Canard stalls at 60 mph indicated (airspeed may not be accurate at slow speed) will climb with canard stalling & unstalling, and is fully controllable. Side slips well.

Actually, it flies just about like yours. I must say I really get a heck of a kick out of flying it. I will enclose some pictures. I painted it off-white with dark green trim.

Sally sends her best regards. Thank you again, Burt, for making it possible.

Three issues later (nine months), Rutan reported that Mike and Sally have really been giving their Viggen a workout:

They visited RAF in May during a 600-mile trip. Mike and Sally were alternating front/back seat pilot chores. They were loaded down with baggage and handled a 9,000-foot density altitude takeoff at Albuquerque with no problem. His summary after arriving home: "Once again the Viggen has proven to us what a really practical cross-country machine it is. We love it and would not trade it for anything."

Mike designed and built a very clever angle-of-attack instrument for his Viggen. Instead of a potentiometer on the vane (the one that's so hard to find), he made up a wiper with three electrical contacts. These go to three lights on the visor arranged in a vertical format. When the center light is on (green), the airplane is "on speed." When the top light is on, you are too slow; too fast if the bottom one is lit. This system automatically makes you fly the correct approach speed regardless of weight. It works exactly like the indicator lights in an F-4 jet fighter, yet Mike built it for $5.00!

We have been able to inspect the Melvill drawings for the worm-drive main gear modification. They do add some complexity, but in the long run we feel that it's well worth it. We highly recommend it and plan to incorporate it when the Viggen plans are updated in the 2nd edition.

Four more issues went to press and then Mike penned the following report for VariViggen and VariEze builders:

I flew N27MS to Oshkosh this year and had a super trip, flew in formation all the way there and back with a 180-hp Grumman Tiger, piloted by Sally. The Viggen had to be flown at quite a low power setting in order to stay with the Tiger at ground speeds around 140 knots (162 mph). I only burned 7.8 gph average for the whole trip. Not bad for 180 hp.

We flew from Mojave via Las Vegas, NV, Provo, UT, Scottsbluff, NB, Rochester, MN, to Oshkosh. The Viggen joined up with the defiant and Long EZ for several airshows during the week. From Oshkosh Sally and I flew (Tiger and Viggen) to Indiana to visit family and then via Coffeyville, KS, Tucumcari, NM, Abq, NM, to Mojave. It was a most enjoyable trip. I put 37 hours on the Viggen; she now has 366 hours and apart from adding two quarts of oil, she required no maintenance. The only new Viggen flying since the last newsletter is a French VariViggen, built as a flying test bed for the Microturbo jet engine. This very beautiful aircraft is powered by two of the diminutive jet engines (same as BD5-jet) located one above the other. The aircraft has only flown a few times, but reportedly is quite fast.

Unfortunately, since the last newsletter there have been two VariViggen accidents. Although causes are not known for sure, pilot proficiency still appears to be a problem. You must be current and *sharp* in several airplanes before attempting a first test flight in any new airplane. *Do* follow the owner's manual to the letter. *Do not* omit the high speed taxi and runway flights. If possible, get a checkout in a Viggen with an experienced Viggen pilot. All of you are spending several years and several thousands of dollars; don't throw it all away with careless flight testing.

I have a hunch that several Viggens are almost flight ready. When you are, give us a call; we will be glad to help you with your test program or provide a Viggen checkout.

In the next newsletter, Mike had this to report about Sally:

N27MS has flown regularly and on June 19, Sally soloed our Viggen for the first time. She had flown it regularly from the front seat, but I have never had the guts to get out and let her go solo! I finally could not put it off any longer, and she went out and made three perfect landings. Sally's total flying time is 120 hours, mostly in C-150s and with a little Grumman Tiger time. The only problem is now our Viggen will not always be available for me to fly! Congratulations, Sally.

With the many and varied activities at Mojave,

there may be more aircraft than pilots come Oshkosh time. Thus, when Mike Melvill flew the Grizzly east in 1982, Jeana Yeager volunteered to fly the No. 2 Viggen. Mike gave her a short checkout and she spent an hour or two shooting landings at Mojave. A load of 25 pounds of lead shot was needed in the nose because of Jeana's weight of under 100 pounds.

Mike reported that "Jeana did not have any problems with the Viggen. I demonstrated the pitch trim change with power changes and also the high sink rate with power off. We practiced a few simulated power-off landings, then she was ready and she honestly never made a bad landing. Jeana had a ball on the way to and from Oshkosh. The only squawk was a short in the number one com radio,

caused by water. Just over 30 hours was added to the logbook, bringing the Viggen's total time to 560 hours."

BUILDING THE VIGGEN: NOT VERY EASY

George Craig is a retired school psychologist living in Milpitas, California (Fig. 3-9). He is one of the VariViggen builders whose airplane was perhaps ¾ completed at the time we contacted him. Craig has been a pilot for many years, working on his own Cessna 172, including rebuilding the engine. He installed the popular 180-hp Avcon engine conversion kit on his Cessna, doing the majority of the work on it himself.

We asked George to share his reasons for

Fig. 3-9. George and Madge Craig work together on this homebuilt design. Without family cooperation like this, many homebuilt projects never fly.

choosing the Viggen for his first homebuilt project and any other thoughts or suggestions he might have. Here's what he had to say:

As to why I selected the Viggen—that goes back to when I was in high school and was doing designs of airplanes before WWII. I had always wondered why one puts the tail behind the airplane. If you look at an airplane, it's like an arrow in reverse. The wing should be the stabilizing part of the airplane and instead you put the tail in back, and you end up with a negative lift component. In other words, you're always dragging that tail along behind you and, in order for it to control the airplane, it has to work in reverse so that you actually lose lift. That doesn't really seem reasonable to me and the Wright Brothers must have felt the same way because they certainly put the tail out in front.

In selecting the Viggen, I wanted an unusual design. I had heard that the VariViggen would go very slow and make quite steep turns without the possibility of stalling. And I found out later, in the two times I flew Burt Rutan's airplane, that this was the case. So, on the basis that it was an unusual design, one which would theoretically be very efficient and the fact that I had an interest in the canard concept dating back to high school, I selected it. Another factor is I felt comfortable with woodwork as that is what I was most proficient with and had the most tools for. So there again, since the fuselage of the VariViggen is spruce and plywood, it appealed to me.

Another point: at the time that I started the Viggen, there wasn't the complication of having the choice of the VariEze—though for reasons I'll indicate later, I wouldn't have chosen it anyway.

It was very obvious to me from the beginning that the cost was going to be in the thousands of dollars. There was no possibility of this being built with any degree of efficiency and not buying all the possible components prefabricated that you could. As you are probably aware, in the homebuilder movement the majority of the homebuilders are 'scroungers,' and as a result they take great delight in taking something and putting hours on it and modifying it and making do with it. I still feel that I'm essentially first a pilot and then a mechanic. As a result, I want to get the airplane in the air—I want to see it fly. And I've taken all the shortcuts I can, though they're quite expensive. Offhand, I'd say that probably the Viggen will turn out to be one of the most expensive homebuilts that a person could approach.

Here is some idea of the cost of the Viggen. On mine, I find that the instrumentation and the wiring on the airplane alone (unless you try to scrounge the parts) will cost you very close to $2,000. The engine—in my case I've always rebuilt a first runout engine—will cost me $2,400 to obtain and probably another $1,000 in parts. That's very conservative. I think by the time I have the alternator, generator and the whole thing, I'll be well into $4,000 for the engine. And that, believe me, is cheap because these engines are selling up between six and eight thousand dollars.

Engine availability depends on what you put in them. The Viggen as it's originally designed was intended to use the 150-hp Lycoming or the current 160. Now those engines are a dime a dozen; you can pick them up almost anywhere because that's the engine that is replaced when you go to the Avcon conversion. I found that the 0-360 180-hp Lycoming makes it possible to use original wing plan—the swept wing—rather than the later high-performance wing. This retains the airplane's flying characteristics; it retains the better stall characteristics of the airplane, and by adding the 180 horsepower, you get performance so that you can fly in and out of high mountain summer strips.

An additional, but certainly very individual reason for my choosing this airplane is perhaps a little bit curious also. You may have been around enough fly-ins to run across airplanes like the ones labeled "nostalgia," and you find airplanes that while they are not an exact replica of war planes of the pre-WWII era (the biplane era), they are obviously intended to be very similar. You'll see planes painted up in Army colors and attempts to have something like those early planes. You'll see a J-3 Cub painted to look like it was being used as an observation plane for D Day—that sort of thing. Well, for me, I haven't seen any airplane that could mimic with any degree of reliability a modern military jet fighter. But if you take a look at the Vari-Viggen, with the exception of the canard, you'll find that that airplane very much resembles the F-14 Tomcat fighter and the later F-16 Air Force fighter.

To my way of thinking, it has the possibility of being dressed up in Navy colors and Navy stencils for emergency exits, etc. What I'm saying is that for me it is a further step along the line of imitating military airplanes, which has been part of the movement for a long time. Now, I admit that it's certainly taking on the nature of a toy. But that's what you're in the homebuilt movement for. I certainly don't want to be in this for work. I want to get all of the fun I can out of it, and part of the fun for me would be to fly it into Moffett Field (U.S. Navy airfield in California) on Navy Day sometime and have some of those young military pilots come over and gawk at it and 'ooh and ahh!' Well, that's my specific reasons for wanting the Viggen. Because so far as I know, there's no other airplane that really resembles a jet. There just isn't any. None of them have the wing far enough back, and you don't sit far enough forward in splendid isolation, you know, as you do in the VariViggen.

I've been over to Mojave to see Rutan and I've always been treated very nicely over there; I appreciate what they've done in back ups and support, although the Viggen, it seems to me, is losing some of that support. It's probably as much as anything the fault of the VariViggen builders. They do not communicate their progress to Rutan. There are dozens of VariViggens around the country that are in the process of being built. But all of us, I think, are a little ashamed of how long it takes us. This is a fearfully complicated airplane, and it is going to take you time and time and time. A good example will be my experience with the retracting mechanisms. I was very clever in setting my entire retracting mechanism up on the main spar and making sure that it worked well before I installed the main spar in the airplane. And, if I do say so myself, I had a beautiful installation which was exactly according to the plans. Well, I found that there were some aspects of the plans that in small

details were causing problems—such as the fact that the cables were rubbing and an additional pulley would have had to have been installed. But worst of all, I discovered that the entire gear system had problems. I was playing around with the apparatus one day and let the electric motor that potentially raises the gear get a little bit beyond where it should have and snapped the cable. They are very tiny cables. Then I began to hear that other people were having trouble with these cables and the only way that you could get the gear down was to pull the handle, drop the gear, and hope it would go down and lock. I didn't like that idea. And there were more problems of this kind.

So what happens? Here's this complicated mechanism which has taken me months to build and the whole thing, or 80 percent of it, has to be junked. I started over from scratch again to build a different mechanism which was developed by Mike Melvill and involves worm gears and little transmission cases and this sort of thing. This is again fearfully complicated and required you to have several friends who are machinists or you're going to be in trouble.

I feel one of the problems is that I don't know how many parts of the VariViggen were simply designed by Rutan but had never been tried out. If you take a look at the original VariViggen, you'll find that it is built differently than the plans. Mike Melvill, who is the only one that I know whose Viggen is flying (although I understand that there are others) had to depart from the plans. There's a friend of mine now down in Texas, Leonard Dobson, who completely revised the retracting mechanism. He did this on the basis of a complicated transmission case and he uses a bicycle chain. There are a lot of airplanes that use that on the retracting mechanism. Leonard uses that on his main gear. [*See Chapter 13 for Dobson's first flight.*]

"I think that some of us have been ticked off and discouraged by the fact that we've had to go back to square one on the most difficult and complicated part of the airplane. However, mine is now well on its way; I've got everything out to be machined and I think we're in pretty good shape. On the whole, I know very well and I feel quite confident that if I have any problems, I can go directly to Rutan and get a good answer and a good fix for the airplane. I feel confident of this, and as long as he's in the airplane business, I'm sure he will provide generously that kind of advice and consultation. In addition, Mike Melvill, who's in charge of the VariViggen project in Mojave, is equally an excellent person to consult. He is a very practical person and I have enjoyed my contacts with him.

I'm not going to use the canopy as it's in the plans. Using Mike Melvill's new type of retraction mechanisms, I'm making the rear cockpit so that it will have brakes and, as Mike says, it will be possible to fly the plane to a full stop from the back seat, which is not the case with the plans. I've changed the seating and the interior, which I think everyone who works on the Viggen has. I'm much more elaborate in instrumentation because I want to be very sure I know what's happening back in the engine compartment. However, I've stuck as closely as possible to the original plans, and it's been possible to stick fairly close. Like, for instance, the plans have a hinged nose cone—I plan on attaching mine with camlocks. That sort of thing—nothing major.

As to how much time and money I've spent on the project to date. I have spent parttime for a period of four years, off and on. I've spent the last six months purely on the VariViggen. But I've found something important to me personally. I've found that what I'm missing as a person who comes from a professional area (social service profession, for example) into working in a mechanical field is the shop techniques. For instance, what do you do when a hole is drilled off-center and you need to redrill a hole; or you find your countersink doesn't center on the hole and starts to drift off because it isn't a piloted countersink? Well, you find out that people who are shop 'pros' know that you just take a thicker piece of steel, bore a hole in it and use that as a drill guide for countersinking with no problem.

I think that Rutan's designs are excellent. I really feel that they are in the process of development, and anyone who gets the idea that he can take a Rutan design when it first comes out and follow that design and get through the projects without making changes and without some frustrations because of design difficulties, is out of his head. It's going to have to be a process of modification. I don't see that as a weakness. I think that's true of any aircraft development. You simply have to continue to make changes.

And as to hard-to-get parts—for the most part, they're available. The machining that's required for the new Melvill-type landing gear is extensive and if you do not have available a machine shop with at least an end mill, you'd be out of luck. You just couldn't do it with hand tools." [*This gear is now available from Ken Brock.—Ed.*]

As far as flying the Viggen is concerned, there have been too many people who have had trouble with the Viggen due to the fact that the engine produces a high thrust line which causes the airplane to act in reverse. You increase the power and the nose goes down; you take off the power and the nose comes up. I think the plane is moderately sensitive on the controls; I think it is just about right. The controls are much better balanced than they are, for example, on the Hyper-Bipe which is an acrobatic airplane and will drive you wacky trying to control it. But to take on the whole, it's this peculiarity that gives trouble. and unless you're used to flying Lake amphibians or some other high thrust line airplane, I think it would behoove you to take the precaution of going over and flying with Mike Melvill or getting one of the Rutan factory pilots to come over and check you out. I think you need to fly that airplane from the front seat with somebody in the back seat who has previously had VariViggen experience because I'm quite positive that it's no more difficult to fly than the original Cardinal which had the problem with over-sensitive longitudinal stability. You simply need to have just a little time to get your muscles in tune with the idea that when you pull that throttle off, you by gosh better shove that stick forward. It becomes a reflex after you're used to it with a little bit of training. As far as the landing in this airplane is concerned, I think it must easily be the easiest airplane of the homebuilts to land that you could possibly get. There's nothing to do with it except close the throttle, hold the stick back in your lap, use the throttle to increase or decrease your glide angle, and you simply bring it down and land it. There is no stalling of this airplane so that the landings become quite simple.

I do not think that this design is too much airplane for many builders. It's simply that if the person is a 172 driver, he's gotten used to the idea that when you pull on full flaps and apply full power, the nose just comes the hell up and you've just about got to push that wheel through the instrument panel to get that nose down. Now, we don't consider that as being a difficult airplane to fly. You can check with other people and verify this, but I think you'll

Fig. 3-10. Every available space is being used for instrumentation and nav/com equipment. George Craig is spending $2,000 just for instruments to monitor the engine compartment and provide for occasional IFR.

find that the VariViggen is no worse than a 172 with full flaps. But believe you me, all the person needs to do is get over that one psycho-motor learning experience, which is no more difficult than a 172 full-flap-go-around and you're in business. So you see, it's not a case of there being too much airplane. The airplane when it's properly handled and under normal flight conditions is practically stall-proof. You can't get into the problems you get into with most airplanes, and it's an easy airplane to land. What does it leave you with—just that high thrust line problem.

You ask whether I could go into the Long EZ and/or VariEze design. This, incidentally, was not on the market when I picked up on the VariViggen. My answer is a definite and resounding *no!* First, let's take the VariEze. As I pointed out, it's costing me about $2,000 to adequately equip my airplane with sufficient instruments to monitor the engine compartment and to provide for occasional IFR (Fig. 3-10). There's no way that I could afford to properly equip the VariEze, even though I am planning to spend approximately $15,000 to $18,000 on this project. For example, an electric artificial horizon will cost two to three times as much as the war surplus type. Besides that, the instruments on the VariEze (the Long-EZ I'm sure is in the same boat) have got to be miniaturized. They've got to be the very most expensive instruments that you can get for that airplane. The VariEze, itself, is absolutely out of the question for a person like myself who weighs 200 pounds. That airplane simply will not carry me with any amount of baggage; it's absolutely crowded. You have to use special luggage—the whole bit. Now, it's a wonderfully efficient airplane for someone who wants to stay on smooth pavement. Well, I don't necessarily always want to fly that way. The VariViggen with its 550 main gear can, according to what I've been told, be used on a fairly rough field—nothing excessive— but it certainly is a lot more adequate than the little tiny wheels that you'll find on the VariEze. I presume the Long EZ will use a comparable landing gear.

I imagine the VariViggen can possibly be operated for about the cost of a 172; it's a little bit more efficient than the Avcon conversion. It's about 25 miles faster. I think that by cruising the Vari-Viggen back to about 8½ gallons an hour for cross-countries, it will do quite well. With our gasoline situation, I'm hopeful that gasohol for aircraft engines might be our solution in the future. It would seem to me that the most one might have to do would be some minor modifications to the carburetor. Besides, most homebuilts are not flown a great deal—they're mostly for hobby and sport flying to fly-ins, and spend an awful lot of time in the hangar.

As far as help from other people, I get a great deal of help from my brother-in-law, Paul Schillerstrom, who is a machinist, retired, and from Ray Stevens, another homebuilder. They both have helped me a great deal. And when I need another set of hands, my wife has been extremely generous. Madge comes out in the shop and helps (Fig. 3-11). She has been very supportive. The EAA has been helpful as well. John Winters who was our EAA designee before he started to work on United night time, would come around periodically and make inspections. On the whole, I think the EAA Chapter is more socially oriented. I don't get an awful lot of direct help, and it is not necessarily reliable because many of the people in the organization are floundering as much as I am.

You ask me if I would build another aircraft after I completed the VariViggen. I most certainly would. Now you know the VariViggen allows you to do all the mechanical and instrument and radio and wood work and the composite construction, but it doesn't really give you the opportunity to work with fabric.

As this second edition goes to press, Craig's VariViggen is still not in the air but he is still working. He feels that he is now within six to eight months of completion and pointed out that the remainder of the work should require no re-engineering. Craig has been meticulous, even to the point of rebuilding his own engine. "When I do finish, my Viggen will be far and away the best-equipped one around."

By the end of 1983, between 500 and 600 sets

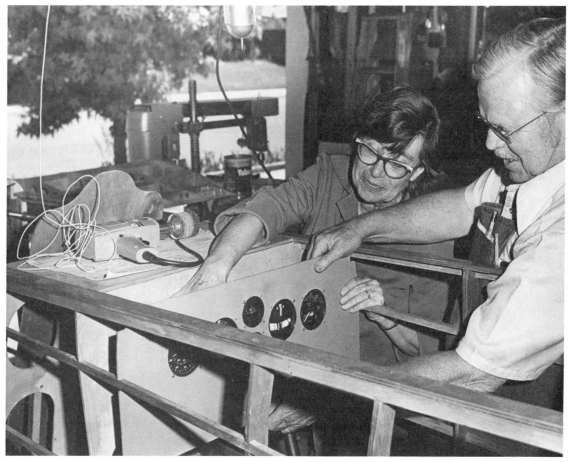

Fig. 3-11. George and his wife, Madge, check out the front panel in their VariViggen. The couple owns a Cessna 172 that they use for extensive cross-country flying.

of plans had been sold for the VariViggen; some 32 are reported flying. This total was increasing rapidly as many long-time builders finally were reaching completion.

After developing a dozen major projects since the Viggen was designed in 1968, Burt now feels that this design is only for the truly dedicated homebuilders who enjoy the challenge of construction more than the completion. He feels that even a dedicated builder will take five to six years to complete the project and is recommending that a Viggen not be started unless the builder enjoys the challenge of building a very complex machine.

"The efficiencies of the Viggen are not all that good," said Burt. You're burning 11 gph for only 150—160 mph. At this stage of the game I'd recommend the four-place Defiant as a much simpler airplane to build and one that has many advantages going for it. The Viggen is still a fine airplane and the owners who are flying swear by it, but the time involved is terrific. We've learned a lot since I started that first one 15 years ago."

Chapter 4

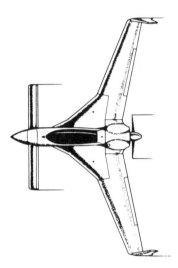

VariEze—It's Really Very Easy

Building and flying a VariEze is certainly a new way of life. Nat Puffer of Minneapolis penned the following account of the airplane that changed his life. We reproduce it, incomplete sentences and all. Then we'll look at where this design came from:

This is a special "thank you" letter. The VariEze has really changed our lives. Much has been written about how easy and satisfying it is to build a VariEze, and much has been written about how delightful it is to fly a VariEze. With all of this we concur. But not enough has been said about how owning and flying a VariEze can change your personal lives.

When you are building an airplane, you live in relative obscurity, except for other builders. You tend to shun social obligations to get the plane done, and tend to drop out of things going on around you. But once the airplane is completed, especially a VariEze, it is an instant passport to fame. You become an instant celebrity! It is very ego-building and in stark contrast to what has gone before.

It starts with offers of free use of airplane trailers, free hangaring and/or reduced rates. Very prompt attention from the FAA, etc. Every time we open the hangar doors, an instant crowd of admirers gathers. People come back time and time again, and just stand and look. Special recognition by the control tower. All kinds of people anxious to help in any way possible.

Being reported as a UFO, and being interviewed on the radio. Being the subject of a sound movie, and being interviewed on the local TV station.

At Oshkosh, receiving a very warm and friendly reception by the control tower, and being personally escorted to a parking space right in front of the main gate. Being asked to participate in a fly-by. Being asked to participate in photo flights in formation for *Popular Mechanics, National Geographic* and *Sport Aviation.* Being asked to announce on the Oshkosh PA system for the VariEze fly-by just before the airshow.

On return home from Oshkosh, having Minneapolis Flight Watch carry on a running conversation for 90 miles asking if I could land at Minneapolis International so they could see my VariEze. At Voyageur Village being swarmed with kids. At a local fly-in at Osceola drawing the crowd away from all the other airplanes. Not being allowed to pay for my gasoline. Having the 3M employee magazine editor asking for an interview, and having to fly a special photo flight for the company photographer.

Having everyone who flies in the other plane on a photo flight ecstatic over how much the VariEze excels any other plane in the sky. (I make gunnery runs and fly circles around the chase planes.) Being very proud to be part of the VariEze program.

Best of all, how ecstatic my wife is about being a part of it all, and how she simply eats it up! She delights in explaining all the intimate technical details to people, and how wonderful it flies. (She has never even had her hands on the stick and would be terrified if I asked her to fly.)

There is no indication that any of this will ever let up. It has truly been one of the nicest things that has happened to us in our lifetime. (See Chapter 10 for Nat Puffer's Cozy)

HOW IT ALL BEGAN

Burt Rutan detailed the development of the VariEze in a first-person report published originally in *Sport Aviation*, the popular and colorful monthly magazine of the EAA. The evolution of the VariEze as described by the designer-builder follows, with permission of both author and publisher:

The VariEze (pronounced "Very Easy") design started in early 1974 (Fig. 4-1). At that time it was a high wing/low canard configuration. Its structure was all metal. The prototype was never completed, partly due to complexity and weight problems with the structure and due to spiral instability discovered during model tests.

Further wind-tunnel model tests (Figs. 4-2, 4-3) conducted in the fall of 1974 led to the general arrangement of the VariEze. This aircraft, N7EZ, was built in four months and made its first flight in May 1975 (Fig. 4-4). The main aerodynamic benefits sought were the following: the canard and wing systems could be carefully designed to provide natural passive angle-of-attack limiting to make the aircraft departure and spin proof. Inclusion of the new NASA-developed winglets could reduce in-

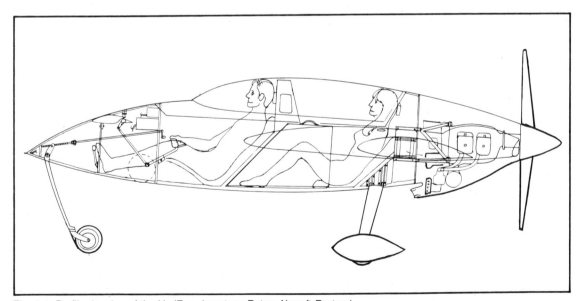

Fig. 4-1. Profile drawing of the VariEze. (courtesy Rutan Aircraft Factory)

Fig. 4-2. A recent scale model of the VariEze is "flown" in the NASA wind tunnel. This ¼-scale model produced excellent data for further canard development. (courtesy NASA)

duced drag and thus provide better climb and cruise efficiency. The layout, using canard elevons for roll and pitch control resulted in an unusually simple flight control system. Packaging of the two occupants was efficient and resulted in a considerably lower wetted-area airplane than a conventional design.

Oddly enough, the decision to use the all-composite glass-foam-glass sandwich structure was mainly an expedient, rather than an attempt to develop improved technology. Because of the many unknowns, the prototype (N7EZ) was considered a research airplane to develop the canard aerodynamics, not the prototype for homebuilder plans. In addition, it was decided to attempt several distance and speed records in its weight class. The structure then, was merely an easy-to-build expedient to allow quick construction of the prototype. It was not known if it would be light enough or durable enough for anything beyond the prototype. However, we found during the detail, design and construction of N7EZ and through the many lab tests of the materials that the structure offered some real possibilities. Structural design philosophy was to

Fig. 4-3. Early car-top wind tunnel model of the VariEze was photographed in front of the RAF at Mojave. (courtesy Burt Rutan)

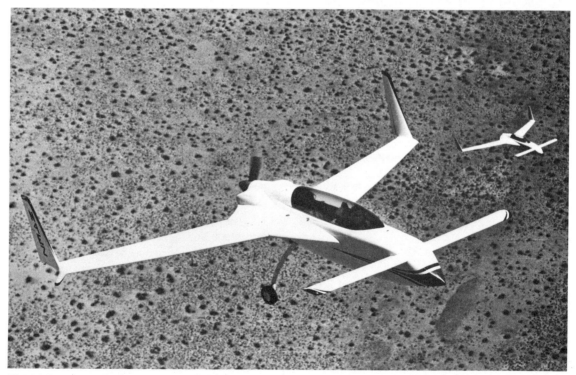

Fig. 4-4. Early air-to-air photo of N4EZ with N7EZ (the No. 1 VariEze) in the background near Mojave. (courtesy Don Dwiggins)

design to a much greater strength than normal to encompass variations in workmanship and unknowns about long-term degradation (moisture absorption and ultraviolet deterioration). Then, to provide an acceptable structural weight, the structural configuration was closely optimized by using unidirectional spar caps following the maximum thickness contours and by using the skin to absorb bending and torsional loads. The extra beef for the conservatism was put in the skins to resist surface damage. The result was gratifying—a structure with excellent surface durability, a 12G ultimate load factor and competitive weight. N7EZ with its 62-hp, 139-lb. Volkswagen engine had an empty weight on its first flight of 399 lbs. This later grew to 420 lbs. after the addition of extra equipment and had a limited electrical system.

Due to doubtful engine reliability, N7EZ never demonstrated its range capability as originally intended for distance records. It did set a world's distance record in August 1975, of 1638 miles, only slightly over the old record, using 241 lbs. of fuel at low altitude without a mixture control. To attain its full capability in the 500 kg weight class would require burning 495 lbs. fuel, using a mixture control, an optimum prop, and flying at optimum speed. This would be a 35-hour, 4,000-mile flight, requiring flight at heavy weights in darkness. We had found that, even at reduced power settings, the poor reliability of the VW engine made this attempt too risky. N7EZ had, on two occasions, experienced failures requiring immediate landing to avoid total loss of power. Also, maintenance was high. Dick Rutan installed a 60-hp Franklin in N7EZ to again address a distance record attempt. However, vibration and other engine installation difficulties canceled that plan.

The performance and efficiency of the VW-powered N7EZ was excellent. Its top speed was over 180 mph. It could achieve over 40 mpg at high cruise speed and over 60 mpg at 95 mph. Its span efficiency (e) at 1.15 was greater than anticipated due to the local aft wing upwash (induced by the canard) increasing the benefits of the winglet system. It had to be parked in the nose-down position to provide adequate ground stability without pilot.

To minimize the disadvantage of this unusual procedure, a ball-screw device was installed to allow the pilot to raise or lower the nose gear to kneel the aircraft with him aboard.

In the summer of 1975, after flying N7EZ 100 hours, we addressed the feasibility of offering a VariEze-type aircraft to homebuilders. Several problems needed to be solved:

(1) There was no suitable engine available.
(2) The stall speed was too high.
(3) Roll control at low speeds was poor.
(4) The pilot-in-kneeling system was inadequate, requiring too much effort.

Problem No. (1) was a difficult one, since the VW's reliability above 60 hp was in question. The Franklin 60 aircraft engine was out of production. The only alternative was the 173-lb. A-75 Continental. At that time they seemed to be in adequate supply on the used market. At 173 lbs., the A-75 was too heavy for N7EZ. It was decided to scale up the design to a size correct for a 173-lb. engine. This increased the wing area from 59 sq. ft. to 67 sq. ft. Every dimension in the airplane was changed requiring a completely new prototype.

Problems No. (2) and (3) were both due mainly to the poor lift of the GAW-1 airfoil on the canard. This airfoil with plain flap at the low Reynolds number (half million) had a max lift coefficient of less than 1.6. A new canard wing was built for N7EZ using a new airfoil developed at the University of Glasgow. This G U 25-5 (11) 8 section promised a max lift coefficient over 2.6 when used with a slotted flap, a value unheard of at this low Reynolds number. I did not believe problem (3) would be adequately solved, so I designed ailerons to be installed on the rear wing.

Problem No. (4) was attacked by developing several nose gear retraction devices ranging from electric screwjacks to oscillating mechanisms like a car jack. None of these were satisfactory. The decision was then made to require the pilot to raise the nose, lock the gear down, and then climb in the airplane. With this in mind, the simplest system was selected—a one-piece rod attached to a block running in a guide for up and down locks.

New flight tests were then done with N7EZ to

test the modifications. The new canard wing performed excellently, lowering the stall speed nearly 8 mph and considerably improving roll rate at low speeds. We now considered the roll authority to be adequate and thus decided to retain the elevons. The simple control system with roll and pitch on the front wing would be used on the second prototype. We were satisfied with the simplified nose gear retraction system.

The second prototype (N4EZ) (Fig. 4-5) was designed in the winter of 1975, built in four months and made its first flight in March 1976. Our search for an A-75 Continental engine was not successful, but we found a good deal on a Continental 0-200. We removed its starter but retained its alternator, resulting in an engine weight of 206 lbs., which required a nose ballast of 10 lbs. to achieve the proper CG.

The structural redesign for the second airplane involved additional conservatism in allowable stresses and some other weight penalties for items changed to simplify construction. We had anticipated that N4EZ would weigh about 540 lbs. with the 0-200 engine with alternator and NAVCOM radio. The "basic" Eze with an A-75 and no electricals would weigh about 500 lbs. To our dismay, N4EZ tipped the scales at 585 empty. We then anticipated that the average homebuilder's VariEze with an A-75 and no electricals would weigh about 535 lbs.

N4EZ completed its 85-hour flight test program including engine and systems development, flying qualities optimization (all weights and CGs), performance determination, dive tests, spin tests, environmental qualifications, etc., in ten weeks.

The tests indicated few modifications. The aircraft was not susceptible to stall/spin. Overall flying qualities were satisfactory.

As we went to press with the plans in July, 1976, the VariEze was a very basic, simple configuration with adequate useful load to allow 700 miles range with two crewmen. Single-place with one hour's fuel, is a true "hot rod" with an initial rate of

Fig. 4-5. N4EZ, second of the VariEze prototypes, was built in four months. It was powered by a Continental 0-200 with the starter removed. Note rear wing leading edge cuff.

climb near 2,000 fpm and a demonstrated ceiling above 25,000'. However, as the homebuilder's airplanes started hatching from the various basements and garages, we quickly found the "average" homebuilt Eze to be much heavier than anticipated. Whereas we always pitched the Eze to be light, basic and simple, a large percentage of the builders were loading them up with extras. Of the first five to fly, two had full IFR instrumentation/electrical systems (Fig. 4-6), extra gadgets and heavy finishes, resulting in empty weights near 700 lbs. These were, unfortunately, single-place airplanes due to their low useful load. Despite our nonstop preaching about weight control in our newsletter, many of the Ezes continued to be built overweight. In April 1978, we conducted a survey of Ezes flying and found that while a few are at the desired weight, the average Eze is 30 to 50 pounds overweight. Twenty-five percent of them were marginal for two-place operation due to more careful weight consideration by the average builder. We later removed the alternator and the nose ballast from N4EZ to lower the empty weight. The heavy 0-200 and 0-235 engines are recommended only in the stripped-down condition without starter or alternator.

Our most serious problem with the VariEze surfaced when the initial homebuilder's airplanes began flying in March 1977. We found that relatively minor rigging errors in setting the back wing incidence and twist could overpower the elevons' ability to roll the aircraft. Of the first six Ezes to fly, two required full roll control to maintain level flight and had to be assisted with rudder to remain upright! These aircraft flew normally after rigging errors were fixed or corrected with trim tabs. If the pilots had not been proficient, accidents could have occurred. This problem, of course, indicated the need for an immediate major modification to increase roll authority. Roll control on the front wing is only about 25 percent as effective as on the rear wing because aileron deflection on the front wing causes a down wash change that makes the aft wing oppose the roll input. Adding to the problem was the fact that an elevon, when doubling as aileron *and* elevator, is a poor aileron at large elevator

Fig. 4-6. Instrument panel of N4EZ.

deflection (slow speed). Clearly, we had to abandon the elevons and put ailerons on the back wing. The front control surfaces would be used only as elevators, like our previous VariViggen aircraft. Working under the pressure of a major flight safety consideration, we did all the following within two weeks: design and build ailerons and aileron controls for N4EZ; flight test them throughout the envelope, including stall/spin and flutter qualifications; prepare owners manual data and installation drawings, and arrange for the availability of parts and materials. This development blitz was very successful, giving the flying qualities an important improvement, allowing a backseat stick and extending the allowable forward CG range. Three months later, four of the five Ezes at Oshkosh had the new rear wing ailerons. The other one was modified shortly afterward. I know of no Eze now flying with elevons.

Another problem that surfaced during the homebuilder's operational experience involved stall characteristics. The majority of airplanes we tested and reports from others indicated that the stall-proof flying qualities were indeed being realized. The airplanes could be flown in good stable flight indefinitely while at full aft stick. While holding full aft stick, the pilot could use power to climb or descend and could even sideslip with full controls without experiencing a stall break or departure from controlled flight. However, we had several reports from pilots who indicated they experienced divergent wing rocking at the stall or a roll-off when approaching minimum speed. These were occurring at aft CG but within the allowable CG range. Tests conducted by NASA with a Vari-Eze model showed that the wing rock was caused by aft wing stall and that a small leading edge extension (cuff) on the back wing would eliminate it (Fig. 4-7). In November 1978, this departure (roll-off at minimum speed) occurred while demonstrating stalls in N4EZ. We then began a new flight test program to further investigate what was happening. We tufted the wing to observe airflow, and did high angle-of-attack tests with and without the wing cuffs. We found that the stall margin on the back wing without the cuffs was quite low at aft CG. Tolerances occurring during construction were enough to allow some airplanes to induce a stall on the back wing which results in a roll-off and loss of several hundred feet of altitude. Since tests showed this was eliminated when cuffs were installed, we then recommended them for all Ezes. Noting the large number of Ezes still flying without cuffs, it is seen that it is difficult to convince many owners to install them, particularly since most are very pleased with stall characteristics. However, because we found a departure stall on N4EZ only after nearly two years and hundreds of stalls, we still consider the cuffs to be a mandatory addition.

Operator experience indicated the need to increase the pitch stick forces, as many of the pilots were not comfortable with the sensitive controls. A modification introduced in July 1978 increased the pitch control forces and greatly reduced the tendency for some pilots to overcontrol the Eze during their initial flights.

Performance variations experienced by the homebuilders have been large. Only a few airplanes can meet or beat the cruise speed listed in the Eze owners manual. The average Eze cruises 12 mph slower than the book. Small variations due to external additions, surface finish and fits can have a large effect on performance on an aircraft that has only 1.4 sq. ft. of equivalent flat plate drag area.

Fig. 4-7. Wing tip cuffs are installed on Mike Dehate's VariEze. Mike is one of a group of San Diego, California builders who attend various fly-ins.

While most Ezes can match the take-off and landing performance listed in the Manual, many suffer large losses due to improper propellers, wheel toe-in or pilot technique.

Many Ezes have experienced collapse of the nose gear when the downlock failed to retain the retraction mechanism. This problem was initially addressed with cautions and recommendations regarding rigging, checking for interferences and operating techniques. The problem, though never experienced with our prototypes, persisted on as many as 20 percent of the flying Ezes. The nose-gear collapse generally resulted in only minor damage to the skin under the nose, but, at times, major damage to the pilot's ego when he found his airplane on the nose closing a major runway. In late 1978, the nose gear retraction system was redesigned to a worm-gear mechanism which has eliminated the collapse problem and raised the gear-extension speed by 30 mph.

Several examples of failure or deterioration of landing gear attachments indicated that inadequate allowance was made in the original design to account for variances in workmanship and vibration loads due to wheel or brake imbalance. These resulted in recommended beef-ups of the attachments. These changes were not incorporated in the prototype.

[*Author's note:* There have been no airframe structural modifications required. The Ezes had a perfect record of airframe integrity, with no reported failures until mid-1982 when a VariEze winglet ripped off at some 200 mph during a reported buzz job. The right winglet was found about 1,900 feet short of the wreckage. Within two hours of the report of this crash, Burt and Mike Melvill headed for the Texas crash site nonstop in the Defiant to investigate. What they found did not lead to the grounding or flight restrictions to any of the VariEes.

Careful analysis of the structure indicated that the major tension layup No. 8 was omitted and layup No. 9 was not extended to the lower skin. The only structure opposing the bending (of the winglet) was the foam core. Rutan stated that the structural strength of the winglet-to-wing joint was less than 1/20th of what it should have been.

Prior to this accident, the VariEze type had amassed approximately 150,000 flight hours without inflight airframe failure, even though many of the aircraft had relatively poor workmanship according to the designer's standards. However, the omission of important primary structure was considered clearly to be the cause of this structural failure.

Several incidents of violent flutter at high speeds have been experienced due to improper elevator mass balance. In each case, the airframe was not damaged. (Flutter generally results in catastrophic airframe failure.) A canopy opening incident resulted in an Eze tumbling out of control while 25 mph over its maneuvering speed. No structural damage occurred. The pilot was quite complimentary about the airframe structural integrity. Enough experience has now been accumulated to assess the structural success of the composite structure. Environmental exposure has included the extremes of tropical salt water areas and Alaskan cold temperatures. Fred Keller's beautiful Eze, which has flown to Oshkosh twice, is parked outside year-round at Anchorage. The oldest airframe is now nearly eight years old.]

(Burt Rutan's narrative continues:)

I am often asked what it is like to provide support for the over 3,500 builders. The answer is often challenging, often frustrating, often rewarding, but in general a lot of fun. My workload on support was reduced considerably in 1978 when Mike and Sally Melvill joined my brother Dick and myself here in RAF. Sally is our office manager. She handles the calls and letters, funneling them to Mike, Dick or myself. Mike has built a VariViggen and a VariEze and is in charge of builder support. Our quarterly newsletter provides the primary builder-support function and is the formal means to distribute any modifications and improvements. Since the VariEze program started in July 1976, we have published a total of 36 newsletters which include a total of approximately 400,000 words through 1983!

Now for some statistics: If the "average" builder calls us every five months for assistance and writes for help every five months, we get a phone call every 20 minutes of our working day (Monday through Saturday) and we get 24 letters per day. If only 1 percent of the builders have a problem with a given aspect of construction, thirty people will need help! As you can see, the builder support function is an enormous task. It is aided considerably by our requirement for all written correspondence to include a self-addressed stamped envelope and by our builder's cooperation in keeping calls brief.

One of the expanding problems in mailing out ever-increasing numbers of newsletters at a single shot is keeping a current mailing list. To solve this, Jeff Hiner, Burt's son who is studying computer technology at California State College, Fullerton, spent part of the summer in 1983 at Mojave working on computer programming. Now names and changes have been brought up to space-age speed and hooked into the Apple's memory bank.

Jeff has had just one dual flight with his Uncle Dick, but he's eager for more. Burt's daughter Dawn is in a pre-nursing course of study at California State College at Stanislaus.

THE VARIEZE DEVELOPS

Rutan's initial announcement on the VariEze was prepared within a month of its first flight. The designer prepared the following rundown on the then-new concept and sent it along to the EAA's *Sport Aviation*. We have excerpted the following with permission:

The VariEze (Very-Easy) prototype has logged over 45 hours in its first three weeks of flying and performance is exceeding expectations. The aircraft was designed for maximum-cruise efficiency and an extremely long range. Major design features which make this possible are (1) light, yet rugged, structure using fiberglass in a composite form using rigid foam as core material, (2) compact tandem seating made possible by the broad CG range attained with the canard configuration, (3) modern airfoils—surface contour is maintained under load with the composite structure, (4) no control surfaces on the main wing, (5) Whitcomb-designed winglets reduce induced drag and halve the apparent parasite drag of the vertical fins, (6) high aspect-ratio wings with distributed loading between wing and canard, (7) unique engine-cooling system that results in low drag, low oil temperature and longer accessory life.

The prototype has already demonstrated 70 miles per gallon with two people aboard—an unprecedented 140 miles per seat! That mileage is at the economy-cruise condition of 30 percent, 8,000', 135 mph TAS. At 75 percent power, it will deliver 48 mpg at approximately 185 TAS.

The low induced drag necessary for optimum cruise efficiency results in quite spectacular climb performance with the 62-hp Volkswagen engine: 2,000 fpm single place, and 1,200 fpm with two aboard and fuel for 1,000 miles. Empty weight is 390 lbs., normal gross is 890 lbs., which includes full fuel, two 6'4" people and two specially-designed suitcases.

The prototype was built in only 2½ months; thanks, of course, to Carolyn, who handled the VariViggen program, Phil Rathbun, who built the machined parts and Gary Morris, who donated most of his evenings to help with the glass lay-ups and finishing. That time included some tooling work also and we expect that a plans-built project can be completed in less than 350 man hours using supplied components. Components to be supplied include a canopy, landing gear (molded fiberglass), molded foam seat/bulkhead, cowling and wing spar/center section which will provide a "one-pin" wing removal similar to European sailplanes.

Flight testing is now being conducted to test modifications required to correct a canard flutter experienced with the original configuration. The present plan is for my brother, Dick Rutan, to fly the prototype to Oshkosh non-stop (1,800 miles) with a 25-gallon fuel tank in the rear seat and, if time permits, attempt to set a new world, closed-course distance record during the '75 Oshkosh Convention.

This winter I plan to build another VariEze, using the manufactured parts intended for the homebuilt market, in order to fully test the supplied components and further simplify the basic structure. Plans and parts will not be sold until the entire development program is completed and parts are on the shelf. I expect this will be early in 1976.

True to Burt's fast-moving plans, the initial VariEze went nonstop to Oshkosh in 1975 and proceeded to make its name in the record books. EAA *Sport Aviation* Editor Jack Cox thrilled the thousands of homebuilt enthusiasts with his report of the record flight. In part, here's what he had to say in an article that was written right at deadline following the VariEze's inital record flight:

VARIEZE FOR THE RECORD

5:30 is a brutal hour in the morning for anyone to be up and about after a week of endless tramping up and down the aircraft display lines at Oshkosh. Yet, a score or so of us have summoned the strength from somewhere and now find ourselves huddled around this pale apparition of an airplane, intently watching.

Harold Best-Devereux, the NAA/F.A.I. Official Observer for all that will hopefully transpire this day, jots down the numbers. Harold's crisp British accent snaps everyone back to the matter at hand.

"Now, gentlemen, will you please step back—completely away from the aircraft?"

As the rest of us back off a few grudging steps, Harold strides forward, reaches deep into the rear cockpit of the VariEze—behind the hulking fiberglass auxiliary fuel tank—and starts the barograph (Fig. 4-8). Then he proceeds to tape over the filler caps, affixing his initials to each with a flourish worthy of his station and the occasion. Taking all this in with a slight bemused expression on his face is pilot Dick Rutan, waiting calmly in the front seat, already strapped in and ready to go. Dick is the only one in the crowd who really looks like he is up to the occasion. Decked out in a powder blue turtle neck pullover, he is downright dapper as compared to the rest of us who have the disheveled appearance of a bunch of sleepyheads who have just been rousted out of bed . . . which, of course, is exactly the case.

Draped over each of Dick's shoulders are several stout strings each attached to some unseen object behind his seat back—plastic bags containing

Fig. 4-8. Dick Rutan, Burt Rutan, and Harold Best-Devereux check the barograph to assure that it will operate properly. (courtesy EAA by Dick Stouffer)

a couple of Baby Ruth candy bars, a package of cheese and crackers, three pull-top cans containing Beenie-Weenies, chicken gumbo and chocolate pudding, a Chap Stick, Rolaids and some aspirin and a couple of plastic bottles full of water laced with just a dash of lemon juice, three-quarters of a gallon in all. One string leads to a large, empty plastic bottle.

Not exactly an Apollo life support system, but simple, effective and, most important, lightweight.

A short exchange of pleasantries between Dick and Harold ends with a groping with the canopy support rod and a lowering and locking of the Plexiglas bubble through which, if all goes well, Dick's only sensory contact with the rest of us will be possible for the next 12 to 14 hours, except for intermittent use of his battery-powered Escort 110 radio.

With brother Dick properly and officially encapsulated in the VariEze, Burt Rutan takes charge.

"Okay, let's have lots of hands under the canard and the main wing—anyplace except the control surface on the canard—and s-l-o-w-l-y ease forward off the scales and down the ramps.

"All together, now . . . lift!"

Effortlessly, the tiny bird, its pilot and 279 pounds of gasoline are palm-powered up, forward and gently down on the taxiway . . . its first "flight" of the day a total success.

Now Burt assumes the position at the rear of the craft and addresses the Monnett VW and Ted Hendrickson prop.

"Make it hot."

Flip . . . flip . . . flip. Come on you little Wolfsburg prima donna—this is no time for dramatic pauses! Flip . . . flip . . . broooom!

"Okay, just as a precaution, let's walk him out to the end of the runway. Keep the nosewheel light over the bumps and tar strips."

Burt and John Monnett climbed aboard the VariViggen. Now they have fired it up and are taxiing along behind the VariEze, preparing to accompany it on the first lap of this attempt to break Ed Lesher's World's Closed Course Distance Record of 1554.279 miles set back in 1970.

Dick's Air Force training makes him a believer in airspeed above all else . . . he levels out just after lift-off and accelerates in ground effect right down to the end of the runway. As Dick smoothly brings up the VariEze's nose, the rate of climb is far in excess of what even the new long-winged VariViggen is capable. I can't believe it; that little son-of-a-gun is carrying over 126 pounds more than its own empty weight, propelled by a 1700cc VW.

Leveling off, Dick throttles back to his programmed rpms and begins cruising up the shore of Lake Winnebago, heading for his turn point at Menominee, Michigan. Only then can the VariViggen catch up and slide in under the VariEze for a look-see to determine if all is well in the engine compartment. Finally, both have disappeared and those of us on the ground drift back toward the Control Center trailer to sit out the expected hour and twenty-five minute lapping of the Oshkosh/Menominee course. If that VW continues to purr away, we can expect to spot that unmistakable VariEze profile overhead at about 7:20 or so.

Burt Rutan had flown east in the VariViggen a few days before, leaving his brother Dick with the task of flying the VariEze to the EAA Fly-in at Oshkosh, hopefully in one big hop. The little bird had nearly 100 hours of flying time on it when Burt left and all manner of flight testing, fuel consumption tests, etc., had been accomplished. All that was left was for Major (Lt. Colonel by the time you are reading this) Richard Rutan, USAF, Field Maintenance Squadron Commander of the 355th Tactical Fighter Wing at Davis-Monthan AFB near Tucson, to get away from his duties, get up to Mojave and blast off on Wednesday. Flying nonstop to Oshkosh would be the grand entrance of all times for a new homebuilt design, Burt and Dick had figured.

In the wee hours of morning, Howard Gann and other local EAA types strapped Dick in and fired up the 1834cc Barker VW . . . only to have oil come gushing out of the cowling. The start-up had ruptured the oil cooler. A quick decision was made to remove the cooler, plumb the system "straight" and attempt the flight anyway. This wasted a precious hour or so but still left just enough time to make Oshkosh by sundown—if winds were favorable.

Taking off with nearly 50 gallons aboard, Dick climbed to 7,500 feet and headed east, accompanied the first 100 miles by Howard in his T-18. The route to be flown was a gentle curve out across the Sierras, southern Nevada, through the heart of Utah, clipping the corners of Wyoming, Nebraska, South Dakota, Minnesota and, finally, a dash across the mid section of Wisconsin to Oshkosh. The course was selected partly because it overflew major interstate highways and partly because it allowed some pressure system flying that promised tailwinds.

Settling back in the semi-supine and super-comfortable seat, Dick could see nothing ahead except clear sailing—visibility was unlimited, all the gauges were in the green and he was indeed picking up a tailwind.

A ground speed check somewhere over Utah revealed that the tailwind was really picking up. Later checks showed that a full 45 minutes had been picked up. Call a pre-selected FSS that Burt will call later in the day to let him know that ETA at Oshkosh will be about 20 minutes before official sunset. What luck! This called for another Life Saver from the package taped to the side of the cockpit.

About this time Lady Luck turned her beneficent smile elsewhere. Over Nebraska the tailwinds became headwinds and the oil temperature began to rise. Over southwestern Minnesota the oil temperature and the oil pressure started shooting up. Dick headed for the nearest airport and shortly was rolling out on the runway at Worthington, Minnesota, after 8 hours and 50 minutes of nonstop, non-refueled flying, some 1,500 miles out of Mojave.

A check of the engine revealed nothing that could be seen, except that most of the oil had been consumed. This would explain the rise in oil temperature, but what caused the oil pressure rise? After replenishing the oil supply, a run-up showed everything in the green again—and left a nagging suspicion that in the rush to remove the oil cooler that morning, maybe the oil had not been topped off before takeoff. Better call Burt and give him the bad news.

Burt, meanwhile, had been following the progress of the flight by calling in to the FSS stations along the route that he and Dick had agreed to use as "message drops." Dick was hardly on the ground before Burt knew about it and shortly the two were talking it all over by phone. After hearing about the puzzling oil pressure reading, Burt agreed Dick had made the wise decision, sparing himself and the VariEze to fly again another day.

After a night's rest, Dick flew on to Oshkosh the next morning to the most spectacular reception an aircraft has ever received at an EAA Fly-in. Several PA announcements had been made the previous day keeping everyone informed of the VariEzes progress as it winged its way across the continent, and Burt had talked briefly at the evening program detailing the problem with the oil pressure. An announcement was made Thursday morning when the tower reported the VariEze entering the pattern and it appeared that everyone there was standing on the show line to witness the landing on Runway 18 at 8:40 a.m. There was no way to taxi in through such a multitude; the tiny aircraft had to be walked to its already roped off parking spot beside the VariViggen. There it was to be totally surrounded by huge crowds every minute of the daylight hours that it was on the ground.

A thorough check was immediately made of the engine and nothing could be found awry. After removing the long-range fuel tank from the rear cockpit, a test flight was made with this writer serving as an inadequate replacement for the weight of 35 gallons of fuel. Again, no problems.

On Friday, Dick took the bird out for some more flying and on landing, had to go around to avoid a slow plane rolling out long on the runway. Cranking the nose gear up and then right back down again for the second landing attempt, he apparently did not get the circulating ball system wound up to the stops, although it had felt to him it was "down and locked." On touchdown, the little panel-mounted crank started spinning wildly, slowly letting the nose right down on the pavement. A layer or two of fiberglass was ground off the nose gear leg and the bottom skin, but that was the extent of the damage. Repairs were made by Gary Morris right at the aircraft's parking spot—with a pair of scissors, a paint brush, a can of epoxy resin and strips of glass cloth. By evening, 7EZ was pronounced ready for the record attempt the following morning, Saturday, August 2.

All that day frantic preparations were being made elsewhere on the field for the record attempt. Several weeks earlier, Burt had made application to NAA, the U.S. F.A.I. affiliate, for the attempt. David Scott had been designated as the official NAA observer . . . and he had much to observe even before the first prop was turned. A barograph had to be smoked and sealed, scales had to be certified, turn point observers on the other end of the closed course had to be lined up, communication with the Oshkosh tower had to be coordinated, etc. Fortunately, Bill Turner also became available and pitched in with the legwork. Harold Best-Devereux, who was an old hand at this sort of thing, was there whenever he was needed.

Adding to the last-minute adrenalin level was the fact that the closed course was changed at the eleventh hour. All week the weather had been unseasonably hot for Wisconsin. Gulf moisture was being pumped up the back side of a titanic high pressure area stalled in the east, resulting in a really bad haze condition all over the midwest. The original closed course was to have been from the Oshkosh Omni to the Burlington, Wisconsin Omni—but the rather featureless Wisconsin landscape would make Burlington awfully hard to find groping through the atmospheric goop. The use of omni could not be depended upon because the Vari-

Eze's radio was powered only by a primary system consisting of an 8-amp gel cell and a secondary system consisting of a 2-amp motorcycle battery. Only intermittent use would be possible because the electronic instruments were also drawing off the power supply. The Barker engine was devoid of all but mags and a carb to keep it at a spare 138 pounds. Starters and generators simply meant less fuel, reasoned Burt. Being the Original Interstate/Railroad/Coastline Chicken Flyer, I suggested a course I have often flown: up the west shoreline of Lake Winnebago, over the freeway to the city of Green Bay and up the west shore of Green Bay to Menominee, Michigan and return—a 182-mile, no-sweat navigation run, even in marginal visibility. This met with everyone's approval.

Now, if the weather will cooperate . . .

Saturday morning started at 4:30 A.M. for those of us involved in the launch. A quick breakfast for some of us, none for others, and it's off to the airport, with one eye on the somewhat low overcast, the first since the fly-in started. The weathermen say some scattered showers and maybe a thunderbumper to fly around before the day is done, but ceilings should be VFR. The weighing, sealing of the tanks and barograph, etc., proceed under the direction of David Scott and presently the buzz of the VW is causing heads to peep out through tent flaps in the campground.

As Dick taxied out, Burt ran by and yelled at me, "Jump in the back of the VariViggen and we'll pace him the first lap. Be back on the ground here at 7:30."

I dashed for my camera and hopped in behind Burt, who already had the Lycoming turning. Taxiing out to the end of 18, we lined up behind and to the left of the VariEze and followed him down the runway at a distance that left us some place to go in case he had to abort. It was difficult to see much of the VariEzes takeoff from the rear 'pit, but it was long and climb wasn't initiated until a real head of steam had been built up. We were already off and climbing, but when Dick started a climbing turn back to the northeast, we seemed to be settling as he zoomed up. Burt kept yelling something about how he couldn't catch up, that we were at full throt-

tle. Also, he was laughing a lot.

When Dick throttled back to 3075 rpm, we were gradually able to catch up and finally pulled alongside, indicating just over 130 mph. We then slid up under the VariEze for a look at the engine and were greeted by a chilling sight . . . a brown streak, at least two inches wide, streaming back from the air inlet all the way back to the prop hub. Oil!

Some animated radio conversation between Burt and Dick resulted in the hopeful conclusion that perhaps the oil was merely residual spillage in the cowling, because all the instrument readings were comfortably in the green. But we would keep a close watch the remainder of the lap to determine if the streak became wider or darker.

On we speed, over Neenah, Menasha, past Appleton, over Kaukauna, up U.S. 41 to Green Bay. The overcast begins to break up and by the time we are approaching Menominee, shafts of sunlight are creating luminous, shimmering pools on the otherwise drab green surface of the bay.

Sweeping around the easily spotted airport, we see Paul Schultz, Joe Gypp and others spreading a white sheet near the Enstrom helipad, indicating a confirmation of our pass. Burt has also received the good word via Unicom.

Turn completed, we head southwest toward Oshkosh. Sliding in under the VariEze for perhaps the tenth time, we can detect no change in the size or color of that ugly streak on its belly. As the landscape slides so rapidly beneath us, it is easy to believe our assumption that the oil is spillage—merely spillage.

Over the city of Green Bay, the overcast becomes solid again and as we proceed down towards the north shore of the Lake Winnebago the area ahead of us darkens dramatically. By the time we are over Kaukauna and Little Chute, we are in light rain and the ceiling and ground fog that has materialized from nowhere are ominously close to what will be an illegal merger for Burt and me in the VariViggen. We push on for a couple of minutes, but when the near all-white VariEze starts pulling momentary disappearing acts on us, we know we've been had. A quick call to tell Dick to follow the dual lane road south rather than following a coastline he sees to the west—that's Lake Butte Des Morts—then Burt takes full advantage of the Viggen's turn-on-a-pin-head capability and we are headed back to Green Bay airport. Somehow Dick gropes his way through to Wittman Field, gets confirmation on his turn and starts back north behind us. One lap completed.

Burt and I race the rapidly advancing line of crud back to Green Bay's Austin Straubel Field, land and dash into the FSS to see what the heck has gotten the weather god's bowels in such an uproar. About 15 minutes later, I stepped outside into a light sprinkle and was greeted by, "Hey, where were you guys when I needed you?"

To my utter astonishment, I turned to see Dick Rutan striding up the walk.

"Weather?"

"No, just blew the engine about 20 miles north of here. Made it back by pumping the extra oil we installed last night. Deadsticked in here."

"Deadstick . . . with all that fuel on board?"

"Had to, the oil pressure was reading zilch. Thought you guys would come running out to help . . . had to push the little beast in to the ramp from out there in the middle of the runway."

We walked back into the FSS, turned a corner and confronted Burt. "Thunderstruck" is a pretty good adjective to describe the look on his face when he saw Dick. Out again into what had now become a light shower of rain, we trudged out to the VariEze and hunkered down to view the oil soaked belly.

All the effort, all those people at Oshkosh and Menominee who have helped out—and here we stand watching oil drip-dripping onto the pavement.

"Well, the weather probably would have zapped the flight anyway."

With the downpour getting worse by the minute, some kind gentleman drove out and invited us to push the VariEze into his hangar, which we gratefully accepted. Pulling off the cowling we find . . . absolutely nothing. No gaping hole in the case where a rod has smashed its way out, no ruptured hoses, nothing. More probing leads to the conclusion that the VW had spilled its oil out the number 3 cylinder, but it was impossible to say from what specific point because the entire lower side was covered with the stuff.

I suppose for some this would have been sack cloth and ashes time, but not so with Burt and Dick. Conversation immediately turned to where and how they could get a new engine and be ready to go *Monday morning*! With all the engines at Oshkosh, there's bound to be one that can be used, is the reasoning. It can be installed tonight, test flown tomorrow and be ready to go Monday morning.

By various means, all of us got back to Oshkosh during early afternoon.

Golda had John Monnett waiting for me when I walked in the door at Press Headquarters. Sure, he had a brand new engine in his booth, ready to bolt on . . . but it's brand new, no run-in time, the mags would have to be timed and it had a Posa injector carb. He had a better idea. An hour or so later we caught up to Burt who had finally managed to get the VariViggen back to Wittman Field. Right there in the middle of the busy display building floor, John laid a deal on him that was impossible to refuse.

"I'll send a couple of my friends down to Chicago tonight, have them remove the engine from my pranged Sonerai, fly it back, and my crew will work all night installing it in the VariEze so you can start test flying tomorrow. With a new engine, any new engine, you can't be sure what you have for the first 20-25 hours. With my engine, I know what you've got."

In late afternoon the VariEze arrived on a loaned trailer. After no little searching through the vast EAA grounds, Sonerai builders Charlie Terry of Long Island and Vance Graebner were located and immediately dispatched to DuPage County Airport to remove the engine from John's bent bird. It was after midnight when they returned with the vital organ. John and Mike Core would spend the remainder of the night transplanting it in the pallid body of the VariEze.

By sunup two very weary bug doctors had completed their work and were ready to look for some breakfast and a couple of beds. Burt could handle the final closure, cleanup and bandaging.

Considering the drama of the past 24 hours, it was almost disappointing when the engine simply fired up and ran like it was supposed to; well, almost. It ran, but Burt was not happy with the characteristics of the Posa injector, so off with the cowling, off with the Posa and on with the Barker engine's float carburetor. Whoops! the intake plumbing doesn't fit, and it's Sunday. Probably the only place in the U.S. that day with all sorts of aircraft hoses and hardware for sale was the EAA Fly-in. Within 30 hours of Dick's deadstick landing at Green Bay, the VariEze was winging its way around the fly-by pattern at Oshkosh.

One last dollop of adrenalin remained to be squeezed out of the situation. After landing, Burt eased off the runway, came to a stop, shut down and climbed out to inspect the nose gear leg. The earlier fix had not been enough—a crack had developed. No big deal, however, as the repair, including an additional wrap with glass cloth, took only an hour or so. Most of that was curing time.

At dusk all that could be done had been done, so everyone involved headed for bed. A 4:30 wake-up call would be much harder to take this time around. Come morning the same cast of characters would greet the rising sun.

And that's how we came to where we are . . . standing around or absently walking over to look at a couple of homebuilts, waiting, watching for the VariEze to return. then, finally, there it was—the VariViggen. Can't see the VariEze yet, but the "mothership" must be leading it in. Yep, there it is! What a beautiful sight!

After swinging wide around the Oshkosh tower where Harold is standing by to confirm the turn, Burt peels off and enters the landing pattern. Good sign! The VariEze must be okay if Burt is letting him head back for Menominee.

When Burt and John taxi in, we descend upon them for work on the VariEze, and they report that all seems well. Now they join the ranks of the watchers and waiters. We busy ourselves with the statistics of the first lap: Airborne at 5:55 A.M., Over Oshkosh Tower at 7:20 according to Harold Best-Devereux's watch—an hour and 25 minutes to cover 182 miles.

That's 128.5 mph and includes the climb-out from Wittman Field. Before landing, Burt has gotten fuel consumption numbers from Dick by radio and he seems concerned, but he isn't saying much.

"We'll see how it looks on the end of the next lap."

Lap two ended with Harold Best-Devereux's, "Mark 8:44." That was one hour and 24 minutes—130 mph.

"Too fast," says Burt.

He uses the VariViggen's radio to order a power reduction from 3,075 to 3,050. His brow knits a little deeper when he hears the fuel consumption figure for lap two.

"Ladies and gentlemen, the Oshkosh Tower has just established radio contact with the VariEze. If you will look to the northeast, you will soon see this aircraft completing its third lap."

"Ladies and gentlemen, the VariEze is again approaching Oshkosh. Pilot Dick Rutan is completing lap 4 and will be beginning lap 5. When he passes over the Oshkosh Tower, the VariEze will have passed the halfway point toward breaking Ed Lesher's record. Nine laps are required to set a new mark."

"Mark 11:40" a one-hour, 27-minute lap—125.5 mph. Burt doesn't look quite as worried over the fuel situation.

"Mark 1:09" One hour, twenty-nine minutes—122.5 mph. Funny, the mid laps seem to be going past faster than at the beginning. Complacency? . . . or is hunger dulling the senses? It's been eight hours now since breakfast.

"The VariEze is inbound again. This will be the completion of lap 6. At the turn, the VariEze will have covered 1,092 miles. This is the first time a world's record has been attempted at an EAA Fly-in. We invite everyone to stick around this evening to greet Dick Rutan when he completes the flight."

Harold's mark had caught Dick rounding the Oshkosh tower at 2:36 P.M., an hour and twenty-seven minutes time for lap 6. Same as lap 4. Obviously, wind is not a factor today.

"Mark 4:07. Two more laps for the record, gentlemen." Hmmm, that's an hour thirty-one—120 mph. A check with Burt reveals that, yes, he did slow Dick down again to 2.950 rpms. Fuel consumption?

"Yeah, it looks like we are burning a little more than we expected. Don't think we will be able to go the extra laps we planned. Running too slow now . . . but the record looks okay. Know what? I don't think we had the tanks completely full at takeoff. I couldn't believe the consumption on the first lap, but has settled down some now."

So that's what was on his mind.

"Mark 5:37."

"Ladies and gentlemen, the VariEze has now completed lap 8 and has started the record lap. If all goes well, the aircraft will return over Wittman Field at just after 7:00 P.M. At that point, Dick Rutan will have flown 1,638 miles, 83.7 miles further than Ed Lesher's 1970 record."

Decision time! While Arv Olson is keeping the crowd informed over the PA, Burt is busy taking data from Dick via the VariViggen's radio—speed, fuel remaining, temperatures, pressures—the decision has to be made now on trying lap 10 because now the race is also with the sun. The VariEze is not equipped with lights and a tenth lap at the present lap speeds would get Dick back around 8:30, after official sunset. Is there enough fuel left to speed up?

Lap 8 took an hour and a half even . . . it sure seemed longer than that: 121 mph.

Look at the people who are beginning to gather around the Comm Center.

"He's coming in this time," somebody yells. A dash to the Comm Center confirms it. Dick has decided to call it quits at the end of lap 9; the fuel remaining is such that 10 laps would be slicing things too thin. There's a technicality that has to be kept in mind in these closed course record attempts—you have to land back at the same airport from which you started, otherwise all goes down the tubes. Dick has figured his fuel at the turn at Menominee and has told them via Unicom to call us regarding his decision.

"Ladies and gentlemen, the VariEze will land at the conclusion of the 9th lap, setting a new world's record. When the aircraft lands, everyone is asked to stay back behind the showline barriers. For the record to be official, Harold Best-Devereux, the official observer, must check the fuel tank seals and remove the barograph before the plane is disturbed.

Harold's "mark" comes at 6:58 P.M., officially ending the course time. That is a 1:21 lap, the fastest of the day. Just over 134 mph. We will let the tower mark his official touchdown time and figure his total time in the air from that.

Just over 13 hours aloft is not enough to cool off Dick's enthusiasm before landing on 18! He says the VariEze cockpit is the most comfortable he's ever sat in; must be true.

This time around he has the nose gear cranked down; hope it's locked. That's it, he's down! He's done it!

Dick taxies back up the side of the runway and turns down the EAA access. Harold is out of the car now and is giving him the "cut" sign. Dick brakes to a stop and is lifting the canopy. He is greeted by a resounding cheer from his fellow EAAers (Fig. 4-9). Harold gives him a fast handshake and proceeds to dive into the rear cockpit for the barograph. Presently he emerges and hoists it over his head like a trophy won. More applause.

Dick pulls out his can of chocolate pudding to show what provisions he has left and immediately it is requested by an admirer, who also wants it autographed after the prize is his. This starts a frantic round of autograph signing by both Dick and Burt.

Dick was in the air a total of 13 hours 8 minutes and 45 seconds. The tower officially had him down at 7:03.45 C.D.T. The nine-lap course distance was 1,638 miles. Burt Rutan finally figured that the VariEze had taken off with 46.5 gallons of fuel on board; 6.3 gallons remained when the flight was completed; so 40.2 gallons were consumed in the 13-plus hours. This figures to just over 3.1 gallons per hour for the day's flying. One pint of oil was used by the Monnett VW. The average speed had been 125.5 mph. These were tremendous figures for any small airplane, but more impressive when one reflects that the construction of the aircraft was

Fig. 4-9. We did it! Paul and Audrey Poberezny, Dick and Burt Rutan, Harold Best-Devereux and Bill Turner after the record flight. (courtesy EAA by Dick Stouffer)

started the last of January of this year and that it did not fly for the first time until May 21. The months and years ahead will see the effects of the shock waves that are even now rippling out through the aviation world. We suspect they will be profound. Certainly it can be said, no homebuilt design—or factory design—has made such a spectacular start as the VariEze. It took a lot of help from Burt's friends to get the first record, and he is grateful; but to Burt must go the credit for daring to be different in the design of this aircraft by asking so much of it so soon . . . in full view of so many people.

BUILDERS' EXPERIENCES—FACTS, FRUSTRATIONS, AND FOUL-UPS

The trials and tribulations of VariEze builders differ somewhat from those of VariViggen, Quickie and Long-EZ fabricators in that the VariEze was the first composite construction homebuilt to achieve

true popularity. Thus, many of the problems were those of first time pioneers.

A Mature Builder Speaks His Mind

We met VariEze builder Norm Spitzer (Fig. 4-10) on a hot summer morning in the RAF office in Mojave. We'd met him before, a long, long time ago on a rice paddy in the middle of the Upper Assam jungle in those nearly-forgotten days when both of us were flying C-46s over the Burma Hump. But enough of the war stories.

Norm's VariEze, which he calls *The Rockpile Express* in memory of the India-China-Burma "rockpile" of the World War II days, was completed and flying when we ran into him at Mojave (Fig. 4-11). He was close to having flown his time out in the Central California Bay area near Berkeley and was savoring the idea of taking his new plane on its first long cross-country trip. We asked Norm to

Fig. 4-10. Norm Spitzer, WW II pilot, with his partially-completed VariEze, shown on the porch of his second-story apartment. "It has rekindled a new interest and joy in aviation which I thought I had lost," said Spitzer. (courtesy Jean Spitzer)

share some of his experiences in developing his project. At first, he didn't want his name used because he said that he wasn't reaching for notoriety, but we pointed out that the material was more forceful with a real, live, breathing builder in the background, so here 'tis:

"You asked what prompted me to start the VariEze. After forty years of flying, I found that I was becoming bored with the stock complacent Wichita type of aircraft. I had become more and more interested in the homebuilding movement. The first information on the VariEze captured my imagination with its efficiency, type of construction, and most of all its magnificent appearance. And then, a very close friend (we had been Cadets together and subsequently, fishing and hunting partners) died unexpectedly. He had taken an early

Fig. 4-11. Norm and Jean Spitzer (left) enjoy a picnic lunch at the Watsonville, California, fly-in with friends. The Eze that was built in the bedroom takes them everywhere they wish to go.

retirement from the airlines to do all the things he had put off and shortly after that he was gone. My wife pointed out that I had been talking of building an airplane and not to wait too long, so the decision—thanks to her—was to start the VariEze.

We drove to Aircraft Spruce and brought back the kit in our station wagon. Plans were acquired and my neighbor, Gene Cartwright, recently retired from the newspapers, volunteered to assist.

"Several other builders were located locally and wonderful telephone conversations and visits were initiated with discussions of construction methods, sources of materials, potential performances, etc.

The one frustrating aspect was the constant changes that came during the early period of construction. I had the control system finished when ailerons were added; the fuselage when the dive brake was added; the gear when the retraction method was revised, etc., etc. It got to the point where the quarterly newsletter was received with dread as invariably the changes would set back the completion date by months.

I had built the ship in a bedroom on the second floor, and as each unit was finished, it had to be stored elsewhere because of space requirements. Soon wings were stacked in the entrance way, boxes of parts in the living room—with urethane dust everywhere. Meanwhile, the mailman and UPS brought a constant stream of strange boxes to add to the modifications, such as rejecting and rebuilding items, and the one main tragedy of breaking the canopy after its completion.

Then comes the subject of visitors. The knowledgeable ones are always welcome, with many delightful hours spent displaying plans, parts, and learning from them; then, there are the others with quick advice without knowledge. Actually, the visitor situation is very good preparation and training for your first fly-in when your plane is inspected by a horde of hard-eyed, doubting fellow VariEze builders. On one occasion after looking at the alternator, instruments, radio, omni transponder, etc., one such type said, with his voice dripping with disbelief, 'How did you get it so light?' Thanks to the visitor training period, I was able to instantly answer, 'Oh, I left the main spar out!'

Finally, I took the ship out to the airport ready to fly. Four months later, it did fly, but not before another sad occurrence. My good friend and helper, Gene Cartwright, died of a heart attack. I had decided to fly it when both the ship and I were ready and so did not invite any observers. However, the two local VariEze pilots saw me taxi out and were on hand for the landing. Now if you read *Sport Aviation*, you know the first flight is supposed to be, at the very least, some type of religious experience. In my case, this was far from true. The ship was wing heavy and I was mad at myself to have erred, and I guess after three years of construction I was let down. My friends insisted on congratulations and retiring for a ceremonial drink. I did appreciate their thoughtfulness—I never did find the source of the trim problem and finally corrected it with a fixed tab.

Only as the flight test program progressed did I really begin to appreciate the wonderful experience of developing your own airplane. I have plans for many changes and experiments down the road, and this ship will fulfill my aeronautical appetite and curiosity for many years to come. It has rekindled a new interest and joy in aviation which I thought I had lost. My wife Jean, who has contributed so much in my life, has taken a complete part in the entire endeavor, and I feel sorry for those who start such a project without that support. Finally, the building of an aircraft introduces you to some great people. Buchanan Field's other two VariEze builders, Lyle Powell and Carlos Amspocker, fall in that category.

And finally for me, building this ship was never VariEze. But Carlos, a retired chemical engineer and ex-Marine pilot, puts it very well when after flying, he sits in a chair, lights up a cigar, looks at his VariEze parked in front on the hangar, and says, 'I can't believe it's all mine and that I actually built it!'

Trio With 500 Hours Each

The first three VariEze builders to top the

500-hour mark all lived in California. They are Ed Hamlin of Rocklin; Les Faus of Van Nuys, and Dr. Don Shupe of LaVerne (Fig. 4-12). The trio met and discussed their experiences with a tape recorder running, using a series of questions as a format. Some of their comments and stories, gleaned from an hour and a half of tape, give an interesting insight to these builders of VariEzes. (Ed died in 1983.)

How did you first become interested in the VariEze?

All three credit an article published in *Air Progress* magazine and all were impressed with the mileage and speed of the two-placer. Les Faus started out looking at the original BD-5 and planned to purchase a production model in partnership.

Les: That got me into flying, because the fellow I went into partnership with said I wasn't going to fly his half until I got some time in. I hadn't flown 'til then. Then the VariEze came up about that time, and it looked like it was going to be a long time until the BD-5 was done, so I got interested in the VariEze and went ahead with it.

Ed: A friend came by and wanted some help in building a seaplane in my garage because I had the better shop. My friend was going to buy the materials and I'd go ahead and build it. This was back in the summer of '75. I became disillusioned because there were only five places to land seaplanes in California. Then I saw the *Air Progress* article and said to myself, "That's the airplane I've got to build." I was familiar with the fiberglass material. At that time, I owned a 1/6 interest in a Grumman Trainer but I couldn't afford to own a certificated plane because of maintenance and other problems.

Don: After I saw the article, I went around talking with friends, discussing the specifications that Burt had put on building time and simple construction style. The price tag, including engine, seemed to be within my financial budget, and I had had some experience in fiberglass on boats. It seemed to be the way to go. I had owned a Cessna 150 on a leaseback and it ate me alive. It cost about $4,000 a year to own it and rent it out. I couldn't afford that kind of a plane either.

Les: I was influenced by the fact that you could get a higher performance airplane for a lot cheaper than a factory one. I did get into a partnership with a Cessna 150 for a while just to build time.

How long did it take you to build?

Don: I started in the summer when the plans came out—one of the first sets of plans. I worked steadily for two full summers—about 80 hours a week, and then another full year; it first flew in December '77.

Les: I was one of the first ones to get plans. It took me 10 months to finish and the cost turned out to be about $7,500.

Ed: I got started in the summer of '76 and my airplane first flew in March 1978—18 months. I spent a fair part of the summer of '77 and then laid off of it because I was burned out. Sacramento Valley was hot and it was hard to work. I couldn't keep the shop cool.

What kind of building problems did you have?

Don: Every kind possible. Specifically, I built the canard first to specifications and did all the measurements as closely as possible. I got done and found that the elevators didn't have sufficient travel because the hole they were supposed to go in wasn't big enough. That was because the pivot arms were

Fig. 4-12. First VariEze builders to log 500 hours each in their canard homebuilts are Dr. Don Shupe, left, Les Faus, and Ed Hamlin.

down too far, so I had to cut them all out and put them on again. That was the first thing that I did twice. I did dozens of things twice after that because I was one of the first ones to check out the plans. There were lots of errors in the plans. During the time I built, I found over 30 major errors in the plans for the first time that weren't reported anywhere else. Some of them I found before I made mistakes; but a lot of them I found after I already had the part completed, so I had to do a lot of things twice. That caused lots of frustration and slowed the project down tremendously.

Ed: Well, you had no practical building experience with this type of construction, did you? Actually, there were very few things I had to do twice. I rebuilt one of the back bulkheads simply because I mis-measured one and had it half completed when I finally found my mistake. Other than that, things went fairly smoothly, but I had an extensive background in building fiberglass and foam radio-controlled model airplanes which helped me a great deal in the construction of the airplane—plus, my building partner, Dick Kennedy, had experience working on large airplanes. We had several other homebuilders who were very helpful in our EAA Chapter, and when a problem arose, we could go to several people to try to figure out how to solve it. These people were relatively close at hand. So things really went relatively smoothly.

One of the things that really slowed our project down was that we made all our own metal parts, including wing fittings, which included the unique experience of buying bars of 4130 steel and finding machinists that would turn out our taper pins, finding a tapered reamer of the proper angle and specifications so we could ream the holes. But all totaled, we probably made about eight or nine sets of wing fittings. That is the thing that really slowed my project down.

Don: What slowed me down was that being one of the first people in the area to build, Brock didn't have a lot of the parts done that I couldn't make. I had to wait a long time for wing fittings and had to go ahead with the fuselage before I could do the wing fittings—which turned out to be just fine.

But one of the things that was a major problem was stuff like—Burt said you were supposed to mix the slurry that was supposed to go over the foam to a fairly thick consistency. The ratio he suggested was 50 percent microspheres, or something like that. The mixture I would get when I would mix that would be a gooey mixture that simply would not spread over the foam, and so I would get these chunks of slurry-type stuff that wouldn't even out and I would be starting with a nice smooth piece of foam and by the time I got done putting the damn slurry over it, it would be all chunky and lumpy. And by that time—he told us to use fast epoxy—and I had a 75° room, and the stuff would start setting up. If you didn't get your glass on there quickly, you'd have a horrible mess. Then, later on, I discovered that people were using a much thinner slurry that spread out very smoothly and made all the difference in the world. But see, I didn't have any help. I didn't have anybody to go to to ask how to do things except to call Burt. The first four or five months I was working on it, I had $50 per month phone bills just calling Mojave. They were very helpful, but lots of times I didn't even know what kind of questions to ask. I knew I was having trouble, but I didn't know what to ask.

My layups were taking three times longer than what he said in the book. But by the time I got done with the last wing layup—he said it should take two hours—six of us got it done in two hours. But it took three other wing layups to get to that point.

Another major problem I had was that I didn't know anyone who knew how to cut foam. So when we cut the wings and the canards, the guy who helped me and I were cutting the first piece of foam we'd ever cut in our lives. The wire was too hot— we overburned, and the wings required major surgery to save them. But we tried to salvage them and as a result the wings are just super rough.

Ed: I had the experience of cutting hundreds of sets of foam cores, because once I got involved with a guy who was running a hobby shop. I cut him hundreds of sets of foam for links and delivered them to him as a part of a project. We also had the foam cutting equipment because a friend of mine from the model airplane days had built a very nice rheostat-controlled foam cutter.

Les: The only building problem I had was epoxy poisoning. The airplane went together without any problem, but the epoxy poisoning would keep me from working two to three months at a time. Even now, if I go out and wash car parts with paint thinner, I'll break out the same as I would with epoxy. With the epoxy, it's definitely fumes; with the thinners, I don't know. I don't need to touch the epoxy at all—all I have to do is pour the hardener from one can to another and I break out. I used a respirator after it hit me. I didn't take the precautions I should have like I was warned. I also was working in a closed garage trying to keep the heat up for the epoxy, so I was in a heavy concentration of fumes to start out. But I had most of the airframe done in six weeks. It was a struggle from there to finish the rest of the stuff.

Ed: Six weeks sounds really fast.

Les: Well, it was a week each for the wings, about a week for the canards, and the rest of the time for the fuselage boxes. I was pretty well done with the nose, but I needed fuel tanks on it and the canopy.

Ed: How long were you stopped that first time?

Les: I didn't work on it for a month to get over the epoxy poisoning. Then I started dabbling a little at a time to see what I could tolerate and what I couldn't, and how I could work with it.

What was your level of piloting experience prior to flying your VariEze?

Les had about 200 hours in Cessnas and just before flying his VariEze, he took an hour in a Citabria. Don had 350-400 hours, almost entirely in Cessna 150s, but including 15 hours high-performance retractable time. Ed had about 300 hours, with a majority of time in high-performance aircraft—Beech Sierra and Beech Bonanza. He also had a good portion of time in a 160 Grumman trainer that had similarities to the Eze in high wing loading.

What kind of preparation did you make for your first flight?

Les: Only special preparation was flying the Citabria for an hour and getting familiar with that. Here again, I'm used to running machinery and I have a light touch on things, which makes a bit of a difference compared to somebody who doesn't use their hands.

Burt made the first flight in my Eze and then I made the next flight after the ailerons were put on. I knew the airframe was straight, so I was going to do a lift off and the runway turned out to be too short by the time I got it up fast enough to get it lifted off, so I just poked it and went. I learned to fly it in the air and came back and made a couple of passes for landing. The major thing I found wrong was Burt had the speeds too low for takeoff and landing. That's right at my stall speed: mine stalls about ten miles an hour faster than his figures.

So I was having trouble controlling it at the low speeds, because the wing rocks quite badly at stall. My approaches were too slow and my nose too high. After about four landings, an observer told me it would look better if I went a little faster. I upped the speeds 10 mph and everything went beautifully from there on. In three or four flights I was really comfortable in the airplane. It's more like a sports car; it goes where you point it.

Don: Really, I didn't make any preparation for test flying. I was working on the plane so much and I had very little money. It was just not practical to get out and fly a taildragger or anything else. I did extensive taxiing that I'm sure was not good for the airplane engine, but it was really good for me. I was down at Chino on a long smooth runway and did many, many runs before I finally got it off the ground. I knew the airplane was rigged properly and that it was balanced. As it turned out I required minimal trim. When it went off, it was all ready to go.

Ed: I didn't actually do any preparation. I was flying fairly actively at the time.

Chapter 13 contains some of the test flying experiences of this trio.

A total of 4,500 VariEze plans and construction manuals were sold between 1976 and the rollout of the enlarged Long-EZ late in 1979. The increased size and performance of the Long-EZ dictated that new builders start with this stretched model. Most builders who were well into their VariEze projects went on to complete them. That is the way of progress.

Chapter 5

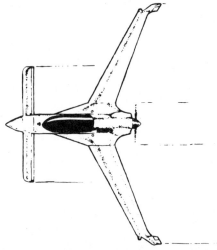

Canard Concept
and Composite Construction

Rutan's basic configuration—whether the Vari-Viggen, VariEze, Long-EZ or Defiant (Fig. 5-1)—is a loaded canard wing designed to provide aerodynamic angle-of-attack limiting and thus be stall-proof.

When the opportunity comes along (as it did to us on several occasions) to fly Rutan's designs, you'll really enjoy this proof of concept in the air.

THAT LITTLE WING UP FRONT

The Rutan crew describes the canard system very simply. A canard airplane has a tandem wing—one wing in front of the other. Generally, the front wing is smaller than the other. Mike Melvill commented that he knew of no canard where the front wing wasn't smaller. The front wing provides pitch control, though the Swedish Viggen's pitch control comes from elevators on the back of the delta wing. Dick Rutan says that this makes it not a canard, while Burt maintains that it is. So you take your choice. The Eze canard design has flaps for landing on the back wing—not elevators.

Both wings on the canard design are lifting rather than having the tail of a "conventional" design with a down load that causes drag. Nothing on the canard design is "lifting down."

The canard, itself, goes back to the days of the Wright Flyer. Canard glider designs included Wolfgang Klemperer's in the 1920s that was supposed to sense rising air currents and pull up into them to gain altitude. In WW II, Curtiss-Wright built a canard interceptor fighter with a pusher Allison engine called the XP-55 Ascender, which was the subject of numerous snide puns.

After Rutan's early success with the complex-to-build VariViggen, he turned to a smaller, cheaper, hopefully less-complex canard. His initial effort in this smaller class of airplane was called the "MiniViggen" (Fig. 5-2). As Burt reported in an article carried in the January 1976 issue of *Sport Aviation:*

It was a high-wing, low-canard, two-place with fixed gear and conventional ailerons. Its structure

Fig. 5-1. Rutan's canards in formation. The twin-engine Defiant, the VariViggen, and the Long-EZ in the desert skies at Mojave.

NASA's yet unpublished research with Whitcomb winglets, contacted Dr. Whitcomb for details, and incorporated them into the design. I had been studying the smooth contoured, efficient glass composite European sailplanes. These all-glass ships represented to me the only really significant advance in lightplane aerodynamics and structures since the advent of the Beech Bonanza—it's a shame they require expensive female molds, exotic materials and skilled craftsmen to build, for a homebuilt composite aircraft would sure be nice with its light weight, wrinkle-free structure, improved corrosion resistance, longer fatigue life, and a dramatic reduction in the number of parts!

In order to demonstrate the efficiency of the configuration, I decided to develop an airplane to capture Ed Lesher's speed and distance records in the under 500-kg weight class. I spent the next two

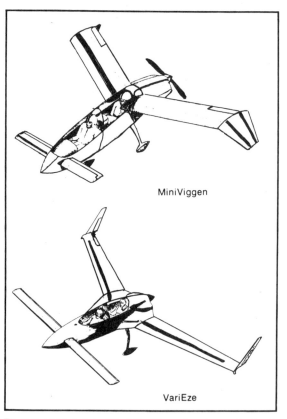

MiniViggen

VariEze

Fig. 5-2. Initial sketch of the "MiniViggen" and an early sketch of the VariEze.

was all aluminum, using forward fuselage formed skins and canopy from another design and single curvature aluminum sheets for the aft fuselage and flying surfaces. The aircraft was designed around the then-available 60-hp Franklin aircraft engine. In early 1974, I built the fuselage and canard of the MiniViggen. I later scrapped the structure because I found that the compound curves of the fuselage made the fabrication and installation of all internal parts very difficult and time-consuming. I was also not satisfied with the lack of insulation, vibration, points of fatigue, and weight of the metal structure. I later found through model testing that the design had negative spiral stability and a region of pitch instability at the approach speed.

During October/November 1974, I learned of

months in detail design of the VariEze prototype, using a simple square-inside box fuselage and solid core flying surfaces. Having no previous fiberglass experience, I built N7EZ (Fig. 5-3) over the next 3½ months. The first half of the construction project was done alone, with occasional help from Carolyn. During the second half, Gary Morris donated his evenings and weekends to help. Phil Rathbun built the machined parts for us.

N7EZ was assembled at the hangar for initial tests on May 21, 1975. That day it made several high-speed taxi runs and one short 10-foot altitude hop down the runway. It was not a good day; nose gear shimmy required repair and redesign; nose gear rotation speed was too high and roll control inadequate due to stalled elevons. That night a close documentation of the aircraft was done and it was found that due to a variety of errors, the canard incidence was too low with respect to the wing and the wing had only about half the amount of washout called for in the design. A temporary strip of sheet metal was taped to the wing trailing edge and bent upward to reduce the wing's pitching moment (this was later removed and the wing's under camber filled to compensate). The canard's incidence was also increased, and the next day the VariEze was off on its first real flight. After some fine tuning to get the proper canard incidence, the airplane was pronounced satisfactory for formation flying and was tucked in under the photo chase required for *Air Progress* magazine four days after first flight.

Analysis and tests indicated that a very poor maximum lift coefficient and early airflow separation existed on the canard causing the high stall speed (60 knots) and poor roll control below 80 knots. The 14-inch chord canard was operating at a very low Reynolds number and the GAW-1 airfoil could not exceed eight degrees angle of attack and 19 degrees elevon position without at least partial stall. A little reference searching and the help of Dick Eldridge of NASA's Flight Research Center resulted in finding an airfoil designed to operate at low Reynolds number—the GU25-5(11)8 developed at the University of Glasgow. The GU25 offered several advantages:

- ☐ 50 percent greater G_L than the GAW-1 at Reynolds number of ½-million.
- ☐ Thicker section resulting in a lighter, stiffer canard.
- ☐ No trailing edge camber, thus eliminated the requirement for external trim tabs.
- ☐ Attached airflow at higher elevon deflection.

"I dusted off the cartop windtunnel and tested

Fig. 5-3. Burt sits at the controls of the original VariEze N7EZ as his mother Irene inspects the back seat for space. She was later to fly in this prototype. (courtesy Burt Rutan)

the two airfoils to verify the published data and to evaluate three different elevon gap configurations. The new canard was then built and flown. The difference in the airplane's flying qualities was the most dramatic change I have seen without a planform change. Whereas before, the aircraft had a nose-down stall break at 60 knots, it could now be flown at 52 knots with full aft stick! Whereas before, the roll rate was poor below 80 knots and had to be supplemented with rudder below 70 knots, it now had satisfactory roll control down to the stall speed. Roll rate at all speeds is now much better than a Cessna, but less than a Yankee. According to wind tunnel data, the cruise speed should have been reduced three knots; however, flight tests showed identical cruise performance and in improvement in low-speed performance (maximum L/D increased to 18.5).

Rutan expanded on the desirable features of the canard design for use:

Regarding pitch stability and high angle-of-attack characteristics, the canard arrangement obviously does not guarantee stability and a safe stall—rather it gives the designer the flexibility to tailor the characteristics to his desires. What is desired? The optimum is a linear airplane in the normal flight regime with a strong stable break in the pitching moment curve near maximum usable lift. The conventional one-wing, tail-aft configuration does not allow a designer to provide natural limiting of angle-of-attack. If elevator power is strong enough to get the nose up at forward CG and is capable of driving the main wing beyond initial stall to where loss of directional stability or massive unsymmetrical wing stall can occur, these, of course, are the causes of spin susceptibility. There is no need or desire to ever operate beyond the initial stall. Any student knows that yanking the stick further aft at the stall will result in you being a pile of mush on the runway. But if the airplane limits itself at the initial stall and has no stall break, then we have real stall safety. The nose on the Defiant does not "drop" at the stall. It stays at its maximum angle and if the CG is aft, it gently "nods" about one degree every three seconds. The pilot retains full control of flight path at this extreme condition of holding full aft stick. Even with a failed engine, he can obtain an instant climb, or descent, or fly indefinitely level while holding full aft stick. By contrast, a conventional aircraft, if stalled, will mush to the ground even at full power, since the elevator power is sufficient to cause massive wing stall with its attendant loss of lift and enormous drag (reference stall/mush accidents on takeoff and landing).

Why can the canard do this is forward and aft CG? The reason at forward CG is simple, since the definition of the forward CG limit is that CG beyond which the low-speed performance is not obtained. Now, let's see how the canard configuration can be designed to limit angle-of-attack at aft CG. Elevator power at aft CG is considerably higher, and the high angle-of-attack is reached with very little elevator. Then, as the canard begins to stall (a gradual loss of lift, not abrupt, if the correct airfoil is used) a great deal more aft stick is required to get only a small amount more angle-of-attack. At aft CG using full aft stick, the canard is actually operating above its maximum lift angle; thus the canard is a stabilizing surface (more angle—less lift), and pitch stability is much 'stiffer' than in normal flight. Thus, at this flight condition, the aircraft will maintain angle-of-attack very accurately. Contrast this with the normally 'sloppy' pitch stability of a conventional aircraft at the stall, and its abrupt loss of lift."

In speaking specifically of the twin-engine, push-pull Defiant, Rutan explained: "The main reason the Defiant outperforms the other light twins is its low wetted area, not its canard configuration. However, the reason it has low wetted area is because of the canard configuration."

The canard configuration drastically reduces the magnitude of the structural loads and eliminates a very large percentage of wasted wetted area. Its simplified design philosophy eliminates many unneeded systems like flaps, cowl flaps, etc. Its control runs are shorter and carry less than half the forces. All the above items contribute to weight savings, which reduces required wing area, again saving weight. The next result is that even though the Defiant's ultimate load factor is 50 percent higher than the conventional twins, it is nearly 1,000 pounds lighter and has less than 2/3 the wetted area. Again, the reason is the canard configuration."

1990 DESIGNS AND CAPABILITIES

Rutan is by no means the only aircraft executive who is high on the use of new construction techniques and material and the canard concept. Malcolm S. Harned, Senior Vice President, Technology, Cessna Aircraft Co., has some very definite ideas on the subject. Some of these were expressed to the American Institute of Aeronautics and Astronautics (AIAA) at a seminar in Washington, D.C. under the title, *General Aviation Aircraft—A Forecast of 1990 Design and Capabilities:*

Several factors will assure a high demand for general aviation aircraft through the decade of the 1990s, namely, increasing airline specialization in mass transport between major hubs and, as a result, greater use of private or executive-type aircraft by businessmen and the affluent for both convenience and comfort.

This trend will foster a need for more feederline aircraft. There also will be broader demand for increased safety, fuel efficiency, comfort, performance per dollar as well as reduced maintenance.

New technologies will be available such as composite materials, new aerodynamics, very sophisticated electronics, fallout from the auto industry's booming technology, and advances in turbo-machinery. New generations of aircraft will materialize, most with pressurization, all-weather capability, and self-monitoring diagnostic systems to minimize failures and maintenance requirements.

Reduced weight, improved aerodynamics and engines will generally increase speeds by 25 percent and kilometers per liter by more than 50 percent. Compound aircraft will provide vertical landing plus high-speed cruise. Efficient short-haul feederliners will also be available.

The airlines will become extremely efficient transporters of masses of people for long distances.

As a result of the recent reductions in air fares here, there were large increases in traffic.

However, worse than the crowded aeroplanes are the congested terminals. These two factors make flying very unpleasant for the businessman and eliminate the possibility of working while traveling.

In addition, there is a continuing decline in airline service to smaller communities. Since the quadrupling of the cost of fuel, the airlines can no longer afford to service their low load-factor routes, which generally are to the decentralized business and industry communities.

In the smaller communities there are rapidly growing numbers of people who want to take advantage of the low-cost, high speed air travel available at the hub terminals. This will create a very large demand for feederline operations. These aircraft need to be relatively small, from 9 to 50 passengers, to provide reasonable frequency of service and be economical to operate to the smaller communities.

Fortunately, there will be a number of new tools to assist the aircraft industry in meeting the stringent demands of the greatly expanded marketplace.

Great promise for general aviation is offered by composite materials, such as the aramid fibers and graphite fibers with an epoxy bond. Both types of fibers offer strength-to-weight ratios and modulus of elasticity-to-weight ratios very superior to aluminum alloys.

Before this potential is fully realized, there are many developments required which include lightning protection, inspection and testing techniques, interfacing with metals, new approaches to structural analysis and design, new manufacturing techniques and methods for field repair. In addition, material costs must be drastically reduced.

However, by the 1990s these problems should be resolved and these materials should be standard production items. The fact that Kevlar® is replacing steel in premium tires today is very promising. They will be used not only for basic airframe structure but for propeller blades, landing gear, etc., with the general result of at least a 25 percent reduction in empty weight.

There should also be significant improvement in aerodynamic efficiency as the result of the universal application of refined versions of the so-called supercritical airfoil sections. These will not only be applied to wings but also to improve the efficiency of propellers.

Aircraft piston engines will be significantly better, both in power/weight ratios and specific fuel consumption. Composite materials will be used extensively for engine structure and components, thereby reducing weight. Lean burning techniques with fuel injection and other improvements should also offer 10 to 15 percent reductions in specific fuel consumption (SFC). Even diesels will become usable with over a 25 percent improvement in SFC.

The use of pusher propellers will be made practical as a result of using composites for lightweight, very reliable drive shafts and gear boxes.

This approach offers several advantages:

☐ The high speed propeller slipstream does not impinge on the aircraft, thus reducing drag.

☐ Mounted on the tail, the inflow to the propeller keeps the air flow attached to the tailcone, also reducing drag.

☐ Nacelle drag can be eliminated by locating the engines in the fuselage.

☐ The aft location substantially reduces cabin noise.

☐ Visibility is greatly improved.

☐ For twins, gearing the two engines to a single rear prop gives centerline thrust, eliminating any yaw with an engine failure. This configuration is also ideal for thrust reversing.

☐ The rear location is much safer on the ground since with the proper tail configuration the possibility of people walking into a propeller can be virtually eliminated.

The twins will all have thrust on or near enough the centerline to eliminate V_{mc} (minimum control speed for twins) as a consideration which will be a real safety advantage.

Most [aircraft] will have engine monitoring systems which will sense vibrations, torsional loading and metal in the oil to anticipate engine failures well in advance. This will not only increase safety but will reduce engine maintenance costs.

The six-place and larger aircraft will have strain gauge systems mounted on the landing gear that will make possible an automatic weight and balance readout from the computer.

The 25 percent lower empty weight, the supercritical airfoil and the full-span flaps all combine to make possible reducing the wing area by one-third. However, the wing span has been retained to give good climb characteristics with relatively low power and a high lift/drag ratio for the higher altitude cruise.

The minimum family twin is illustrated. To provide minimum cost, two turbocharged automotive Wankel engines are used. Their compact size and light weight almost make possible a convenient arrangement for a centerline thrust twin to provide maximum safety. Since these engines are liquid cooled, the radiators will be aluminum leading edges on the wing for the front engine and on the tail surfaces and inlet for the rear engines. This will also provide an automatic anti-icing capability.

Although the Wankel will always be inferior to the piston engine in SFC, its light weight, compact size and lack of vibration will perpetuate its development as an automotive engine with the result that its low cost could make it attractive for personal aircraft. The lack of a valve train and basic simplicity should make it very reliable.

Continuing up the scale in speed, in that decade we'll see the Mach 0.95 business jet (Fig. 5-4). This would offer essentially a 20 percent increase in speed over today's business jets and at the same time provide high fuel efficiency.

It will be necessary to bury the engines, area rule the fuselage, go to highly swept wings with super-critical airfoils, and a canard surface on the nose to minimize trim drag. Winglets will serve a dual purpose, increasing the aspect ratio and directional stabilization.

This aircraft would offer stand-up aisle height, 16 places plus a 965 km/h cruising speed capability at altitudes up to 60,000 feet with ocean-crossing range. Even at this speed, it should offer a fuel

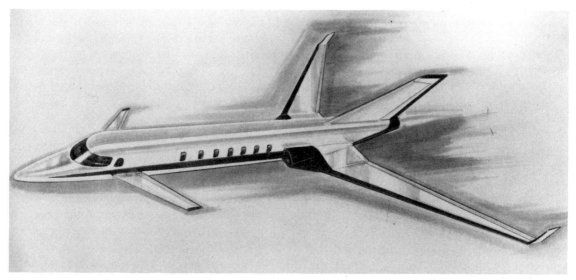

Fig. 5-4. Mach 0.95 business jet of the 1990s as foreseen by Malcolm S. Harned. This artist's diagram shows highly swept wings with super critical airfoils and a canard surface on the nose. Looks a lot like Rutan's designs today. (courtesy Cessna Aircraft Company)

efficiency of 1.7 km per liter. It also offers the safety advantage of essentially centerline thrust plus a cabin free of engine noise.

Another new category for general aviation will be the short-haul commuter transport. Although there has been a limited participation in this field with aircraft derived from business airplanes, this market will grow in size by several times in the next 15 to 20 years. Consequently, there will be all new designs developed in which the principal emphasis will be on the minimum amount of aircraft weight per passenger lifted into the air.

One approach to such a 50-passenger short haul airliner is illustrated (Fig. 5-5). By using a tandem wing configuration, minimum trim drag is achieved with good control power for low take-off

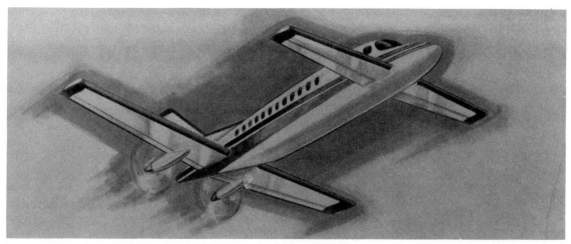

Fig. 5-5. Notice the comparison between Harned's concept from many years ago and SCALED's Starship I developed with Beechcraft shown in Chapter 14. (courtesy Cessna Aircraft Company)

and approach speeds. It also makes possible an aft location of the turboprops, which will provide a very low cabin noise level. The ability to use the aft pressure bulkhead as the carrythrough structure for the main wing minimizes weight.

It would be pressurized to cruise at 25,000′ where it would achieve speeds up to 480 km/h. Even for relatively short routes, it would offer over 42 seat-km per liter.

A principal requirement for future general aviation aircraft will be for improved safety. Consider, for example, general aviation's record with those for other modes of transportation (fatality rates per 100 million passenger-kilometers, based on U. S. figures only):

Overall airline aircraft	0.025
Overall general aviation aircraft	10.0
Overall passenger cars	0.875
Passenger cars on turnpikes	0.44
Cessna aircraft types:	
Skyhawks	4.375
421s	0.94
Citations	0.25

In summary, in the 1990s, we should expect our general aviation aircraft to generally provide 25 percent more speed with 50 to 100 percent better fuel efficiency plus greatly improved safety, reliability, convenience and comfort. They should reduce the accident rate and be safer than cars.

Many of Malcolm S. Harned's visions of the 1990s are already being assembled and flown by Burt Rutan and his army of homebuilders.

RUTAN'S COMPOSITE CONCEPT

Burt emphasizes that he has developed *methods* to simplify fabrication, not *materials*. The materials are those proven through years of aircraft experience.

Burt Rutan gives much of the credit for his new construction procedures to Fred Jiran, who operates a glider repair facility on the Mojave Airport. Burt spent many hours in Fred's shop "drooling over the smooth, contoured, efficient glass composite European sailplanes."

In his initial EAA announcement of the VariEze program, Rutan explained his reasoning for composite structure. We have excerpted portions of the report, which was originally printed in *Sport Aviation*, with permission of the Experimental Aircraft Association:

A *composite* as used in this article is defined as a sandwich of a low density core covered on both sides by a high strength material. A major point I want to clarify is that the VariEze is *not* a fiberglass—it is a *composite* aircraft.

A typical aluminum wing is a combination of a spar, ribs and skin attached in several hundred places by rivets. It is common practice to use safety factors of only 1.5, such that the metal permanently deforms at loads lightly over limit, or the maximum allowable flight loads. Further, the typical metal spar or rib is designed without full redundancy such that one crack can propagate across the piece and result in catastrophic failure. Commercial and military aircraft designed in this way require strict quality control and expensive equipment to inspect for hidden flaws and have a calculated fatigue life. The homebuilder generally uses only the visual surface finish to determine flaws, makes periodic inspections, and takes his chances. All flight loads are transmitted in concentration, not only at specific places (ribs), but at discrete rivets. This results in many minute high stress areas and the majority of the structural weight operating at very low stress. Further, if the ribs do not fit perfectly, they are pulled into position when the skin is installed, resulting in "assembly stresses," or loads, not due to flight loads. The metal skins and ribs also wrinkle and buckle under flight loads. Aluminum under stress has a definite life, beyond which it will crack and fail. To have a long life aluminum structure, the designer must assure that all flight stresses are small, and the builder must assure that flaws do not exist due to tight bends, nicks, assembly fit, or improper fastener installation. Due to constraints of complexity and weight, the designer can use redundancy in only critical areas and trust that adequate quality control is exercised when building parts.

In contrast, the VariEze wing has no ribs, no concentrations of high stress, and a spar which is multiply redundant. It is also designed for safety factors of approximately four, instead of 1.5. There is absolutely no wrinkling or buckling of any component, even above three times the design load factor for the aircraft. With the aircraft operating in its normal envelope, the maximum stresses are only a small fraction of the percentage of allowable stress, which means an exceptionally long fatigue life. Further, cracks cannot propagate across individual glass layers or even to adjacent fibers of a layer. Delaminating stresses are low, but even if a major amount of delamination occurred, the wing would still maintain its integrity for all normal flight loads. The nil-absorbent epoxy used is not susceptible to water absorption and freezing which causes crazing on some fiberglass products. Skin durability is such that you can walk on any portion of the wing with hardsoled shoes and cause no damage.

On the VariEze, I made the entire wing a single composite by using a solid core of low density foam. The homebuilder makes the cores by running a hot wire around rib templates. This method is quick and accurate, and it is easy to obtain any desired airfoil contour and wing twist. Where the box spar is located, the cores are cut with hot wire, the glass shear web is layed up, and then the cores are assembled. The glass spar cap and glass skin are then applied in one horizontal lay-up.

The advantages of this method are many: far fewer man-hours and skill are required, the box spar and the skin are 100 percent foam-supported, all the structure is easily inspected from the outside, and thermal stresses are eliminated since all structure is at the surface and expands uniformly. Foam stresses are very low and not concentrated. There are no stresses that tend to cause the foam to separate. The outer skin is quite stiff compared to the foam; even the foam's normal 2 percent dimensional instability with heat and time cannot give it undue stress. The foam is really just along for the ride, providing local buckling support and cannot change the shape of the wing once the glass skin has cured. The foam's role of providing buckling support is also not very critical to the integrity of the wing. Due to the high safety factors, a large percentage of the foam could be removed or detached from the skin, and the structure would still be adequate.

Do not confuse this construction with the method which uses a wood spar, foam ribs, and non-composite foam skin covered with Dynel. The success of that method is actually a good indication of the safety margin of glass composite, since it apparently does result in a satisfactory structure while breaking most of the rules! First, it is the best candidate for thermal stress; the wood spar is insulated by foam, so when the temperature changes, the skin immediately goes to the new temperature causing thermal stress. Second, bare foam is used in individual ribs to carry lift loads back to the spar, and the skin is foam sheets with one side bare. Thus, the foam is stressed many times greater than with a composite, and foam dimensional changes can affect structural shape. Third, Dynel has a very low modulus of elasticity, so that when stressed, the epoxy will actually crack before the material itself fails. The low modulus means that when the wing is loaded, more stress is dumped into the foam. Dynel is also quite thirsty for epoxy (its weave resembles burlap) resulting in a high weight/strength ratio layup. Dynel's main good point is the relative ease in which it lays down. Dynel or polypropylene *cannot under any circumstances* be considered for a structural application in a composite similar to a VariEze. Graphite or Kevlar® could be used in place of glass cloth, resulting in a 10 to 15 percent weight reduction, but the cost is prohibitive.

The glass spar is more efficient than an optimum metal spar, because the cap is uniformly tapered (using scissors when cutting glass cloth, as opposed to a milling machine for aluminum!), the direction of stress is oriented along the load path (along the spar cap at 34° in the shear web), and complete buckling support raises the strength of the compression cap to near that of the tension cap. A hand-layup of unidirectional fiberglass with the materials the homebuilder will use in VariEze construction has almost the same ultimate tensile strength, more compressive strength, and is 2/3 the weight of 2024 T-3 aluminum! Since the stresses are more uniformly applied, the strength-to-weight ratio of the entire structure is much greater.

Aluminum is susceptible to corrosion, requiring particular protection in humid, salty climates. Wood is susceptible to dry rot if not carefully protected. The glass structure requires no corrosion protection and can even withstand a salt water environment. The composite cannot trap moisture and has no hidden joints susceptible to stress corrosion.

Every homebuilder and every FAA inspector already has the inspection equipment required to check for flaws—his eyes. Visual inspection for voids or dry areas is all that is required. Due to the available adequate inspection method, ease of producing a quality part without high skill, and high safety factors, I believe that glass composite will provide a marked improvement in structural reliability over aluminum, steel or wood.

A composite structure is a quieter structure; there is no buckling or oilcanning, the foam core is a natural sound deadener. The thermal insulation qualities of the composite are beneficial in the cockpit. Whereas, in a metal airplane the radiant warmth from the canopy quickly escapes through the skin, the VariEzes canopy will even keep the pilot's feet warm at high altitudes without a heater.

Probably the best way to show the advantages of the composite structure is to compare it to a contemporary structure. The illustration (Fig. 5-6) compares the wings and canard of the VariEze

homebuilt to a typical all-aluminum set of wings and horizontal tail. The comparison is equal in terms of utility, since both provide all lift, pitch control, roll control, and flap. Both are detachable for trailering. Both are intended for homebuilt construction and are of approximately the same size. Note that although the wings are approximately the same aspect ratio and weight, the composite wing's ultimate strength is 2.6 times that of the metal wing. The canard strength is also much greater, but that comparison is unfair since the canard has three times the aspect ratio of the horizontal tail. Using accepted calculation methods, the expected fatigue life of the composite wing is over nine times greater than the metal wing in their respective applications. The metal structure suffers a performance loss due to airfoil contour deforming and wrinkling under load.

While we believe the skill required to build a VariEze is less than that required to weld or to form sheet metal, the method must be learned and we have the responsibility to educate the homebuilder. Thus, the plans will be much more than construction drawings—they will also include a complete, highly detailed, photo-illustrated construction manual and an education in composite methods.

Originally we had planned to market the VariEze the same as the VariViggen: i.e., market only the plans, construction manuals, formed materials (canopy, cowling, wheel pants and landing gear) and machined parts. Several problems with this plan became apparent. Raw materials shopping can be

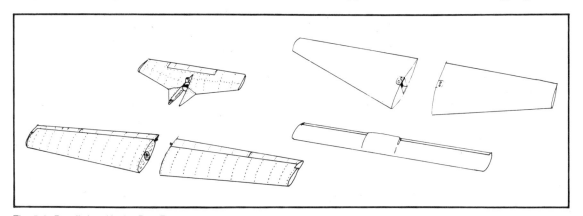

Fig. 5-6. Detail drawing by Burt Rutan.

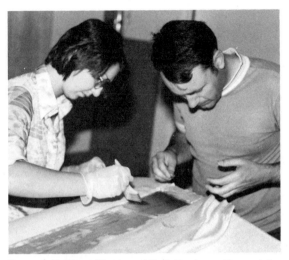

Fig. 5-7. Builders Chuck and Barb Banks wetting out the fiberglass. She's brushing epoxy and he's trimming the glass cloth. (courtesy RAF)

quite a chore for the homebuilder, having to buy a few nuts and bolts here, epoxy there, etc. Substitutions of the wrong materials can result in extra work, extra weight or inadequate structural integrity. I feel that we have a responsibility to assure the complete success of the introduction of composites to the homebuilder by not only completely educating him on the methods of construction, but assuring him of being able to obtain the correct materials.

Further, we are a small organization, presently incapable of handling a large volume of materials and having no ambition to develop a large materials distribution organization. If we did, it would no doubt take years to reach the efficiency and productivity of the best companies now in this business. Therefore, we have contracted with present aircraft materials distributors and manufacturing firms to produce and distribute all the manufactured parts and all the raw materials in the VariEze bill of materials. The companies were selected based on their excellent record of delivery and customer satisfaction. They have all been in this business for a long time and will require very little time to begin volume delivery of kit materials. We are working directly with them, supplying engineering specifications of the materials and as-

sisting with quality control. We will continue to work directly with them to supply and support any changes required in the manufactured items and raw materials.

Thus, we will directly market plans and construction manuals only, and will assist the homebuilder in the use of all materials purchased from our authorized distributors. The homebuilder will then be able to receive materials directly, from the best source, very soon after the inception of the program.

COMPOSITE CONSTRUCTION IN DETAIL

Most readers of this book are not going right out to buy the "makings" of a composite airframe. What we show here is a brief overview of how Rutan's designs are fabricated. Hopefully, this will give potential builders an inkling of what's in store for them should they eventually build their own fiberglass and foam airframe.

Much of the instant popularity of the VariEze and Rutan's follow-on designs comes from a structure made of glass/foam without molds. Homebuilders using this relatively new type of structure are encouraged to do their homework with a primary book entitled *Moldless Composite Sandwich Homebuilt Aircraft Construction*.

Excerpts from this Rutan booklet give a basic concept of glass construction. Readers who like what they see and really want to get into a serious study of glass homebuilding should contact the Rutan Aircraft Factory for their copyrighted book-

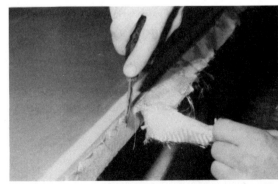

Fig. 5-8. Knife trimming the edges before full cure. (courtesy RAF)

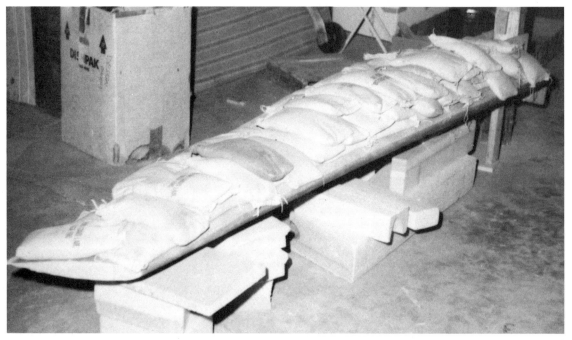

Fig. 5-9. A formal wing static test with lead bags to apply a 10G load.(courtesy RAF)

let. What follows is just a "tester" from the briefing manual and is reproduced with permission of the copyright owner. (Figures 5-7 through 5-13 show some of the steps of composite construction).

Glass

The most basic structural material in your VariEze is glass cloth. Glass cloth is available commercially in hundreds of different weights, weaves, strengths, and working properties. The use of glass in aircraft structures, particularly structural sandwich composites, is a recent development. Very few of the commercially available glass cloth types are compatible with aircraft requirements for high strength and light weight. Even fewer are suitable for the hand-layup techniques developed by RAF [Rutan Aircraft Factory] for the homebuilder. The glass cloth used in the VariEze has been specifically selected for the optimum combination of workability, strength, and weight.

The glass cloth in your VariEze carries primary loads, and its correct application is of vital importance. Even though doing your glass work

correctly is important, this doesn't mean that it is difficult; in fact, it's VariEze!

Two types of glass cloth are used, a bi-directional cloth (BID) and a unidirectional cloth (UND) (Fig. 5-14). BID cloth has half of the fibers woven parallel to the selvage edge of the cloth and the other half at right angles to the selvage, giving the cloth the same strength in both directions. The

Fig. 5-10. An informal test with eight people applying a 7G load. (courtesy RAF)

Fig. 5-11. The Long-EZ wing core in its jig. It is being checked for twist before skinning. (courtesy RAF)

selvage is the woven edge of a bolt of fabric. UND cloth has 95 percent of the glass volume woven parallel to the selvage, giving exceptional strength in that direction and very little at right angles to it (Fig. 5-15).

BID is generally used as pieces which are cut at 45-degree angle to the selvage and laid into contours with very little effort. BID is often applied at 45-degree orientation to obtain a desired torsional or shear stiffness. UND is used in areas where the primary loads are in one direction and maximum efficiency is required, such as the wing skins and spar caps.

Multiple layers of glass cloth are laminated together to form the aircraft structure. Each layer of cloth is called a ply and this term will be used throughout the plans.

Newcomers are urged to cut a square ply of BID and see how easy it is to change its shape by pulling and pushing on the edges. Cut a square with the fibers running at 45° and pull on the edges to shape the piece. It helps if you make fairly straight cuts, but don't worry if your cut is within 1/2 inch of your mark. As you cut BID it may change shape, just as the square ply that you are experimenting with does when you pull on one edge. Plies that distort

when cut are easily put back into shape by pulling on an edge.

The fiber orientation called for in each materials list is important and shouldn't be ignored. UND is characterized by the major fiber bundles running parallel to the selvage and being much larger than the small cross fibers which run at right angles to the selvage. In BID, the cross fibers are the same size as those running parallel to the selvage, giving BID an even "checkerboard" appearance. BID is commonly used for plies cut at 45° to the selvage. Your tailor would call this a "bias" cut.

Epoxy

In recent years, the term *epoxy* has become a

Fig. 5-12. Landing gear attachment layup custom fits landing gear strut to fuselage. (courtesy RAF)

Fig. 5-13. Basic Long-EZ fuselage after drying at Mojave. (courtesy RAF)

household word. Unfortunately, "epoxy" is a general term for a vast number of specialized resin/hardener systems, the same as "aluminum" is a general term for a whole family of specialized metal alloys. Just as the "aluminum" in the spar of a high-performance aircraft is vastly different from the "aluminum" pots and pans in your kitchen, the "epoxy" in your VariEze is vastly different from the hardware store variety.

Epoxy is the adhesive matrix that keeps the plies of load-carrying glass cloth together. Epoxy alone is weak and heavy. It is important to use it properly so that the full benefits of its adhesive capability are obtained without unnecessary weight.

An "epoxy system" is made up of a resin and a hardener tailored to produce a variety of physical and working properties. The mixing of resin with its hardener causes a chemical reaction called curing, which changes the two liquids into a solid. Different epoxy systems produce a wide variety of solids ranging from extremely hard to very flexible. Epoxy systems also vary greatly in their working properties; some are very thick, slow-pouring

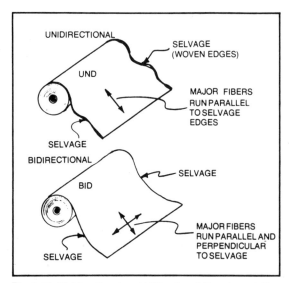

Fig. 5-14. Unidirectional and bidirectional fiberglass cloth.

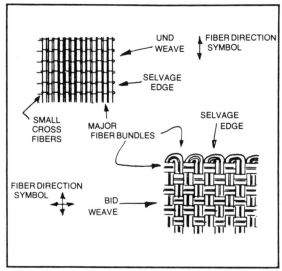

Fig. 5-15. Unidirectional and bidirectional figerglass cloth.

liquids, and others are like water. Some epoxy systems allow hours of working time and others harden almost as fast as they are mixed. A single type of resin is sometimes used with a variety of hardeners to obtain a number of different characteristics. In short, there is no universal epoxy system; each has its own specific purpose and while it may be the best for one application, it could be the worst possible in another use.

The RAF-type epoxy systems used in the construction of your VariEze (Fig. 5-26) are tailored for the best combination of workability and strength, as well as to protect the foam core from heat damage and solvent attack. These systems are also low in toxicity to minimize epoxy rash. These epoxies are not similar to the common types normally marketed for fiberglass laminating.

Three different systems are used in the Vari-Eze for three different types of work: a slow-curing system, a fast-curing system, and a five-minute system. The very fast curing (five-minute) system is used much like clecos are used in sheet metal construction (or clamps in woodwork) for temporary positioning. Five-minute is also used in some areas where high strength is not required, but where a fast cure will aid assembly.

As an epoxy system cures, it generates heat and in some areas the heat buildup of a medium or fast curing epoxy system is unacceptable. Where this is a potential problem, a slow curing system is used. Slow cure epoxy is always used with Styrofoam where heat can melt the foam away and ruin the joint. In other areas where heat buildup isn't a problem and a faster cure is desirable, a fast curing system is used. Both the fast and slow cure epoxies will cure to a firm structure at room temperature within one day. Complete cure takes 14 days.

Epoxy resin and hardener are mixed in small batches, usually six ounces or less, even in the larger layup. The reason for small batches is that, in large batches, as the hardening reaction progresses, heat is generated which speeds the reaction which causes even more heat, which ends up in a fast reaction called an exotherm. An exotherm will cause the cup of epoxy to get hot and begin to

thicken rapidly. If this occurs, throw it away and mix a new batch. The small volume batch avoids the exotherm. For a large layup, you will mix many small batches rather than a few large ones (Fig. 5-16). With this method you can spend many hours on a large layup using epoxy that has a working life of only a few minutes. If the epoxy is spread thin as in a layup its curing heat will quickly dissipate and it will remain only a few degrees above room temperature. However, in a thick buildup or cup, the low surface area to mass ratio will cause the epoxy to retain its heat, increasing its temperature. This results in a faster cure causing more heat. This unstable reaction is called an exotherm. Exotherm temperatures can easily exceed the maximum allowable for foam (200° F) and damage the foam-to-glass bond.

Microspheres

Microspheres are a very light filler or thick-

Fig. 5-16. Here's just about everything a builder needs to complete a composite airplane. Mike Melvill, left, and Dick Rutan used this workbench to prepare the materials for two Long-EZs at Mojave. Note that the epoxy is mixed in many small batches, rather than a few large ones.

ening material used in a mixture with epoxy. Micro, as the mixture is called, is used to fill voids and low areas, to glue foam blocks together, and as a bond between foams and glass skins. Several different types of microspheres and microballoons are available commercially. The quartz-type supplied by RAF distributors is lighter and cheaper than most common types. Microballoons must be kept dry. If moisture is present, it will make them lumpy. Bake them at 250° F, then sift with a flour sifter to remove lumps. Keep the microballoon container covered.

Micro is used in three consistencies: a *slurry* which is a one-to-one by volume mix of epoxy and microspheres, *wet micro* which is about two-to-four parts microspheres by volume to one part epoxy, and *dry micro* which is a mix of epoxy and enough microspheres to obtain a paste which will not sag or run (about five parts to one by volume). In all three, microspheres are added to completely mixed epoxy.

Flox

Flox is a mixture of cotton fiber (flocked cotton) and epoxy. The mixture is used in structural joints and in areas where a very hard durable build-up is required. Flox is mixed much the same as dry micro, but only about two parts flock to one part epoxy is required. Mix in just enough flock to make the mixture stand up. If "wet flox" is called out, mix it so it will sag or run.

When using flox to bond a metal part, be sure to sand the metal dull with 220-grit sandpaper and paint pure mixed epoxy (no flox) on the metal part.

Bondo

The term Bondo is used as a general term for automotive polyester body filler. Bondo is used for holding jig blocks in place and other temporary fastening jobs. We use it because it hardens in a very short time and can be chipped or sanded off without damaging the fiberglass. Bondo is usually a dull gray color until a colored hardener is mixed with it. The color of the mixture is used to judge how fast it will set. The more hardener you add, the brighter the color of the mixture gets and the faster it hardens. This simple guide works up to a point

where so much hardener is added that the mixture never hardens. Follow the general directions on the Bondo can for fast setting Bondo. Mixing is done on a scrap piece of cardboard or plywood (or almost anything) using a hard squeegee or putty knife. A blob of Bondo is scooped out of the can and dropped on the mixing board. A small amount of hardener is squeezed out onto the blob and then you mix to an even color. You will mix the blob for about one minute. You will then have two to three minutes to apply it before it hardens.

Foam

Three different types of rigid, closed-cell foam are used in your EZE (and several densities). A low density (2 lb./ft.^{3}), blue, large-cell Styrofoam is used as the foam core of the wings, winglets and canard. The blue foam is exceptional for smooth hot wire cutting of airfoil shapes. The large cell type used provides better protection from delamination than the more commonly used insulation-grade Styrofoams.

Low density (2 lb./ft.^{3} green or light tan) urethane foam is used extensively in the fuselage and fuel tanks. Urethane foam is fantastically easy to carve and contour and is completely fuel proof. The urethane used is U-Thane 210 or equivalent.

PVC foam in medium and high densities is used in fuselage bulkheads and other areas where higher compressive strength is required. The light red PVC is 6 lb./ft.^{3} and the dark red is 16 lb./ft.^{3}. We considered using the "fire resistant" brown urethane instead of the green 2-lb. urethane, but found its physical properties, fatigue life and fuel compatibility to be much lower than the urethane supplied to VariEze builders. Do not confuse Styrofoam with white expanded polystyrene. Expanded polystyrene is a molded, white, low density, soft foam which has the appearance of many spheres pressed together. This is the type used in the average picnic cooler. It disappears immediately in the presence of most solvents, including fuel, and its compression strength and modulus is too low.

All three types of foams, PVC, urethane and polystyrenes are manufactured in a wide variety of flexibilities, densities and cell sizes. Getting the wrong material for your airplane can result in more work and/or degraded structural integrity.

Sun damages foam. Keep covered.

Hot Wire Cutting

The airfoil-shaped surfaces of your VariEze are formed by hot wire cutting the blue Styrofoam of 1 lb. ft.^{3} density. The hot wire process gives airfoils that are true to contour, tapered, properly twisted, and swept with a minimum effort and the simplest of tools.

The hot wire saw is a piece of stainless steel safety wire, stretched tight between two pieces of tubing. The wire gets hot when an electrical current passes through it and this thin, hot wire burns through the foam. The blue foam used in your flying surfaces was selected for a combination of reasons and its hot wire cutting ability was one of them. Use only the recommended materials.

Urethane Foam Shaping

One of the real treats in the construction of your VariEze will be shaping and contouring urethane foam. Urethane is a delightful material that shapes with ease using only simple tools. A butcher knife, old wire brush, sandpaper, and scraps of the foam itself are the basic urethane working tools. A vacuum cleaner is convenient to have handy since working urethane produces a large quantity of foam dust. The knife is used to rough cut the foam to size. The knife needs to be kept reasonably sharp; a sander or file is an adequate knife sharpener since it's a frequent task and a razor edge isn't necessary. Coarse grit sandpaper (36 grit) glued to a board is used for rough shaping outside contours.

Keep your shop swept reasonably well. The foam dust can contaminate your glass cloth and your lungs. Use a dust respirator mask while carving urethane. Try not to aggravate the better half by leaving a green foam dust trail into the house.

Glass Layup

The glass layup techniques used in your Vari-Eze have been specifically developed to minimize the difficulty that glass workers have traditionally endured. Most of the layups that you will do will be on a flat horizontal surface without the molds, vacuum bags, and other special equipment that are common in glass work. The layups that you do will all cure at room temperature; no ovens or special heating is required. If you have suffered through a project that requires you to build more molds and tools than airplane components, then you are in for a real treat.

The techniques that you will use are VariEze, but they still need to be done correctly.

Before you get started with a layup, plan ahead. Some major layups take several hours and before getting your hands in the epoxy, it's a good idea to make a pit stop at the restroom. Do not start a large layup if you are tired. Get some rest and do it when fresh. It's best to have three people for any large layup—two laminators and one person to mix epoxy. Be sure the shop is clean before you start. Take the recommended health precautions using gloves or barrier skin cream. Get your grubby old clothes on or at least a shop apron.

If you use skin barrier cream, the epoxy and cream will wash off easily with soap and water. When you get epoxy on unprotected skin, Epo-cleanse is used to remove the epoxy. Both of these products are available through RAF distributors and are listed in the bill of materials. Once you are sure your skin is clean, wash again thoroughly with soap and water, even if your hands were protected with plastic gloves. If you get epoxy on tools or metal parts, clean them with acetone or MEK before the epoxy cures.

Quality Control Criteria

One of the unique features of the glass-foam-glass composite construction technique is your ability to visually inspect the structure from the outside. The transparency of the glass/epoxy material enables you to see all the way through the skins and even through the spar caps. Defects in the layup take four basic forms: resin lean areas, delaminations, wrinkles or bumps in the fibers, and damage due to sanding structure away in finishing. Resin lean areas are white in appearance due to incomplete wetting of the glass cloth with epoxy during the layup. Delaminations in a new layup may be due to small air bubbles trapped between plies during the layup. The areas look like air bubbles and are distinctly visible even deep in a cured layup.

The following is a listing of the "critical areas"—the portions of the VariEze that must meet all the inspection criteria:

☐ Center section spar—entire outside skin and spar caps.
☐ All portions of the fuselage within 10″ of the engine mounts and canard lift tab attachments.
☐ All control surfaces.

☐ All flying surfaces in the shaded areas shown plus all overlaps at L.E. and T. E.

Major wrinkles or bumps along more than 2″ of chord are cause for rejection in the wings, canard and winglets, particularly on the top (compression side). This does not mean you have to reject the whole wing—anything can be repaired by following the basic rule: remove the rejected or damaged area and fair back the area at a slope of 1″ per ply with a sanding block in all directions. By watching the grain you will be able to count the plies while sanding. Be sure the surface is completely dull and layup the same plies as you removed, plus one more ply of BID over the entire patch. This will restore full strength to the removed area. Use this method

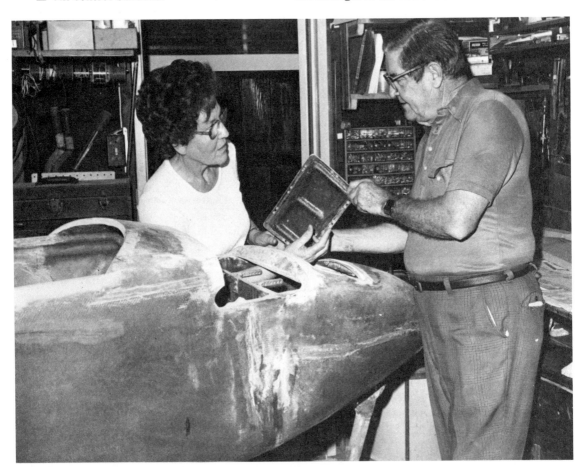

Fig. 5-17. Rutan's composite construction makes it relatively easy to patch areas with the resultant structure as strong as before the "patch." Note rework on the front of this VariEze fuselage as Marshall and Rachel Gage inspect a nose cover panel.

to repair any area damaged for any reason—inadvertent sanding through plies during finishing, taxiing a wing into a hangar, etc. (Fig. 5-17).

Health Precautions

If you work with epoxy on your bare skin, you can develop an allergy to it. This "sensitization" to epoxy is an unpleasant experience and is to be avoided. You generally have to get epoxy on your unprotected skin to become sensitized. If you use a protective barrier skin cream like Ply No. 9 (available from VariEze distributors) or disposable plastic medical examination gloves (also available from VariEze distributors) the allergy can be avoided. The barrier skin cream also allows you to clean up with soap and water after a layup.

The RAF epoxy systems are low toxicity (SPI=2). However, many people (about 5 to 7 percent) are sensitive to epoxy to a great extent and thus will find it impossible to build their airplane without extensive skin rash, facial swelling, etc. These people can get some help by using doctor-prescribed anti-allergy medicines and/or by using elaborate masks/multi-gloves, etc., to reduce exposure; however, in many cases the allergy is sufficiently strong to preclude their ability to make layups. Remember to *always* use skin protection; never let epoxy come in contact with bare skin, even if you have no reaction to it. Sensitivity is accumulative, such that you may later develop an allergy unless you protect your skin.

MURPHY'S LAW IN COMPOSITES

There have been unexpected glitches in composite construction, but it came as a complete surprise to Long-EZ builders when a pseudo-fiberglass cloth came on the market. The cloth, made by a different major weaver, was cheaper, looked virtually identical to the original UND 7715, and was tagged with the same number. Initial RAF testing showed comparable results until a flexure test was run. The results showed that the pseudo-cloth was 19 percent weaker at ultimate load and 31 percent weaker at initial failure.

Builders were cautioned immediately that if they had purchased UND glass from any source other than Wicks Aircraft or Aircraft Spruce, they almost certainly had the wrong glass. Due to proprietary rights, Spruce and Wicks have been the only source of the correct UND. Builders were advised to discard any major structural parts built with the copycat material.

AUTOMATION IN FABRIC WEAVING

In the fast-paced world of computers, it is now possible for machines to impregnate fibers with just the right amount of matrix material and put each fiber in the direction of the load. Rutan reported that the poltrusion process, invented by Dr. Galsworthy, is in production now and produces parts that go out the door at a cost only 30 to 40 percent more than the price of the raw material. "I was in a poltrusion plant recently that had three or four machines running, producing a continuous sample of oriented composite material—and there were only two people working the plant," said Rutan.

NEW MATERIALS JUST KEEP COMING

Since Rutan began his pioneering composites, there have been significant improvements both in materials and in procedures. Carbon fibers were used in the new Lear Fan where the entire fuselage went into an oven for curing. "Pre-preg," a pre-impregnated cloth, was developed to aid the builder.

Many high-technology, exotic fabrics of a few years ago have been replaced by graphite, Kevlar®, S glass, and ceramic heat-resistant fiber.

Graphite fibers are processed so that all the molecules change into long parallel chains of carbon atoms. The resulting cloth is lightweight, stiff, and strong. In 1983 dollars, the woven material runs from $25 to $70 per pound for super strength.

Kevlar® from DuPont is related chemically to Nomex and nylon. Yellow in color, it is super-strong, lightweight, and tough. Somewhat more difficult to work than graphite fibers, its cost is about $10 per pound.

S glass differs chemically from other fiberglass. It costs about $5 per pound and is easy to work with. The Long-EZ uses highly-directional E glass skins, S glass landing gear, and Kevlar® engine cowl.

Ceramic fibers woven into cloth have about the same properties as S glass, but can withstand temperatures to near 3,000° F. Cost is over $90 per pound.

Today's composite designer has the option to pick from a large variety of cloth to build specific portions of a new structure. Some designs call for a different glass on either side of a finished component.

It's a whole new ballgame!

Chapter 6

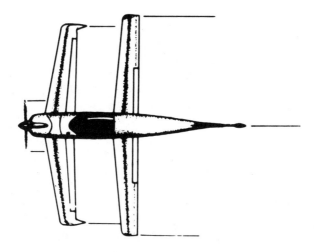

The Power to Go On

Reliable, affordable, efficient powerplants have been the goal of aircraft designers since day one. The history of aviation has many examples of fine, innovative designs that literally never got off the ground because a suitable powerplant was not available at the time the design was developed.

There was one notable exception where two designers searched first for a suitable engine and then had an airframe designed to fit it. And this is where Rutan entered the picture.

QUICKIE: THE ENGINE CAME FIRST

The amazing Quickie (Fig. 6-1) is the brainstorm of Gene Sheehan and Tom Jewett, two development engineers who searched nearly four years to find a reliable gasoline engine in the 12 to 25-hp range with sufficient power for an efficient, single-place sport plane.

Tom Jewett (Fig. 6-2) was a flight test engineer on the Rockwell B-1 bomber. He spent his entire career in flight testing new aircraft, ranging from homebuilts to jets. He was a graduate en-

gineer from Ohio State University. Subsequent to the Quickie project, Jewett was killed at Mojave in the crash of *Free Enterprise*, a design under development for an around-the-world flight attempt. (See Chapter 15.)

Gene Sheehan had worked in the aerospace industry since 1964 and with homebuilt aircraft since 1973. He was involved with several home-built projects, including the BD-4, a helicopter, a gyrocopter, and a BD-5. A former University of Texas student, he is also a private pilot. Sheehan has continued with the Quickie and the two-place Q2 project since Jewett's death.

Since engine development is critical to any new airframe, it came ahead of the Quickie's configuration. Gene and Tom were purposely secretive in their engine project, not wanting to follow the path of some other developers who put plans and kits on sale before the systems had ever flown or been proven.

"This is not the policy of our little skunk works at the Mojave Airport," explained the developers of

Fig. 6-1. Quickie in flight near Mojave. Gene Sheehan is at the controls. N77Q is the original prototype and is being used as a test bed for new improvements.

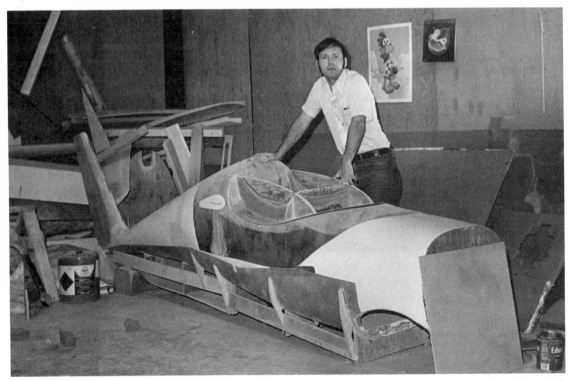

Fig. 6-2. Tom Jewett stands beside the original mold used to form the Quickie fuselage. The cabin is large enough for a 6'6", 220-lb. pilot.

the Quickie in their initial brochure. "The development of the Quickie was one of the best kept secrets in aviation. Until its first flight late in 1977, its existence was known only to a handful of people."

The "skunk works" refers back to famed Lockheed designer Kelly Johnson's super-secret skunk works that developed the P-80, the famed U-2, and the Mach 3 SR-71 Blackbird. Johnson was noted for a minimum of engineering drawing and a maximum of prototype building to cut time and cost in new aircraft development.

The Quickie story really goes back to early 1975 when Gene and Tom began looking for a small, efficient, reliable engine. The search included two-stroke and four-stroke engines used in chainsaws, garden tractors, motorcycles and automobiles. The search was frustrating because lightweight, powerful engines lacked reliability and the ones that had proven reliability were either too heavy or did not develop enough power.

SEARCH FOR AN ENGINE

The search for a suitable engine was outlined by the two engineers in their company brochure:

The origin of the Quickie began with the search for an engine that required over two years. Until it was completed, no serious thought was given as to what the aircraft should look like because the aircraft was to be designed around the engine.

The requirements for the engine were simple enough:

- ☐ 12 hp to 25 hp.
- ☐ Lightweight.
- ☐ Small size.
- ☐ Low fuel consumption.
- ☐ Reliable, reliable, reliable.

Many different types of engines were evaluated prior to making that selection.

Two Stroke: These engines have several desirable features including high power, light weight, and few moving parts. The disadvantages include poor fuel economy, high rpm, high vibration level,

poor mixture deviation tolerance, and questionable reliability for an aircraft application. Several small aircraft are using the McCulloch chain saw engine. It is interesting to note that all of these airplanes are either powered hang gliders or powered sailplanes, and not intended for cross-country use. Two-strokes are very mixture conscious; throttle back with the mixture leaned, descend and forget to richen the mixture, and as soon as power is added the engine is likely to seize. Failing to lean the mixture at altitude, however, may lead to plug fouling. Most dirt bikes powered by two-stroke engines have two spark plugs for each cylinder so that the rider can switch plug wires when the first one fouls.

Rotaries: The small Sach's wankel rotary engine has many of the desirable features of a two-stroke, and it is certainly smooth running. However, these engines have had seal problems when run for long periods at high power settings, and the fuel consumption characteristics are poor in the rpm range necessary for good propeller efficiency. Besides, the engine is no longer produced.

Four-Stroke: These engines are the best ones for aircraft use. They have a good fuel economy and tend to be very reliable. In the low horsepower examples, however, they tend to be heavy, or to require a high rpm, in order to produce sufficient power. One of the four-stroke engines that Quickie Enterprises tested was a Honda CB-175 motorcycle engine. Initially, it was too heavy, but after removing the transmission with a bandsaw and deleting all other non-essential parts, the weight was reduced to about 65 lbs. This engine produced about 18 hp at near 9,000 rpm. While Honda engines have a reputation for being very reliable, the drastic surgery required to reduce size and weight could very well have weakened the crankcase and, therefore, reduced the reliability.

One might ask at this point why not use a reduction drive system with a light weight, high rpm, four-stroke or two-stroke engine? There are several reasons not to do this, including complexity, cost, and torsional vibration. Given enough time, money, talent, and luck, these problems can be overcome. Often, however, the solutions only complicate the aircraft further. For example, a clutch is often used to solve the torsional resonance problem, but then the engine must use an electric starter, which adds about 25 lbs. of weight.

Volkswagen Engines: A number of home-built aircraft have flown using VW engines. However, a stock VW typically requires considerably more maintenance than a normal aircraft engine. This is probably because few automobile or motor-cycle engines are designed for the type of continuous, high speed operation necessary for an aircraft.

Industrial Engines: These engines tend to be very reliable, but also heavy. Most are designed to run near rated power for extended periods and usually are so dependable that oil temperature and oil pressure gauges are omitted. They have reasonable fuel consumption and frequently operate under extremely harsh conditions. Until recently, they were prohibitively heavy, and the single cylinder models have excessive vibration for an aircraft.

The engine selected is a four-stroke, horizontally opposed, two-cylinder, direct drive type used in various industrial applications at a continuous 3,600 rpm (Fig. 6-3).

The Onan Company has made over 1,000,000 two cylinder, horizontally-opposed, four-stroke direct drive engines in the last thirty years for applications from electric generator sets to snow plows. They recently introduced some aluminum versions of their cast iron series of engines. These aluminum engines weigh 98-106 lbs. in the stock configurations, some 50 lbs. lighter than their cast iron counterparts.

After careful examination, it was determined that we would reduce the weight to slightly more than 70 lbs. dry. While this may seem excessive for the produced 18 hp, they are very well built. Further, if the aircraft is carefully designed around the engine as was the Quickie, the results are most satisfying.

Some design features are as follows:

Horsepower	18 @ 3,600 rpm
Type	2-cylinder, horiz.-opposed, four-stroke

Fig. 6-3. Onan engine on a bench at the Quickie factory awaiting modifications.

Bore	3.250″
Stroke	2.875″
Displacement	47.7 in.^{3}
Compression	6.6:1

The manufacturer recommends up to 1,000 hours between major overhauls for a normal industrial application. At this time, there is not enough data to state what the TBO in an aircraft application for a Quickie engine will be. However, it should be noted that in comparison with most industrial applications, the aircraft environment is cleaner and owner maintenance more regular.

Much testing has been accomplished in the areas of induction, exhaust, cooling, mounting, ignition system, and the engine airframe compatibility. The result of all this testing is an engine specifically intended for installation in the Quickie. It is definitely not the same engine one can buy from the local Onan dealer (Fig. 6-4).

Only after the basic engine research and testing was well in hand did Gene Sheehan and Tom Jewett approach Burt Rutan, an old friend, to de-

Fig. 6-4. Onan engine with Quickie modifications ready for delivery to consumers.

velop an airframe tailored around the Onan engine. Rutan was impressed by the demonstrated reliability of the engine and began putting lines on drafting paper. Early attempts were unsatisfactory because a low enough drag in a conventional or VariEze configuration would require a retractable gear with its associated weight and complexity problems. Most pusher configurations had only a narrow range of pilot weights.

Rutan finally came up with a novel tractor canard tailless "biplane" configuration (Fig. 6-5). The pilot sits near the center of gravity (Fig. 6-6). The combined canard and landing gear has low drag and saves both weight and complexity. This compactness lends itself to a "glue together" airplane

that saves weight on wing attachments. Full-span elevator/flaps went on the canard with inboard ailerons on the rear wing. Originally the tailwheel fairing was the only rudder.

Once the concept was established, a detailed plane was agreed upon. Tom Jewett and Burt Rutan did the detailed design while Gene Sheehan continued engine development. Most of the actual construction was done by Gene who had no prior experience with composite construction. This was a simple way to prove out the concept that the Quickie could be put together successfully by a first-time builder.

The construction phase took just two months. All three developers, Burt, Tom and Gene, flew

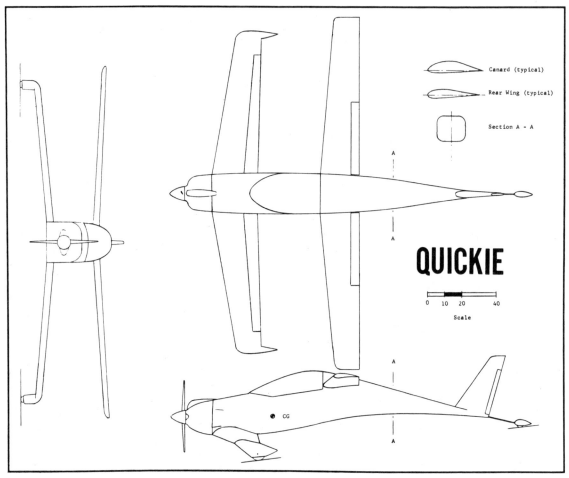

Fig. 6-5. Three-view drawing of final Quickie configuration. (courtesy Quickie Aircraft Corp.)

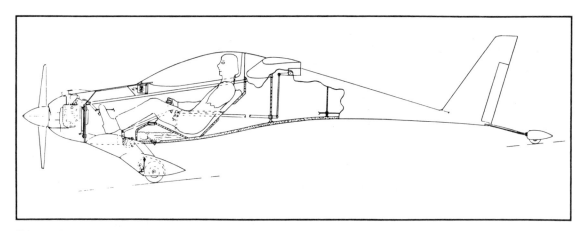

Fig. 6-6. Cutaway drawing of the Quickie sideview. (courtesy Quickie Aircraft Corp.)

N77Q on the first day after completion (Fig. 6-7). Then followed a five-month flight test program to assure that the unusual configuration, coupled with a new-to-aviation engine, would do the job.

Sales of the Quickie kit increased steadily. Shortly after the kit program began, the Quickie received the coveted Outstanding New Design award from the Experimental Aircraft Association (EAA) at the annual EAA Oshkosh, Wisconsin Fly-in. In presenting Quickie Aircraft Corporation with the award, EAA stated that the pioneering of the Onan engine together with an exceptionally efficient aircraft design in order to bring the cost of ownership and the cost of flying down to an affordable level represented a significant breakthrough. As this book went to press, Quickie Aircraft Corp. was no longer in business.

FLIGHT TO OSHKOSH

The trip to Oshkosh was described in the newsletter as follows:

The Quickie was the lightest and lowest horsepower aircraft to fly to Oshkosh in 1978. We (Sheehan and Jewett) firmly believe that any aircraft which is not flown cross country to Oshkosh should not be offered for sale to the general public as an aircraft.

Our trip was spread over 2½ days, with overnight stops in Albuquerque, New Mexico and Kansas City, Missouri. The 2,025 miles were covered in about 19 hours (against the proverbial headwinds!) while averaging 65.1 mpg, also a record. That means that the trip cost us about $30 in gas and one quart of oil! The takeoff from Albuquerque was made at a density altitude of 7,000'. The highest altitude reached was 13,500' west of Gallup, New Mexico. The normal cruise altitude was 7-8,000'.

The trip was both routine and uneventful. Our biggest problem was minimizing the time spent on the ground when we stopped for gas. Usually we had to spend at least 30 minutes talking to the crowd that invariably gathered. In Dalhart, Texas, we had to wait an additional 30 minutes so that the line girl could go home and get her camera.

For a companion aircraft, we took along a Grumman Trainer. We had originally intended to use a Cessna 150 for the flight, but found that it wouldn't keep up with the Quickie! The Grumman is about five knots faster than the Quickie and made a good companion aircraft.

We arrived at Oshkosh two days before the fly-in started so we could relax and take a short vacation. Wishful thinking! From the time we touched down until we left, we were surrounded by people wanting to see the aircraft and ask questions.

It was not unusual during the week at Oshkosh to find a crowd four people deep surrounding both the Quickie on the flight line and our booth in the

Fig. 6-7. Unusual configuration of the Quickie shows up in this formation photo taken near Mojave, California, with Gene Sheehan at the controls.

main exhibit building (in fact, some people complained that they couldn't find our booth).

Gene, Tom and Burt gave forums on the Quickie on both Monday and Friday. The crowd estimate on Monday was over 900 people. As a result, the forums ran long past the scheduled hour.

We were fortunate enough to acquire a flight demonstration slot immediately prior to the airshow on several days. Quickie flight demonstrations were flown by Tom and Burt. When traffic permitted, both flew the aircraft within a box about ¾ mile long by ¼ mile wide by 500 feet high to show off the extreme maneuverability of the Quickie.

Peter Lert (pilot report in June 1978 *Air Progress*) flew the Quickie for a photo session with *Popular Mechanics*. After returning, we asked him in front of a large crowd how he liked the aircraft. His reply was, "Flying a Quickie is the most fun a person can have in public during the daytime!"

The trip home from Oshkosh to Mojave, California, was as uneventful as the trip East. The most important news is that we stopped at Ames, Iowa, to test the Quickie off of a grass runway. We loaded the Quickie to 20 lbs. over gross weight and took off at a density altitude of about 2,000′, and a relative humidity of about 85 percent. The Quickie was off the ground within 100′ of what the Grumman Trainer required.

In explaining the role of the Quickie in aviation today, the developers put it this way:

The Quickie is not intended to be an aircraft for everyone. A Quickie will never win the World's Aerobatic Championship, and it should not be outfitted with wing deicer boots and complete avionics so that it can fly IFR; nor is it the perfect airplane for the pilot that weighs 270 pounds, unless he is willing to go on a strict diet while he is building one.

A Quickie is a fun aircraft; it is a reasonable aircraft for today; it is a creature that brings the exhilaration of flight to individuals unable to afford the machines turned out by Wichita; it is an airplane that a pilot can measure himself against—it does not fly so high that man needs help breathing; it does not require an A&P mechanic to keep it in

perfect order, and it does not require a 10,000-hour pilot to utilize its maximum capabilities.

If you can accept the Quickie in this spirit, you will never be disappointed, and you will be hard-pressed to find a sport that will give you more fun for less money.

ECONOMICS OF A QUICKIE

The developers explained the economics of owning a Quickie very explicitly:

Many pilots who may have been considering purchasing or building an aircraft look only at the initial purchase price when considering how much the aircraft will "cost" them. This is a fallacy since the owner will usually spend more on maintaining a typical aircraft than he spent to obtain it in the first place.

Most pilots will agree that it is difficult to find a production aircraft cheaper to fly than a Cessna 150. Let's compare the cost of fuel and oil for one year of a Cessna 150 and a Quickie. We will assume that each aircraft flies 200 hours a year. Since the Cessna burns 6.1 gallons per hour, as opposed to the Quickie which burns 1.5 gallons per hour, the Cessna uses $4.6 \times 200 = 920$ gallons of fuel more per year than the Quickie. At current prices, that is

Fig. 6-8. Cockpit installation of the Quickie. Round knob in the center is a temporary installation of a controllable pitch propeller drive. This control would be relocated in production planes since it would be a hazard in case of an off-field landing.

over $1,700 more per year to operate the Cessna. In addition, the Cessna uses a quart of oil every 10 hours, whereas the Quickie uses a quart every 50 hours.

To overhaul a Cessna 150 engine will cost about $3,000; to buy a *new* Quickie engine will cost less than $1,000.

Since the Quickie lacks complex systems (Fig. 6-8), and since the owner of a homebuilt can legally do all of his own maintenance, a large savings is realized in maintenance cost over the Cessna 150 owner who pays about $25.00 per hour shop rate, and maybe $200 to overhaul the carburetor. We all know about the inflated prices of components with "Aircraft" stamped on them. Remember, maintenance costs are proportional to the initial purchase price, not the market value.

ONE PILOT'S OPINION

Wayne Thoms reported on the Quickie in *Mechanix Illustrated* magazine, copyright 1979 by CBS Publications, used here with permission. In a report titled "A Plane for Under $4,000," Thoms said, in part, that the Quickie kit represents the easiest-to-build plane in this country, if not the world. "And it's complete even to the engine, requiring only paint and a motorcycle battery before you, too, can be up there winging with the birds."

Moreover, the Quickie is an efficient craft aloft, able to cruise at 121 mph; when you back off to an even 100 mph, she can go 85 miles on a gallon of fuel. Construction time is estimated at 400 hours.

"Flying the Quickie is the most fun you have in the daytime in public without getting arrested," begins the flight report. And the actual flight is described later in the article as follows:

Line up with the runway, push full throttle, hold slightly aft stick and the Quickie levitates at 53 mph, flying off more or less level and going up like a slow elevator. Acceleration feels similar to that of a small two-place trainer. Takeoff distance is 660 feet at sea level, about normal for small aircraft and slightly less than a 100-hp Cessna 150.

Instructed to climb at 70 mph, we lowered the nose shortly after takeoff to accelerate. The idea was correct, but the Quickie is so much more responsive than the craft we usually fly that we pushed too much forward stick, then too much aft. The effect was an interesting porpoise at about 30 feet—that's right, 30 feet!—until we worked out the technique of gentle control movements.

Rate of climb is 425 fpm, but there's no gauge to indicate this. The instruments built into the canopy panel are airspeed, altimeter, compass and voltmeter. Tachometer, cylinder-head temp and oil temp and pressure are on the left. Our test plane had a bell to indicate coordinated flight but it did not agree with the seat of our pants. After a while we ignored it and later on the ground we were advised that our pants were correct.

Once the Quickie levels off, the speed builds slowly behind 100 mph indicated. The advertised cruise of 121 mph true airspeed can be achieved, but we weren't off on a cross-country trip and didn't try.

The idea of being strapped into a powered flying machine that weighs little more than the pilot and has the ability to respond instantly to the pilot's wishes was mind-bending. Never has this pilot felt more in control of his destiny than with the Quickie.

Approach to landing is made between 70 and 75 mph, adjusting throttle as required to reduce speed and maintain glide angle. Contact is made at about 55, tailwheel first with stick full aft. In theory, at least, this is simple. After all, the main wheels are clearly in view on the wingtips, and with a long runway there is no reason to drop the airplane in. A kiss-soft landing should be within the grasp of even a novice pilot.

We goofed slightly, and we were glad that the main gear/canard wing is stressed to 12 Gs. Our drop was only a matter of inches but it felt like much more. The canard took up the shock, we steered carefully with rudder pedals and applied the brakes.

ENGINE, ENGINE, WHO'S GOT AN ENGINE?

Rutan's development of the VariEze faced the usual problem of engine availability. While there are many VariEzes flying with VW engines (Fig. 6-9), a motorcycle engine, and various cut-down automotive engines, Rutan had consistently urged

Fig. 6-9. VW installation in early VariEze.

his builders to stick with proven aircraft engines until a proven, dependable automotive or other design is available. Early in the program, Rutan singled out the popular 100-hp Continental 0-200 as being the best power package for his design (Fig. 6-10). This reliable, high-production engine has powered the Cessna 150 and several other trainers so that used and rebuilt engines are more-or-less readily available. Older Continental engines ranging from the A65/A75 through the C85/C90 have been used successfully.

Through newsletters, lectures, and flight demonstrations, Rutan has stressed engine reliability. The designer and his knowledgeable builders shared valuable engine experience, just as they did in the building and in the flying of these homebuilts.

Concerning the pusher engines, Rutan said, "As you engine experts know, the Continental 0-200 (100 hp), C85, and C90 engines have a special crankshaft for an FAA-approved pusher installation. These special cranks are rare and expensive. We don't believe that these special parts are necessary for the VariEze. The difference between the 'pusher' 0-200 B and the tractor 0-200 A is a reinforced flange to take the high static thrust loads that you find in amphibian type or the slow aircraft. The O-200, C85, C90, C75, A80, A75 and A65 crankshafts are almost identical (not interchangeable) and the A65 engine is approved as a pusher without modification. Because of the fixed-pitch prop, designed for 200-mph cruise, the thrust loads on the 100-hp 0-200 A are lower than they are on the 65-hp A65 in a 'normal' installation."

After 150 hours of flight testing in N4EZ, Rutan reported that there had been no measurable increase in crankshaft end play which would reflect thrust bearing wear. "Everything looks good for the 0-200 A on the VariEze aircraft. Do not conclude from this that the 'A' engine is suitable on other pusher aircraft."

As the VariEze project developed. Rutan developed a perspective that he passed along to his builders:

We are probably going to hear a lot of anguished cries from would-be engine developers,

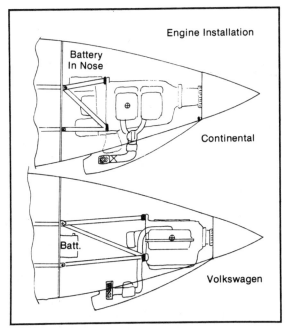

Fig. 6-10. Sketch of rear-mounted engine installation for both the Continental and VW powerplants. (courtesy Rutan Aircraft Factory)

but we are taking a hard line on 'other' engines in the VariEze. We have had many calls and letters from people wanting to install all kinds of converted boat, snowmobile, auto, turbocharged trash compactor, etc., engines in a VariEze. Also, there is an interest in all kinds of unproven modifications to the VW (fuel injection, turbocharged, electronic ignition, etc.).

Frankly, we're scared stiff by this. Aircraft engine development is a very risky, horribly frustrating and enormously expensive business. Please don't kid yourself and think your new engine conversion isn't going to fail a few times during initial flight testing. Even a professionally trained, educated, and experienced engineering organization with a barrel of money can't do these things, so don't try it in your garage. Moreover, don't believe anybody who says he can do it for you, unless he can show you excellent maintenance records taken during hundreds of hours of *flying* with the engine.

We are very much afraid that if a lot of homebuilders start trying to develop new engines on homebuilt airplanes, that EAA's accident record

will look horrible. Doing engine development on an amateur-built airplane hurts every one of us by further endangering the lenient rules that we now have. Please don't do it.

This isn't to say that some very good engines aren't hiding out there, waiting to be developed for aircraft use. We wish the best of luck to those who have the funding, ability and ambition to do the job well. Doing an engine development job well implies that you have the professional ethics not to endanger the hard-won privileges of others.

EXPERIMENT WITH A CUB—IF YOU MUST

Now, if you have an engine that looks good to you and you really want to prove it out for aircraft use, here's what you do: fly it! There is no substitute for flight experience. Not in a *homebuilt*, though! Get yourself a Cub or Champ that is a very forgiving airplane, easy to land safely in a pasture. You are going to make several emergency landings, so plan on it. If things really get bad and you have to plant your test vehicle in the trees, then for the FAA, it's just another Cub that crashes—not a *homebuilt*. Also, you can buy another Cub and get your test program rolling again, quickly. If you had used a homebuilt, you would have to build another airplane instead of getting on with your engine development work.

A comparison between the Continental 0-200 and the original VW in N7EZ (Fig. 6-11) was detailed. Rutan compared the cooling of the two engines as follows:

Fig. 6-11. VW hanging on half-finished VariEze prototype.

The 0-200 Continental engine (Fig. 6-12) has been trouble-free, requiring no modifications, adjustments or unusual maintenance. This has not been true of our VW installation on N7EZ. We have flown the VW VariEze a total of about 280 hours (two different engines), which is a lot of flying for one year for a VW homebuilt. We have had its cowling off an average of once per five flights, making minor carburetor adjustments, trying to find oil leaks, adjusting or repairing valves, cleaning plugs, checking the magneto coupling, tightening loose bolts, etc., etc. The VW-powered VariEze has never had an inflight power failure, but it has twice had to be landed within a few minutes or it would have had a failure. Once it was due to low oil pressure; another time it was due to an impending failure of the prop hub/extension. We have conducted an informal survey and found that our VW experience is quite similar to others who have high time on VW aircraft conversions.

SAVE MONEY ON YOUR PURCHASE

New engine cost is approaching the ridiculous.

Fig. 6-12. Ken Swain, Travis AFB, California, has a scimitar prop on his Continental-powered VariEze. He turns his combination at 2750 rpm and wants 3000 at sea level.

Cooling on the 0-200 has been excellent. Ground cooling is better than on most factory-builts. At a recent fly-in, we had to sit in a long line on a hot ramp awaiting takeoff for over 30 minutes. Many of the factory-builts had to shut down to avoid overheating, but N4EZs temperature stayed under the normal values for cruise.

Fig. 6-13. Two-cylinder, 60-hp Franklin engine, a 2A-120-C, was installed in the prototype VariEze. Here Dick Rutan cleans the cowling on the installation that did not work well. "This engine is not recommended for the VariEze," said Dick.

But, if you can find a partially run-out engine, it can be more of a bargain. The Long-EZ has a Lycoming 0-235 that had 1,400 hours, and it cost us $1,500. It was installed without modification or repair. The Lycoming has a 2,000 hour TBO, so we can expect 600 hours flying on this engine (3-4 years). When it is run-out—2,000 hours—it will still be worth what it cost us. Thus, it's truly a *low* operating cost engine (zero $)! This newsletter lists a 400 hour C90 at $2,800. If you run it out (1,200 hours left), then sell it for $1,500, you have spent $1.08 per hour for engine. If you buy a new or newly over-hauled engine at the high going cost and sell it for run-out costs, you will spend $2 to $3 per engine hour. Remember the majority of you will take years to put a few hundred hours on an engine. So consider a ½ or ¾ run-out as a bargain. Run an ad in *Trade-a-Plane*—it works!

Not all engine projects end in success. This cryptic note was included in the *Canard Pusher*:

Franklin engine 2A-120-C, 2 cylinder 60 hp, 30 hours SMOH. Rebuilt bendix mags and carb with pusher prop. $1,900 FOB Mojave. This is the engine out of N7EZ original prototype. The aircraft engine is EAA museum bound and engine is available. This engine is NOT recommended for a VariEze. Ask for Dick, (Fig. 6-13).

At least one VariEze was flown with a Chevrolet engine. This East Coast ship was later wrecked under icing conditions when the engine quit cold 40 minutes after takeoff. This was not due to engine failure, but rather to fuel starvation in the fuselage tank.

"We've received a lot of flak over our selection of the Continental engines (Fig. 6-14) for the VariEze, since most models have been out of production for years," said Burt in detailing his engine preference. "The most common question is 'How about the Lycoming engines?' And this is our answer: They are too heavy. The 0-290, 0-320 and

Fig. 6-14. Gary Hertzler of Tempe, Arizona, tops off his Continental-powered VariEze at Bullhead, Arizona. Note exhaust stacks mounted out the trailing edge of the wing. Reliability of the aircraft engine is far higher than automotive conversions.

0-360 engines are *totally out of the question.*"

The 0-235 models could be used only with some *strict* limitations. The normally equipped 0-235 is 242 pounds which is much too heavy both structurally and from C.G. considerations. If the 0-235 is *stripped* (mags and carburetor only remaining), its weight can be reduced to 211 pounds which is marginal but can be lived with (as is the Continental 0-200 with alternator but no starter); the 0-235 has some advantages in lower cost, and it is available in a 100 octane burning version.

Weight is critical in a small airplane like the VariEze. Rutan had some specific comments for builders who insist on installing an electric starter:

Look at what you're doing to your airplane. First, you add a 16-lb. starter to your engine; then you add a 25-lb. battery in the nose to balance and power it; then you add six pounds of cable to connect the two both ways. (You can't ground to glass and foam.) Presto, you've added 40 pounds of empty weight that does nothing except in the first five seconds of a flight. A small seven-pound battery gives you everything you need for avionics and lights. For the privilege of pushing a button once each flight, you have reduced your useful load-carrying ability 10%. Look at it this way: your starter-equipped airplane will go 330 miles *less* with the same takeoff weight as my hand-propped model.

When N4EZ had 300 flight hours, its 0-200A had 1,500 hours since major overhaul. It required no maintenance besides oil changes since it was installed in N4EZ two years ago. It rarely requires more than two flips to start. Oil temperature runs at 170° F. Cylinder heads run 420° in a long climb, 360° at cruise, and do not exceed 300° on a continuous hot-day ground run. It has never had a starter while on N4EZ and its alternator was removed a year ago. These two holes were covered with 3/16" aluminum plates. The logbook shows that the starter failed twice on the previous owner and the alternator once, costing him over $400! As you know, starters are not recommended on VariEzes. Only one has flown with a starter and that builder has since removed it. About ½ of the Ezes to ini-

tially fly with alternators have removed them also, to reduce weight. We strongly recommend that you first fly without starter and alternator. Add them later if you desire, but do initial flying as light as possible. Do use a carb accelerator pump or primer for easy starting.

The following is a quote from Warren Curd, Raytown, Missouri: "I originally had full electrical. The airplane flew well enough, but I had to carry weight in the nose; then when I started adding weight in the passenger seat I was less than satisfied. I finally took your advice and removed the starter, alternator, two solenoids, 22 feet of 1/0 cable, and heavy battery—weight reduction, 65 lbs.! The airplane now flies and handles so much better I hardly can believe it. Takeoff and landing speeds and distance are greatly reduced; climb improvement is amazing. Take it from me—save yourself a lot of work later. Don't install a starter or generator in your Eze. Starting is easy and the trickle charger keeps the small battery sufficiently charged for radio needs."

Caution: Do not ever hand prop a VariEze (or any airplane) that does not have at least one functioning impulse mag. An impulse mag allows the plugs to fire at or slightly after top dead center; without an impulse mag it will fire up to 25° before top dead center, which can lead to broken thumbs at the very least. If you only have one impulse mag, be sure you select only that one until the engine is running.

PROPELLERS TO MATCH

Since engines and propellers must work well together, Rutan also monitored this development carefully:

We have tested several propeller types and studied several others. Fortunately, the best prop has been the lightest and lowest cost—a fixed-pitch, all wood, two-blade with plastic leading edge for rain erosion protection. These are available through several vendors. The owner's manual will specify prop sizes, specifications and recommended vendors for all recommended engines (Fig. 6-15).

Fig. 6-15. Ken Swain, Nut Tree, California, hand props his Continental powered VariEze. Swain carved this scimitar prop himself. "If you can build the airplane, you can certainly build the prop," he commented. He is a USAF Captain flying C-141s from Travis AFB.

The three-bladed prop tested resulted in less takeoff, climb and cruise performance as compared to the two-bladed props.

We haven't gotten too many requests for variable pitch/constant speed/adjustable props from our builders which is a tribute to their good sense and intelligence. However, for those few who have asked about them, this is why we are down on them: safety, cost, weight and maintenance. First, it is a very definite risk to install a variable pitch prop on a pusher aircraft. The development of a variable pusher prop for the VariEze could easily run hundreds of thousands of dollars and still be a failure. The cost of a proven variable prop, even if one were available, would be over a thousand dollars each. The lightest controllable prop would weigh about 25 pounds which would create a CG problem requiring ballast, further increasing the weight growth. The maintenance and upkeep required on a variable prop is unbelievable.

In answer to a specific question about the use of constant or variable speed props on the EZs, Rutan replied: "We do not recommend the use of this type prop for several reasons: weight on the tail; complexity; and the prop on a pusher like and Eze gets a fore/aft bending load on each blade, twice per revolution, as the propeller passes through the wake of the wing/center section. This input can resonate and fail a metal prop or a metal hub assembly. Only the solid wood prop is known to have an adequate safety history for this application. An 'experimental' variable pitch prop destroyed the Q2 prototype."

From overseas we heard that Rudi Kurth of Busswil, Switzerland, who has a VariEze, has been working on an electrically-actuated variable propeller. When completed, he tried it in the Eze as a ground test stand. The propeller came apart within a few moments and ripped the engine out of the mounts, doing considerable damage to the aircraft. Whether this was due to poor design of the hub or the whirl mode is not known.

Because of the geometry of a pusher design, propellers are prone to damage or failure by anything that either falls off the aircraft or that is thrown up by the tires. A comment in a very recent Rutan newsletter cautioned:

"Remember, flying a pusher airplane, anything that comes off the airplane might possibly go through the prop. This includes cowling screws, loose pieces of safety wire, nuts and washers left loose in the cowling—even wrenches inadvertently left in the cowling! A cowling screw or a fuel cap going through the prop can cause sufficient damage to the wooden prop that you may have to land and wait for a replacement prop."

After completion of Solitaire and Starship I, we asked Burt if he saw any sort of a breakthrough in propeller material. He felt that there was some promise in using the newest composites but that anything useful would still take considerable development. In the meantime, he feels that wood is still the best material to use with some sort of erosion protection added along the leading edge for rain damage.

THE FLYING HONDA

One of the more memorable efforts to obtain reliable power from an existing engine was developed by Jim Cowley and a team of engine experts from Santa Paula, California. With a glib, tongue-in-cheek approach, Cowley details the development of this water-cooled engine and airplane combination. The project began in 1976 and continued on—and on, and on.

Cowley and his group followed Burt's advice and first put their Honda engine in a J-3 Cub that was flown to Oshkosh and back by Jim Kern, later to become President of TASK Research Incorporated (see Chapter 12). There were over 25 precautionary landings caused by overheating, but that's another story . . .

Eventually the Honda was installed in a VariEze that the group threw together in a record four months at Santa Paula, and Cowley reported on Burt's flight in it:

The FAA inspector was scheduled to meet us at Mojave at noon. Shortly after noon on January 14, 1977, we had one VariEze Honda-Powered Aircraft, N344SP, inspected and ready to fly. Whoopee!

It was mutually decided by everyone (except Burt) that Burt should have the honor of flying the first plans-built, Honda-powered VariEze. After chasing him down, we strapped him tightly in the cockpit, wound it up, and pointed him in the direction of the runway. We all stood back and with encouraging words and cameras pointed, watched this great flight. It actually took off, made turns at the proper times, flew several times around the airport, and came in and landed just like it was designed to do.

Amazing! When we let Burt out of the cockpit, he was mumbling something about it not being right for us to have a quieter and smoother-running engine than he had. Jim Kern had the honor of going around the patch with it next. We then decided it had been a long (January 19th) and a longer four months. We gave N344SP a friendly pat on the nose and put her to bed. Then we all went out to toast Burt, Hondas, VariEzes, Cowley, Inc., Kern, and anyone else we could think of.

How does the VariEze fly with a Honda Civic engine? We wish we knew. About all we can tell you is that it's very, very quiet and smooth. We have flown with an old T-Craft prop. It's in no way near the pitch and diameter we need for the best performance. This prop *was* 72 inches long, but on one of the trial runs the ship was over-rotated and the prop was trimmed about an inch—and the winglets about a half-inch.

Cooling problems plagued the combination during 250 hours on the test stand, in the Cub, and in the VariEze. Eventually it was replaced by a C90. Thus ended another noble but ill-starred effort.

LONG-EZs LOVE LYCOMINGS

As the larger Long-EZ evolved, the popular 100-hp Continental just wasn't powerful enough and Burt recommended the 115-hp Lycoming. With larger versions of the four-cylinder Lycoming in use on the VariViggen, Defiant, and Grizzly, the designer feels that the builders of the popular Long-EZ can do no better than the Lycoming 115-hp for which the airframe was designed: "I'd strongly recommend that builders don't do anything other than use this Lycoming. It has to be one of the best powerplants ever built!"

Fair enough.

Chapter 7

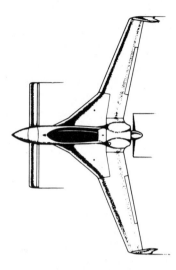

Long-EZ: A Best-Seller

The Long-EZ design is the most popular homebuilt airplane yet to be developed. Within the first two months that the plans were available, 500 sets were sold! Sales continue at a record-setting pace and Long-EZs are sprouting up all over the world to continue the success record of the VariEze.

Rutan's initial announcement of the Long-EZ explained:

We decided to design a new aircraft around the Lycoming 0-235 with starter and alternator. It would have unusually long range, thus the name "Long-Ez." It would have good forward visibility on landing and a lower approach and landing speed than the VariEze, making it more suitable for the low-proficiency pilot. The original configuration of the Long-EZ used VariEze wings placed on a center section spar that was four feet longer than a Vari-Eze. The wings were swept more than a VariEze to support the heavier engine. It had a "rhino" rudder on the nose and no control surfaces on the winglets. That aircraft, N79RA (Fig. 7-1), was built in four

months in the spring of 79 and made its first flight in June, 1979.

The Long-EZ really started out in life as a training project for Mike Melvill (by then working for Burt Rutan), who completed the first Vari-Viggen. As the project got underway, Burt decided to modify the VariEze design to accept the popular Lycoming 0-235 115-hp engine. Thus the fuselage was widened 2″ and beefed up to handle the extra weight; wingspan was upped to 26′ and the Long-EZ was soon in the air. Following first flights, extensive modifications were made in the design because it did not fly well. As Burt explained:

Directional stability was weak; dihedral effect was excessive; adverse yaw was high; roll rate was sluggish; early airflow separation on the wing caused pitch instability at low speeds, and the stall speed was too high.

During the next five weeks, N79RA made 51 flights, testing the effects of over 30 different modifications. Modifications included many configura-

Fig. 7-1. Dick Rutan with passenger Bob Weston in flight near Mojave. This represents the completed configuration of the Long-EZ with the new wing installed.

tions of wing leading-edge cuffs, wing fences and vortex generators. The winglet "cant" angle was changed. The ailerons were rigged to various neutral positions. Some of the changes resulted in improvements in pitch stability and lateral-directional flying qualities. However, we were unable to improve the stall speed, landing attitude and roll rate to a satisfactory level. By August, we were convinced that to get the Long-EZ we really wanted, we would have to build an entire new aft wing.

The new aft wing, first flown in October '79, had the following improvements:

☐ Less sweep.
☐ More area.
☐ A new Eppler airfoil similar to that on the Defiant.
☐ Longer ailerons.
☐ Improved winglet juncture to eliminate airflow separation at wingtip.
☐ Overlap-type wing attachment to center-section spar, allowing incidence adjustment.

The new wing performed excellently in test. Approach and stall speeds were lowered. The lower approach and landing attitudes allowed "full stall" landings with good runway visibility. Roll rate was superb. Directional stability was still weak and rudder power at the new lower landing speeds was inadequate. We then built new, larger winglets with rudders and removed the "rhino" rudder from the nose. That configuration completed flight tests in December '79 with very excellent results in every respect.

It has been shown to be resistant to departure during every conceivable stall entry, including tailslides. Its stability is firm even at maximum aft CG (obtained with a 120-pound pilot with starter, alternator and vacuum pump installed on the 0-235 Lycoming). Even though it has a wing area 41 percent greater than the VariEze and a 26 percent greater gross weight, it cruises at 183 mph at 75 percent—only 14 mph slower than the VariEze.

The Long-EZ is now the recommended airplane for the 0-200 Continental and 0-235 Lycoming engines. Complete electrical systems, including starter and night lighting are approved.

The first sets of completed plans were taken by Dick Rutan and Mike Melvill to build twin Long-EZs. They purchased the material package from Aircraft Spruce, rented a small section of a barracks building and spent every night for several weeks in the fabrication of two identical Long-EZs (Fig. 7-2).

"We're using this project to prove out the plans," explained Melvill. "By the time these two airplanes are complete, we should have every problem eliminated in our working plans. And besides that, we'll each have our very own aircraft."

In April, 1981, Dick Rutan published the following letter in *The Canard Pusher* about Long-EZs #3 and #4.

Last summer Mike Melvill and I decided to build ourselves one each Long-EZ. We agreed to work together on the basic structure, then split off and finish individually. On 15 June 1980, we started and with a lot of help from Sally and Jeana, both aircraft are now flying. Mike's (N26MS) was finished in late December 1980, and mine (N169SH) in early April 1981.

Mine took longer to build for two reasons. First, Mike worked harder, but the biggest reason is all the changes I made to mine. I thought I wanted more power, more roll rate, more negative Gs, and IFR equipment. I installed a bigger engine, longer ailerons, different canard airfoil, and several other changes. All these mods took more time to build, cost more, and after first flight, I found they didn't work. While I should have been very happy after it flew, I was not. Instead of having an aircraft I could

Fig. 7-2. Dick Rutan and Mike Melvill used the first set of plans to begin construction of two personal Long-EZ aircraft for their own use. The fuselages, shown here, took two weeks of after-hour and weekend work. Note rolled glass in the background that was used for construction.

use, I found I had a prototype that needed work. The big engine overheated, the revised canard airfoil resulted in loss of speed stability at high speed, and very poor stall characteristics (a nose drop). The standard Long-EZ rolls about as fast as mine and because of a poor prop match, Burt's Long even outran me on the first flight! I was then faced with finding fixes for all the problems.

I'll fix the problems, but it will take some time and effort. But in retrospect, I wish I had stayed more standard. My airplane now is a compromise, a whole bunch more effort that I feel is not worth it.

If you see my light-blue modified Long-EZ at fly-ins and airshows, remember the mods were not approved by Burt or RAF. In fact, Burt was not aware of most of them. Please don't bother RAF about my mods. They have enough to do just to support those building from the basic plans. I do not intend to do as complete a test program on my airplane as RAF did on N79RA. Thus, they are in no position to verify or recommend my modifications.

I am now deeply involved in the Voyager round-the-world program and will not be able to get involved in any way assisting builders.

I don't recommend any of the changes I've made and wish I had not. The best advice I can give is to keep it stock, build it light, and resist the temptation to change, especially anything structurally.

Dick eventually did fix the problems, and his light-blue modified Long-EZ is quite well-known for its record-breaking speed flights in the CAFE 400 as well as the Anchorage-Grand Turk distance flight, as detailed in Chapter 1.

Fortunately, Dick had all the facilities at Mojave available to rectify his problems. Other builders do not and his advice in the letter is still valid: *Don't change the plans!*

LET'S BREAK A RECORD!

At 7:27 on the morning of December 15, 1979, Dick Rutan lifted the Long-EZ prototype off Mojave, California's Runway 12 . . . and 33 hours, 33 minutes and 41 seconds later landed on 24 after covering an incredible 4800.28 statute miles, a new

world's closed-course distance record for aircraft weighing between 1,102 and 2,204 pounds (Class C-lb.).

This narrative of the Long-EZ's record flight was prepared by Jack Cox with background information from the Rutan family, Burt, Dick, George and Irene. Excerpts are from Cox's article carried in the February 1980 *Sport Aviation*, from which we continue to quote with thanks:

The flight eclipsed the old record of 2955.39 miles held for the past 20 years by Jiri Kunc of Czechoslovakia. Rarely is a world's record exceeded by such a wide margin as Dick's 1844.89 statute miles.

The facts and figures of the flight are as follows:

- ☐ The aircraft—Rutan Long-EZ, N79RA, powered by a 108-hp Lycoming 0.235.
- ☐ Fuel on board at takeoff—143.6 gallons.
- ☐ Weight at takeoff—1,904 pounds, 604 pounds over the normal gross of 1,300 pounds. The take-off weight, however, was 300 pounds under the weight limit of the F.A.I. class—which means an additional 50 gallons of fuel could have been carried.
- ☐ The course—Mojave to Bishop, California and return equalled one lap. Fifteen laps were flown.
- ☐ The average speed for the flight was 145.7 mph.
- ☐ Average fuel flow was 4.17 gallons per hour, or about 35 miles per gallon.
- ☐ 3.75 gallons of fuel remained in the aircraft's tanks at the conclusion of the flight; 2.3 quarts of oil were consumed.

On December 7, Dick flew the dive/flutter tests and investigated the aft CG limits. Finding everything to agree with the computer, the design was frozen that day and, at last, preparations for the record attempt could begin.

Dick had already been working on an auxiliary fuel tank—one that would fit the rear seat area like a hand in a glove (Fig. 7-3). This was finished—in foam and glass, of course—and installed in the airplane. In short order other mods followed.

Fig. 7-3. Roger Houghton of the RAF holds the 74-gallon fiberglass back-seat fuel tank used on the record flight. Total fuel aboard at takeoff was 143.6 gallons.

The fuel system was altered to route the flow from the tanks to the front cockpit and back to the engine. This was done because a Sears fuel flow meter was installed in the instrument panel to keep the extremely accurate tabs on gasoline consumption that would be absolutely essential for the successful completion of the flight.

Since about 14 hours of the projected flight would be in darkness, a lighting system had to be installed. Jack Gretta of Whelan made up a custom rig that could operate on just 6 amps. Included was a retractable landing light in the belly of the fuselage that would serve double duty, as you will soon learn.

An ac dyno from a Kubota tractor was installed. Including a small belt to the engine and the regulator, it only weighs about five pounds and produces 6 amps. (It has worked so well that RAF may offer installation drawings for homebuilders.)

The 604 pound over normal gross take-off con-figuration was too much for the fiberglass landing gear legs—they could handle the weight, but would spread out too much. Burt's fix was to install a sturdy cable bridle between the main gear axles to restrict their tendency to spread apart. There was no living with the drag this would produce, so a 1/16 inch cable was rigged up so it ran from a T-handle inside the cockpit, down through the open landing light hole and back to the gear legs. After takeoff, the 1/16 inch cable would be given a yank, which would pull pins to release the cable bridle between the mains. Then all of it would be reeled into the cockpit for stowage for the duration of the flight. It sounds like a page from Rube Goldberg—but it worked like a charm and added negligible weight.

Very heavy duty industrial rib 6-ply Goodyear tires were installed on the mains, inflated to nearly 100 pounds each!

The same auxiliary oil supply system that had been used on N7EZ in 1975 was installed on 79RA. It contained .8 qt. of oil and could be pumped via a hose into the crankcase in flight.

A heat muff was fitted around an exhaust stack with a hose extending up to the front cockpit. This was intended only as a backup source of cabin heat at the project cruising altitude of 11,500 feet where a nearly constant 0°C temperature was expected. Heavy clothing was intended as the primary means by which Dick would keep warm. The heater on/off "valve" was a rag stuffed in the end of the hose.

A glare shield was installed to prevent a fishbowl effect from the instrument lights on the canopy at night.

And at the 11th hour, a compression check on the 1500+ hour Lycoming brought the heartbreaking news that two cylinders were below acceptable standards. This resulted in one of the world's fastest top overhauls. Two new Slick mags were also purchased, however, one was found to be defective. Out of desperation as much as anything else, a replacement was dug out of RAF's junk pile, checked out and found to be in working order, installed and has been working to perfection ever since.

Two test flights were made, one during the day and the other at night, to check all the new systems—including the landing gear bridle release. Everything worked, so the aircraft was pushed in the hangar for one last exhaustive stem to stern inspection. The day before the flight, Friday the 14th, was spent attending to all the last minute details: getting the NAA observers briefed and sent to their stations, assembling the required clothing, food, extra batteries, and so forth, that would be needed.

The Long-EZ was impounded about 7:00 P.M. on Friday evening, and Dick hit the sack at 9:30. He left a wake-up call for 4:30 A.M..

Before dawn the crew, led by Burt Rutan, of course, converged on the RAF hangar and began setting the next two days' events in motion. N79RA was rolled out, started and warmed up, then taxied to the end of Runway 12. There, the tanks were carefully topped with STP treated gasoline and sealed.

As planned, Dick showed up at the last minute—ostensibly having had the chance to sleep right up to strap-in time. As the crew would later learn, however, he had been up for some time and had done his usual jogging before heading for the airport.

Donning gloves and an Arctic coat over his other clothing, which included thermal underwear, Dick had himself literally stuffed into the cockpit. The airplane was gingerly pushed up ramps to the scales and was given its official weigh in . . . 1,904 pounds for everything down to the GatorAde chewing gum. Well within the 2,204 pound FAI Class C-lb. limit.

The all-important barograph had been smoked and sealed, wound and set ticking. The Lycoming was started at 7:15 and the lift-off was marked by the NAA observer at precisely 7:27 A.M. A lot of breaths were being held as the Long-EZ hammered down the runway. Everyone who knows anything about flying realizes what an ultra-dangerous calculated risk a pilot is taking in an overgross takeoff such as this.

Dick was amazed at the Long-EZ's willingness to fly. Without hesitation the little beast settled into a 600 to 700-fpm climb and held it as Dick arced around to the right to pass the start/finish pylon to officially begin the record run. This done, he assumed his heading toward Bishop—and began reeling in the gear leg bridle. The retrieval was accomplished on what was a climbing downwind, just in case it somehow got back into the propeller.

Burt was pacing Dick in a Grumman Tiger and came in tight to watch and videotape the bridle retrieval. He accompanied Dick, in fact, for the entire first lap to insure everything was proceeding according to plan. Frequently Burt would slide under Dick to examine the belly of the Long-EZ to look for tell-tale streaks of oil or venting of fuel.

Depending on what sort of rate of climb the airplane had left after lugging its fuel load off the runway, Dick had had the option of flying up and down the Owens Valley at low altitude until enough gasoline was burned off to permit his climbing to a more efficient cruise level. However, with the EZ climbing so well, he chose to streak right on up to 11,500′ where he planned to spend the next day and a half. The Owens Valley is a very narrow and very deep fold in the tallest and most rugged mountains in the "lower 48." To the east rise peaks of over 11,000 feet and to the west is the very backbone of the Sierra Nevada. On each leg of every lap Dick would cruise past...and below...the 14,494-foot crest of Mt. Whitney. This is the valley that attracts sailplane pilots from the world over to test their skill and daring against what are believed to be some of the most powerful mountain wave conditions on earth, but the air was calm.

After the chase plane departed at the end of the first lap, Dick settled into a routine that consisted of a lot of chatter with the ground observers at each end of the course and a lot of fuel flow/leaning experimentation at mid course where he was out of radio contact. He soon found the particular EGT system installed in the Long-EZ was virtually useless as an aid in leaning. What worked was a little routine in which he established the fuel flow using a stopwatch and the Sears fuel counter, then matched this against various combinations of throttle and mixture settings. He found he used the least amount of fuel when he set up a constant rpm and then leaned until he got a 25 rpm drop. Any more or less used more fuel. Relaying the numbers back to

Burt who ran them through his computer, it was soon evident that a very long flight was in reach. It would take 10 laps to break the record and they were shooting for at least 13—14 if things were going really well. Now, however, came the exciting news that if he could maintain the present fuel consumption, a full 15 laps might be possible.

Generally, the first day went well. The form-fitting, semi-supine seat of the Long-EZ was extremely comfortable with no pressure points developing. The engine continued to run smoothly and Dick was able to pass the hours with his fuel computations, log entries, checkpoint chatter and admiring the scenery.

"I swore up and down during the night that the stars were stuck in the sky," he recalls.

On one occasion while fishing down in a leg well for something he could keep on his stomach, Dick inadvertently bumped the mixture control and shut down the engine. The sudden silence instantly jerked him into a state of alertness.

"I looked and saw I had fuel and oil pressure, and for the life of me I couldn't figure what was wrong. The ol' adrenalin was flowing again, though, and after scrounging around the cockpit for a few seconds I discovered I had kicked off the mixture. Actually, it was a godsend because I was really fighting fatigue at the time. It gave me about an hour and a half of fatigue-free flight, which really helped.

"Having the moon come up about an hour before sunrise was a big event. I was very happy I got myself up for it and I was okay for a while. Then the sun came up and that was a big event—that lasted two or three hours. I felt good again, I felt normal."

Fig. 7-4. Certification by the Federation Aeronautical International (FAI) of the Long-EZ distance record. This plaque is on the wall of Rutan's front office at Mojave.

About midnight, Dick had pressed on the left toe brake and had it drop to the floor. The next time he overflew Mojave, he advised Burt that he should be devising some way to retrieve a Long-EZ without a left brake. (The aircraft is steered on the ground with the brakes.) Burt said he would work something out.

In the early afternoon the decision was made —go for Lap 15. It would be tight, but more of a race with the sun than with dwindling fuel. Dick did not want to land without brakes after dark. If he could keep his speed up, however, he should touch down just after sunset but with adequate twilight remaining.

On the next to last lap, the Defiant joined up and escorted Dick the rest of the way. At long last he made his final turn at Bishop and headed down the home stretch.

"About halfway on the last leg, I climbed up to 13,500' and when we determined we had plenty of fuel, I pushed the throttle wide open and set up a 200 feet per minute rate of descent. The airspeed pushed up to 180 or so, coming down hill all the way. After the last ridgeline, I got it right down on the deck. Everyone was waiting down there and I wanted to end it with something special—it was a little treat I had been saving for myself. I was really feeling good as I came across the field at about Warp 3, and once past the pylon I did a steep pull-up and roll-off and came around to set up for a landing."

The landing, of course, was with an emergency. Dick slowed the aircraft as much as possible on approach and after touchdown held the nose high to get maximum aerodynamic braking. As the Long-EZ decelerated to the minimum speed that rudder control was still available, he came in with just enough power to maintain that speed. At that point, a motorcycle ridden by Burt and with Mike Melvill seated behind him came roaring up on the left wing. After neatly synchronizing their speed with the Long-EZ, Mike reached over and took a firm grip on the left winglet. Seeing this, Dick cut the power and allowed Burt and Mike to quickly guide him to a stop—right in the middle of the runway.

Dick sat there for a second listening for the

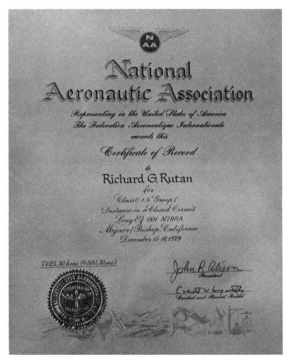

Fig. 7-5. Official recognition of the Long-EZ record was also made by the National Aeronautic Association. The plaque is also on display in Mojave.

barograph, then gave a yell when he could hear it still tick-ticking away.

"I knew then we had all the squares filled, that we had a record that could be certified!" (Figs. 7-4 and 7-5)

FROM THE OWNER'S MANUAL

A complete 66-page Owner's Manual was prepared for the Long-EZ, which contains several comments unique to this design. The following are some examples:

Engine Start: Engine starting may be accomplished by hand-propping. While you have undoubtlessly been horrified by the accident statistics on hand-starting antique aircraft, remember that the Long-EZ is a totally different story. Antiques are generally tractor aircraft, which means that they tend to chase you, once started. Long-EZs, on the other hand, try to run away from you. The traditional hand-start airplane has to be chained down and main wheels blocked for marginal safety (the tractor prop still tries to suck you in). The Long-EZ with nose-down parking chocks itself, and the pusher prop blows you away from danger. With modern, impulse-coupled magnetos, it is not necessary (or desirable) to make a Herculean pull of the propeller for starting; just pull the engine up on compression and give it an EZ flip through. In the unlikely event that your Long-EZ does run away from you after starting (if you leave the throttle open), it won't carve the first thing it comes to into hamburger, but will give it a bump with the nose instead.

Rough Field Caution: Although the Long-EZ may use the larger 500 × 5 tires, this does not make the aircraft totally suitable for rough, gravel or unprepared fields (Fig. 7-6). Since the Long-EZ is a pusher, the aircraft cannot be rotated as easily as a conventional tractor aircraft. You still must accelerate to normal rotation speed, 50-60 knots, depending on CG, before the nose wheel comes off, and during this time the nose wheel can kick debris into the prop. The small nose wheel tire, high rotation speed and prop damage possibility make the Long-EZ less suitable for unprepared field operation than a conventional aircraft.

A standard non-turbocharged Long-EZ (N79RA) attained an altitude of 26,900 feet in December '79. Caution: The altitude capability of this aircraft far exceeds the physiological capability of the pilot. Use oxygen above 12,500 feet.

Caution-In the Rain: When entering visible moisture (rain) the Long-EZ may experience a pitch trim change. The Long-EZ prototype (N79RA) has a significant nose-down pitch trim change in rain. The VariEze prototype has a mild nose-up trim change. Some VariEze owners report nose up and some nose down. This phenomenon is not fully understood and your aircraft may react differently. Our flight tests on the prototype Long-EZ have found a slight performance loss and the pitch trim change forces could be trimmed hands off with the cockpit trim handle at airspeeds above 90 knots when entering rain. Once the aircraft is in visible moisture conditions, it can be retrimmed and flown normally. There may be a disorientation factor during the transition from visual to instrument

Fig. 7-6. Large 500 × 5 tires are tested on the Long-EZ as Burt Rutan takes documentary footage with a videotape camera. The 2 × 4 plank under the aircraft was used to simulate a rough field before the aircraft was actually taken into a small nearby airport.

125

flight that the pilot must be ready for, especially if your trim change is significant. If your rain trim change is found to be significant, install a placard to notify pilots of this characteristic.

Landing: Make your approach and traffic pattern very cautiously. Most pilots and controllers are accustomed to looking for more conventional aircraft of gargantuan proportions (like Cessna 150's) and may ignore you completely. Best pattern speed is 70-75 knots (80-85 mph), slowing to 65 knots (75 mph) on final approach (70-75 knots in turbulence or gusty winds). The Long-EZ is a very clean airplane and you can double the runway length required if you are 10 to 15 knots fast on your approach.

Caution—Parking: With the nose gear extended and without the pilot in the front cockpit, the Long-EZ may fall on its tail. The aircraft may initially sit on the nose wheel, but may tip backwards when the fuel bleeds through the baffles towards the aft of the tank. Be sure to brief all ground handlers that the aircraft can fall on its tail unless parked nose down and could also get away from them while moving the aircraft. If your aircraft is subject to being moved by unknowledgeable people, ballast the nose or attach a sign to caution them about the possibility of tipping over.

Pilot Experience Requirements—Pilot Checkout: There is no such thing as a minimum number of total hours a pilot should have to be qualified for checkout solo in a new aircraft. The best pilot qualification is variety. He should be current in more than one type of airplane. The Long-EZ is not difficult to fly, but it is different; like a Yankee is different from a Cessna, or a Cub is different from a Cherokee. A pilot who is used to the differences between a Cessna and a Cub is ready to adapt to the differences in a Long-EZ. The Long-EZ has entirely conventional flying qualities. However, its responsiveness is quicker and its landing speed is faster than most light training aircraft. It should not be considered as a training airplane to develop basic flight proficiency.

ANOTHER HEADLINE

While a two-airplane flight, nonstop—one

starting from Cape Canaveral and the other from San Francisco—to the mecca of homebuilders, Oshkosh, isn't too challenging, it probably hasn't been done before. Thus, Johnny Murphy, Mayor of Cape Canaveral and the sixth VariEze builder to fly, teamed up with Dick Rutan just as soon as his second-to-fly Long-EZ was completed to plan the details of the above flight. Johnny took off with his son for the nonstop flight to Oshkosh; Dick took off from San Francisco to meet up with them. Both Long-EZs arrived at Oshkosh at about the same time in what was even then beginning to be an almost-routine performance for the Long-EZ.

LADIES' FIRSTS

The first woman to solo the Long-EZ was Sally Melvill (Fig. 7-7). She was also the first lady to solo the VariViggen. Between answering the phone at the RAF and opening the day's mail, Sally expressed her feelings with the Long-EZ checkout this way:

Fig. 7-7. Sally Melvill was the first women to solo the Long-EZ. She had 150 hours at the time.

"It was all so easy! I had approximately 150 hours when I soloed the Long-EZ. Dick Rutan gave me two check rides and turned me loose. The first impression I had was a feeling of being a part of the airplane, and of wanting to dance in the sky. The Long-EZ needs very little hands-on flying—it seems that you think of what you want and where you want to go, and it does it. I had had the feeling that it would be a sensitive airplane to fly, but I found that if you did over-control, just let it go! The airplane seemed to know how to fly better than I. It is not a difficult plane to fly—just different. Sweet is a word that fits for me. A great feeling of being a part of the airplane. I enjoyed the Long-EZ so much that Michael and I are busy building one for ourselves. It is going to be hard to keep me on the ground. Long-EZ—WOW!!"

The lowest time pilot to solo the Long-EZ to date has been Patricia (Pat) Storch (Fig. 7-8). Not counting passenger time in other Ezes, she had 24 1/2 hours of dual and solo before Dick Rutan gave her an hour and a half of dual instruction. Thus, she had logged just 26 hours flying time when she soloed the Long-EZ at Mojave. Here's what Pat had to say:

"Incredulous—that was my feeling when they told me they wanted me to solo the Long-EZ. Tiny insecurities worked their way out in the form of protests: 'But I'm only a student! I've only soloed one other airplane! I have less than 30 hours!' It seemed that I was the only one lacking in confidence, because they would not be dissuaded.

The day came when it was time to give it a try from the front seat. The cockpit looked foreign, almost hostile. Instruments were not where my eyes wanted them to be. Throttle and stick were in the wrong hands. With my heart in my mouth, we started the pattern work. Soon I was thankfully too busy to be nervous, but I still felt I was reaching for an unattainable goal. Control of the Long-EZ felt so different, and the full stall landings I had practiced so diligently in the Tiger were to be forgotten.

Then, amazingly, little pieces started falling together. Each landing felt better; the cockpit looked familiar, and a tiny seed of confidence started to bloom. Could it be? Would it really happen? Down to refuel and then came the words I wanted to hear: 'You're ready to go!'

I was full of anticipation and busting with excitement. The takeoff was smooth and felt good; the plane felt fantastic. Then I wanted to play in the sky—up, down, turns and steep turns.

I never expected an experience to equal my first solo, but this surely surpassed it. Flying never felt so good. Then came the final test—the landing. A little long, but a good one.

A Long-EZ pilot! I may have landed, but I was still in the air. In fact, I haven't come down yet. It was the most satisfying exhilarating experience I've ever had.

What better way to prove the docile flying characteristics of the Long-EZ than to kick a chick out of the nest, and do it safely, with just 26 hours of flying time?

WE FLY THE LONG-EZ

You can do all the research on a project, study its history, talk with builders and share their experiences; however, there's nothing like flying the product to make all this information fall into place. That's what we did on a crystal clear day at Mojave with Instructor Dick Rutan sitting lightly in the back seat of the No. 1 Long-EZ, N79RA.

Fig. 7-8. Pat Storch has only 26 hours flying time when Dick Rutan checked her out in the Long-EZ. However, she had logged many hours of passenger time in the canard aircraft.

None of the VariEze series has been designed for training purposes and the "stretched" version is no exception. In the bare back seat, Dick had a side control stick and that was all. There were no rudder pedals and brakes, no throttle, no mixture control, no radio and no intercom. Dick Rutan checked his log book on 79RA and noted that he had "checked out" 24 other pilots since original flight testing and the 33-hour, 34-minute record flight.

"Everyone we put in the front seat has to be a well-qualified pilot first. Most of our pilots are Eze builders who have flown their own ships extensively and really have nothing new to learn," explained Dick. "I've given many of these Eze pilots just a systems check and sent them out in the Long-EZ. Nobody has had any trouble. Some pilots who have never been in a canard before will tend to level off too high, but we have plenty of runway here at Mojave."

Yes, there was plenty of runway, and I used most of it! We'll explain why later on.

The Long-EZ cockpit is quite comfortable once you begin to get accustomed to the supine position. The cockpit, two inches wider than the VariEze, is wide enough and adjustable rudder pedals will give sufficient leg room. I'm a long-legged 6'2" and we should have taken the time to extend the rudders for my long legs. Instead, we removed some seat cushions and went on from there. My shin bones and the bottom of the instrument panel had a

Fig. 7-9. Instrument panel on the Long-EZ. Essential blind flight instruments are installed, along with a single nav/com radio.

speaking relationship by the time we had landed.

Dick Rutan has been a flight instructor for nearly 20 years, and he does an excellent job—both in pre-flight briefing and later in the air. He helped me unfold inside the cockpit and get the seat belt and shoulder harness adjusted. Then came a systems check of all the goodies in the cockpit—and it is quite "busy." Starting left to right, we found the canopy latch and emergency locking system, a firm reminder that it is extremely poor policy to take off with the canopy not fully down and locked.

Both the canopy lock and gear down system are wired into a warning horn and light in the middle of the panel. A small switch next to the throttle will disarm the horn, but not the light, for throttle-off, nose-gear-up practice.

The instrument panel is straightforward (Fig. 7-9). The super-dependable Lycoming 0-235 has an adjustment for carburetor heat, but Rutan advised that it wasn't necessary in the dry desert climate.

A typewritten checklist taped near the pilot's left elbow reads as follows:

Before Takeoff:
1. Fuel caps/oil locked
2. Controls free and correct
3. Seat belts fastened
4. Trim for take-off
5. Circuit breakers IN
6. Dyno ON
7. Lights as required
8. Fuel - fullest tank
9. Master ON
10. Boost pump ON
11. Start - left mag only.
12. Ground run-up
     Mags 2000 rpm
     Oil pressure - green
     Fuel pressure - green
     Dyno - load check
13. Canopy locked

Climb—Cruise
1. Gear up
2. Boost pump off
3. Mixture lean as required

Before Landing
1. Fuel - fullest tank

2. Circuit breakers IN
3. Mixture RICH
4. Boost pump ON
5. Landing gear down - indicator check

After Landing - Engine Shut Down
1. Boost pump OFF
2. Lights OFF
3. Dyno OFF
4. Radio OFF
5. Master OFF
6. Mags OFF
7. Record tach time

The "dyno" used for electrical power on the Long-EZ is a four-pound unit from a Kobota tractor that produces unregulated alternating current. A standard alternator weighs between 15 and 20 pounds.

Not listed on the checklist, but used in practice, is to plug in the headset and microphone after the pilot is seated and removed it before deplaning because the plugs were installed between the pilot's legs. "We'll change that location later," explained Dick.

One other cockpit placard lists "Front Seat Pilot weights: Maximum 250 pounds; Minimum 120 pounds."

Beside the pilot's right elbow was a hand-calculator-type "Long Ezcale" being developed for

Fig. 7-10. Dick pulls the prop through as "student pilot" Downie sits up front. (courtesy Bob Weston)

functions of TAS, GPH, Fuel used/remaining, time, battery voltage, inside/outside temperatures, and other cockpit calculation functions. The Rutans plan further development of the "Ezcale" with a view to marketing in the near future.

Soon it was time to flick on the right mag switch and Dick walked around the Long-EZ and cranked up the sturdy 115-hp Lycoming (Fig. 7-10). I had the throttle cracked a bit too far and it took a few pulls on the prop to get ignition. Then the other mag switch came on and Dick walked to the front of the ship where he lifted the nose easily and I cranked down the nose gear with about 10 turns of the easy-to-reach knob in the middle of the instrument panel.

We kept the radio on Mojave's 122.8 unicom and handled in-flight instruction just by voice. The pusher's cabin was surprisingly quiet so that an intercom headset system was really not required.

After having read voluminous material on the non-standard "side stick" control, I'd expected some problems. However, by keeping your right elbow snugly in the arm rest, there was little tendency to overcontrol.

Rutan slid up on the leading edge of the wing and told me to taxi out. The rudder and brake attachments take some getting accustomed to, particularly when you wear a big size 12 shoe.

The nose gear casters so that all steering during taxi is done with the brakes. Pilots who have spent considerable time with the American Grumman series of trainers and four-place Grumman Tigers will find this sort of transition fairly easy. To others, there is a learning curve.

The sun was warm, but there was only a three-knot wind reported as we taxied along the rough ramp toward Runway 7. Dick remained on the wing until we neared the run-up area and then eased his frame into the back pit of the Long EZ. This was the location of the 74-gallon auxiliary fuel tank used on the initial record-breaking 33-hour, non-refueling distance hop.

Runup really doesn't amount to much: fuel boost as a back-up for the engine drive pump, a mag check, controls free, and you watch the trailing edge of the canard move in front of you as you pull back on the side stick. Then carefully close and lock the canopy. There have been fatalities as the result of VariEze take-offs with the canopy unlocked, even though the aircraft is fully controllable with the canopy open.

We called Unicom, were given a clear shot and taxied into position. As the power eased on, it was a bit of a guessing game to keep off the brakes and try to get a feel for when the tiny rudders were useful. With a high-performance cruise prop (58 × 72), acceleration was not extremely rapid, but our altitude was 2787 and the comfortable 75° day put our density altitude at 4,472 feet.

We used up considerably more of Mojave's runway on take off than was really necessary because of our unfamiliarity with the novel rudder and brake system on the Long-EZ. On a subsequent solo flight, take off was in just about 1/3rd the distance and reasonably close to the 550 feet shown in the specs.

In any event, the rudder/brake pedals on the Long-EZ are completely independent of each other. Push in left rudder and you get just that; push harder and you get both left rudder and left brake. Push easily on both rudder pedals and you have both winglet rudders deflected. Dick uses this procedure in lieu of flaps or a dive brake for rapid letdowns. Tense up on touchdown and push hard on both pedals and you lock both brakes—and probably blow both mainwheel tires.

On takeoff, I had some problems with directional control and snubbed the brakes a couple of times to keep the nose going down the runway. This, of course, extended our takeoff roll.

As soon as the rudders began to take over and I eased my feet off the brakes, we picked up speed more rapidly. With the stick full back, the nose started to pick up as the airspeed went through 50 mph. The Long-EZ flew itself off the runway smoothly and I eased off the back pressure to go to a 90-mph climb speed. As soon as we were over the far end of the runway, Dick advised me to turn off the fuel boost pump and crank up the nose gear.

Our rate of climb with full throttle was close to

1,000 fpm at 1,300 pounds gross weight and density altitude as we circled out away from the airport. The control touch of the Long-EZ was smooth and comfortable. The supine position—actually your back leans 42° from vertical in level flight—would probably become completely comfortable in time.

There is something completely different about flying behind the stubby canard airfoil. After years of boring holes through the sky, you become accustomed to a conventional engine cowling or, in larger twins, vast nothingness in front of the windshield. But to have that stubby wing breaking the air ahead is quite different. Even piloting an open biplane from the back seat where wing structure is ahead and above you has little bearing on the view from the front seat of the Long-EZ. Visibility is excellent.

On this first flight, I felt that I had to carry a little "bottom rudder" in turns to keep the ball in the center. We discussed this on the ground with Dick during the two-week period between two flights. Dick advised that his tests found only a slight amount of adverse yaw with aileron use and almost no torque or "P" effect during the slight pitching moment found with power changes. But more about these fine points during the second flight.

We leveled off at 7,500 feet and Dick asked me to lean the engine to best power (maximum rpm) on the fixed-pitch prop. We went back, and back, and back some more on the mixture—almost to the idle cut-off position—before the little Lycoming began to roughen up. Then forward to a smooth engine and a try for maximum cruise speed. Full throttle at 7,500 rpm with a non-turbocharged engine equals 75 percent power and is permitted indefinitely on this engine.

The airspeed picked up to 163 mph or 164 calibrated. Compensate for altitude/temperature, and we were doing 187 mph—and on 75 percent of 115 (or 86 hp) this is *really* moving. This same engine will drive a conventional two-place Citabria at 116 mph. The Long-EZ is clean-clean!

We throttled back to a comfortable cruise of 19 to 20 inches (60 hp) and tried some turns. Visibility is excellent and all the controls were most responsive without being "touchy." Rate of roll was ex-

cellent. In medium-to-steep turns, the canard up front made an easy reference for both pitch and turn angles. The long main wing with its tiny rudders at the tips took some rudder going into a turn, much like a long-spanned sailplane.

After a high-speed run, Dick suggested sampling the slow speed end of the dial. We cut back to 15 inches and then to 12 inches to let the engine cool slowly. Then the power came all the way off and I eased the pitch trim lever full aft. The air speed dropped into the "approach" segment of 70-80 mph and it felt so slow that I thought we were about to fall out of the air. Dick has fixed up an idiot-proof overlay on the airspeed indicator. He has marked cruise climb in the 100-110-mph range, best rate of climb at 87, pattern speed at 80 mph, and final approach at 72-75 mph.

"Now bring the stick all the way back and see what happens," counseled Rutan.

I eased back on the stubby side stick until it hit the aft stops. The 11.8-foot canard came up slightly and our airspeed finally dropped to 60 mph. There was that mushy feeling of an impending stall—but perhaps all in my mind. The nose dropped slowly, perhaps a degree or two. The Long-EZ picked up perhaps 2 mph, and we were right back flying again.

Dick then asked for more turns. "Make them as steep as you wish with the stick all the way back."

I tried turns up to 70-80° and we still didn't stall—though our rate of descent increased dramatically. The rate-of-climb needle dropped to 1,000-1,200 fpm before roll out, but there was no tendency for the ship to duck a wing or roll inverted.

We tried stalls and promptly found that you just don't stall one of Rutan's canards. We tried accelerated stalls and the Long-EZ would merely "nod" its canard slightly when the front wing "stalled" and with an increase of a mile or two an hour, the wing promptly unstalled. You can fly around all afternoon, turns or not, with the stick all the way back and all that will happen is that you'll develop a mild rate of sink, perhaps 600 fpm, with power off. At 15 percent power, you hold level flight with the stick full aft. That's your practice for the pattern and landing.

"We have this designed so you can't force a 'departure,'" explained Rutan. A "departure" is departing from controlled flight and can result in a Lomcevac maneuver where the airplane will tumble completely uncontrollably until it makes up its own mind to start flying again.

Then came steep climbs, full stick back, both straight ahead and in turns. With the supine seating, it felt that you were going straight up, but a check out the side indicated at 45-55° angle of climb. As the airspeed dropped, stick full back, the nose would drop slightly all on its own and the Long EZ would be back flying again.

It was all most impressive!

"This trick will help get you killed in a conventional airplane," grinned Dick from the back seat. And he was quite correct.

The air over Mojave was busy on a clear weekend. A gaily painted AT-6 and a surplus British Vampire jet fighter were rolling around in the sky near the airport. Mojave is both a sport plane center and near the Edwards AFB restricted test area, so many unusual things occur in this airspace. And we had more than our share of non-standard operations that afternoon.

Dick pointed out the jet as it circled off to the north of us. As we watched, the jet began a slow left turn that seemed destined to intersect our flight path. We dumped the nose on the Long EZ to get out of the way and the fighter dropped his nose slightly. Dick swore quickly and we kept going down. However, our 185 mph was no match for the turn rate of the jet, and we had a far-too-close look at the air intakes as he flashed just behind our twin tails. At that time, Dick didn't know whether the jet was "playing with us" or if the other pilot never saw us. In either event, it was too close.

In the quiet cockpit of the Long-EZ, Dick and I exchanged irreverent and unexpurgated comments to unwind our nerves a little. Then we circled back to make a landing.

On a previous "check ride," I had been at the end of the runway shooting pictures and watched a VariEze owner make three passes at Mojave to get the Long-EZ slowed down enough to "make the field." At the time of this flight, the Long-EZ did not have a speed brake. The plans have already been drawn and all Long-EZs will have an under-the-fuselage speed brake.

We cranked down the nose wheel and could see it extend through the small plexiglas window in the cabin floor. The boost pump went on and I punched the transmit switch on the EdoAir radio to check traffic at Mojave Unicom. There wasn't anything reported, but we were still very wary of a T-6 and an old jet fighter. Once was enough on that routine!

Because the EZ is so clean, and without the speed brake, Dick recommended only a 500-foot traffic pattern. Had we flown the standard 800-foot circuit, we'd have never gotten to the ground. However, Unicom at Mojave was accustomed to this procedure. I chopped the power and waited and waited, all the time easing back on the stick so that we could slow to approach speed. It took the whole downwind leg. That miniscule 1.6 square feet of frontal area is certainly noticeable when you try to get this bird slowed down.

Over the railroad town of Mojave, we looked around and turned on a wide base leg. Visibility from the front seat is excellent in all attitudes except during landing flare. We rolled out slowly to line up with Runway 7. We were still a little fast according to Rutan's "idiot-proof" airspeed overlay, but Dick said, "You're in the groove; just stay with it."

We crossed the numbers at perhaps 20 feet and 65-67 mph. Then came the problem of slowing down. We eased back more on the side stick and the canard came up to cover our view of the far part of the runway.

Dick's voice came from the back. "You're still ten feet in the air; let her down a little."

I eased off the back pressure just a bit and we continued to eat up runway. It was a good thing that we had 7,000' to work with because the little 3.40 × 5 main tires didn't touch until almost the midpoint.

"Now let the nosewheel down and begin to use some braking," advised Rutan. We followed instructions. We played with the brakes gingerly to avoid skidding the tires and let the ship roll to the far end of the runway.

As we turned off to taxi back, Dick asked for the canopy open so that he could stay cool. It seemed like a good idea, though the glass house was not really uncomfortable even on the ground.

We taxied back to Rutan's ramp and closed the mixture control. As the engine stopped, Dick slid off the wing and lifted the nose. I cranked the nose wheel up and he eased the stubby fuselage to the ground. It's certainly an unusual way to park an airplane—any airplane but Rutan's designs.

I snapped all the switches off, unhooked the harness and belt and slowly extricated my long legs from under the instrument panel. It was only a short step to the pavement.

As we re-hashed the flight, Dick handed me the log book of the Long-EZ, put the date and my name on a vacant line and said, "Tell me what you think of the flight." There wasn't much space, so I

signed it and said, "Great ship!"

You'd think that was enough excitement for one day, but we decided to shoot some air-to-air formation pictures of both the Long-EZ and Mike Melvill's No. 1 VariViggen (Fig. 7-11). Dick took my flying buddy Bob Weston in the back seat of the Long-EZ and Les Faus, who had flown his VariEze up from Van Nuys, went along in our Cessna 170 to do the flying while I shot pictures.

"I'm not current in taildraggers," said Les as we taxied out, "so you please make the takeoff and landing." That's the way we did it.

We took off first with the two canards right behind us. As the Long-EZ "formed up" with the Viggen and climbed toward our camera platform, Mike came up on the 122.95 air-to-air frequency we were using. "Did you see that F-4 go past us and then go right straight up?" Dick Rutan acknowledged and back-seat passenger Bob Weston told

Fig. 7-11. A familiar sight at the EAA air shows. Rutan's Defiant and Long-EZ in formation with the VariViggen joining the group.

later of seeing the supersonic jet go past the two canards and pull straight up out of sight. But more on that in a minute.

According to plan, Mike came in alone first for a load of 11 black-and-white shots from my 6×7 Pentax (200 mm Takumar lens). Mike flies a great formation, and we had to keep admonishing him to move away a little so that we'd get the entire airplane in the photo.

Then we changed film and Dick moved in behind Mike with the Long-EZ. We shot another 11 pictures and a few assorted color shots with a second camera. As Mike pulled away, we noted a large black ball of smoke erupting from the desert floor north of Mojave toward California City. Since Mike's camera posing was finished, he headed for the smoke while Dick and his passenger came in for solo pictures. We soon finished the roll and Dick headed toward the fire that was billowing from the desert floor.

"That looks like a plane crash," said Mike on our plane-to-plane frequency. "Let's change over to 'point eight' (122.8) and advise the airport. Dick and I "rogered" and we all went to the busy Unicom frequency. We followed the two canards toward the fire and I could hear Mike talking with Mojave's Airport office. He confirmed that the smoke was a burning aircraft.

"It looks like an F-4," said Mike. "It's probably out of Edward [AFB]."

Mojave Unicom, with Airport Manager Dan Sabovitch behind the radio, said, "Please change over to 120.7 and advise Edwards Tower of what you see."

About that time, Mike came on the air from the front seat of the Viggin. "Hey, there's one parachute coming down, but he's still way above me." Sure enough, we could see the red and white 'chute drifting lazily toward the calm desert floor. Below, streams of dust converged on the burning F-4 and the probable touchdown of the survivor. I don't know where all the motorcycles, campers, dune buggies and standard cars came from.

Later, Dick Rutan commented wryly, "It was just like North Vietnam all over again. Whenever a 'chute came down, there were people crawling out

from under rocks headed for the impact site."

The airwaves were busy with queries about a second parachute since the F-4 always flies with a two-man crew. There was no second 'chute.

Yes, it had been an unusual day.

The first flight of the Long-EZ was in mid-1979. Final flight testing was accomplished in December and the initial record flown December 15-16. After the successful record flight, the first passenger in the Long-EZ was Burt and Dick's mother, Irene. Since that time, the popular ship has been giving demonstrations and flight checks. Dick had just returned from Florida's annual Sun-'n-Fun Fly-in at Lakeland where he flew a waivered airshow in the Long-EZ for each of the seven days of the program. He logged 52.2 hours on the two-week trip. Flight time to Florida from Mojave; 4:20 to El Paso and 8:10 non-stop into Lakeland. Average true airspeed was 183 mph on 5.5 gph. Altitudes ranged from 9,500 to 13,500 feet. The engine, now with 1,534 hours total time (it was purchased used and put into the Long-EZ with 1,350 hours when it was removed from an American Yankee trainer) required a main oil seal that was replaced in Dallas, Texas, on the way back. Aside from that, it was just gas and oil.

After the Long-EZ returned from Florida, we had the opportunity to fly N79RA again—this time without Dick's 170 pounds in the back seat. On any initial orientation flight in a new style airplane, the pilot is somewhat overwhelmed with new operational procedures, new reference points, and a whole new cockpit arrangement. After the first flight, we had roughed-out the copy and had shown it to Dick.

"You'd better go out on your own and correct a few of your misconceptions," suggested Dick after reading our rough draft. He then suggested a mini-test program to prove or disprove to my own satisfaction some of my initial impressions. Before flight, the former USAF fighter pilot suggested that I pay particular attention to solo rate of climb, any yaw abnormality, adverse yaw with full aileron and feet on the floor, torque, "P" factor pitch trim changes with full power application, visibility at various climb and approach speeds and simulation of a "Hormel-handed" pilot who might tighten up his turn in the traffic pattern when a strong wind was blowing on the ground.

Rutan opened the nose compartment and readjusted the rudder pedals to full extension. It was a great help to me. I shoehorned into the cockpit and slid the back cushion as far aft as possible. Then the paper listing the items to be checked in flight went under one leg and I followed the cockpit checklist. Dick propped the Long-EZ while the nose was still on the concrete. Then he and a friend lifted the nose and I cranked down the nose gear, squirmed in the seat, called Mojave Unicom and taxied out. The group of aficionados who regularly congregate at the Rutan hangar on Saturdays wasted considerable film, and undoubtedly even more envy. Flying the Long-EZ solo is a real treat!

There had been a wind shift and noontime thermals were starting to pop. Unicom advised either Runway 22 or 30. I taxied out slowly, waiting for two aging British jets to exhaust their fuel with fast passes down the runway. Both finally landed as I completed my run-up. After a call to Unicom, I lined up on the spacious 9600-foot Runway 30 and eased in the power. I "worried" the rudders and applied brakes as required to keep the nose pointed more-or-less down the runway while easing in full power. Acceleration solo and with low fuel was much more rapid than on the previous dual flight, and there was less inadvertent brake dragging.

I hopped into the air, adjusted the trim, retracted the nose gear and made a slight left turn to parallel the parking ramp. With full power, the rate of climb swung between 1200 and 1500 fpm in moderately choppy air at 90-100 mph. Rate of climb is actually better at 80 mph, but forward visibility is poorer.

I shut down the fuel boost pump, came back on the power to about 22″ and climbed to 6,000 feet indicated. After leveling off, my first test was to take both feet off the rudders and roll the wings quickly, checking for adverse yaw. With an abrupt roll to the right, the nose tended to go up and to the left, but ever so slightly—not more than 4° or 5°.

Next I throttled back and let the speed bleed off, watching how visibility was affected as the nose

and its canard came up. The higher the nose, the more obstruction to vision. At pattern speeds, the canard was clearly visible but presented no problem; on a straight-ahead, full-stick back stall, it was a slight obstruction. I let go of the controls with full aft trim, let the ship stabilize and briskly applied full power. The nose slowly dropped perhaps 5° and wandered off to the left very slightly. With power reduced, the nose returned to the horizon. Good, safe, docile.

While I was slowed down, I simulated the careless pilot trying to "hurry" a turn toward the airport. With full back stick and ample rudder, the Long-EZ turned calmly. Holding the stick back in a continuing turn, there was a mild oscillation as the canard stalled, lost just a bit of its lift and the nose dropped slightly. Just as soon as a little bit of speed was picked up, the ship was flying again smoothly.

I had taken off with only about 1/3 fuel and Dick had suggested that I return within 30 minutes. I called Unicom and was advised that Runway 22 was now in use. That's the shortest of Mojave's three runways, but it is 5,200 feet long with nothing but sagebrush on approach.

I flew a long pattern, slowed to the 75 mph marked in the airspeed box for approach and held perhaps 70 indicated across the numbers. During flare out, it was still a bit hard to see around the canard, and I found myself taking a quick glance or two out to the side as I let down through about 10 feet. There was a minimum of float and the mains were on. Even without Dick's weight in the back seat, there was no holding the nose gear off with full back stick. It plopped to the runway and I let the Long-EZ roll out. It took several power applications to reach the end of the runway.

I cleared the active, opened the latch on the canopy and pushed it up to keep the desert heat tolerable. The taxi back was with one hand holding the canopy open.

Yes, the Long-EZ proved out all the questions I had from that initial demonstration flight.

Then Dick checked for oil leaks, added a little fuel and went out to work on his air show program while a dozen VariEze builders and would-be builders watched.

It's a great airplane!

Popularity of the Long-EZ design has led to more than 3,000 sets of plans and construction guides being sold in just over three years, despite an economy that was not considered robust. It is only a matter of time until the record 4,500 sets of plans sold for the VariEze will be topped by its big brother, particularly with the advent of prefabricated components that cut building time on the Long-EZ drastically.

No wonder the name Rutan has become a household word in aviation circles.

Chapter 8

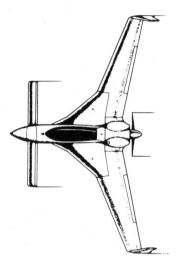

Everybody Gets into the Act

There's much more to joining the homebuilt scene than sending your check for a set of plans, stopping at the neighborhood aircraft supply house, and moving one car out of the garage.

Homebuilding is a people-on-people experience. There's the designer working with the builder, the builder working with the designer, and builders working with other builders.

THE CANARD PUSHER

Faithfully every quarter, Rutan produces a mimeographed newletter that goes to all builders of any of the various projects. This newsletter is a mandatory publication for active builders since it is the only way the homebuilt designer can communicate officially with any update on plans.

This newsletter is the primary clearing house for ideas, shortcuts, vendor information, fly-ins, and just about everything a builder wants to know.

Originally called the *VariViggen News* (the first six issues being concerned with the VariViggen exclusively), the name was changed with the advent

of the VariEze to *The Canard Pusher*, in October, 1975. The newsletter name, which has continued for at least eight years, was picked over a number of other interesting mastheads submitted by builders. These included: *The Canard Line, The Canardian Club, Vari New-Z, Canard Time News, The Vari Forum, VariUnique Aircraft News, Canard Capers, Canard Contrails, Glass Backwards News, Vari-Vignette, The Canard Rumor, Canard Disclosure, Canard Gas Line, Canard Trend, Canard Courier, The Backward Flyer, The Canard Leader, On the Nose, Canard Tales* and *Canard Forward.*

"The new name should last for some time now, until we come up with an aircraft without a canard," said Burt Rutan.

The evolution of the unique landing gear on the VariEze and Long-EZ is an example of how the designer helps supply hard-to-fabricate parts. This change was duly noted in the builder's newsletter:

"The vendor for the VariEze fiberglass parts notified us that he was modifying his business operation and would discontinue manufacturing the nose and main gear parts. Since tooling for the main gear was wearing out, we would not arrange for the new manufacturer to produce this same item. Instead, we developed a new gear, which is 40 percent stronger and made with an improved process. This gear is designed specifically for the Long-EZ, which has a gross weight 24 percent heavier than a VariEze. We plan to have only this new gear produced by the new vendor, and use it on both the Eze and the Long-EZ. It is three to four pounds heavier than an Eze gear. We have also developed an improved main gear attachment design which

is now being tested on the Long-EZ.''

After testing, Rutan advised that "The search for a manufacturer was difficult—the normal fiberglass production shops do not have the necessary ovens, instrumentation and impregnation machines needed for this work. The shops that do have the equipment and engineering capability to produce these parts are those who only make expensive aircraft components and they have bid excessive prices on these items to cover the development costs. We were faced with either no landing gear, or a price increase.

"We felt that the price of the gear, having been

Fig. 8-1. Long-EZ landing gears are formed here at the RAF in Mojave. A special production method was developed by Rutan to wind filament and which uses a new epoxy system. The new gear is 40 percent to 60 percent stronger and 24 percent heavier than the original.

raised 20% in the three years, so excessive, we decided to tackle the job ourselves—the only alternative available to provide a reasonable gear for the builders. We knew this job would result in delays in plans preparation for Long-EZ, but it really was our only alternative. Within six weeks we produced patterns and tooling for the new strengthened nose and main gear (Fig. 8-1), developed a new production method, built a convection oven and filament winding machine, set up a quality control process, tested a new epoxy system, and began production of the new parts. Our new method, which winds roving and tapers it for accurate mold filling, requires fewer man-hours and results in more uniformity than the previous process. Thus, we are able to sell the parts for only 70 percent of the previous price per pound.

"The new main gear is 65 percent stronger than the old VariEze gear and should not be susceptible to the long-term creep (spreading and loss of camber) experienced on some of the heavier VariEzes. The new gear is 3 inches longer on each end to raise the prop clearance on the Long-EZ. VariEze builders using the new gear will saw off the 3 inches. The old main gear weighed 16 pounds. The new one weighs 21 pounds. While we regret any increase in empty weight, experience has shown that many VariEzes are being operated heavier than expected and need the extra beef in the gear."

One might call this an enlightening report from one of the builders:

"I have installed the Long-EZ nose and main gear on my VariEze so I am sure I will have a lot better landing gear system, but it is making me even more overweight than I already was. I decided the best thing to do about it was to lose 30 excess pounds off of my 230-pound body, which I have almost accomplished. Also, my wife has lost nearly 20 pounds, so the 17 or 18 extra pounds I picked up on the bird is more than compensated for by the combined 50-pound weight loss. I attend Weight Watchers and you can rest assured I am the only one in the class who isn't losing weight because of a woman or a man. My white, red, and blue mistress has put on weight, so in order to be compatible with

her, I had to lose or else become a single-place pilot."

Contributions to the newsletter by the builders indicates a wide spread in the age spectrum. It was reported that VariEze N9036G was built by George Gilmer, age 73 years young. Three years total time at Santa Paula Airport, California. Total cost was about $3,600. George made almost every part, wing fittings, wheel and brake system, throttle quadrant, etc. George advised all builders that if Burt gives a measurement or method, there is a reason. George started flying in 1929.

On the other end of the age spectrum is this report on a first flight by Stuart Kingman, of Paicines, California, age 18:

"After three years of blood, sweat, and tears, I had my own airplane! I taxi-tested for two or three days just to get the feel of the airplane, and also because I was scared, and rightfully so after reading of all those experienced pilots getting killed in their Ezes. All of my experience rested on 150 hours in a Cessna 150 and one hour in a Grumman TR-2. After the taxi tests, my Dad took out a $10,000 life insurance policy for me, and I lifted N222SK off the pavement and around the pattern. The feeling I had during those few moments were completely void of any fear—it was the most fun I had ever had. The plane flew as if it had been flying for years. Absolutely no problems whatsoever. What surprised me even more was the landing. I had never flown an airplane with a stick, much less a side stick. That first landing was the smoothest landing I've ever made. Every other landing since then has also been smooth, too. N222K cruises at a true airspeed of 180 mph at 6,000 feet and 75 percent throttle. The engine is a Continental C-90-12F turning a Bruce Tifft prop. Empty weight is 597 pounds. I am extremely pleased with the airplane. I have never flown a plane even similar to it. Like I've said many times before, it flies like an airplane should."

Non-intentioned "first flights" are also duly reported by the builders. Lee Roan of Temple City, California (Fig. 8-2), really hadn't planned to make his first flight, at least not that day, as he had not flown in the past six months and had not yet had his planned Yankee checkout. He said, "I made a high-

Fig. 8-2. Lee Roan, shown here with his fully IFR-equipped VariEze, reported in the newsletter that his first flight was purely an accident. Control stick is snubbed by a bungee cord and a special Sigtronics headset is stowed between flights in the right rudder well.

speed taxi, got to 70 mph with nosewheel off, then was flying. I pulled the throttle back but floated past the half-way mark, still floating. I decided it was time to fly, so I took off and flew around the field and came in too fast the first time. So, I went around and made a good landing the next time." Roan is an electronic designer for Sigtronics, Inc., and naturally has the latest Sigtronics intercom system and voice-actuated headsets in his Eze, which he demonstrates at the drop of a decibel.

In 36 issues of *The Canard Pusher* and its predecessor, there have been some gems of information and interesting questions and answers. Some examples follow:

Use a plastic garbage can liner to keep epoxy off clothes. Cut three holes, one for your neck and two for arms. - Phil Supan.

Be careful when storing foam blocks; not only can sunlight ruin them, but rats and mice love to dig tunnels in them!

Q. My wife is 6'5" tall. Can she fit the back seat?

A. The front seat allows "stretch out" comfort (feet in front of the rudder pedals if you desire) for pilots to 6'7" and 210 lbs. Back seat is comfortable for pilots' passengers up to 6'5" and 220 lbs. In fact, those of you who were at the Watsonville Fly-in may have seen a 6'9", 210-lb. man get in the back seat with the two full suitcases. His comment was, "relatively comfortable." Even he was not pressed up against the canopy.

Q. I want my Eze to look more like a Defiant. Can I eliminate the lower winglet?

A. Performance-wise, yes; it only gives about 1 percent induced drag reduction. But do not leave it off— it protects the rudder and cable in case you drag a wingtip on takeoff or landing.

Wilma Melville—possibly the only woman VariEze pilot at this time—has completed her 100th hour in the airplane which she and her husband John built over a period of 1½ years. A physical education teacher from Torrance, California, she included the EAA Oshkosh Fly-in in her schedule. John built the Eze with Wilma's help, but he is not a pilot and is thus confined to the back seat.

Q. Are dual controls planned?

A. No. Again, I do not plan to compromise the design simplicity to do a mission other than that of efficient cruise. Learn to fly in an airplane which was designed as a trainer. Dual controls would triple the number of parts in the control system and eliminate one suitcase. Also, controls could be jammed when flying solo with baggage in the back seat. Currently there is nothing in the back seat which moves. Four pilots have been successfully checked out in N7EZ to date—none of them had side-stick experience.

Q. What is the minimum size door in the shop to hatch a finished VariEze?"

A. If you leave the main gear off until after the airplane gets out of your shop, a 30" × 68" door or window is enough.

A few builders have asked what the weakest

part of the landing gear is, and the answer is the attachment pads. Don't misunderstand, it is strong enough to do the job and then some, but it is the part we expect to break first if the system is overloaded. On N7EZ (VW prototype), its trip through a ditch at 75 knots last summer tore the gear free of the airplane (Fig. 8-3) by failing the attachment layup, but the gear strut itself was not damaged and will be reinstalled on the airplane. We specifically tailored the attachment layup to fail first in a crunch because it is the easiest and cheapest part to replace.

A border patrol Cessna Citation picked up a suspicious target cruising toward Florida from an island in the Caribbean. Its strange configuration was a complete puzzle to the radar operator, so the aircraft was tracked to its destination in Florida. Law enforcement officers were waiting to nab the pilot and his load of marijuana. The airplane? A VariEze.

FOREIGN IN NATURE

Worldwide interest in the VariEze shows up in the columns of *The Canard Pusher.*

From Mick Hinton, Kororo Via Coffs Harbour, Australia:

"I would like to inform you that my VariEze VH/EZH is now flying (fantastic to say the least). It weighed out just under 600 pounds with alternator and limited IFR panel.

"Thank you very much for your help, which has allowed me to build this magnificent machine. It flies hands-off and I just can't stall it, but will be going back into the workshop soon to install the wing cuffs.

"After the necessary flight tests in March of this year, I was able, accompanied by my wife, to do my longest flight in EZH and enter my Eze in the SAAA convention of the year at Bowral, N.S.W. I am very proud to say it won the Reserve Grand Champion homebuilt of Australia. This was my first attempt at building so mere words will never express how I felt that day.

"Since the air show, my phone has rung constantly with enquiries from future builders of the VariEze.

"Hope to see you at Oshkosh this year."

Fig. 8-3. The VW prototype N7EZ went through a ditch at 75 mph—when the pilot undershot. The landing gear tore free of the airplane, as it was designed to do, since it is the easiest and cheapest part of the airplane to replace. Dick Rutan later rebuilt this airframe. (courtesy Don Dwiggins)

And from Switzerland, we hear from Dana and Rudi Kurth:

"Our VariEze flew for the first time at Sion Airfield in Switzerland. We used Sion for the tests because it has a longer runway than our local airfield at Grenchen.

"I have been pretty busy. I translated the Eze plans into German and I also translated *The Canard Pusher* for a group of Eze builders here. So what with all that, plus teaching Grenchen Tower personnel English, teaching at the local school, and a 10-month-old baby to chase after, you can see why we haven't written sooner.

"Our registration number is HB-YBG. HB is Switzerland, Y is the prefix for homebuilts here and BG is just the letters which came next in sequence—you can't choose special letters here, like they can in the U.S. So we just tell people that it means, '*Hey Burt, You're Bloody Great!*'

"For your information, over forty Ezes are being built in France, ten in Italy, about five in England, about eight to nine in Switzerland, and I believe one in Holland. Further, four or five are building in Germany."

Since it was flown for the first time, we have had 78 different passengers in it, have landed at 29 different airfields, and she has been flown by six different pilots, including a Swiss Air Force pilot, the Swiss Ministry Chief Flying Instructor, and Inspector for homebuilts from the Swiss Air Ministry, the Tower Controller from Grenchen, and the French Army test pilot who test-flew the Mirages. The Inspector did a belly landing (nose gear up) at Grenchen, and got out of the Eze very red-faced, but having done very little damage, to our relief, and to the amusement of the many on-lookers.

"We will be flying to Germany, France, England, Holland, Belgium and Denmark this year—a flight we had planned to Israel, via Italy, Greece and Cyprus has had to be canceled because they have no av/gas, and can't fly through Turkey, Lebanon and Syria. In August, we will be flying with our daughter with us. She will be 16 months old then, so we hope she's not too heavy.

"It's wonderful to be able to get into the plane and fly to Grenoble for a coffee, or to be able to fly off and land in England less than 2½ hours later— even SwissAir can't beat that, when you count the check-in time, luggage-finding, queue for the Customs, etc." [A full account of the test-flying of HB-YBG is carried in Chapter 13.]

One builder in England shared his thoughts with other canard builders. Ivan Shaw of South York said that building his VariEze was an exciting and satisfying period in his life. However, he recommended that before starting any project, the would-be builder should decorate that bedroom, mend the washer and/or tidy the garden. Since builders need all the support possible from their wife, lover, or mistress, it is for the builder's own good to get all these little jobs done first.

Shaw considers his Eze a challenge, something to pit his wits against. He expounds the joy to be had from working with your hands, using tools, and actually producing something. While flying a rented club 150 is enjoyable, traveling in an aircraft you have purchased is more enjoyable, but the ultimate is flying the aircraft that you built by yourself. He still finds the thrill and sheer magic there in every flight.

The VariEze with the call sign G-IVAN travels to the airport on a special trailer the builder designed. When not flying, it is in a heated workshop at home. Time required to install the two main wings and the canard is just 15 minutes. He fuels at the corner petrol station on his way to the airport. Imagine the hangar fees he saves!

Since plans for the popular Long-EZ were announced, there have been finished units flying in Italy, France, Sweden, Japan, Australia, New Zealand, Switzerland, West Germany, and Denmark. Some 300 quarterly newsletters are mailed overseas.

Bill Allen from England reports that a landing fee at London's Heathrow Airport is three pounds—about $4.50—for each touchdown, including touch-and-goes.

In France, homebuilders get a break from their government. They are refunded half the out-of-pocket cost after the airplane flies.

Sources of builder supplies are beginning to develop on the Continent. Dane Jurth-Rowe in

Switzerland stocks PVC foam, urethane and Styrofoam, and the required weaves of fiberglass. He can also translate plans and instructions into German.

Graham Singleton in Holmesfield, England, stocks EZ canopies and has a set of Lycoming Long-EZ cowlings in Kevlar®.

Henri Christ in France reports that F-PYIP, the VariEze he built, is now being used by his flying club and flown regularly off a grass runway without problems. He is impatiently awaiting plans to start another canard composite.

Neil and Gary Hunter and Al and Mabel Coha took their two Ezes as far as Sao Paulo, Brazil. Both pilots were formerly U.S. Navy aviators, so the long overwater hops seemed no problem. The two aircraft were featured on the Brazilian Global News TV program with footage of the two homebuilts (called "housebuilts" in Spanish-speaking countries) over Sugar Loaf.

VARIEZE NEWS EXCHANGE

A regional newsletter, the *VariEze News Exchange* ($V_E N_E$), has been developed by George Scott, Jr., of Cummin, Georgia. Calling himself "The Real George Scott," he is one of the charter members of EAA Chapter 611 in Georgia.

In his Christmas newsletter several years ago, George Scott commented:

The VariEze rumor mill has a new model being developed by RAF! It is to be tested December 25th by an elderly gentleman with a white beard in a red jump suit. It is reported that the new aircraft was built in six weeks by 365 elves, none of which were allergic to epoxy. Stellar instrumentation negated any use for flaky gauges and the tach was reported to be accurate to ±.000994 percent. Cruise speed is reported to be 186,000 mph on eight horsepower and fuel consumption is four bhph (bales of hay per hour).

The plane has room for ten pounds of luggage in a five-pound sack and the front cockpit is extra comfortable since the seat is constructed of a filler of Preparation H covered by non-itching fiberglass cloth.

Approaches to landings are accomplished via a remote TV camera located on the non-steerable, non-retractable Teflon skid. The lower .9 of the TV screen is blocked from view to simulate the visual approach of older style canard-type aircraft.

So, if a futuristic appearing aircraft makes a low pass over your house on Christmas Eve, don't call the FAA; just smile and wave.

Northpole Unicom. This is Experimental 1979 EZ entering a left downwind for Runway 36. This will be a full stop and the last flight for this year.

Merry Christmas and Happy New Year!
The "Real" Santa Claus.

TYPICAL MUTUAL AID SOCIETY

The assembly of your very own homebuilt airplane becomes a very personal thing. When you begin a project that can take from one to five years (or even longer), you're committing a substantial part of your time and complete interest. Anywhere that two or more Eze builders live within commuting distance, there becomes instant comraderie; as the numbers grow, self-help groups develop (Fig. 8-4). We attended a recent meeting and reported to *Homebuilt Aircraft* magazine. We have excerpted from that article with permission:

Meetings are completely informal, centering on new and successful techniques in composite construction. Questions and answers cover what problems have developed and how some of them have been solved. It's a roundtable information exchange.

The "San Diego Bunch" began in mid-1976 when a group of 15 would-be VariEze builders met at Stan Levine's home to discuss the then-new Rutan design. About that same time, Burt Rutan had flown his prototype VariEze to San Diego to give a talk before a joint meeting of the AIAA and EAA. The San Diego Bunch liked what they saw and heard.

The result was a flight to Mojave by one of the original members to purchase 13 sets of plans, then $105 each. Of these 13 sets of plans, there are 11 completed airplanes and one nearing completion. The group has grown with composite projects ranging from eight VariEze to 36 Long-EZs. A

Dragonfly or two, a Quickie, a Quickie 2, and a two-place twin push-pull called the Gemini that's nearing completion.

With a large monthly attendance, it takes a good-sized room to handle the group. Fortunately, Navy Commander Ralph L. Gaither owns a VariEze and teaches flight psychology in the military survi-

Fig. 8-4. VariEze builders check what other builders have done. Here a couple peer through the canopy of a parked VariEze to see what ideas might be used in their own ship. Note solar panel in front of canopy to power radios in daylight.

val school. Commander Gaither is particularly qualified to teach survival after spending seven years as a POW in Southeast Asia. He has been able to find meeting rooms for the group on base at the Miramar Naval Air Station.

Early squadron meetings showed FAA films and had regular speakers, but the builders soon found that they didn't have time for these types of programs. They were more interested in the "here and now" of building their composite aircraft. During every Eze Squadron meeting, each member is polled on the status of his project and asked to detail current problems or solutions. The meetings soon become a lively exchange of information ranging from the prices charged by various vendors, to where surplus stores have useful material, to the latest techniques in mixing and applying epoxy.

Squadron Director and one of the original 15 members is Al Coha, who is just retiring from Teledyne Ryan as head of the material composites group.

There is considerable group sharing in the EZ Squadron. For example, Dick Posten excels in welding and makes parts for many of the members. Roman Wasilewski has his VariEze flying and has cranked out 13 sets of wing fittings for others with his lathe and milling machines. Marshall Randall, a machinist at the University of San Diego, is working on a Long-EZ; he built a jig for aligning landing gear legs and another for drilling wing fittings for the VariEze.

Mrs. Liz Todd is the member of her family who is building the Long-EZ. She's reacting to the challenge to build it all on her own while husband Larry watches with hands-off interest.

Many of the original 13 remain active in the group even though they have completed their initial aircraft and have them flying.

INTERNATIONAL VARIEZE HOSPITALITY CLUB

The International VariEze Hospitality Club (IVHC) was founded by Donald and Bernadette Shupe in 1979 to encourage and promote hospitality, travel, and support for builders and flyers of Ezes and other composite airplanes (Fig. 8-5).

A quarterly newsletter contains letters from

Fig. 8-5. Don and Bernadette Shupe in their VariEze "Puff"—the Magic Dragon—during a fly-in at Mojave. Other VariEze owners ease the nose to the ground after the Shupe has retracted the nose gear.

members on safety, first-flight data, better how-to instructions, accident reports, and information on fly-ins.

Members are expected to provide shelter and comforts to other members in need only according to the hosting member's ability and desire to provide these considerations.

The IVHC sponsors fly-ins several times a year at various locations around the country and across-the-borders. The complexity of these gatherings varies from the highly-organized extravaganza at Taos and the Bahamas to the more informal "do-it-yourself" fly-in coming up at Loreto, Baja California.

IVHC members support other members by lending, replacing, and/or repairing parts and extending aid to any member who has become stranded in their vicinity.

This organization began with 20 members; 12 of the founders are still with the club. The group has grown steadily with 95 members in 1980, 134 in 1981, and 194 a year later. These totals caused the Shupes to buy a computer to handle the paperwork and mailing.

Irene Rutan volunteered her services from the beginning to be Historian, and she maintains an ever-increasing collection of color prints and first-flight dates of builders of her son's designs. Whether members or not of IVHC, builders with fledgling flyers are urged to send a photo and the true scoop to Mrs. Irene Rutan, 8526 Calmada, Whittier, California 90605.

After three years of club development, Don Shupe summarized his feelings about the Ezes and the people who build them:

"I've met a lot of fantastic people and had

Fig. 8-6. Bruce Tifft flies his pod-equipped Eze near Santa Paula, California.

bunches of super experiences. I've seen the people associated with EZs change, too. In the beginning it appeared that EZ people were different than other people in aviation; different even from other homebuilders. They seemed to know what they wanted and dug in and did it. Not many were like the seven-year builders I had seen so often with other homebuilts. Now I *know* that EZ people are different. There seems to be more aviators among us than among builders of other types of planes. We like to fly as much or more than we like to build. We like to talk, too, as much as anybody, but we like to fly more. Bernadette and "Puff" and I have met a lot of great people in our travels. We didn't notice that we were changing even though we were probably different from other people to start with, having chosen to build this unusual plane. The people most deeply involved with the EZ have changed even more. Burt is warmer and friendlier. Dick is happier, and I don't think that success alone accounts for all of this."

Bruce and Bonnie Tifft expressed warm memories of their 7,000-mile trip across the U.S.A. and visits with IVHC members along the way:

"We were welcomed in each and every instance like long-lost friends or relatives. There is a tremendous, warm bond between the people with these airplanes, and we thoroughly enjoyed our stay with each and every one of the Hospitality Club members. It was great for us to have the opportunity to get acquainted with all these interesting people, and they seemed to enjoy the chance to swap EZ stories, get building hints, chat about the fly-ins, etc. Of course, back-seat checkout rides were a must for all the would-be EZ pilots and it was such fun to see the reaction from the fellas and gals who have never had the thrill of flying in an EZ before. They were so excited and enthusiastic about the wonderful flying characteristics of the EZ. It's especially fun to get this reaction from the high-time pilots who have flown lots and lots of different kinds of aircraft over a period of many years. They are as impressed as the brand-new pilot. It's really rewarding for us to share this experience."

And there is a strong feeling of involvement among the families of EZ builders. When Ron Walters' VariEze was destroyed by fire after engine

146

shutdown in front of his hangar, his wife wrote the following poem:

You were the diversion he needed in times of stress.
You were solace to him when he was not at his best.
When the world was too much for him to cope,
He turned to you, and you gave him hope.
In the wee small hours when sleep wouldn't come,
You were there—always something to be done.
You and he saw the world from a different view
When you soared together to the distant blue.
You're gone now—no more obsession;
Only memories left—the only possession.
You were the joy and pride of his life.
I can't fill the void. I'm only his wife.

HAMLIN AWARD

After builder Ed Hamlin, one of the original members of the Hospitality Club, was killed in his EZ, the club established a perpetual trophy in his name to be given annually to a member who gave unselfishly of time, energy, knowledge and spirit, as did Ed Hamlin.

Nominated for the first trophy were Al Coha of San Diego, the "Real" George Scott, Nat Puffer from Minnesota, and the eventual winners, Mike and Sally Melvill. The initial presentation was made before a full banquet room at Butch's restaurant, Oshkosh, 1983.

INNOVATIONS FOR PERSONAL NEEDS

One of the inherent compromises in the efficient EZ designs is the lack of baggage space. This problem was solved by at least two builders working independently.

Bruce Tifft, one of the early finishers of a VariEze, now carves wooden propellers for homebuilts. His company is B&T Propellers in Mariposa, California, and he wanted to have the capability to deliver propellers up to 68 inches long by air. They just wouldn't fit comfortably in the back

of his Eze, particularly when he was carrying a passenger.

Tifft modified a tip tank mold developed by Forbes Simpson of Mariposa, California. (Forbes is completing a homebuilt of his own design.) The tanks were mounted on pylons and hung beneath the wings. The prop builder limits his loads to 15 pounds maximum, with no more than 10 pounds on each side. The tail section of the tanks is removed by turning three fasteners (Fig. 8-7).

There appears to be almost no change in performance, according to Tifft, who tuft-tested his installation extensively. He has exceeded 210 mph with the tanks installed. Tifft has logged more than 550 hours on his VariEze.

In a completely separate development, Ed Hamlin of Rocklin, California, built up a set of cargo pods to carry his tent and other camping gear on his travels in Mexico. Actually, Hamlin was the first to install a cargo pod, flying just one at a time on the initial installation on his VariEze. He reported almost no change in trim with just one tank installed.

Hamlin consulted with designer Burt Rutan before starting his project and stated that while Rutan wasn't particularly enthusiastic about the idea, he did advise that the tanks should be mounted at least one diameter away from the wing. Hamlin's tanks are designed on a 1:4 ratio, 12 inches in diameter and four feet long. At the suggestion of an F-86 pilot, he added a single outboard stabilizing fin similar to those used on F-86 drop tanks. Hamlin called them his "fun fins." He figured his installation so that the center of the pod was directly on the CG of his aircraft.

Hamlin mounted the pylon supports for his cargo pods to his wing with a series of nut plates under the skin. He reported that he continued to record 165-175 mph block-to-block while pulling 2,500 rpm on his 0-290 Lycoming engine and he couldn't tell any difference in performance versus no pods. He logged more than 830 hours on his busy homebuilt. (The cargo pods had been removed at the time of Hamlin's fatal crash.)

Other builders, including Wes Gardner of Redlands, California, have copied the idea of the pods developed by Bruce Tifft. Gardner flew to

Fig. 8-7. Tifft loads a wooden EZ propeller into one of his cargo pods.

Oshkosh and reported a 3-5 mph speed penalty.

The range and duration of Rutan's designs call for a certain pilot stamina and self-control but enough is enough. A standard Long-EZ with normal fuel tanks can stay in the air well over eight hours, but how many pilots can fly that long without a pit stop? Thus one issue of Rutan's quarterly gave the following relief information:

"We used ⅜-inch plastic line from the local hardware store and left about two feet in each seat. We ran it down the length of the fuselage through the aft bulkhead to the trailing edge of the gear. Then it was run down the trailing edge of the gear and left long enough to protrude out of the wheel pants. To use the relief tubes, uncoil them and plug a rectangular plastic funnel into the end of the tube (Figs. 8-8, 8-9)."

In this era of complete equality, we can pass along an account from one of the long-range feminine pilots from Mojave. It seems that she was flying a Long-EZ on a solo cross-country flight in close formation with two other EZs. When she throttled back and broke formation, one of the other pilots wanted to know if there was a problem.

"No," she replied over the radio. "I'm just going to make a pit stop."

During our discussion, she added that "the only real problem about this whole arrangement is

Fig. 8-8. Long-range plumbing installation shown in the front pit of a Long-EZ.

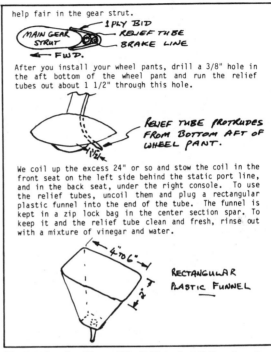

help fair in the gear strut.

After you install your wheel pants, drill a 3/8" hole in the aft bottom of the wheel pant and run the relief tubes out about 1 1/2" through this hole.

We coil up the excess 24" or so and stow the coil in the front seat on the left side behind the static port line, and in the back seat, under the right console. To use the relief tubes, uncoil them and plug a rectangular plastic funnel into the end of the tube. The funnel is kept in a zip lock bag in the center section spar. To keep it and the relief tube clean and fresh, rinse out with a mixture of vinegar and water.

Fig. 8-9. Details of Long-EZ relief tube installation. (courtesy *Canard Pusher*)

getting your slacks back up in that small cockpit."

FLY-INS FOR CANARDS

By no means is all the designer-builder interface on paper. What is becoming an annual meeting keyed on Burt's birthday is a Mojave Fly-in. First there were only a handful of Vari-Ezes. The number grew to 25 aircraft that showed up for Burt's 37th birthday, the largest of the regional meetings to that date. The surprise party (Burt never remembers his birthdate) was put together by his parents, Dick's wife Emily, Pat Storch and Mike and Sally Melvill to honor three birthdays in the Rutan family: Burt, his brother Dick, and their 91-year-old grandfather, Jessie Clyde Goforth from Fresno, California (Fig. 8-10). The cake's inscription was "Happy Birthday, Orville, Wilbur and Grandpa."

VariEzes on the flight line came from near and far. Norman Ross of Victoria, B.C., Canada, brought his grand champion Eze. Gary Johnson came from El Paso, Texas, Ray Dullen was from Tillamok, Oregon, while Charlie Richey flew in from Las Cruces, New Mexico. When you have an Eze, distances really don't seem to matter that much.

A catered lunch was served in the hangar and a magician performed "flight of hand." Builders compared instrument panels (Fig. 8-11), special modifi-

Fig. 8-10. Family portrait on a birthday at Mojave. Standing, left to right are Dick; parents, Dr. George and Irene; sister, Nellie; Burt. Seated is the Rutans' 91-year-old grandfather, Jessie Clyde Goforth.

Fig. 8-11. USAF pilot Ken Swain, Nut Tree, California, shows off his simple VFR instrument panel and side-stick installation. Captain Swain, who flies military for a living, has limited his "for-fun" Eze to a basic panel. He logged 400 hours on this ship in its first two years, including one trip to Oshkosh with his wife when she was five months pregnant—with twins yet!

cations (Fig. 8-12), and generally swapped flight experiences. Five San Diego-based Ezes made a formation fly-by. Later in the day, Burt flew passengers in the Defiant, Dick was in the Long-EZ, Mike Melvill performed with his VariViggen, and several pilots joined up with VariEzes. This was strickly a homegrown fly-for-fun gathering.

Three years later, at another "surprise" birthday party for Burt, there were 45 EZs despite Mojave winds up to and above 40 knots (Fig. 8-13).

Not long ago, 17 VariEzes, one Long-EZ, a VariViggen and a couple of store-built aircraft attended a fly-in at Bullhead, Arizona, organized by the International VariEze Hospitality Club. Members Bill and Julie Lermer of Spring Valley, California, picked the site for this fly-in. The Ezes came from California, Arizona, Utah and New Mexico,

logging a total of 9,000 miles to attend this social and mutual admiration get-together.

Jaded casino gamblers spent considerable time watching the antics of "those funny looking little airplanes" as builders swapped rides, took pictures and watched Dick Rutan perfect his aerobatic routine in the Long-EZ. Non-flying airport visitors asked all the usual questions: What are they? How much do they cost? Where can you buy one? One casino van driver was reluctant to drive behind a VariEze that was warming up because he didn't know which way it was going to go.

The VariEzes proved again that they require a minimum amount of parking space as 12 grouped nose-to-tail in a ramp area usually reserved for a single Beech Queen Air (Fig. 8-14).

The International VariEze Hospitality Club presented awards to Jack and Marilyn Day for the longest distance flown—some 550 nm. Recognition for the most hours logged in a VariEze went to Ed and Joanne Hamlin of Rocklin, California, with more than 500 hours. An all-in-fun Pterodactyl Award went to Mike Melvill who flew in with his Vari-Viggen. The Grand Champion Award for this regional fly-in went to Gary and Betsy Hertzler of Tempe, Arizona. The Galoshes Award for courageous aviating went to Charles and Joan Richey who took off in the snow from Las Cruces, New Mexico, chased an errant compass that was 30° off, and viewed some new scenery enroute to Bullhead.

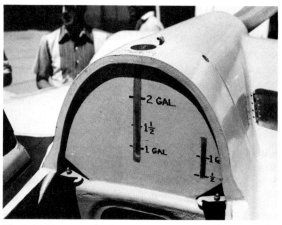

Fig. 8-12. Here's the gauge reading for the two-gallon header tank above and aft the rear seat on a VariEze.

Some 30 VariEzes were expected in Bullhead, but strong Santa Ana winds over the Sierra Madre Mountains discouraged a number of pilots. Dr. Shupe reported his outbound flight to be the roughest he has yet encountered in more than 450 hours in his VariEze, "Puff," decorated with a dragon design. "I was too scared to turn around," he admitted later.

Bullhead City is becoming an increasingly popular fly-in destination since a new ferryboat landing was completed directly across the highway from the airport office. Free 24-hour shuttles take no more than a minute to the Riverside Motel and Casino at Laughlin on the Nevada side of the Colorado River. They replace the six-mile drive over the top of Davis Dam and back down the Nevada side. Shuttle boat service is also provided between the Riverside Casino and the River Queen Motel in "downtown" Bullhead.

First of the new resorts and casinos, the Riverside was begun in 1966 by pilot Don Laughlin.

He named the area after himself and at one time had a 2,800-foot flight strip partially on his property. Laughlin spent a great deal of time admiring the covey of "strange homebuilts" and talking with the Rutans.

The 4,000-foot paved, lighted Bullhead Airport has Unicom on 122.8. The best windsock in the area, however, is the plume of smoke trailing from the tall steam-generating plant just downstream from the airport.

As the fuel crunch increases, VariEze pilots tend to smile most of the time. A survey of visiting pilots at Bullhead indicated that the average VariEze with a 0-200 Continental engine (100 hp) uses 5.8 to 6 gallons per hour, with an average speed of 165-170 mph! That's 28½ mpg or almost 57 seat miles per gallon.

Burt Rutan's efficient canard design becomes increasingly popular, particularly for pilots making long cross-country trips. Two builders who have VariEzes now flying are seriously considering a

Fig. 8-13. Record fly-in of 45 EZs shown on the ramp at Mojave for a birthday celebration.

Fig. 8-14. Twelve VariEzes park nose-to-tail in a corner of the tiedown area at the Bullhead City Airport. Long-EZ is parked in the foreground. Note shadow of camera plane.

round-the-world, two-plane flight in 1981—and their wives plan to go along!

Perhaps it'll all be VariEze.

Hooray for Hollywood

With their futuristic appearance and the proximity of many of their builders to Hollywood, it is not at all surprising that film directors, always looking for the unusual, have put many of Burt's designs on the screen.

The first appearance of one of the aircraft on film was in a 1974 low-budget epic titled *Death Race 2000*. The script covered an auto race of the future; Sylvester Stallone played one of the drivers in one of his early roles. The original VariViggen was flown by Burt in a chase sequence, and a small model of the Viggen was crashed in the film.

Dick Rutan and his blue Lone-EZ were featured in a *Guiness Book of World Records* TV series segment. Film footage showed the Long-EZ flying up the side of the Angel Falls in Venezuela with a

subsequent interview on camera with Dick.

VariEze builders Wes Gardner and Don Richards of Rialto, California, had their pod-equipped Ezes used in an episode of *Blue Thunder*. The planes were fitted out with bright red paint; to portray drones, their canopies were covered inside with darkened Mylar to obscure the pilots. The "bad guys" were scripted to manipulate the drones into ramming the helicopter featured in the weekly TV series. Motion picture pilots Art Scholl and Brad Cantrell did the flying and again, models of the Ezes were blown up on the screen.

Early in 1984, Dick again flew for the movies, this time in a two-hour pilot for Warner Bros. called *Midas Valley*. Again the film depicts the future in a high-technology "Silicon Valley" setting. The ultimate goal for *Midas Valley* is to be chosen for a weekly *Dallas*-type television series.

Undoubtedly, you'll be seeing more and more Ezes—and probably a Defiant or two—on your movie and television screens in the future.

Chapter 9

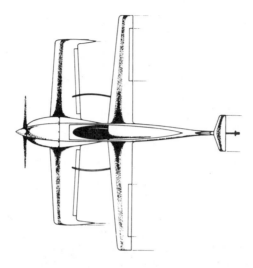

Variations on a Theme

Most people love a change of pace and Rutan is no exception. He has enjoyed completely the development of innovative, one-of-a-kind machines that explore unplowed fields of aviation. Here are two such projects.

GRIZZLY: THE SLOW-SPEED CANARD

Rutan's press preview of his first new project was a jewel worthy of the best of Madison Avenue's press agents. The designer mailed out a simple mimeographed announcement to perhaps 20 of the nation's top aviation writers, advising that a rollout was scheduled.

The Grizzly concept was one of aviation's best-kept secrets. The veteran press crew who assembled at Mojave as a result of Rutan's limited invitation to a scheduled rollout, coupled with a wine-and-cheese buffet, was completely in the dark as to what would be seen. It is a credit to Rutan's reputation that working press representatives of virtually every aviation publication in the country trekked to Mojave to see what was new. Even the

weather cooperated.

Rutan held a pre-inspection briefing inside his hangar on the flight line. First, he introduced Herb Iversen of Ames Industrial Corp. from Bohemia, New York, and announced that this entire company was moving to Mojave to develop new scale model vehicles for flight testing.

Rutan advised that the IO-360 Lycoming powerplant on the Grizzly had been run for the first time on the evening preceding the unveiling for about 30 seconds. The press rollout was actually performed in reverse, with reporters being briefed inside the hangar and the radical new airplane being taxied up in front of the closed doors by Rutan's test engineer Mike Melvill at precisely 2:30 P.M. The hangar doors were opened and the reporters swarmed outside to view the new creation (Fig. 9-1).

The Grizzly is fitted with a sliding canopy with bulging side windows, allowing "straight-down" visibility for the pilots (Fig. 9-2). Fuel is carried in the wing outriggers (Rutan calls them "interconnects"). This novel arrangement keeps fuel away

Fig. 9-1. Press preview of the Grizzly at Mojave. In the background, left to right, are the other Rutan designs: VariViggen, Long-EZ, Defiant and AMS/OIL Racer.

Fig. 9-2. Interested spectators view the Spartan interior of the research vehicle. Note bulged side windows.

from the cabin and provides the torsional bracing required for the forward-swept wings. Deep Fowler flaps average over 50 percent of the chord of each wing and add over 45 square feet of wing area when deployed.

Conventional ailerons are installed at the tip section of each main wing with no spoiler ailerons installed. The tail is completely conventional, with a small ventral fin in front of the large-diameter tailwheel. The Grizzly's cabin converts quickly into a comfortable sleeping compartment for two people. By folding the rear seat forward, there is an unobstructed 78-inch level area for sleeping bags.

Rutan hopes his new Grizzly concept will result in "a rugged bush airplane that will fly just about like a Cub, except maybe slower. If the Grizzly proves not to be a good slow-flying airplane, we won't go ahead with it. That's what a flying test bed is all about."

The prototype was built in Rutan's "back room" and moved to a nearby T-hangar in the middle of the night to keep it away from prying eyes. It had never even been run or taxied until the evening before the press conference.

The Grizzly's double-wheel configuration with four low-pressure tires on the main gear is designed for soft and unprepared fields (Fig. 9-3). Prop clearance with the taildragger configuration is more than adequate for the Hartzell constant-speed Q-tipped propeller.

Stressing again that the Grizzly concept is strictly a test bed, Rutan pointed out that the right wing is of a hollow, sandwich-skin configuration while the left wing is the full-core construction technique pioneered on the VariEze back in 1975.

"Our previous canard aircraft have not been designed for short-field operation," said Rutan. "Thus, many have concluded that tandem-wing aircraft may not be suited for STOL performance. We do not have the definitive answers on this subject, but hope to gather the necessary data during the test program to considerably expand our technology base. We expect the knowledge gained by testing this proof-of-concept aircraft will be invaluable to future designs."

The Grizzly concept is planned to include amphibious floats, but Rutan said frankly that he had not yet figured out their design nor how they will be attached. He plans to make the floats out of low-density foam sandwich core, covered with fiberglass and carbon fiber facings. Float construction will be similar to that of the airframe, except the float will not be hollow. Wheels and brakes will be integral within the float structure and not retractable. Rutan is seriously considering using three individual floats—"just like Glenn Curtiss did back in 1910."

At the time of the rollout, we reported: "Whether the new Grizzly concept ever claws its way into popularity or remains a one-of-a-kind de-

Fig. 9-3. Grizzly lines up at Oshkosh to tow the Solitaire without an engine. Note four-wheel main gear.

Fig. 9-4. Grizzly in flight near Mojave looks like nothing ever seen before.

sign concept, it is certainly a breath of fresh air in the world of light airplanes to see something new—really new—come along. While most of today's production aircraft seem content to make only cosmetic changes in designs that go back for a quarter of a century, it is stimulating to see new concepts like the Grizzly being developed. Who knows, one of these may very well be the general aviation airplane of the next generation!"

When all the Rutan Aircraft Factory airplanes at Oshkosh '82 were ready to fly home, Burt took Grizzly and battled a 20-knot headwind most of the way home. He was heard to mutter something to the effect of "Gimme my Defiant back!"

Several months after the Grizzly first flew, we were talking with Burt at Mojave on a rare day when things were leisurely. He looked at me and asked, "You've never flown in Grizzly, have you?"

I shook my head and we promptly went out and climbed aboard. The cockpit is big and you sit up high. The broad outriggers cut into your peripheral vision as foreign objects, but don't really create blind spots (Figs. 9-4, 9-5).

Rutan fired up the durable Lycoming and we taxied out in one of Mojave's average 25-knot breezes. Of course, the wind was quartering to the close-in runway, so Burt took off on a bias, showing the unusual STOL capability of Grizzly. We aviated slowly upwind and Burt relaxed by flying a series of figure eights around the tall tails of the mothballed Boeing 707s that line Runway 22 at Mojave. Burt had a rare, relaxed smile as the Grizzly handled the choppy winds with ease. For a dedicated designer, Burt is a surprisingly good pilot and maintains his proficiency well.

When it came time to return, we landed across the parking ramp into the wind. Mojave is an uncontrolled airport and many a non-standard flight procedure is condoned, sometimes even encouraged.

AND STILL NOT A HANGAR QUEEN

During a recent visit to Mojave, we saw the Grizzly tied down in the lee of one of the large WWII hangars. The ship has achieved its main research goals, but is still flown on occasion.

"I had an errand down at Agua Dulce just the other day and took Grizzly," said Burt. "We've always planned to take it out on a back country aircamping trip, but just haven't yet found the time.

"I still want to put it on floats, and maybe one of these days we'll have the time to play with it."

However, the never-ending line of new Rutan projects would appear to preclude the Grizzly on floats for some time to come.

BURT DESIGNS A RACER

Another of Burt's one-of-a-kind designs was in an entirely different flying arena—air racing. He designed a competition racing biplane for Dan Mortensen late in 1979. Sponsored by a synthetic lubrication company, AMS/OIL, the racer was built by a team in Sacramento, California, and first competed at Reno in 1981. The new racer finished only third in the biplane race due to several pylon cuts. Later analysis indicated these cuts were due to roll deficiency and the racer was returned to Mojave for rework.

The little competition airplane had a 250-mph straightaway capability with good handling characteristics once the travel and stiffness of the controls were modified. Basic design was similar to the Quickie, with reversed stagger wings and landing wheels in the canard tips. A small horizontal T-tail was added to operate with the canard elevator control system to increase pitch control at high speeds and in 4G turns. This was the first use of a horizontal tail on any Rutan-designed aircraft (Fig. 9-6).

The AMS/OIL racer was at Mojave one day when we were there. Since publicity is the name of the game with a racing sponsor, Dan Mortensen asked if I'd like to fly the one-of-a-kind competition airplane. Our report of the resulting flight was first

Fig. 9-5. Grizzly with flaps extended is capable of extremely slow controlled flight.

Fig. 9-6. AMS/OIL Racer flown by Dan Mortensen is shown in flight near Mojave.

printed in *Homebuilt Aircraft* Magazine and is presented here with permission:

LET'S FLY THE AMS/OIL RACER

Way down there outside the clear bubble canopy, it was a beautiful scene at Mojave, California. On the broad high-desert airport, Mike Melvill was shooting landings with Burt Rutan's brand new Grizzly; a Volante flying automobile was making fast taxi runs with careful liftoffs on the spacious 9,600-foot main runway, and a Long-EZ or two were cavorting in the calm morning air. It was an ideal day for boring small holes in the sky.

I circled the field leisurely, enjoying being a part of this ideal aviation location where many of the truly new developments in flying machines are in process. I was part of the scene, to be sure. I was flying the sleek new AMS/OIL biplane-class racer that Rutan designed for Dan Mortensen.

It all began with a casual comment during the press conference when Burt Rutan rolled out his Grizzly STOL concept. A string of Rutan's creations were parked out on the ramp for reporters to ogle when they had exhausted viewing on the new contours of the Grizzly. Way down at the end of the line was the AMS/OIL Rutan competition biplane racer, with owner/pilot Dan Mortensen keeping an eye on the festivities.

We all admired the sleek little competition machine and commented casually to Mortensen, "Man, I'll bet that thing is really fun to fly!" Then Mortensen took off and made a couple of passes down the runway and I was sure that it *would* be fun—but I also felt that was the end of the daydream.

Not so! A week or so later there was a letter from Mortensen, who lived in Newcastle, near Sacramento, California, at that time. It began, "I would be more than happy to bring the plane down to you for an evaluation for an article. The insurance requires that you have a commercial rating and belong to EAA and its IAS (aerobatic) division . . . What would be a good day for you, and what is the best airport convenient for you?"

We picked the Mojave Airport where Rutan lives because it has broad runways, sparse desert surrounding the area, no control tower, usually little traffic, and ideal high-desert weather—when the wind doesn't blow. We picked a day before Mortensen was due in Southern California to attend an AMS/OIL Convention at Disneyland. Mortensen took an hour and 45 minutes from Sacramento to Mojave at 10,000 feet, cruising an economy 160 mph at 2,350 rpm on 6.5 gph. I took almost an hour coming up over the hill from Cable Airport with my Cessna 170B. We landed just a few minutes apart.

Looking at the canard racer this time was an entirely different matter. It wasn't just an interesting little airplane that looked like an overgrown, overpowered mean-machine relative of the Quickie. It was a novel, one-of-a-kind competition machine that is perhaps the fastest racing biplane in the air today. Redline speed is tentatively 250 mph, and Mortensen was clocked unofficially at 232 mph around the three-mile course at Reno in 1981 on the first race in which he ever competed.

There was more activity than usual at Mojave when we met Mortensen. Melvill shouldered into a parachute and climbed aboard the brand new

Grizzly for a test flight to explore the travel of the elevator trim. Burt Rutan flew Mike's four-place Grumman as the chase plane with Pat Storch shooting documentary pictures out the open baggage compartment door. Out on the main 9,600-foot runway, a flying automobile (reportedly the Volante) was making high-speed taxi runs and, from a distance, it looked like an occasional liftoff. Research surplus jets prepared for a day's work as one F-100 taxied down the ramp. Yes, Mojave is where things really happen!

Before our flight, only four other pilots had flown the new racer and the plane had just 60 hours total time. Dick Rutan and Mike Melvill did the initial flight test program. Owner/pilot Dan Mor-

Fig. 9-7. Race pilot Dan Mortensen and Burt Rutan compare performance figures at Mojave.

tensen (Fig. 9-7) and his competition racing friend Don Beck have soloed the single-placer. It was a unique experience to join this group.

Before we got down to a serious checkout, I cornered ex-fighter pilot Dick Rutan, who had checked me out in the prototype Long-EZ shortly after it was completed. "What does that little racer fly like?" I asked in private. "It's a creampuff, a piece of cake," he replied with a big grin. "Be sure and make a long, flat approach for landing, but you won't have any problem. Go and enjoy!"

Just about then Mike Melvill taxied in with the Grizzly and I went for another independent evaluation. I'd flown with Mike Melvill previously in his sleek VariViggen, the first to be built from Rutan's plans. He replied candidly, "Well, it doesn't fly like an overgrown Quickie. Those airfoils are designed for 90 degree banks at racing speeds of over 200 mph, so they're not nearly as forgiving as the designs we use on the VariEze and the Long-EZ. They bite you if you get it too slow, but as long as you're a little careful, it's a fine little flying machine."

Well and good. I'd done my homework and had filled out an application to join the EAA's IAC group. That seemed an unusual insurance requirement, since no pilot qualifications are required for membership, but that's what they wanted and that's what they got. When Mortensen and I began to talk, he casually asked, "How much taildragger time do you have?" I nodded toward my Cessna 170B tied down on the flight line, admitted to about 1,700 hours in that ship alone and a "tail-dragging history" going back to Aeronca Ks, a year in the front pit of U.S. Army Stearman trainers, and an overseas tour in the Curtis C-46. (Unbeknownst to me at the time, Mortensen had also done his homework. He'd asked the Rutans if it was okay to turn his one-and-only racer over to me. Fortunately, I was given the nod.)

And so out to the flight line. Mortensen's racer came about after he asked Burt Rutan if he could design a biplane racer that would beat Don Beck's *Sorceress*. Mortensen had the performance numbers for Beck's racer that were printed in a racing book for sale at the Nut Tree Restaurant located northwest of Sacramento. Rutan fed these numbers

into the computer and told Mortensen that he felt he could come up with a winner. The contract was for Rutan to do the designing, with Mortensen having permission to build two airplanes only. Rutan retains the design rights.

Rutan's initial computer runs showed that his new design would beat Sorceress by seven to eight mph on the straightaways and 30 mph in the turn. The initial computer runs called for 240 mph on the race course; Mortensen has already clocked 232 mph.

During the final race at Reno in 1981, Mortensen hit low altitude wind shear and propwash that almost put him out of control on a pylon. Full top aileron was insufficient for a speedy rollout, and further investigation showed that the original aluminum tube aileron linkage was inadequate. Steel tubing of the same diameter and three times the strength is to be installed, aileron stops will be removed, and the aileron travel that was 6 degrees is now 12 degrees, with a design criteria of 16 degrees. At the time we flew the airplane, 12 degrees of aileron travel was much more than adequate.

An estimated 4,000 man-hours went into fabrication of the racer. At least 40 members of EAA Chapters 52 and 526 at Sacramento and nearby Roseville, California, helped on the project. Mike Arnold built the fuselage. Larry Lombard and Mike Dilley spent so much time on the project that both eventually went to work for Rutan at Mojave. Lombard, who worked throughout the project with Dan, has the distinction of receiving a Master's degree in sculpture from a California state university for building a Teenie Too that now resides in the Mather Air Force Base Museum. Lombard and Mike Dilley have a part-time business of carving propellers (Revolutionary Propeller Manufacturing—RPM), which has enough backlog that they're not accepting new orders.

At one time, Dan had five people working full-time on the prototype. The largest part of his cost for development was labor. While the aircraft is technically a homebuilt, it was done as a prototype. Fabrication of the racer was done in a hangar at the Sacramento Executive Airport, where experimental first flights have been a definite no-no since a tragic jet fighter crash several years ago. So the racer was carried on a flat-bed truck to Franklin Field with four pickup trucks as "outriders." First flights were made from Franklin Field.

On one of his early flights, putting time on the new airframe, Mortensen decided to go up to altitude and made an easy cruise climb to 20,000 feet. At that time, the engine had short exhaust stacks that routed hot gasses over the top of the canard in climb. After landing, Mortensen found that one wing panel had been severely damaged from the heat and had to be rebuilt. That's the main reason the racer didn't get to Oshkosh in 1981.

The T-tail on the racer is no add-on. Rutan designed it right into the initial project to provide more elevator authority when you want it for 6G vertical turns. Use of the T-tail makes the structure less susceptible to aeroelasticity loads (bending in flight).

NASA research teams coated the wings of the racer at Reno during a test flight and reported a laminar flow of 60 to 61 percent of the wing area in racing conditions. Thus the experimental airfoil sections, used for the first time on this racer, are doing the job they were designed to do—and doing it well.

Biplane racing specifications call for a minimum 75 square feet of wing area. The Rutan design has 76.5 square feet; that figures out to 14.72 pounds per square foot and a power loading of 20.9. By comparison, a Piper Tomahawk II has a wing loading of 13.39 and a power loading of 14.9.

The actual checkout in a single-place airplane is always an interesting operation. Since most single-seaters are small, you first have to find out if you can physically get into the cockpit. However, Mortensen is almost six feet tall and Rutan had tailored the cockpit to fit Dan (with a reserve for Burt's 6'2" frame), so this didn't prove to be a problem. In fact, both the small seat and back cushions remained in place. After one look at the hardware-store-type canopy latches, I didn't go looking for a parachute. Mortensen assured me that these super-safety latches were on the list for replacement.

For a little airplane—22-foot span on the upper wing and 20'5" on the lower—there is a surprising amount of room in the 22-foot-long fuselage. A 16-gallon fuel tank sits behind the pilot under the turtledeck, and there are two recently-added 7½-gallon tanks in the check cowlings (fairing aft of the engine cylinders) to give a total of 37 gallons (2½ unusable) and enough range to compete in this year's Oshkosh 500.

The instrument panel was fairly standard, with a small radio hanging underneath (Fig. 9-8). Switches for master, radio, and mags were protected by a flip-over lid protruding from the floor. There was more than enough room to get my size-12 shoes up to the rudder pedals. Brakes were the old-fashioned heel variety and just barely adequate. More braking is also on Mortensen's clean-up list.

The rudder pedals are not interconnected and you feel the slack until you put a little pressure on both feet. The heel brake tabs are just a little inboard of the rudder pedal center and this location requires a little jockeying to assure that you're really on the brakes. Mortensen assured me that the brakes would not hold on a mag check over 1500 rpm. He was right!

There's a five-point harness system with a push-to-release similar to that used on Indy cars. One strap comes up from the floor, two over the shoulders, and two across your lap. Put it all together and you have a very close connection with the airframe. Mortensen assured me that the cockpit section was designed to withstand a 22 G load while the entire frame was good for +/−12 Gs. (Later proven the hard way when Mortensen demolished the racer during the 1983 Reno Air Races; he was only slightly injured.)

Mortensen also supplied the background that he had lost one brake during a rollout at the 3,400-foot runway at Lincoln Field. It seems that a hydraulic line was cut by the wheel rim and, after landing, he found that only the right brake was working. Rather than risk a nose-over in the plowed field off the end of the runway, he slowed as much as possible and then locked the right brake. The racer spun 90° to the runway and slid sideways for about

Fig. 9-8. Cockpit interior shows AMS/OIL Racer instrumentation.

400 feet, stopping at the end of the runway with no damage. "After all, there's no way to get a wing tip with this design," he grinned. "You're already landing on the tip."

Unlike most racers, the AMS/OIL biplane has a battery starter and alternator. It seems that Rutan's original specifications called for the battery far back in the tailcone for weight and balance, but Mortensen's crew built the fuselage hell-for-strong, so it was much heavier than anticipated. To solve the weight and balance problem, the engine was equipped with these heavy accessories and the battery mounted forward of the firewall. Total empty weight of the racer is 865 pounds with 1,226 for gross.

Mortensen explained that he preferred carrying the weight of the electrical system because the very low centerline of the racer would make it difficult and potentially dangerous to hand-prop. "You'd almost have to get down on your knees to spin the prop," he commented.

After I settled down in the cockpit, Mortensen helped me slide on his crash helmet and plug in the radio leads. He leaned in, flicked the master switch, and turned on both mags; then a quick burst with the electric fuel pump charged the injected engine—which promptly didn't start. This engine has a novel injection system installed by Duke Dodge of Sacramento. The IO-320-A2B 160-hp Lycoming was built up by Dodge from two run-out Super Cub engines that had already flown 8,000 hours. He added the Bendix fuel injection system with the lines going to the individual cylinders through the original primer line fittings in the non-injected engine. Perhaps this system has been tried by other engine specialists, but Mortensen doesn't know of it.

Finally, using the conventional hot-start procedure (full throttle, mixture off; hit the starter and then quickly decrease the throttle and increase the mixture as soon as the engine begins firing). We were in business; with 80-87 fuel and a 7.5 compression ratio, the engine ran very smoothly.

Both mixture and throttle are on push-pull rods with the throttle on a vernier. I'd have expected a conventional left-hand throttle, but Mortensen doesn't worry much about anything but full bore in racing, so the vernier is satisfactory for him.

Dan had the engine set to idle so slowly that it had quit a few times during rollout. "Don't worry about it in the air or when you have any appreciable groundspeed. However, if it quits as you roll to a stop, take your time and make a normal hot start. If that doesn't work, we'll drive out and help you out. We'll set the idle faster when we beef up the brakes."

There's a conventional Long-EZ-type canopy lock that slips down into a catch in the cockpit. However, because of the high speeds involved, Mortensen had added two breadbox-type latches at each end of the canopy that flip over small brass fittings on the fuselage. There's a certain finality as you latch those down.

Visibility on the ground is excellent. You can see everything except directly over the nose, and by pushing your crash helmet up against the canopy, what's directly ahead is almost visible. The tiny two-inch+ tailwheel made a hollow grinding sound as I taxied out slowly over the rough parking ramp. That tiny tailwheel is from one of Bill Boland's Mong championship racers. With wheels in the lower wing tips, you've got to be careful not to taxi over any of the semi-submerged lighting fixtures implanted in the cement. Maybe they would clear, but I didn't want to find out.

The wing tip landing gear of the AMS/OIL Rutan design is not at its best in a strong crosswind. Dan figures that anything over ten knots, 90 degrees, is a problem, Fortunately, our flight was in super-still conditions.

I called the Mojave Unicom and advised that "Racer 301LS" was taxiing out from Rutan's. Runway 7, parallel to the parking ramp, was in use, so it was only a short taxi to the end of the active strip. With the fuel tank mounted high in the aft fuselage, the auxiliary pump is not used for takeoff or landing. There's no operative trim tab, no gear or flap retraction system, no controllable prop, and no checklist. About the only thing to do is run up to 1500 rpm, check the mags, take a very deep breath—and go!

I waited until Mike Melvill came in for a short-field landing with the Grizzly. As soon as he'd taken off again, I rolled into position and eased in slowly on the power. With spongy brakes and a little tiny rudder way back there somewhere, I didn't want to have a mess of torque to fight. Thus, acceleration was fairly slow.

Directional control seemed to be no problem as the throttle came all the way on. I eased forward on the side-mounted stick in an effort to cut down on the high-angle drag. Eventually the tail came up just a little and I was in the air.

I made a slight nose-up correction—and that was *too* much. The nose began to go up quickly, and I learned immediately that the elevators were very, very sensitive. After a couple of shallow oscillations, I began to get the feel of the thing and I eased—and I do mean *eased*—into a modest climbing left turn out of traffic. When I had a chance to scan the instrument panel, I was already showing 140 mph and going up at what seemed like 2500 fpm. There was no rate-of-climb instrument aboard.

I eased back off the power and established a less spectacular climb while circling the airport. Now was the time to try to get really acquainted with this little beastie. Elevators sensitive? Yes! Rudder and ailerons—normal. Acceleration with throttle application—great! Deceleration with power off—next to nil. Visibility in any attitude, steep turn to climb—excellent. That front canard doesn't get in the way of any viewing.

When about 4,000 feet over the airport, ground elevation 2,787 feet, I decided it was time to explore the slower speeds. Mortensen had recommended 80 mph on final approach, "but you'll probably be doing 90 on your initial approach." It took at least 30 seconds with power off to slow from 140 to 80 mph because of the super-clean little airplane. At 80, I kept coming back very slowly on the side stick. The needle came down to 70 and, as it was approaching 60, the left wing dropped abruptly—no burble, no buffet, no nothing. I was about 60° to the horizon as I instinctively applied power and eased off the back stick.

The ship picked up a little speed and promptly responded to all three controls. We rolled carefully back to straight and level. There would be no slow approach in this airplane.

I circled around, admiring the desert, listening to the Unicom chatter of the incoming pilots and marveling that the reported winds remained calm. That's a rarity at Mojave, where we've taken off in the 170B from the parking lot because I felt it was unsafe to taxi crosswind.

The AMS/OIL racer was a joy to fly. With no parachute and a complex canopy latch, there was only a fleeting thought of aerobatics. Maybe some other time. Rolling in and out of turns required just the thought of moving the controls and a suggestion of pressure. The racer is sensitive to touch—much like a thoroughbred horse—but not what I'd consider too sensitive. After all, its design is for one use only—getting around a three-mile course just as quickly as possible.

With a cruise power setting of 2,350 rpm, I eased the nose down just a little and the airspeed soared from 160 to well past 200 in just a few seconds. Then ease back on the stick and we went up, up, and almost away—great sport, and exclusive as hell!

But all good things must simmer to a halt, and I didn't want to give Mortensen too much ramp-walking anguish watching for his pride and joy to return. So I called in for a landing advisory and began an easy letdown to the active Runway 7, with winds still calm. Runway 3/25 is a mere 5,950 feet long and I remembered Mortensen's caution that I'd probably float all the way to midpoint before touching down with an 80-mph across-the-numbers speed.

The more I looked at the airport, the more the mile-and-a-half of Runway 12/30 looked good. The flying automobile was just completing a run, so I advised Unicom that, at pilot's discretion, I'd elected to use Runway 30. With the first third of 30 off in an area well away from the other runways, there was no traffic conflict.

My approach was high and wide, out over the little railroad town of Mojave, down past the highway that leads to Edwards Air Force Base and into a wide base leg, airspeed still at 130 to 140 mph. I advised Unicom that the racer was turning on a long final for three-zero and boresighted the little biplane toward the numbers. The approach was long and flat. The speed was more than fast enough but the runway was very long. It looked like a friendly situation.

Flicking across the numbers at the end of the runway, I still was indicating 110 mph, so I knew I'd float for a while. I eased all the way off on the power, let the bipe down to what seemed to be about five feet off the runway, and attempted to hold it there. As the speed spilled off, I let down just a little more. The racer is a lot like a sailplane in that there isn't all that much distance between your fanny and the runway on touchdown. I floated a little more and eventually run out of back stick. We dropped in perhaps a foot. About that time I wished that I'd landed out in front of Burt's hangar where the owner could have admired the touchdown, but what the heck—this procedure seemed the safer of the options.

It was a long way to taxi to the approach end of Runway 25 and all the way up the ramp—past the research jets and WWII relics, around the areas where lines of weary jet passenger transports await export or cannibalizing for parts—back to the Rutan ramp.

Dan Mortensen walked out and gave a thumbs-up with a grin. I taxied back to our starting point, pulled the mixture control, cut the switches, and opened the canopy. Only then did I flex my fingers and rub the perspiration from my palms.

And that's what it was like to fly the AMS/OIL Rutan Racer.

KEEPING TABS ON THE RACER

It is always interesting to follow the exploits of an aircraft once you've flown it. Mortensen's AMS/OIL racer had more than its share of excitement. While returning from an airshow in Beckley, West Virginia, Mortensen had a metal racing prop shed a part of one blade.

"The vibration was tremendous," said Dan. "It only lasted four or five seconds, but the wing tips must have been flexing three to four feet. I had double vision while my life flashed before me. I pulled throttle and mixture and hit all the switches in that order almost immediately. Then it finally stopped. Initially I thought I had lost the tail and gone into flutter, but when the prop stopped, I could

see about 17 inches missing. One or two seconds passed, and then I realized that it might burn so I turned off the fuel. I was not wearing a chute.

"I headed down in a steep dive for the Volk Air National Guard runway when the prop started to rotate, causing the engine that was now lying inside the cowl to shift. I immediately returned to straight and level flight and then took what seemed like forever (actually five to six minutes) to get down."

The landing was uneventful and Dan continued on his trip after installing a new engine and prop. However, vibration had broken loose the 22-gallon main fuel tank behind the seat—and it was full at the time. Had the tank shifted another half inch back, it would have jammed the control system.

It took a team of four builders a full month of intensive work to get the racer ready for Reno '83. Dan managed to qualify third at 210 mph and matched the qualifying speed of 217 in gusty winds

Fig. 9-9. Pilot Dan Mortensen walked away from this crash at the Reno Air Races. (courtesy Dan Mortensen)

during practice. Dan was confident that this was his year—but that was not to be.

The AMS/OIL racer was in the ground before the scatter pylon had been passed. Dan was in the pole position at about 35 feet when another pilot turned in front of him. Dan reacted to avoid a midair with two other pilots out of sight just above and just behind him.

"If I had pulled up or gone in any other direction, I would have hit one of the other planes," Dan told us later. "I was trapped. I almost made it through underneath, but my ground track must have carried me through the propwash of one of the other racers. I hit the ground left wheel first and almost level in about a 3 to 5 degree nose-down attitude at 200 mph. The airplane must have bounced and slid along pretty much in a straight-ahead situation until just before stopping, when it pivoted 180° and rolled once. Amazingly, the fuel tanks were intact and did not break. My deceleration was slow and intermittent, which saved me. My five-point Indy seatbelt did not fail . . . I had black-and-blue marks to show where I was wearing it."

Mortensen called Burt to verify the 22G cockpit since there was no G-meter in the airplane. From the looks of the wrecked airplane, very substantial forces were withstood (Fig. 9-9).

In looking ahead, Mortensen plans to have the University of Illinois rebuild the airplane since the fuselage was intact. As a school project, this may take several years.

Dan feels that the canard will never race again since its particular race class has been disbanded. However, Dan plans to race again in his venerable Mong that is being rebuilt with new airfoils and new powerplant.

And that's what happened with this one-of-a-kind Rutan design.

Dan Mortenson now runs a weekly aviation radio show in Southern California and handles a series of aviation ground school courses. His AMS/OIL Racer, battered and bent, is in a warehouse in Duluth, Minnesota, awaiting finalization of an insurance claim. "I'd like to rebuild it and fly it again sometime," said Mortensen.

Chapter 10

Side-by-Side

There isn't an aircraft designer alive who really likes to have builders change his plans, and Burt Rutan is no exception. However, he does recognize that builders have the inalienable right to assemble their planes any way they want, and the designer can't do a thing about it except disown the effort.

On at least two separate occasions, Rutan has cooperated with designers who made a conscientious effort to modify Rutan's original design and come out with a variation that had merit. One such variation was the Cozy, Nat and Shirley Puffer's side-by-side modification of the Long-EZ. The other was Dave and Kathy Ganzer's Gemini, a two-place, side-by-side, push-pull variation of the four-place Defiant.

COZY WITH THE PUFFERS

The side-by-side Cozy was developed by Nat and Shirley Puffer of St. Paul, Minnesota, originally as a one-of-a-kind modification of the Long-EZ for their own use. However, a number of homebuilders are buying Puffer's plans to modify the basic

Long-EZ during construction to come out with a side-by-side airplane (Fig. 10-1).

Prior to the Cozy, Puffer had begun a BD-5 before the VariEze appeared, but soon changed his game plan. He spent 22 months in completing the conventional VariEze, then began looking for another project. At this time, Burt was just starting on the Long-EZ project and was anything but enthusiastic about a drastic modification that the side-by-side concept could involve—particularly center of gravity problems that might arise from either a single pilot or two heavy aviators along the same weight reference point.

Puffer bought a set of Long-EZ plans and went to work on his own. Perhaps a year later, Burt became a bit exhausted answering questions about "Why not a side-by-side model?" and agreed that the Cozy might be acceptable.

Puffer feels that there are at least four basic areas where the Cozy has a personal appeal to many pilots:

□ Side-by-side seating, which is more inti-

Fig. 10-1. Nat and Shirley Puffer have ample room in the side-by-side cockpit of their Cozy. The Puffers (photographed at Oshkosh) have an investment of $15,000 in their airplane (1984 dollars).

mate, allows better communication between pilot and passenger, allows passenger to share piloting and navigating work loads, and provides more space for chart work.

☐ Full dual controls, which allows the aircraft to be flown equally well from either side. The passenger can learn basic flying skills more easily, and there is less danger to passenger and pilot if pilot is incapacitated.

☐ Larger instrument panel, with ample room for good instrumentation and avionics, plus someone to help operate them, provides an added margin of safety over an airplane not so equipped when deteriorating weather is

encountered, as it sometimes is on long cross-countries.

☐ A large luggage compartment in the rear, which could alternately be used as a third seat, subject to weight-and-balance limitations.

Rutan checked the original Cozy drawings, calculated the flight characteristics, and discussed possible marketing of the package. Construction took one year longer than Puffer's VariEze, and the Cozy was first shown at Oshkosh in 1982. The width of the fuselage was measured from a Cessna 150 and built at 38 inches across the shoulders. The wider fuselage required adding additional structure, including a keel the entire length of the fuselage.

All engine and flight controls, except sticks on the outside of either pilot, are mounted in a center console. There are dual rudder pedals and brakes, a full set of IFR instruments, and a complete stack of King Silver Crown avionics. All antennas are homemade and buried in composite structure. The ADF loop antenna is under the front seat. The cockpit canopy came from a KR-2.

Puffer, a former chemical engineer for duPont and a WWII Navy pilot, checked with several other aeronautical engineers and then decided on eight inches more canard span to compensate for any heavier-than-normal front seat loading. The engine went aft 1.75 inches to help offset any extra front seat weight. The final empty weight was 904 pounds, including instruments and avionics.

Puffer had hoped to turn the package over to Rutan to supply plans and product support, but Rutan had other projects under development, including the SCALED effort. He offered Puffer a license to commercialize the Cozy using Long-EZ plans and technology. Since Puffer was set to retire from 3M shortly, he took up the challenge and is putting together a Cozy package for interested builders.

While prices tend to escalate, at the time the Cozy was proposed as a homebuilder's project, all the raw materials were valued at about $3,600 with a building time estimated at 1,700 hours. Using prefab parts common to the Long-EZ—landing gear, cowling, welded engine mounts, etc.—you can add another $3,000 and save 500 man-hours, some all-up weight, and weeks of frustration. The cost of the 118-hp Lycoming 0-235 engine depends on condition and hours logged; overhauled engines are between $3,000 and $6,000. Including all available prefab parts, IFR instruments, and a zero-time or new engine, Puffer can see an investment of $15,000 (1984 dollars).

In a newsletter to potential Cozy builders, Puffer stressed not changing the design and other limitations as follows:

We have had questions such as folding the fuselage in half for trailering, expanding the fuselage to carry four people, installing larger engines, using a turbine, and even installing floats. We are going to have to take a hard and fast stand. We will not condone any changes, because we cannot predict what the effect might be without first testing it ourselves. We are optimizing our design, and it works well. If you follow the plans, you can build a very nice airplane, and it should perform like ours. If you don't follow the plans, you cannot call it a Cozy, and you are on your own. You will have to assume the responsibility of proving that it is safe, and all the expense and flight testing this entails.

We will also have to take a hard and fast stand on the limitations of this design. It is suitable only for two average or smaller sized people in the front seat. That means 340 pounds maximum, fully dressed, in the front seat, period. Not 345 or 350, counting on squeezing in just a little more than the designer intended—340 pounds, period! And of course anything less is all for the plus. Large people have almost every advantage in life, but flying a Cozy is not one. This limitation is not arbitrary. It is a fact of life in a canard configuration where the pilot and passenger sit 40 inches ahead of the CG. And don't expect me to privately test this airplane way beyond these limits, because you don't reach my age taking reckless chances.

The other limitation on the Cozy is minimum front seat weight. Each airplane might be slightly different, depending on how the individual builder builds and equips it. I have a minimum limit of 185 pounds, but I only weigh 150 pounds. This means that when I fly solo, I have to add ballast to the compartment in the nose to compensate for the absence of my normal passenger (my wife). . . Anyone who is not willing to accept the responsibility of CG management should not build a Cozy (or any other airplane, for that matter). I made this decision three years ago and have not regretted it one second since. I considered it a small sacrifice for all the benefits and pleasures this configuration offers. However, Burt was quick to point out that there might be some who would ignore the rules for long life, and who are prone to take unnecessary chances. If you are responsible, you can have the best of both worlds with a Cozy.

Cozy Specifications/Performance;
engine, Lycoming 0-235 118

Span	26.1 ft.
Area	95.6 ft.^{2}
Empty Basic	850 lb.
Empty Equipped	900 lb.
Solo Weight	1,100 lb.
Gross Weight	1,500 lb.
Max. fuel	52 gal.
Cabin L/W/H	100/40/38
Max. front seat	340 lb.
Takeoff solo/gross	670/1,050 ft.
Climb solo/gross	1,500/900 fpm
Cruise 75% 8,000 ft.	180 mph
Cruise 40% 1,200 ft.	143 mph
Max. range* 75%	1,200 mi.
Max. range* 40%	1,800 mi.
Ceiling solo/gross	25,000/20,000 ft.
Ldg. Dist. solo/gross	550/950 ft.

* 1 hr. reserve

The side-by-side Cozy is proving to be a popular variation on a theme. The Puffers took their prototype N22CZ to Oshkosh in 1983 and promptly sold 15 sets of plans at $200 each. Nat Puffer advised that the complete plans include 30 large drawings and a 20-page, 11 × 17-inch builder's manual. This step-by-step book has nearly 200,000 words and 1,000 illustrations. An additional 400 information sheets were sold at Oshkosh.

Cozy builders will be provided with a quarterly newsletter with any corrections or changes in the plans, plus builder support material. An example of these tips is that "an inexpensive substitute for peel ply is to buy mill ends of nylon, polyester, or Dacron at your wife's fabric shop. Make sure it is a hard, plain, non-fuzzy weave. Test the swatch first before committing an entire layup. Fuzzy or stretchy weaves will not release."

Not all Cozy builders are after the side-by-side seating. Nat reports that one rather large gentleman—over 6 feet and perhaps 240 pounds—was admiring the Cozy at Oshkosh and asked about building it. As subtly as he could, Nat advised that he was a little too large. The gentleman replied,

"You don't understand. I am going to just put a *single* seat up front!"

"What a clever idea," thought Nat. "Why didn't I think of it? A Cozy fuselage with Long-EZ control arrangement—what a natural! It would be like a first-class seat on a 747!"

From a purely personal standpoint, we viewed the Cozy at Oshkosh on two successive years. This mammoth EAA Fly-in has what is called a "Dead Grass Award" that arises from the packing of grass under the feet of people who have circled any plane tied down in the display area. If the Cozy didn't win that award, it was a strong contender.

On our way home from Oshkosh '83, we heard the call sign "Cozy Two Two Charlie Zulu" on an FAA Flight Service Station frequency somewhere over southern Iowa or northern Missouri. As soon as Nat had completed his radio transmission, we cut in briefly on the same frequency, requesting that Two Charlie Zulu go to 122.75. We both changed frequencies and compared last-minute notes in flight before the Puffers headed for Minnesota and we continued on to California. Yes, it's really a small world when you fly.

A SENTIMENTAL ATTACHMENT

Anyone who has ever owned an airplane for any period of time has developed a rapport, consciously or otherwise, with that inanimate piece of machinery that has taken you safely over some horrendous terrain in all kinds of weather. Thus it was not really surprising to find the following note to Rutan's builders from Nat and Shirley Puffer as they watched their VariEze head out with a new owner:

We stood there with tears in our eyes as our VariEze, N2NP, took off, dipped her wings at us, and disappeared in the southwestern sky. What a proud airplane she was, gleaming in the early morning sun, waxed to showroom quality, with her new crank-up nose gear and freshly topped engine with its throaty powerful sound. We had been such close friends.

She had been like a child, needing to learn a few things at first, but rapidly instilling confidence and executing every command with safety and dispatch. We had shared many fond experiences—the envying admiration of many friends, her Oshkosh debut, the LBF races, sailing over vast plains and tall mountains—and we loved her. Perhaps she, too, felt a touch of nostalgia as she waved goodbye but she could feel the firm and confident hand of Lt. Col. Bill Looke on her stick and was ready to go wherever he commanded, like the faithful and obedient servant she was.

Perhaps it was for the best, because in recent months she had waited patiently in the hangar for a chance to fly, and she was repeatedly disappointed when the hangar door would open and her owners would choose instead the Cozy.

But it was love at first sight when she met her new owner, and here was the chance she had been waiting for, to get back in the sky and fly—to be off to new and exciting places once again. She is a proud airplane and deserving of respect and admiration for what she is and what she can do.

It was good for her. We had brought her into the world and trained and sheltered her. Now she was ready to go out and prove herself to others. *Arriverderci*, N2NP; our best wishes go with you!

GEMINI: A PUSHER WITH PULL

The scaled-down Gemini push-pull was developed in San Diego, California, on a shoestring basis by Dave and Kathy Ganzer. We had the opportunity to fly the ship briefly with Dave Ganzer shortly after Oshkosh '82. The following report of that flight was originally prepared for *Homebuilt Aircraft* magazine and appeared in its December 1982 issue:

When Rutan introduced his four-place Defiant push-pull to the aviation community back in 1978, he started a whole new way of thinking for sophisticated homebuilders. As a direct result of Defiant, Dave and Kathy Ganzer of San Diego, California,

Fig. 10-2. Dave and Kathy Ganzer stand beside their push-pull Gemini at Oshkosh. The camping gear beneath the aircraft came with them from California.

started with just a dream and developed Gemini, a two-place push-pull with a 165-mph top speed and range of 1,200 to 1,400 miles.

The Ganzers are full-grown people and designed their homebuilt to fit. The Gemini has a large 17 cubic foot baggage compartment behind the seats that is accessible in flight (Fig. 10-2). The wide instrument panel has all the room that's needed for a full and expensive IFR package. Powerplants are inexpensive Type IV VWs used commercially on vans and the 914-4 Porsche. The engines are modified for dual ignition, and electrical systems are independent on each engine (Fig. 10-3).

The Gemini was flown to Oshkosh '82 by Dave and Kathy Ganzer shortly after the required 40 hours were flown off. Its first flight was just six weeks before Oshkosh.

The Ganzers logged 13 hours dodging weather to Oshkosh and 14 hours on the return flight. Their first leg was nonstop from San Diego to Albuquerque, nearly 700 statute miles, in five hours on 30 gallons of fuel (6 gph).

While Gemini didn't win any of the new design awards at the EAA Fly-in, there was enough interest in the new airplane to convince the Ganzers to go ahead with their flight-test program and to plan providing plans and bills of materials to Wicks Aircraft Supply in Illinois about the beginning of 1983. Dave Ganzer reports good cooperation from Wicks throughout the project. They have not accepted any advance orders and will not accept any money until the flight-test program is completed and plans are drawn professionally. At that time, they will be able to quote a realistic price for plans. At the present time, Dave says that he has over $18,000 and almost one year of full-time work on the project, plus part-time efforts for another year.

Dave is quick to credit his wife with a large portion of the effort in getting the Gemini project into the air. "She was right in there mixing epoxy and helping on lay-ups," he said. "Fortunately, neither of us is allergic to the composite materials." Kathy also went to work full-time in an auto parts

Fig. 10-3. Gemini is powered with two VW Type IV engines, each weighing 188 pounds complete with starter and alternator.

Fig. 10-4. During construction of Gemini, Ganzer was assisted by Richard Hodgkins. This photograph was taken before engines were mounted.

shop during the final year of the project to keep the family bills paid.

During the final rush to the wire to get the new push-pull to Oshkosh, Dave and Kathy were helped by Wayne Smith (a Q-2 builder), Mark Clements, and Dan Sutherland. Richard Hodgkins also shelved work on his Long-EZ to help the project along (Fig. 10-4). "They're all airplane nuts like me," commented Ganzer.

The Gemini design was aided by Burt Rutan almost from the start. Ganzer showed Rutan early drawings from a 20-day class on aircraft design conducted in San Diego by Ladislao Pazmany, designer of the P1-1, P1-2, and P1-4, and many other homebuilt designs for the EAA Chapter 14.

"My wife and I wanted a side-by-side airplane," explained Dave. "We had built a VariEze and found that Kathy wound up in the backseat with all our baggage carried in her lap—the longer the trip, the higher the pile of baggage. That wasn't so much fun, so we decided to design and build our own side-by-side airplane."

The main cabin of the Gemini is 41 inches wide, but elbow room in the strakes goes out to 64 inches. During a subsequent flight with Dave, I found the cockpit to be plenty large enough for a 6'2" frame. The cabin structure is such that the seat backs cannot be removed, so overnights at the airport will require camping out, "but my wife and I don't mind that at all," said Ganzer.

"We are thinking about a Dragonfly, but began kicking around the concept of a push-pull. Burt looked at the original drawings and ran them through his computer. He also did the structural engineering on the canard. The main wing panels are the same as on the Long-EZ except that the entire structure is 18 inches wider with a different center section," explained the designer/builder. "The front canard is altogether different from the Long-EZ and has the same airfoil as the AMS/OIL biplane racer that Rutan designed. The landing gear is made of the same material as the Long-EZs and was built by TASK Research in Santa Paula, the outfit that builds gear legs for Rutan's designs—but a new mold was required."

Continuing developmental work in propellers,

adding gear doors, and modifying rear engine cooling is expected to pick up cruising speed to the 165 mph called for in the original design.

Dave Ganzer is a foreign automotive mechanic by trade and chose the Type IV VW engines because of their reliability and small frontal area. They were powerplants he knows, as well as how to work on them. The engines were modified by Custom Aircraft Engines in North Carolina and then put on Gemini. Ganzer was well satisfied with the basic modifications, including replacement of the No. 4 main bearings. However, he did have more than his share of engine accessory problems during ground runs and initial flight testing at Brown Field, just north of the Mexican Border.

Each VW Type IV engine weighs 188 pounds, complete with starter and alternator. These engines are 30 pounds heavier than the Type I, II, and III engines. Ganzer plans to install RaJay turbochargers on each engine as an option before the project is completed.

While talking about engines for homebuilders, Ganzer commented that Continental Motor's new proposal to sell 100-hp engines in knocked-down kit form is "the greatest thing to come along for a homebuilder. If you can build your own airplane, assembling the engine is really a piece of cake." (Of course, Ganzer is already a top automotive mechanic.)

Gemini has completely redundant electrical systems. There are two separate fuel systems, with the front engine drawing from the left tank. A crossfeed system is built into the airplane so that the entire 50 gallons can be used (25 gallons in each wing). However, in the event of a fuel pump failure on either engine, it is presently impossible to get fuel from "the other can" to the operating engine.

Presently, the new push-pull has a fully castering nosewheel and is steered simply by brake application. Ganzer plans to install a conventional steerable nosewheel interconnected with the rudder pedals. He may also expand the wing tip rudder area to improve directional control.

Dave has used a number of off-the-shelf items with good success. For example, the carburetors are from a Datsun 240Z; power for nose gear retraction is supplied by an outboard motor power tilt unit; the alternators are from a Honda, and the oleo system for the existing nose gear is from an Aero Commander Lark.

When the project is ready to put on the market, Ganzer plans to have approved subcontractors prefab the landing gear, molded cowls, and all welded structure. The canopy is from a Dragonfly, so that's already available.

On his first flight, Dave found it necessary to change the angle of incidence on the canard from .5 to 1.5 degrees. He still plans to make an additional change in the airfoil on the elevator of the canard so that it will trail more smoothly in level flight. During my flight with Ganzer, the canard was still trailing low in level flight, resulting in somewhat restricted up-elevator and adding considerable drag.

Ganzer spent more time flying single engine than he would have preferred in initial testing. Even before his first flight, the oil cooler blew off the engine on startup. On his second flight, after a minute and a half the front engine began sputtering and "really got my attention," he said. "It would run okay at 20 inches, but at full power it would cut out. I thought I had a classic fuel-flow problem, but it wasn't until I switched mags front and rear and retimed the engines that I was able to find the problem.

"On one of the early flights, both engines quit at 500 feet and I was barely able to get back to the runway safely. Fortunately, I'd begun my flying in sailplanes and was quite familiar with a broken-towrope technique. When you're out of thrust at low altitude, there's no time to fool around—drop the nose and begin turning. The problem proved to be spark plugs in the wrong heat range. Now that I've changed plugs, I've had no further serious problems except enroute to Oshkosh after a night at Liberal, Kansas. The rear engine wouldn't start and Kathy and I tore it down on the ramp in about 15 minutes. The problem proved to be an exhaust valve stuck in its guide by lead deposits from 100/130 fuel. We were shortly in the air again."

"Actually, I believe that the Type IV VW is a fine engine for aircraft just as soon as you get the bugs out of a new installation," he explained. "This 2000cc engine will put out an honest 65 horsepower at 3100 rpm and is designed to redline at 3600 rpm, where it should develop 75 horsepower. It is much stronger structurally than the little Bug engines and can be bored out to 2600cc. Anyway, I've wanted VW power for a long time rather than installing 30 to 40-year-old aircraft engines."

Ganzer is doing some long-range thinking about setting up a small shop to modify the Type IV VW for use in his aircraft, but that project is still a year or two away. First he wants to complete his flight testing and get a set of plans drawn and approved. He also wants to have Burt Rutan fly the Gemini and make an evaluation. He feels that Gemini is particularly suited as a follow-on project for VariEze builders because the structure and assembly techniques are similar.

Prior to his first flight at Brown Field, Ganzer did many runway flights, lifting off to 10 or 15 feet and flying for 20 seconds or so. He reported that he still had 3,000 feet of runway ahead when he chopped the power.

Actually, the airplane was signed off for cross-country by the FAA on the Tuesday before Oshkosh. "We almost didn't make it," said Dave; "but the FAA Inspector Jerry Berube from Long Beach was decent to work with and knew overall systems quite well."

During his initial eight hours of shakedown time, Ganzer reported that most of it was single-engine because of the engine problems discussed above. Because of these problems, the designer is even now considering prepackaging VW Type IVs for builders who eventually purchase his plans.

Dave admitted that the stretch run to complete Gemini so that it could be displayed at Oshkosh was a strain. "I was pretty well burned out after a month or two of working full-time on the airplane. Aircraft homebuilding is supposed to be fun, not just work."

However, the effort to complete Gemini before Oshkosh appears to be paying off. The Ganzers report that many of the people who viewed the new Gemini commented, "We want to start building this. It's ideal for a VariEze builder." At least a half-dozen people are impatiently waiting for drawings.

According to Ganzer, it doesn't take a twin-engine rating to fly Gemini. He says that FAA personnel have read FAR 61.31 and feel that a twin rating is not required for a homebuilt flying with an experimental certificate.

Dave Ganzer grew up around airplanes. His father Ray Ganzer learned to fly in the late '50s and owned a 1946 Ercoupe from the time Dave was six years old. Dave designed, built, and flew a rigid-wing monoplane hang glider when he was 19 years old. He didn't get banged up because the ship had three-axis controls. It was soared at Torrey Pines for 30 minutes at a time, but Dave reports that it was such a hassle to transport the ship back to the top of the 300-foot cliffs after a beach landing that he went ahead into conventional gliders and had an FAA license at age 20. He went on to solo the Ercoupe and picked up his private license in 1979.

When the VariEze first came out, Ganzer saw one at Tulare, California, and decided that was the airplane for him. His dad and his wife helped with the VariEze project, which was completed in 2.5 years.

Ganzer explains that he is not a high-time pilot; he has about 600 hours in power and 20 hours in gliders, but he feels completely at ease in the new Gemini. However, he is a surprisingly adept formation pilot, as we found out later on an aerial photo session. He explained that he learned formation flying while touring with a group of VariEze pilots from San Diego who delighted viewers at Gillespie and other airports with their formation takeoffs and fly-bys.

Kathy Ganzer has yet to log any formal flight instruction time, but that's on the family agenda just as soon as finances permit. She should learn quickly, having spent more than 200 hours in the backseat of the VariEze plus the hours on the tip to the EAA Fly-in in The Gemini. There are no right-hand rudder pedals on The Gemini, providing additional leg room for the passenger/copilot but the ship can be flown quite comfortably in the air without rudders by using the stubby center-mounted control stick.

When it came time for me to fly with Dave, I slid up on the left wing strake and swung over into the amply sized cockpit. The canopy is hinged down the right side, so you've got to get in from the left. Once you settle down in the cockpit, you feel like you are in other Rutan designs with the supine seating. Ganzer says that this tilt-back posture is comfortable on a long trip and that he likes the arrangement. As in earlier flights in Rutan's Long-EZ, once I had been in the air for a few minutes, I forgot all about the slanted seat.

Ganzer fired up the rear engine, and we taxied out between the hangars to call Gillespie ground control. The cockpit of The Gemini is very noisy at the present time since no effort has yet been put into soundproofing or engine exhaust modification. The elbow room in each strake is very comfortable and there's no feeling of being cramped. In fact, I would have preferred an inch or two of cushion under my tailbone to improve visibility over the nose, particularly in climbout.

As we neared the run-up area, Ganzer fired up the front engine and closed the canopy to within a couple of inches of the locked position. He checked the mags, front and rear, looked at fuel quantity and pressure gauges, and locked the canopy carefully. An open canopy in flight is the number one no-no! The tower gave us the verbal nod to go, and we cleared out on the main runway.

Initial ground acceleration was not as fast as I had anticipated. I can see why Ganzer has not yet firmed up his prop configuration. The full-castering nose gear (like the defunct American Yankee) requires noticeable braking to get a smooth rollout started. The rudders are not particularly effective until shortly before liftoff.

Since Ganzer is already working on a canard elevator modification, perhaps a fully-slotted elevator for more efficiency, it wasn't surprising that he was not able to lift off the nose gear until we were passing 70 mph. Shortly thereafter, the mains came unstuck and we climbed out indicating 85 mph. The weather was a scorching 95° F., so our rate of climb was averaging between 600 and 700 fpm. The nose gear came up quickly—in just two or three seconds—with its seagoing hydraulic electric actuator doing the pushing and our rate of climb increased perhaps 75 to 100 fpm.

The weather was hot, humid, and hazy. At 4,000 feet we were out of most of the haze, and I tried my hand at Gemini's stick controls. The ailerons were comfortably light while the elevators are heavy and sluggish. That deficiency is due for a change. Ganzer wants to develop a relatively equal control touch for each of the three axis surfaces. He will lighten the elevator touch by changing the camber of the surface and perhaps increasing the angle of incidence of the canard. Increased rudder area can't help but improve directional control. However, these changes are minor and are to be expected in any complex prototype.

Dave demonstrated single-engine performance at 4,000 feet by cutting the mixture on the front engine, using the short left handle just forward of the longer-handled throttles. The engine slowed up but continued to windmill clear down to a mild stall that occurred at about 70 mph indicated. Dave has since installed a new prop on the front engine that greatly improves single-engine rate of climb, and this prop can be stopped in flight at about 80 mph.

Airspeed readings are still somewhat of a mystery because there isn't any spot on the airplane where the air isn't moving rapidly. Presently, the static source is merely inside the cockpit so that indicated airspeed numbers are merely guesstimates. As an alternate method, airspeed parameters have been installed with a calibrated chase plane. Minimum speed at aft CG is 58 mph.

Single-engine climb appears to be about 200 fpm on the rear engine and 150 fpm on the front powerplant, according to Ganzer. Such small rates of climb are difficult to calibrate accurately, but Ganzer has proven to his own satisfaction that he can maintain 6,000 feet on either engine at full gross weight.

We tried a couple of full stick-back stalls with the predictable canard response—the front lifting surface runs out of speed and drops slowly to pick

Fig. 10-5. Gemini in flight over smoggy Southern California.

up the needed three or four miles per hour to put it back flying again. This basic canard design, as old as powered airplanes themselves, never ceases to amaze me with its simplicity of aerodynamics.

Visibility on letdown was very good, and we swung into a wide pattern to space ourselves behind a Cessna 150 with a student pilot. There was no speed brake on the Gemini, so a very wide, flat approach was in order. Ganzer plans to install a speed brake, about 12″ × 36″ of flap surface that will extend aft of the nose gear, before the drawings are finalized.

The nose gear came down and its green light so indicated. This slowed us up, but not very much. Dave held a conservative 90 to 92 mph turning final and 85 across the numbers. The clean push-pull floated a ways, and we touched down between 65 and 70 mph indicated. However, with only minimal braking, we made the first turnoff, so it seems that Gemini will be easily at home at any field where a pilot would put a Long-EZ.

The whole concept of the Gemini (Fig. 10-5) is intriguing. You have readily available powerplants, reliable once they're debugged. You have a roomy cabin with centerline thrust simplicity. You have that ever-lovin' multi-engine security blanket that makes night and overwater flights no sweat. Once it is completely finished, you will have a transportation machine with the space for a full panel and a fuel range of up to 1,400 miles.

The Gemini fills a much-needed gap in aircraft development.

Subsequent to the above-reported flight, the Ganzers put a total of some 150 hours on the Gemini before an engine went sour. Refinements on the canard design were started at about the same time that Dave Ganzer went to work at SCALED Composites, Inc., at Mojave, trading working on VW engines for building such state-of-the-art machines as Starship I.

At this writing, the Gemini is in a hangar in San Diego and refinement efforts are again in the planning stage.

Chapter 11

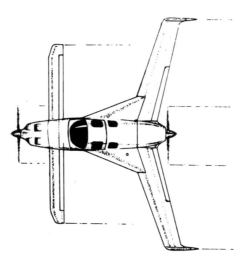

Defiant: From Alaska with Love

The Defiant design was developed as a new-concept light twin with an engine on each end. Right from the start, its fuel economy, safety, and performance were outstanding. The original Defiant was built as a proof-of-concept prototype that worked so well that it has continued to perform with no major modifications as the RAF workhorse for many years.

FIRST FLIGHTS

Within a few days of the Defiant's first flight, Rutan had a newsletter on the way to his builders. Some of his youthful enthusiasm spills over in the words describing this first test flight:

Our new light twin made its first flight on June 30, 1978, with Burt at the controls (Fig. 11-1). Within one week Burt and Dick had logged enough flying for FAA to remove its area restriction and had obtained all basic performance verifications. The only maintenance or adjustments required has been changing the stiffness of the nose

gear steering pushrod. This has been the cleanest initial test program we have seen on any type aircraft.

Curtis Barry, Port Jervis, N.J. won the Name-the-Plane contest. He added that Defiant infers, "the aircraft defies all the common assumptions about current production twin engine aircraft—in pilot skill required, safety, performance, construction, and handling." We waited until after the aircraft had flown to name it, as we wanted to be sure it did indeed meet the above definition. As those of you that have recently visited know, we are extremely excited around here, since we are finding that Defiant actually is exceeding the estimated performance and is verifying the no-procedure-for-engine-failure design goal. It doesn't take a lot of study to realize the impact on flight safety of a twin that not only has no appreciable trim change at engine failure, but requires *no pilot action* when it does fail. You can fail an engine at rotation for takeoff or during a go-around in the landing flare. The pilot does nothing; he climbs out as if nothing happened. He has no prop controls to identify and

Fig. 11-1. The Defiant makes a low pass near a crowd at the Mojave Airport. Even in hot desert air, there are no cooling problems.

feather. He has no cowl flaps to open, no wing flaps to raise, no minimum control speed to monitor (he can climb better than the other light twins even if he slows to the stall speed), no retrimming is required; he can even leave the gear down with only a 50 fpm climb penalty. The only single engine procedures are the long-term ones: (1) cross feed if you want to use all fuel on operative engine, (2) magnetos off. Note that, in general, you do not lose the alternator or vacuum pump on the failed engine since the engine windmills at 1,000 rpm (fixed pitch prop). Why no cowl flaps? The two undraft cooling systems (Fig. 11-2) were designed to have large positive cooling pressure increases with power and angle of attack. When you are cruising, the cylinder head temps stabilize at 370° F. If you then fail an engine and execute a full power climb and slow to best single-engine climb speed, the full-power engine will cool to 350° with no pilot action (same mixture). The engine installations are simpler than the most simple single. Baffling is less complex,

blast tubes for mags or ram air plumbing for carb and carb heat are not required. There are no oil coolers. Oil temps run to 200° F during a climb to 15,000′ and stabilize at 190° F at high cruise at outside air temperatures of 40° above standard conditions!

The most surprising good news is that the Defiant does not have the annoying, loud, out-of-sync noise common to the Skymaster. The pilot has to split the throttles considerably to detect out of sync at high power, and at low or medium power the sync noise is not detectable. The sync noise is more objectionable on other twins than Defiant, even though they use constant speed props mounted on wings. We feel the main reason is the high damping of the Kevlar®/wood props and composite structure. Using Flight Research mufflers, the Defiant makes less perceived noise for a ground observer than the average medium performance single.

The airplane is a stable IFR platform (Figs. 11-3, 11-4), with less trim changes than conventional twins. It has a very solid "big airplane" feel. Approach speed is 75 knots at light weight and 85 knots at gross. We are withholding detailed performance data until it is completely generalized and presented for all weights, but the following is typical of that being obtained: cruise at 65 percent power (maximum cruise) at 12,000′ is 188 knots (216 mph) without wheel pants. Single engine climb gradient (foot increase per mile) is almost twice that of the new light-light twins at any given loading condition. Single engine service ceiling is well above these aircraft even with the gear down and the airspeed 15 knots off the best climb speed, and

this is obtained *instantly*—not after a clean-up procedure! We gave Joe Tymczyszyn, FAA test pilot from the Los Angeles GADO a ride that included single engine go-arounds initiated in the landing flare. His comments: "Unbelievable, single engine procedures are refreshingly simple."

The Defiant is big inside—2 inches wider elbow room, 8 inches longer cabin, 6 inches more knee room in back seat and 3 feet 3 inches more baggage volume than the Beech Duchess. To get to gross weight in a Defiant you can top the tanks for 1100 NM range, add four 175-lb. adults and add 75-lb. baggage to an IFR-equipped airplane.

Fig. 11-2. Nose-to-nose with the Defiant. Little or nothing has been done to improve this design concept since it first flew in mid-1978.

Fig. 11-3. Left side of the Defiant as it has been instrumented. The aircraft is fully IRF equipped, has redundant electrical and nav com systems.

We have no plans to market Defiant at this time. It is merely a proof-of-concept prototype for aerodynamic research.

DEFIANT MEETS THE PRESS

The Defiant first flew in June 1978. Almost immediately it was shown to the aviation trade press and a mass of laudatory semi-technical information was available to every aviation enthusiast in the world. Full-color covers blossomed throughout the flying publications.

We had the opportunity to be one of the first handful of reporters to share the Defiant's cockpit with Burt Rutan. Actually, it was as a result of this first Defiant flight that Burt finally agreed to go ahead with the book project that you are now reading.

There were only 30 hours logged on the Defiant when Burt Rutan met us at Brackett Field, just east of Los Angeles. A group of interested spectators appeared out of the woodwork as he taxied in alone and shut down the engines. Ground control had a list of questions as long as your arm. Here's an airplane that was *news* from the time it started on the drawing boards.

Before flight, Burt went over many of the design concepts that were outlined earlier in his *Canard Pusher*. Burt emphasized that the new

"push-me, pull-me" design was nothing more than a "POC" (proof of concept) test bed.

Since the project began there have been a couple of "almost starts" toward FAA Certification and a production line. "Pug" Piper initally wanted to finance the development, but Burt decided to do it on his own. After the Defiant first flew "Pug" Piper wanted to set up a very large production, as Burt describes it, "with a lot of retired Beech and Piper people and 'improve' the aircraft, making it closer to the Baron or the Cessna Skymaster in terms of systems. I felt that was the wrong way to go. You can't or you'll wind up like the Lear Fan 2100 which may put composite construction back for years. The Lear needs a low parts count, not the 1,400 present number of parts."

Then Burt met a multimillionaire who offered to finance the project himself on a partnership basis, but he wanted the majority interest in the project for his money and Burt didn't think that was fair. "He was also a pilot and wanted to 'influence' the design," explained Burt; "things like retracting the gear. We didn't go that way."

On another "deal," the proposal was a joint venture with an established composite company in Southern California. This proposal had adequate financing and proper facilities, but the merger of

Fig. 11-4. Right side of the Defiant's cockpit. Notice novel throttles at the bottom of the picture with the pointer on the throttle indicating the appropriate engine. Dual mixture controls are vernier knobs just in front of the throttles. The co-pilot's side stick is at the far right.

talents didn't work out either. "We worked in 180° opposed positions," explained Burt. "We work in a direct way with not many people to make a few sheets of paper. They wanted many people to produce fewer sheets of paper."

As we discovered on our initial flight with Burt, the Defiant does not have the fatiguing out-of-sync propeller beat of most twins. There is a high damping effect of the fixed-pitch Kevlar® wooden props.

In flight, the main wing and winglets are far aft of your normal vision. It takes a look far around your shoulder to even assure that the second wing is following you. Aside from the canard in your field of view, flying the Defiant for me was much like riding the nose of a Northrop T-38 jet trainer where what little wing you have is way back there somewhere.

When Burt demonstrated stalls out of steep climbing turns, there was a certain pucker factor as you waited for this weird bird to fall out of the air. It didn't take long to find out that the Defiant wouldn't stall nor would it spin.

With its clean design, it was a problem to slow down in the traffic pattern. A dive brake would help.

Single-engine procedures were completely straightforward and the number one safety item in the design. A high percentage of conventional twin-engine accidents are caused by slow-speed, engine-out operations, either in checkout or under actual conditions, when the off-center thrust of the "good" engine pulls the airplane up and over into a wild gyration that is frequently fatal. In single-engine operations with the Defiant, the main problem is ascertaining which engine is out. The front

Fig. 11-5. Detail of the nose gear and "rhino" rudder of the Defiant. The state-of-the-art push-pull is tied down outside the RAF buildings at Mojave while other work is done on the single-engine canards.

prop will stop only when the Defiant is slowed to 70 mph.

Just about the only thing that isn't goof-proof in the Defiant is the retractable nose gear. If you forget the gear on the VariEze or Long-EZ, about all that is hurt is your pride, a few coats of paint and maybe a little fiberglass ground off the bottom of the nose. With the Defiant, you'll also prang the front prop and ding the front-mounted "rhino" rudder (Fig. 11-5). Thus, Rutan has a carefully prepared checklist, and he's used it from the beginning.

Aside from the problem in getting slowed down on final approach, landing with the tri-gear is a piece of cake. The canard's up elevator is not strong on the ground and the nosewheel gets to the pavement very shortly after the mains. On that first flight, we shot landings at Chino and Brackett, much to the delight of tower operators and airport hangers-on. Even at this early stage, flying the Defiant was something to remember.

After this first flight, there was a personal feeling that we'd just jumped ahead into a new dimension of safe, simplified efficient flight. The Defiant, or one of its kinfolk, should be the new format for tomorrow's twin. We had that sort of a gut feeling after our first exposure to the Defiant—we still have that same feeling today.

In 1977-78, Rutan designed and built the Defiant in 7½ months with 1½ to 2 people working on it. He estimates between 1,800 and 1,900 man-hours on the prototype. On a production line, he feels that the Defiant could be built for 350 man-hours—about the same as a Cessna 150 or the Beech Duchess in production. Rutan estimates that he had $150,000 invested in the project at first flight.

The future of Defiant was not ultimately finalized until Oshkosh '83 when Burt, in a surprise announcement, advised a forum tent full of eager builders that plans were being drawn and would be available shortly. Fred Keller, veteran Alaskan homebuilder, would complete the plans and act as builder liaison.

FRED KELLER BUILDS SECOND DEFIANT

Since announcement of the Defiant plans was

the No. 1 news item at Oshkosh '83, we arranged to meet with Fred Keller during his stop at Mojave on his trek back to Alaska to talk, take pictures, and fly. The following account of Defiant II was published in *Private Pilot* magazine in November 1983, and is reprinted with permission of the publisher:

Now you can plan to build your own twin-engine, four-place, 1,600-mile-range homebuilt from a proven design. Burt Rutan has just teamed up with Alaskan homebuilder Fred Keller to put Rutan's popular Defiant design into do-it-yourself form. An agreement recently finalized will make detailed plans and bills of material available to interested homebuilders by February 1984.

Fred Keller (Fig. 11-6) was awarded the top honor of Grand Champion at the 1981 EAA Convention at Oshkosh, Wisconsin, for his VariEze. At that time, Rutan approached Keller with a proposition to build a second Defiant and incorporate a number of changes that the designer wanted made. Part of the agreement was for Keller to keep extensive documentation on the entire project. The end result is a slightly larger airplane designed around 150-hp Lycoming O-320 engines. The prototype is powered with two 160-hp Lycomings.

"Wow, was I flattered when Rutan approached me to build the Defiant!" exclaimed Keller. "However, I asked to think about it for a few days. I went back to Alaska and talked the project over with my wife Sharon. It was a big project, and I'm cautious. I wanted to be sure that I had the dedication, the finances, and the space to handle this big development project. It didn't take long to decide to go ahead with the job and I flew to Mojave, California, where I took at least 175 photographs of Burt's machine. I went over all the available drawings and shop notes that he had retained and discussed the changes to be made. Then I returned home, cleaned out my two-car garage, and made up a bill of materials.

"Now that Starr Thompson has retired as a 747 Captain with the Flying Tiger Lines, I can thank him publicly for helping airlift all the original materials from Aircraft Spruce. Those crates included over 500 yards of glass cloth and filled up my complete

Fig. 11-6. Fred and Sharon Keller stand beside their Defiant after a cross-country flight from Anchorage to Oshkosh.

station wagon, even to the top of the cab. We had our problems unloading them in Anchorage.

"Actually, building the Defiant is just about the same as building two VariEzes or two Long-EZs," continued Keller. "The techniques are identical and both airplanes build really fast. With this No. 2 vehicle, there were many details to work out that the builder with a set of plans won't be bothered with. All the wiring and plumbing will be drawn out where I had to make it as foolproof as possible."

Keller prides himself on being self-sufficient. While the average VariEze or Long-EZ builder calls Burt or Mike Melvill at least eight times during construction, Fred called only five times in the

19-month construction period. Fred advised that some of those calls were just to let Rutan know that the project was still alive.

Estimates of cost and construction time depend on the dedication and ingenuity of the builder. Keller feels that a serious builder would take between 2,000 and 2,500 hours to build a Defiant (Fig. 11-7). Previous experience with the Long-EZ, VariEze, or other composite aircraft would be useful because many of the construction techniques are identical. Actually, Keller considers the push-pull project to be just about twice as complex as the Long-EZ. It takes roughly twice the material as well as twice the number of engines and accessories. Fred said that he spent $18,000 on his Defiant before the last package of radios. However, it should be noted that Keller is one of the better "homebuilder-scroungers." He started the Defiant project with four O-235 engines in various stages of disrepair under a table in his shop. These were earmarked for trading material.

Specific changes in the new Defiant design included adding two feet to the canard and 27 inches to the main wing. Winglets were set four inches to the rear on the main wing tip and canted inward 8 degrees for dihedral effect. The hinge and balance point for the ailerons was re-engineered, resulting in a vastly improved rate of roll. The strakes (tapered fillets at each wing root) are four inches wider and begin one inch farther forward than on Rutan's original model.

Keller explained that a great deal of the thinking in the Long-EZ design came from the original Defiant. The wing is similar, as are the attach points.

The cabin has more headroom as a result of squaring the top of the cabin. The front seats are permanently installed as structural members. The backseat folds up like a station wagon, providing a 71-inch flat area for storage or sleeping. "I can almost stretch out in it with my shoes on," said Keller, who admitted that he had actually slept in the cabin a couple of times during construction (Fig. 11-8). Both Keller and Rutan looked at the possibility of a walk-in cabin, but felt that it was not practical for a homebuilt of this size; thus the simplicity of the fuselage "tub" was retained. Because both men are well over six feet tall, there is ample room in both seats.

How do you build a 24-foot wing section in a garage that is just 24 feet long? Keller first built a 24-foot table in four sections—two eight feet long and two four feet long. These were moved around to provide a flat working area and the canard was lined up on a diagonal across the garage.

Keller built the 20-foot canard first and hung it up in the rafters for 16 months. The first time the airplane was fully assembled was when Rutan was

Fig. 11-7. Fred Keller's glistening new Defiant in flight near the Rutan Aircraft Factory.

Fig. 11-8. Builder Fred Keller demonstrates the 71-inch flat area in the back of his Defiant can be used for sleeping as well as storage.

coming to visit and inspect the final progress.

Keller's Defiant has two complete electrical systems—one from each engine—that can operate independently. There are more than 1,000 feet of wire in the airplane. There are two alternators and two batteries with one each navcom working on each system that can be connected together in case of an engine or alternator failure.

Each fuel system is completely independent but plumbed with a crossfeed. Each strake aft of the main gear has a fuel tank plus a four-gallon sump tank. There are two mechanical and two electrical fuel pumps. Each fuel system has four screens. Keller isn't quite sure of his total fuel capacity, but estimates that it is just over 100 gallons. The fuel system is identical with that used on the Long-EZ.

Keller installed a dynafocal engine mount in front and the less expensive conical mount in the rear. Dynafocal mounts are more readily available in the contiguous 48 states, but the final plans will provide for either combination of engine mounts.

The engines in Keller's Defiant are second-hand; one came from a Cherokee 140 and the other from an older Cessna 172. The rear engine came as a basket case and Fred overhauled it to zero-time specifications. He recommends two midtime engines that are already running as the ideal power package.

Both windshield and side windows of Keller's aircraft have a definite bronze tint both for aesthetic purpose and for Keller's sensitive eyes. The windshield design was modified from an Emeraude by Walt How of the Airplane Factory in Dayton, Ohio.

The design calls for a warning light on the panel when the canopy is not latched. A high percentage of VariEze and Long-EZ accidents have resulted from an attempted takeoff with the canopy unlocked. The main gear is fixed, but the nose gear retracts. Keller is able to actually see the latching mechanism from the left side of the cockpit.

The most difficult part of building the Defiant, according to Keller, was installing the landing gear. This required taking the fuselage outside his garage, hauling it nine feet up into the air (with a block and tackle hooked to the side of the house) and then slipping in the gear. The design is being modified to create a cut-out section in the fuselage tub so the gear will slip in more easily.

Keller feels that many builders may remove the "rhino" rudder that hangs down under the front engine and will install tip rudders similar to the Long-EZ. "That rhino looks like hell," he said, "but that is the simplest way to build a rudder system. It hooks directly to the rudder pedals. The Defiant does not have a dive flap." Keller feels that you don't need one as long as you plan your approaches carefully.

Keller's basic homebuilding policy is simple: "You must stay with it all the time. I make it a rule to do something on the project every day."

George Pappas, an Anchorage aircraft rebuilder who had his restored Widgeon at Oshkosh in 1983, said that "Keller is a true craftsman. He won't compromise. When he put the first coat of paint on the Defiant he was racing against the clock, but he felt it wasn't right so he went home, sanded it all off, and redid the job."

Keller stresses that an understanding wife is essential to families who build airplanes at home. Sharon picked up her private license in 1980 and is a member of the Ninety-Nines. She helped on the Defiant project primarily with the paperwork, expediting parts and in the cockpit layout (Fig. 11-9).

Keller is employed as telephone construction superintendent in Anchorage. He was an avid model builder and grew up on a farm in Kentucky, where

Fig. 11-9. In-flight photo of Keller's instrument panel shows attention to detail. The Defiant is capable of 185 knots.

his father had a '45 Aeronca Champ. He was given a block of time for a birthday present. Later, he bought a 1946 65-hp Taylorcraft. "I loved that little aircraft," said Keller.

"I used to go flying after work on warm summer evenings with the windows open. I'd fly down the river banks between the trees and really feel that I was part of the aircraft."

Subsequently, Keller purchased an Aeronca Sedan which he flew until he began his first homebuilt project, a Revmaster-powered KR-1. "I started this project in 1973, flew it 235 hours, and then donated the ship to the air museum in Palmer, Alaska," Keller explained. "My VariEze took 18 months to build and won the Outstanding Workmanship award at Oshkosh in 1978. This 85-hp Continental-powered ship is still flying well after 376 hours, but it needs a bit of TLC. I wish I could

sell it and get my out-of-pocket expenses back, but the liability potential is just too great. I don't know just what I'll do with it.

"So before you commit to building the Defiant or anything else, look downstream to see how you might dispose of the ship if and when you're through flying it," advised Fred.

Keller noted one of the most serious drawbacks in building your own airplane is the product liability if and when you wish to sell it. "I've talked to two different judges on this subject and received two different answers. Rutan has advised his builders not to sell their aircraft, even in parts, for this reason.

"I believe completely that the Defiant is the safest airplane ever designed," said Keller. "This was proven on the very first flight that I took in my ship with Burt Rutan aboard. We were climbing out of Anchorage and Burt said quietly, 'There's something wrong; we should be climbing faster.' It took us a short while to figure out that we'd lost the front engine. We circled back around the field and landed easily. We found out later that a carburetor float had stuck."

Rutan made the first flights in Keller's airplane and came up with three pages of data in the first hour. After the engine failure, Burt gave Fred nine hours of dual and then the Alaskan took another seven hours of dual with a local CFI, Dave Bailey. Because Keller does not need a conventional multi-engine rating, he had a centerline thrust rating added to his regular license. The same rating is required to pilot a Cessna Skymaster. Keller now has 1,100 hours total time with an instrument and seaplane rating added to his private certificate.

When Keller visited Rutan's Mojave, California, headquarters on his way back to Anchorage from Oshkosh '83, his new Defiant had logged just 67 hours. The Alaskan FAA officials okayed his departure for Oshkosh when the new plane had only 15 hours shakedown time. Final assembly had taken place at the Anchorage International Airport in the Troy Air hangar with the FAA offices right upstairs.

The Kellers took their complete camping gear—everything but the lawn chairs—and did camp at Oshkosh. On that trip, their first landing was at Whitehorse, Yukon Territory, Canada, just after a 737 had aborted because of a crosswind. Fred reported no problem, adding that "this is the easiest airplane I've ever landed. Ninety-nine percent of the time I grease it on." Later, during a flight at Mojave, he showed us a super-slick touchdown.

On their initial flight from Alaska, the Kellers cruised on 17 inches Hg. manifold pressure on the front engine and 18-19 inches Hg. on the rear to true out at 160 knots at 8,000 feet. Keller feels that a program to "tweak" both propellers will result in greater speeds. Because of weight, cost, and complexity, controllable props are not planned, and fixed pitch wooden props are initially recommended.

The empty weight of Keller's Defiant is 1,680 pounds and gross is 3,000 pounds.

BUILDER NEWS AT OSHKOSH

Some indication of the interest in the Defiant homebuilt project can be obtained from a head count on the first general announcement meeting during the 1983 EAA Oshkosh Convention. With word-of-mouth-only announcements at three of Rutan's regular seminars, more than 400 people showed up for an after-dinner meeting in a tent on the airport. It was here that Burt gave a history of the Defiant and the various factors that influenced his decision to go the homebuilder route.

Rutan explained that his original existing prototype, the Model 40, with the potential of five places and 180-hp engines, was designed in 1979 and built concurrently with the prototype Quickie. "Originally we called it 'the Doctor-Saver'," Burt quipped and added, "when it was decided that included saving lawyers, too, we almost canceled the project." (Burt has spent an inordinate amount of time and money defending himself against lawsuits following mishaps in his various designs.)

"We looked at all kinds of approaches on how to build the Defiant because I felt that everyone in the world should have one," he explained. "Late in '79, fuel was critical. We thought it might go to $5 per gallon and that we weren't going to be able to fly. However, we redesigned the Defiant as the Model 74, non-pressurized, with retractable gear, five-place with club seating in the back. We went as far as a cabin mockup and stopped. We didn't know what to do. Should we go ahead and certificate it, produce it with investor money, build it on a shoestring, let Mooney or Piper do it, or what?"

With considerable candor, Rutan admitted, "I was scared because I could see myself getting into a production situation which would require a company of hundreds of people and where 80 percent of the work does not involve design, structures and aerodynamics—the things I like to do. This would take Burt Rutan and lock him in a jail cell for three, four, or five years, and that is what scared me!"

Rutan decided to improve the VariEze and developed it into the Long-EZ. Then he decided to get the Voyager project started. (Voyager is a nonstop, non-refuel, around-the-world project that

Dick Rutan and Jeana Yeager are actively pursuing at this time. See Chapter 15.) Then the other projects came up and the Defiant collected dust except for the times that Burt flew it.

"I kept telling myself that I enjoy what I'm doing," Burt continued to the crowd in the tent, "doing research and development programs, working with EAA people, studying interesting aerodynamics and making some contributions like the projects we're now doing at SCALED. (See Chapter 14.) These are relatively short programs that take less than a year. I enjoy this a lot more than trying to make myself into another Cessna company.

"I wanted to study the feasibility of this airplane for the homebuilder. Remember, we built the first Defiant in a 30 × 50-foot shop and we weren't sure how well it could be built by one person. A lot of the things we did first in the Defiant later showed up in the Long-EZ, particularly in the wing. We took what we had learned in structures and methods of putting things together and applied it to the Long-EZ."

When co-worker Paul Stritlin, who was on the Defiant project, was killed in an ultralight accident, Rutan found himself with no one in the shop who knew what was really inside the aircraft to provide builder support. "I don't think that it is ethical to hire somebody for builder support if that person hasn't built one with his very own hands. I was stuck with offering the Defiant to a homebuilder and needed to work out a cooperative arrangement with someone else who would work up the drawings and document the project. Depending on how well this worked out, we would decide whether or not we could go ahead at all.

"If you can build a Long-EZ, you can build this aircraft," Burt stated firmly.

There are a number of changes from Burt's prototype. The original airplane had the front engine canted about ½ degree to the left rather than 2½ degrees to the right. "I just completely forgot about P-factor," said Burt, "and I never got around to fixing it. At low speed and high angle of attack, the original ship needs a lot of rudder."

"What we're going to do is offer a Defiant program that is very similar to the Long-EZ. Suppliers and prefab parts will be described. We're going to supply the plans and builder support like the VariEze. The interpretation of plans and expertise gained from building it with his own hands will come from Keller. Specific builder questions, mail or phone, will be to Fred Keller in Anchorage."

The number and sophistication of prefab parts will depend on the popularity of the program. Companies such as TASK in Santa Paula, which now builds Solitaire and Dragonfly fuselages, Long-EZ landing gears and other components, are ready to produce hard-to-fabricate parts for Defiant if a sufficient volume can be generated.

Rutan describes the performance at 185 knots. "We're going to talk knots, not mph. We're big boys now," he advised. "The Defiant is a beautiful, stable platform for instruments; I'm not going to holler and scream if you want to fly it at night."

The present design can be equipped with 150-, 160- or 180-hp engines with fixed-pitch propellers. It is considered possible to adapt constant-speed propellers for better takeoff performance, though there will be both weight and cost penalties.

Rutan explained that his push-pull twin was overpowered. It must be when you can lose 50 percent of your available power and still maintain a climbout. Most of the nearly 1,000 hours that Burt has put on his airplane has been at power settings of 50 percent. "I wind it up tighter for races or for just having fun," he commented.

Rutan expects much of the cross-country work with the Defiant to be in the 18,000-foot level, above the general aviation aircraft and below the jets. "When you're on oxygen up there, above most of the weather, it's a real nice sensation," he mused.

When the designer wanted to find the service ceiling, Dick Rutan put a bottle of oxygen aboard and took it to 28,300 feet. When the range was to be calculated, Dick took off from Mojave at 7 A.M., flew all around California, and landed 15½ hours later with two gallons remaining. The fuel system calls for two independent fuel sumps that hold the last 40 minutes of fuel for each engine. "We can safely come down to one or two gallons on each system; actually, we can feed right down to the last cupful at any normal altitude. The average light twin is carrying 10 to 12 gallons as a permanent reserve.

"With twin-engine reliability and over 14 hours of endurance with 90 gallons of fuel, you have a very safe aircraft."

Rutan brought a chuckle from his attentive tent-meeting crowd when he discussed obtaining either a multi-engine rating or the required centerline thrust rating that is applicable to the Defiant. "I didn't have a multi-engine rating for the first year and a half I flew the Defiant. I just kidded the onlookers that I was flying a single-engine airplane with a big APU (auxiliary power unit) in back!"

Rutan points out that a popular demonstration maneuver in his push-pull twin is to simulate an engine-out on takeoff after the spot for a balked landing on the runway had passed. "There's no procedure," explained Burt. "You have no flaps to monkey with; raising the single nose gear won't make much difference. All you do is build up as much energy as you can and then zoom. You can stay in the air for a short period of time at the top of a zoom below stall speed. Once you've passed the initial obstacle, all you do is lower the nose slightly for a little more speed and then pull out. Do that in a conventional twin and you'll hit the trees surrounding the field upside down.

"This is an extremely safe airplane. It's a real pussycat—a real old barge! It is very easy to fly and the easiest airplane in the world to land," Rutan iterated.

As planned, Keller will act as the builder support person for those who start on their own aircraft. Rutan used a similar system with Mike and Sally Melvill, who built the first VariViggen (see Chapter 3). Both Melvills now work with Rutan at Mojave. Keller, however, will remain in Anchorage and keep his 8-to-5 job. He is now cleaning up the plans and written portion to send to Burt for editing and then printing.

Keller says that the Defiant plans will be similar to those of the Solitaire self-launching sailplane with large drawings, fewer words, and photograph reproductions printed to scale.

As builders get underway, Keller will set up specific hours when he can take telephone calls to discuss personally any problems that may develop. Anchorage is five hours behind New York in time zones, so Keller's evening long-distance calls will come on the "after 5 P.M. rate" from the Lower 48.

"Helping put the Defiant within reach of serious homebuilders gives me a good feeling," said Keller. "There have been 800 to 900 hours of testing on the prototype and it is a fine airplane. However, both Mike Melvill and Dick Rutan have flown mine and feel that it is an improvement over the original.

"Both Burt and I are looking forward to the time when we'll see a whole line of Defiants at Oshkosh. This design should have an important impact on future general aviation development. I'm glad to be a part of it," said Keller.

STOPOVER AT MOJAVE

The enthusiasm developed around the Defiant is contagious. I wanted to get in on the ground floor and fly in this new ship, emulating a very early flight with Rutan when his prototype had 30 hours in its log. When Fred Keller stopped by Mojave on his way back to Anchorage, from Oshkosh, we made arrangements to kick tires and fly.

Keller stressed that his airplane needed a lot of cleaning up, but it looked mighty good to me. When he shows how you can see the weave of some of the cloth beneath the hard resin, you must move your head from side to side so that the sunlight hits just right and then you might see it.

During a walk-around, he meticulously wiped a tiny stream of oil away from the aft engine cowl. He pointed out that the intake scoop for the rear engine is offset to the left so that it will not pick up what little smoke and oil comes out of the front engine.

The disarmingly simple two-step arrangement up into the cockpit took considerable cut and fit. Keller wanted the cabin access to fit a lady wearing a skirt. There is, however, a simple learning curve in where to put which foot and in what sequence (Fig. 11-10).

Once inside, you find both cockpits remarkably

spacious once you're seated. However, there is no wasted space inside or out. The cockpit arrangement is functional, with a sub-panel canted at the left of the left front seat. Throttle and mixtures are in the center console, with a side stick at the outside of each cockpit. Keller had yet to install brakes on the right side.

We settled comfortably into the seats and Fred fired up the rear engine for taxi. Mojave Unicom gave us Runway 22, a distant taxi run out past the long line of mothballed older jet transports. Sitting up front during taxiing, you begin to get a feeling for just how big this centerline twin really is.

At the time I flew with Keller at Mojave, there

Fig. 11-10. Sally Melvill demonstrates the simple two-step entrance into Keller's Defiant.

was just one basic change yet to be made. It has been decided to shorten the main landing gear by at least two inches to produce a more positive angle of attack during takeoff. With three of us aboard and low fuel, we used up almost two-thirds of Mojave's Runway 22 before liftoff. However, once climb was established, we averaged nearly 1,000 fpm in the usual moderate turbulence of a desert midday.

"We're so satisfied with the total harmony of the design that it would be foolish to do anything else," said Keller with a barely restrained smile.

We cruised over the Mojave Desert, climbing to 7,500 feet where it was calm. A few miles away, secure in its own restricted area, was Edwards AFB, where so much of the U.S. aviation development has taken place in the past 40 years. Now Mojave, right next door, is providing a civilian parallel with innovative canards, new composite structures, and finished products like the Defiant and Voyager. This is still the place where the action is!

Keller's airplane was shipshape, functional, and designed to travel long distances in comfort and safety. Its rate of roll was smooth. Even though the nose gear was yet to be sealed and soundproofing added, the cabin noise level was surprisingly low.

Our letdown into Mojave was strictly routine. Drop the nose gear and check both visually and with a warning light that the wheel is down and locked. With no flaps and a very clean airframe, final approach is long and low. There is sufficient mass to make flare and landing greasy-smooth.

Keller continued on to help Burt develop a full set of plans for homebuilders. He set up his schedule to devote two evenings a week to builder support over the telephone from Anchorage. There were somewhat less than 50 sets of Defiant plans sold before Burt decided to close down RAF. A number of these aircraft have been completed and are operating successfully. Keller has continued to assist the plans holders and is going ahead on his own to develop a composite bush airplane.

Chapter 12

Solitaire—Best When It's Quiet

When it comes to covering the aviation spectrum, Rutan is hard to beat. He's designed everything from small two-place transportation machines all the way to a state-of-the-art executive transport. So why not create a high-performance, almost-competition sailplane with a fold-up powerplant—and win a contest at the same time?

This is the story of Solitaire. First, test pilot Mike Melvill tells the background of just how Solitaire was created. Mike prepared an in-depth report of the conception and birth of Solitaire and it is reprinted here from *Sport Aviation* by permission of the Experimental Aircraft Association:

THE TEST PILOT TELLS ALL

During August of 1980, personnel of the Rutan Aircraft Factory were building the Grizzly STOL plane in a shop that was closed to the public. We knew people were speculating as to what was going on in our skunkworks. . . and that if someone about to buy plans for a Long-EZ got the idea we were developing a new, more advanced model, he would

likely hold off on his purchase. Although the Grizzly was strictly a research project, we were concerned it would be mistaken for a new homebuilt. So when the Soaring Society of America announced its competition for a homebuilt self-launching sailplane in November of 1980, we saw this as a means of killing two birds with one stone. For a long time Burt had wanted to design a sailplane, so we announced that we were entering the competition. People would assume it was the sailplane prototype under construction in our skunkworks . . . which would give us some breathing space to work on the Grizzly and Burt would have time to start designing the sailplane (Fig. 12-1).

I feel very fortunate that Burt includes me in a lot of the facets of conceptualizing, aerodynamic, and structural design. It is fascinating to watch Burt at work. He got out his yellow legal pad and began to sketch. Should it be a canard? What about a forward swept wing? A tractor or a pusher? What engine should we use?

Burt initially settled on the Zenoah engine; however, we changed to a Robin within a few weeks

Fig. 12-1. During early stages of development, the prototype Solitaire shared the RAF hangar with the NGT, shown hanging from the roof.

and, still later, switched to a single-cylinder 215cc Cuyuna. Of seven or eight conceptual sketches, Burt liked the canard or tandem wing, with the canard mounted right on the forward end of the fuselage, its leading edge in line with the tip of the nose. Done right, it can theoretically reduce interference drag to zero. For the same reason, the main (rear) wing is mounted at the widest vertical point of the fuselage, which does not start to taper in planform until well behind the trailing edge. The parameters of the original three-view were assessed and revised, using computer programs for stability and performance to refine the planform and

control surfaces. The aircraft was designated as Model 77, the 77th design by Burt.

Glide path control on a canard design is a real challenge. Flaps or spoilers cannot be easily used due to the large pitching moments produced by such devices. Spoiling or increasing lift on the back wing of a tandem wing or canard type will pitch the aircraft, possibly beyond the control authority of the elevator. This dictated a "spoilflap," a main wing trailing edge device that is tailored to provide high drag without a lift change. The flap on the bottom increases lift while the spoiler on the top kills lift. This one-piece, simple surface is designed to not pitch the aircraft. Burt built the spoilflap and we built a full scale section of the main wing four feet long including Burt's trailing edge spoilflap. An outrigger device was built to mount the section of wing about eight feet away from the side of our van while we were measuring lift. An airspeed indicator was also set up with pitot/static out on the wing section. We drove the van up and down the 9,600-foot runway at Mojave at speeds varying from 40 to 90 knots while Burt actuated the spoilflap. From these tests he was able to verify that the spoilflap design was correct.

Burt initially elected to install the single-cylinder Cuyuna engine buried in the fuselage. The prop, driven by two-V-belts, was mounted atop a steel tube arm that pivoted up and out of the top of the fuselage (Fig. 12-2). A test stand had been utilized earlier to break in the engine and look at our folding prop mechanism (Fig. 12-3). With a 2.4 to 1 reduction drive and a 42-inch diameter prop, we measured right at 100 pounds of thrust.

To design the fuselage, Burt wrote a program for his Apple computer that could loft the complex compound-curved shape. Task Research made the male plug and from it pulled the female molds. The prototype fuselage was made from oriented prepreg glass skins with PVC foam cores.

One of Burt's major design goals was to put the

Fig. 12-3. The propeller is shown completely retracted in an early version of the Solitaire propulsion system.

pilot right at the CG, thus eliminating the requirement for ballast depending on pilot's weight normally associated with sailplanes. This requirement is primarily what dictated the canard configuration with the cockpit to be located between the wing and canard, allowing the pilot's "bellybutton" to be right at the CG of the sailplane.

We started construction on the sailplane in December of 1981 and it was completed and ready to fly on May 28, 1982. I was the test pilot for the project. All the taxi tests and initial liftoffs from Mojave's long runway were documented with videotape shot from a van. The first few runs were devoted to checks of ground handling, a cursory airspeed check, and flights in ground effect to evaluate control authority and response. After several runs, I just kept climbing and flew around the airport for 15 minutes with the engine running. Solitaire handled well. We were particularly happy with the spoilflap drag device. Later the same day, we flew again and this time I climbed to 2500 feet AGL with Burt chasing me in the Grizzly. Stalls, power on or power off, were as predicted: no tendency for wing rock or altitude loss, just a mild pitch bobble. A low altitude turn back to the airport with full aft stick will not result in a stall/spin. This is a common sailplane hazard due to rope breaks, etc. At altitude, I shut down the engine for the first time and folded the prop away to fly as a pure sailplane; it

Fig. 12-2. During early development, the engine for Solitaire was mounted permanently in the nose. The propeller was driven by a series of belts. Left to right: Burt, Mike Melvill, Roger Houghton.

was intoxicating! I then extended the prop and, using a rope pull, restarted the engine and climbed back up to 3,000 feet AGL. I did not know it at the time, but this was the only successful air restart ever to be made with the buried Cuyuna installation. Later attempts were unsuccessful due to various engine problems which made it clear to us that we would need either a very easy-starting engine or an electric start capability. During one of the flights, we had a fuel leak that spilled gasoline into the engine compartment. Only five flights were made with this engine before we decided that the fire hazard with it buried in the fuselage was too great. Later design work would focus on extracting the entire engine. In the meantime, we worked on airplane tow launch development.

We removed the engine, installed ballast to account for its missing weight, and, with the loan of a towplane and pilot from Fantasy Haven Glider Port in Tehachapi, were ready for our first attempt at towed flight. We did this in spite of gusty crosswinds right up to the limit of the Super Cub tow ship. On the first try, I aborted due to an unexpected pitch sensitivity. On the second try, I got to 300 feet—and the rope broke!

I turned, made an abbreviated pattern, and landed into the wind (which was gusting to 30 knots). The third try was the charm; we towed to 3,000 feet AGL and spent an enjoyable 30 minutes evaluating the "door closed" clean sailplane configuration.

Since we felt we needed to tow the sailplane ourselves, we worked with our local FAA to get the Grizzly signed off as a towplane and get Burt checked out as a towplane pilot. This sent the local FAA into a bit of a whirl, since they had never licensed an experimental to tow another experimental! With these goals accomplished, we made our first Grizzly tow. By now we had officially named the new bird "Solitaire," a name suggested by RAF employee Roger Houghton. We towed many flights with the Grizzly and some were to 10,000 feet AGL in order to obtain L/D data, with and without spoilflaps, and to open the envelope. These were great flights—early morning over the desert with cool, crystal-clear air and very smooth

conditions prevailed. Our remaining problems were the lack of a good self-launch capability and an overly sensitive pitch control system. The basic static stability of the aircraft was excellent. The control system was the culprit, needing lower friction and gearing revisions.

Soon we felt confident enough to invite an experienced sailplane pilot, Hannes Linke, to try Solitaire and give us his opinion. Hannes liked Solitaire, thought it was a bit pitch sensitive and that its L/D was more than enough for an entry level sailplane. He was particularly complimentary about the spoilflap system. The FAA signed off our area restrictions, so we were ready to take Solitaire to Oshkosh.

We obtained a prototype Normal/Aire Garrett two-cylinder, two-stroke engine, recommended to us by Englishman Colin Chapman of Lotus auto fame. This was installed on a fixed pylon for evaluation purposes and the first flight in this configuration was made. All of the next ten flights were to get carburetion, exhaust system length, and prop to the best we could to see if it was promising enough to develop a retraction capability (Fig. 12-4).

Michael Dilley and Doug Shane towed the Solitaire to Oshkosh behind our van . . . and Burt towed me aloft with the Grizzly on four different afternoons during the airshow periods. One afternoon I took off under power to participate in the fly-bys . . . and had a short trip indeed; I took off on Runway 18, turned crosswing over the woods near Steve Wittman's home—and had the engine seize solid! I turned for the airport with barely 200 feet under me. I did not believe I could make it back to the runway, but I had underestimated the Solitaire's glide capability. Even with the engine mounted on a fixed pylon, I made it back easily, flying downwind, base and turning final to line up with the taxiway. At the last minute, I decided my wings would strike the tall taxi lights, so I closed the spoilflaps, pulled up, and glided over to make a smooth landing on the grass between the taxiway and the runway.

The factory representative tore the engine down and rebuilt it with new pistons and barrels, and we were able to make several successful demo flights under power in the fly-bys (Fig. 12-5).

Fig. 12-4. Solitaire in flight in its final configuration.(courtesy RAF)

Soon after returning to Mojave, Burt made his first flight in the Solitaire. It was getting close to contest time. The rules of the SSA contest stated that although proof of structural integrity by analytical means (stress analysis) is normally acceptable to the FAA, this would not be acceptable for the purpose of the contest. A static load test was the only basis acceptable to prove the structure. The contest rules defined the limit load for our category of sailplane as a minimum of 4.67 Gs. Because the Solitaire was considered by the judges to be "unconventional," we were required to proof load to 4.67 × 1.5 = 7.0 Gs. This load was defined as "ultimate." Tests to ultimate generally yield or destroy structure, making it unairworthy; however, the Solitaire has sufficient margins to allow using the prototype for the load tests.

We mounted Solitaire upside-down on foam block supports on top of a strong work table. The main wing tips were 48 inches above the floor. We static-loaded the canard first, using 25-pound bags of lead shot. These were carefully placed simultaneously, one on each side, at exactly the butt line Burt had called out. We took the canard to limit (4.67 Gs) in bending, then limit load in both bending and torsion by moving the lead shot bags aft 3.5 inches. At this point, all weight was removed to check that the canard tips returned to their original position. Then it was taken to "ultimate" (4.67 × 1.5) in bending and torsion combined. For the

canard, this required careful symmetrical hand loading of the 910 pounds of lead shot. No noise or signs of stress were apparent, so we off-loaded and went on to the main wing (Fig. 12-6).

The main wing at ultimate bending and torsion looked quite scary! The tips bent to within 2 ½ inches of the floor, meaning they had deflected 45 ½ inches! Of course, the "downhill slope" of the wings means that in order to get the lead shot bags to stay in the correct position, each bag had to be duct-taped into place. This is a tricky operation, because any bouncing induced can apply massive overloads. Putting the last lead bag on the wing tip brought the

Fig. 12-5. Mike Melvill, left, and Burt Rutan work on a temporary engine installation at Oshkosh.

196

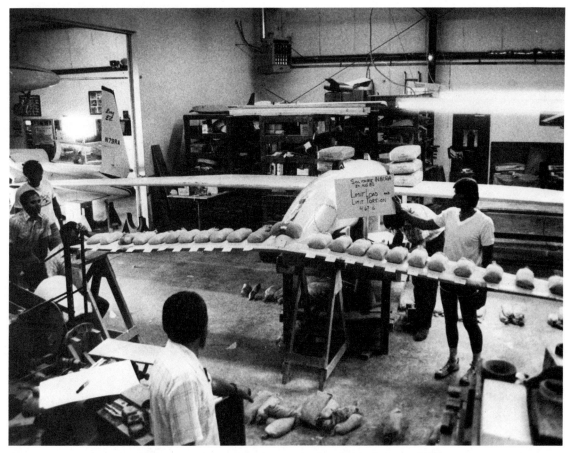
Fig. 12-6. Ultimate load on Solitaire's canard totaled 910 pounds of lead shot. (courtesy RAF)

total weight on the wings to 1932 pounds and was really a teeth-gritter (Figs. 12-7, 12-8). As it turned out, like the canard, the wing did not make a sound and returned to its normal relaxed position as soon as the weight was removed.

The fuselage was then jigged on its side and braced at the main wing and canard attach areas, after which the vertical tail was loaded with 168 pounds to test it to ultimate.

Flying the Solitaire early the next morning, I must say I felt a tremendous confidence in the structure. Even when I opened the dive speed out to its present 120 KIAS and pulled out full spoilflaps at the dive speed, I had no doubts at all. Loops (4 Gs), rolls, split Ss, and wingover turns all seemed easier now that I had seen the airplane at 7.0 Gs.

The SSA contest was held in Tehachapi, California, which is only 20 miles west of Mojave, so we elected to fly in. Burt and Grizzly towed Solitaire and me over the ridge where I released and soared around out of sight of the crowd at the Fantasy Haven airport. Burt landed and parked the Grizzly and then called me in on the radio. Of course I had to show off a little, so I did three consecutive loops and a series of wingover turns while losing altitude to make a high-speed low pass, entered the pattern, and landed.

We took the Solitaire apart for the contest judges and the public to inspect the insides. We later flew with power and tow. Two of the contest judges, Einar Enervoldson and Walt Mooney, flew the Solitaire, as did Larry Barret, owner of the

197

Fig. 12-7. Static load on the Solitaire's main wings totaled 1932 pounds. (courtesy RAF)

Fantasy Haven facility. Burt also flew at Tehachapi, his first flight under tow. The final day of the SSA contest, Solitaire was declared the winner. The whole purpose of our design was realized: that it is the best homebuilt available to promote soaring.

Later that afternoon, I fired up the Normal/Aire Garrett and flew my first powered cross-country back to Mojave. The same week, Sally Melvill, an RAF employee, and Burt's brother, Dick Rutan, flew the Solitaire. Both were delighted. We were invited to fly the Solitaire at a Society of Experimental Test Pilots air show, a prestigious event and quite an honor.

By now, we were close to freezing the design.

We had in the course of testing increased the span of the elevators and reduced elevator system friction. We had increased the span of the ailerons (better roll), reduced the height of the vertical tail (directional stability was more than needed), and tested several different wheel brakes. We had not figured out a way to fold the engine. The Normal/Aire Garrett simply would not physically fit into the available space. Besides, it did not have a starter, a mandatory requirement in our opinion.

At this point, a KFM 107E was obtained from Don Black in New York. We mounted it on the fixed pylon for evaluation and soon decided that this was the way to go. We had to rotate the KFM 90 degrees to place the cylinders vertically instead of horizontally as they normally are, and also had to come up with an exhaust system that would allow us to fold the engine/prop/exhaust assembly into the nose. Dale Fischer of Fischer Engineering put our KFM on his dyno and developed a super exhaust system that has done the job (Fig. 12-9).

Many flights were conducted with the KFM mounted on a fixed pylon to develop props, carburetor jetting, etc. During December 1982, Einer Enervoldson, who is a NASA test pilot, asked if he could conduct an extensive flight test of Solitaire with a view to writing an article for *Soaring*. Burt readily agreed.

Einer installed his own calibrated instruments, an eight-foot long pitot boom, and conducted eight towed flights ranging from 35 minutes to over an hour duration.

Meanwhile, Michael Dilley and I were alternately working on the Solitaire plans and trying to make the KFM engine retract. We settled on an electro hydraulic unit used as a trim motor on an outboard speedboat, with a double-acting ram. This does the job beautifully. It is so simple and had been flawless to date. First flight was with the retractable engine but with no doors to close it in. It worked great and was quite a kick to be able, finally, to retract and extend the engine with just a flip of a switch! The next several flights were used to clock the prop so it would stop vertically oriented, or nearly so. We installed a small cam that could be manually extended so that the prop would windmill to the vertical and a lobe on the prop hub would engage the cam, at which point the engine could be retracted.

Michael and I got busy on the last item not yet

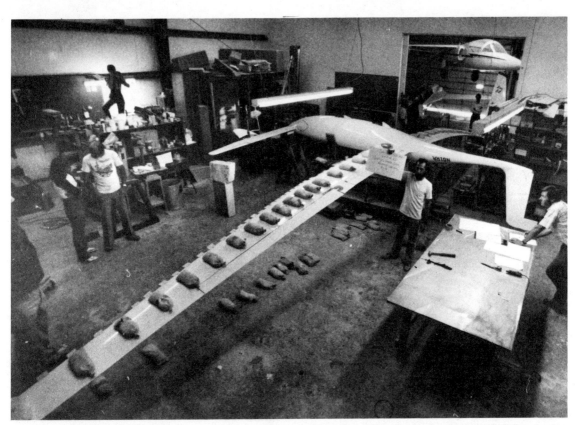

Fig. 12-8. Under final loads, Solitaire's wings were deflected 45 1/2 inches. When the loads were removed, the structure returned to normal. (courtesy RAF)

Fig. 12-9. Engine retraction on Solitaire.

showed a reduction in directional stability with the doors open and engine out. The added vertical surface ahead of the CG was the culprit. We went back to the original vertical tail height and had the required stability for powered launch.

Then I flew the Solitaire to the California City air show with surface winds gusting to 40 knots! I arrived there at 2,500 feet AGL and gave the customary couple of loops and a few wingover turns before making a high speed low approach with the engine folded away. I pulled up to downwind where I extended and started the engine, flew base, final, landed, and taxied around several aircraft and many

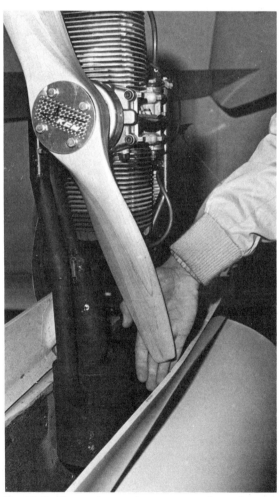

Fig. 12-10. Close tolerance between propeller and engine doors is shown.

worked out—the engine compartment doors. These are split in the middle and held closed by bungee cords. The engine pushes them open as it comes out and holds them open while it is out and running. We have limits of travel, as well as microswitches that disable the starter and ignition unless the engine is all the way up and in the proper position for running (Fig. 12-10).

With the engine cover doors, test results

people to my tiedown spot, unaided and with no requirement for any ground crew. The following day we flew back to Mojave in even worse wind conditions with no problem.

Recently I climbed to about 3,000 feet AGL, shut down and folded the engine, and worked a little lift over the Mojave Airport. I was up for over two hours before an over-full bladder forced me to land. Several flights have included over two hours unpowered. Burt flew a self-launch flight, working weak lift for over two and a half hours, using the engine for about 25 minutes. I plan to use Solitaire to achieve several of the altitude gain and duration pins offered by the Soaring Society of America.

When you're writing about aircraft, you fly in them and hopefully fly them yourself. Only after actually experiencing the feel, the smell, and the sound of an airborne vehicle can one really get close to the new craft. Burt Rutan has been generous in letting us get off the ground at Mojave and fly his creations.

LONESOME AND LOVING IT

Pure soaring has several inherent obstacles. Soaring takes a towplane with pilot and suitable weather. There is the ever-present possibility of an off-airport landing with, at best, a lengthy drive for ground crew and trailer to retrieve pilot and plane. Thus soaring in a single-place, high-performance machine is really a team operation. This required combination of people and equipment has made soaring a complex task for the dedicated few.

Self-launched sailplanes and motorgliders solve these basic problems. The recent Soaring Society of America self-launch competition was won by Burt Rutan's canard with its fold-down engine, the Solitaire.

The sun was actually setting before I taxied out with Burt Rutan's Solitaire at Mojave. It had been a long and busy day for the Rutan crew culminating with a long test flight in the new Beechcraft Starship. The flying day had been extended when both the canard Starship flown by Dick Rutan and the King Air chase plane flown by Mike Melvill made an unscheduled stop for fuel in Bakersfield. It seems that the King Air was getting down into fumes.

After the two ships returned to Mojave and the Starship was trundled into the sanctity of its hangar, there was an extended debriefing. Only after that concluded was there a chance to broach a Solitaire flight. Burt Rutan grinned, shrugged his shoulders and said, "Go ask Mike. He's been in charge of the Solitaire project."

Mike was still unwinding from flying the two-million-dollar chase plane. He asked how much I weighed. I told him that I was just over 190 pounds.

"That's getting close to the top weight, but it is getting cool this time of the year. I guess that it'd be

Fig. 12-11. Cockpit detail of Solitaire. The pilot's feet up to his knees go through the two small openings below the instrument panel.

all right," he commented. "Come on over and I'll show you where the goodies are."

Earlier in the day, I had tried the cockpit of Solitaire to make sure that I'd fit in it. Since Burt Rutan is about my build and he had flown the ship, I was expecting a tight fit but no real problem. After removing all but one bottom cushion, I stepped over onto the seat and slid one foot at a time through the cutouts in the instrument bulkhead. On a first go-around, there's a little fumbling and sliding to get both feet and trouser legs through those holes while supporting yourself by your arms, but once "inserted" in the cockpit, there is a surprising amount of room (Fig. 12-11).

Rudder pedals are adjustable, with space to spare for even a long-legged pilot. With rudder pedals fully extended, your feet are level with the arc of the propeller, but many layers of fiberglass are available for protection should the wooden prop shed part of a blade.

The cockpit is typically sailplane—stick on the right, wheel brake in the middle, and spoilers (called *spoilflaps* on the Solitaire) on the left. Of course, however, Solitaire is a self-launching sailplane so there are engine controls. The throttle is at the far left; this can produce a little busywork if you're making a landing with the engine out and want to play power against spoiler drag.

The spoilflaps are a smooth-operating set of dive brakes that extend both up and down on the trailing edge of the wing inboard of the ailerons. They are extremely efficient, as I later found out, and produce surprisingly little pitch change.

Mike Melvill, who was the test pilot on the entire program and designer of the intricate KFM engine fold-out system, gave a very quick cockpit check as the sunlight slipped into the mountains like the last reel of a travelogue. Outside the Rutan hangar, the air was dead calm, and that is a rarity at Mojave (Fig. 12-12). So we figured that it was best to fly now and talk later, even if there was only time enough for a couple of circuits around the field.

Fig. 12-12. Solitaire is prepared for a demonstration flight during a Saturday program.

Fig. 12-13. Where else but at Mojave can one taxi out in front of a B-25 and an F-104?

Solitaire has neither strobe nor nav lights since sailplanes are not normally flown after dark.

Mike showed me the flexible clear fuel line and filter bowl in full view of the pilot. "If that fuel bowl gets low, just flick the fuel pump switch over at the far right. The engine starter is under a safetied switch low on the panel and the engine retract/ extend switch is located just to the right of the spoilflap handle."

The canopy design is similar to Rutan's Long-EZ, with a double safety feature to assure that it is locked. I slipped into the three-point shoulder harness and Mike closed the canopy. I hit the starter, which appeared to have plenty of crank-power from a Japanese motorcycle battery. However, after perhaps 30 seconds, the engine quit and was reluctant to restart. Mike, who was helping his wife Sally start their Long-EZ, trotted back over, opened the canopy, and flicked the fuel on/off switch.

"I never use that thing," he commented. "Either Michael Dilley or Einer Enervoldson must have left it in the off position."

After a restart, the KFM barked noisily with all 23 horses snarling. Neither crash helmet nor headset was used on this flight. There was no one else in the non-towered airport pattern that time of night, and the Solitaire had been flown sufficiently so that the hard-hat routine seemed an added encumbrance.

The two-wheeled tandem landing gear of Solitaire is augmented by tiny tip wheels. Mike had cautioned that it was easy to hit the temporary plastic cone runway markers used during construction of the airport. After all, the wing is 41¾-feet long 'and the tips drag on their tiny 2½-inch model airplane outrigger wheels until you have enough speed to pick up a tip with the ailerons (Fig. 12-13).

I taxied out slowly, getting the feel of the short-handled throttle. With the engine running, the cockpit is noisy. However, the foldable engine pylon is surprisingly stable and the two-cylinder, two-cycle engine does not shake, rattle and roll as do some non-folding engine installations on today's

203

breed of ultralights. At the end of Runway 7, there was little to do except line up down the 5950-foot strip.

Mike Melvill had cautioned me not to expect rapid acceleration or a spectacular rate of climb. "Sometimes, when I hit a sinker after takeoff, I just don't climb at all and the sagebrush looks awfully uninviting. However, it is cool and calm, so you shouldn't have any problem." (Mike is probably 35 pounds lighter than I am.)

When you're moving 620 pounds gross weight with 23 horsepower, nothing really happens very fast. The bicycle landing gear with front-wheel steering makes holding the centerline no problem. There is no tendency for the Solitaire to swerve or drag, even when the little tip wheel is still dragging down the runway. Just as soon as any speed is obtained, the ailerons become effective and the ship quickly comes up to a level attitude.

Mike had advised that best rate of climb was between 35 and 38 mph so when the airspeed passed 40, I eased back on the stick and watched the elevator on the canard deflect downwards. The nosewheel lifted off smoothly, followed in perhaps two seconds by the main gear.

Pitch control on the Solitaire is sensitive, but should be a delight for thermaling. To keep away from any PIO (pilot induced oscillation), you very soon relax any ham-handed hold on the stick and go to your fingertips. The control touch is similar to Rutan's AMS/OIL racer—light and authoritative, but not really touchy.

Rate of climb was much better than I had expected, and I was high enough to start a turn back into the field as I crossed the intersection of Runway 30. By that time, I could have made it back onto Runway 21 on the three-runway layout with no problem.

Mike had advised that an off-field landing out in the sagebrush would damage the Solitaire but probably not hurt the pilot. Because N81RA was at that time the one and only Solitaire flying, I was most conservative and stayed close to the airport. There was a substantial investment in plans and tooling and already more than 70 packages of plans on their way in just the first three months after Oshkosh;

anyone would be more than embarrassed if that slick new airplane were to get bent up.

One of the things the pilot doesn't have to worry about is power setting. You run the engine at full throttle—close to 6000 rpm—and keep a watchful eye on the temperatures. When it comes time to land, you either throttle back or completely stop the engine, stow it away, and make like a sailplane.

The two-stroke engine stops against the same 11:1 compression stroke every time. Thus the prop hub is drilled so that the prop is vertical and ready for stowing, in most cases without further adjustment. However, the KFM engine had only about 60 hours on it at the time of my flight, and the designers felt that it might not center completely as the powerplant loosens up. A quick push on the electric starter moves the prop enough to center it. With the prop blades within three feet of your eyeballs, there's no problem in assuring that the engine is ready to retract.

Retraction time is just six seconds, and popping the powerplant back into position is the same. Thus soaring pilots can work much lower and much farther afield with this airstart capability than would be prudent with a pure sailplane.

There was some little time to explore the control touch and check on the spoilflaps before shooting a dusky landing. Rate of roll actuated by full-blown ailerons is very good, with the adverse yaw usually associated with long-winged sailplanes cut to a minimum. Just a little encouragement from the rudder isolated somewhere behind you is all that's needed for a fully-coordinated turn.

The engine is mounted with a 3 degree nose-up angle so that pitch change with power change is hardly noticed. As you take your hand off the throttle and pull back on the long spoilflap handle, you'll find a slight pitch-down tendency, but nothing that isn't handled easily by just a touch of back stick. Rutan is particularly proud of his new spoilflaps. "This is the neatest drag device you'll ever fly," he explained. "It doesn't dump you onto the runway when you pull the spoilers; it doesn't pitch the airplane when you pull flaps. You can go out with the device at dive speed and go just about straight down if you want to exceed dive speed. The plane doesn't drop or pitch when the spoilflaps are extended, it just slows down. You can leave the handle in an intermediate position and let go. It just stays there! It does have a spring that assists and holds it over center when it is all the way down. It really works much better than we had hoped for. Remember that this airplane can't have conventional flaps or spoilers; they're not usable because of the [potential for] pitch change."

The Solitaire is light enough on all controls to be considered a "hands-on" airplane, not one that you would trim out and forget about. After all, in thermaling or working ridge currents, the sailplane pilot is constantly making adjustments to get the most out of Mother Nature.

Engine out-of-the-way performance is a sparkling 32:1, making the Solitaire capable of even some competition flying (Fig. 12-14). In fact, soaring pilot Einer Enervoldson had special instrumentation in the cockpit during my brief flight, and he will be attempting to establish some records with this new ship.

Even at pattern altitude, it was getting dark enough that the instrument panel was becoming a bit difficult to read. Considering the inescapable fact that it would be darker on the ground, I decided to head for home. I flew a wide pattern, came back on part of the power over the lights of "downtown" Mojave, and rolled out on a long, high final for Runway 7. There was some straight-ahead visibility problem with the engine extended, but nothing like that of an open biplane.

Sixty miles per hour felt solid down final, and I eased in partial spoilflaps for glidepath control. Just as with any other spoiler-equipped sailplane, you don't haul on full flaps close to the ground or you'll spill much of your lift and hit hard and/or short of the runway. Remembering that I was sitting much closer to the ground than in a conventional aircraft, I made my flare close in and kept coming back on the controls, watching the canard elevator increase its angle slightly and marveling that such a small amount of control surface could handle the pitch of the craft with ease.

We squashed in the last foot and I came back on the spoilflap handle as the Solitaire touched to make sure we stayed down. The nosewheel came down easily, since there is not sufficient elevator authority to keep it off the ground for an extended roll.

Braking is with a handle next to the console, but I was already rolling past the runway's midpoint

Fig. 12-14. Solitaire in flight with the engine retracted. Isn't she a pretty bird?

and elected to let the ship roll out to the east end of the field. It was a long, murky taxi back on a taxiway that was under construction.

I played with the throttle, adding just enough speed so that the ailerons would pick up the low wing. I could then taxi on the level and not grind the tiny tip wheels on the course surface of the taxiway.

"Well, what did you think of it?" Dick Rutan asked after the engine was shut down and the two canopy latches opened.

"It's different. It does the job it was designed for," I answered as I climbed out of the cockpit.

"Now you want to get a chance and make a couple of more flights, sometime when the weather is such that you do a little soaring," Dick advised.

Later, designer Burt Rutan affirmed, "Now you've had the dirty part of the flight . . . wait 'till you can shut down that noisy engine and enjoy!"

"Sounds like a great idea; let's do it very soon," I responded. And I will!

One of the breakthroughs with the Solitaire is the provision and requirement that certain hard-to-build parts be purchased on a prefabricated basis from an approved supplier. TASK, Inc., for several years the sole source for Long-EZ landing gears, has put a sizable investment in top-quality tooling for a prefabricated fuselage shell, turtle deck, wing spars with fittings, and seat pan as well as a canopy installed in a frame. These parts are not even detailed in the plans package. You must purchase them prefab if you're going to build a Solitaire. The essential kit costs $3,726.65 (1983 dollars).

A visit to both TASK facilities shows the time and effort in tooling for building intricate molds for the contours of Solitaire. TASK is based on the airport in Santa Paula, California, with a new second-source production hangar on the airport in Eloy, Arizona. TASK President Jim Kern stated that he will not break even on his tooling until 400 sets have been ordered.

Working on the theory of trading money for time, TASK has added a list of prefabricated "frills" that can be purchased individually or as a package. These time-saving products include a series of bulkheads, main wing fillets, wing tips (including wheels), and a foam wing core kit. Using the complete frills kit and all available prefab parts, Rutan estimates that the Solitaire can be built in 400 hours of a total cost between $7,000 and $9,000.

TASK is also developing a trailer kit for their Solitaire parts. Builders can save the freight by buying the complete package and towing it home from Santa Paula, California. With an eye toward expanding business, Jim Kern and his associates are looking into the possibility of also providing financing for the tow-away package. They'll even sell you the KFM engine.

The refinements developed by Rutan Aircraft, TASK, and other parts suppliers constitute a breakthrough that bridges the gap between years of building and a few hundred hours of labor to put a do-it-yourself pilot into the air with his own homebuilt flying machine. Present sales indicate the builders are completely willing to trade money for building time, particularly when showpiece construction is available.

The Solitaire is one of the most fascinating aviation projects ever to come along. It should be reasonably easy to build. It is reasonably easy to fly. It should develop into an extremely popular soaring vehicle unburdened by towplane and ground support.

And so, another rare bird is added to a dog-eared logbook. Again, it was a ball!

Chapter 13

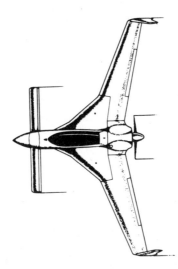

Flight Testing and First Flights

Homebuilt test flights and first flights by a homebuilder are similar, yet different. Test flying of a prototype homebuilt is frequently handled by high-time professionals with years of testing experience between their logbook covers. They explore the flight envelope of an entirely new design concept.

The individual homebuilder, working from a proven set of plans, frequently makes his own first flight, usually against the advice of the designer. After a year (or much more) of painstaking effort to create his brand-new shiny and unflown machine, the builder is emotionally involved and judgment in making those first hops can be impaired. "I built it; I can fly it!" is sometimes called the homebuilder's syndrome.

Some builders take far too much for granted. Take the case of an Australian VarieEze pilot who made a normal takeoff to about 20 feet and then dove back to the runway hard enough to hit the prop and wheel brake disks. Then the aircraft pitched up nearly vertical, rolled inverted, and crashed from about 100 feet. This was not only the pilot's first

flight in the aircraft; he had logged only one hour of solo and three or four hours of dual instruction in the preceding two years! Prior to this crash, the Eze had been flown five hours by a qualified pilot, including stalls, and the ship was considered normal.

The pilot currency suggestions for a VariEze or Long-EZ are merely the same as would be used by any other pilot going up for the first time in a new-to-him airplane. Fly a minimum of two types of airplanes in the previous four months and put in a minimum of five hours in the preceding month. Beg, borrow, or steal a backseat ride in another Eze for a first-hand look at the flying characteristics. Understand that on the Ezes you don't rotate on takeoff at an angle so high that the canard is on the horizon or above it. This same caution applies on landings.

And, of course, parachutes are recommended.

There's a step-by-step procedure for any new aircraft that proceeds from ground testing to low- and then high-speed taxi runs, including nosewheel liftoffs. Runways should be at least 3,500 feet long. The testing should not be attempted in gusty winds, particularly crosswinds. The pilot should be physically alert. There's nothing new here that isn't just good sense.

However, there are two items on the EZs that are nonstandard. The pilot can deploy both rudders at the same time and create a high drag situation—something that you can't do on a Cessna 152. In addition, the EZs have a rapid response, particularly in pitch, to very little input on the side stick. Pilots learn quickly to hold the forearm in the arm rest and control pitch with the wrist only. Only by this light-fingered technique does one avoid PIO (pilot induced oscillation) (Fig. 13-1).

HOMEBUILT FLIGHT TESTING OVERSEAS

In England, those who build a homebuilt air-craft do not get to fly their airplane the very first time, according to EZ builder Bill Allen. An assigned pilot does the first test flight, then he takes the builder along after the test pilot has checked out the airplane. Only then does the builder get to fly it all by himself.

A report of this flight-test procedure was submitted to *The Canard Pusher* by Dane and Rudi Kurth after test pilot Gion Bezzola, a Swiss Air Force instructor and jet pilot detailed the flight program:

After putting the plane together and carrying out a comprehensive preflight check, according to the American Handbook, I did two taxi tests with

Fig. 13-1. Light controls on the EZs call for extremely small pilot input. The pilot can inadvertently deploy both rudders and cause a high-drag situation.

the nose up, and another with about 30 percent power to test the elevators and to get used to them. The nose allowed itself to be lifted from the ground at about 50 mph, and to be held there. The VariEze began to dance about on its toes as if she couldn't wait to get into the air. I wished to remain captain in charge, so we stayed on the ground a while longer to test the steering. I had to remember to bring my feet back when I wasn't using them; otherwise, I would have inadvertently used the brakes. The acceleration was very good. We were very excited before the first lift-off, but this was carried out with no cause for alarm. I got used to the lateral position of the stick very quickly, and then the Eze was flying, one meter above the ground down the runway. I held the speed at about 80 mph. I decelerated by throttling down slowly, lowered the plane and landed like a feather. The steering felt finely balanced and the brakes were adequate. After four more short flights at a height of 1-2 meters, the inspectors from the Air Ministry arrived and then I was ready for the first big flight of HB-YBG.

The five short flights, the taxi tests, the performance of the engine, and the faultless work that the builder had done gave me a lot of confidence in the machine. We worked out that the center of gravity lay in the allowed area when I was wearing a parachute. The motor was running quietly, and so I asked for starting permission from the tower. That moment was here again—the first big flight in a new plane—a fantastic exciting moment. I had already experienced such a moment when I test flew my own construction, the Lutibus, HB-YAY, and now I was looking forward to it again. I opened the throttle, lifted the nose at 50 mph; at 70 mph I lifted the Eze from the runway and held the resulting angle of climb. The angle of climb came as no great surprise to me; as a jet-fighter pilot, I am already used to such a steep angle of climb! But the fact that this was a homebuilt machine powered by only 90-hp—that was a fantastic surprise.

We, the Eze and I, had hardly started, and already I was crazy about her. The steering reacted marvelously, and I trimmed it out with short blips on the electric trim switches. I had to keep watching out that I didn't exceed the permitted maximum speed for a wheel-out flight, because the plane kept wanting to go faster. The Eze was a real little thoroughbred. The air-brake worked very well when it was out and showed this by slightly noticeable buffeting.

I realized something pretty quickly; this was probably the most phenomenal plane that I had flown, and I had flown forty different types, Mirage and Hunter included.

After about twenty minutes, I carried out a simulated touch and go and could judge my imagined landing point very well, a fact that was later supported by the actual landing. On final, at about 90 mph, then over the beginning of the runway with about 80 mph on the clock, the Eze was landed with enough pilot visibility. I landed the Eze and held the nose up in order to brake aerodynamically. Rolling down the long runway gave me time to savor the thrill of that first flight. I was also pleased for the builder of HB-YBG, who had, through his extremely clean work, given me one of the best flying experiences of my life.

The yells from the spectators who had gathered in the meantime, the happy smile of the builder, Rudi Kurth, the congratulations from friends and from the officials of the Air Ministry, were payment enough for the preparation made for this flight, that was threatened at no time by an uncalculated risk. The knowledge that the VariEze designer, Burt Rutan, knew exactly what he was recommending to future Eze pilots through the handbook, proved to me that a very conscientious pilot was the spiritual father of a brand new type of plane. This knowledge grew stronger as the days passed, especially when I took the Eze through the stall test and through the largest part of the tests. How many crashed planes and their pilots could have been saved had this type of plane been designed earlier, because the behaviour of the Eze in extreme conditions is simply fantastic. That a plane can still fly controlled turns when it is stalled, and climbs with full throttle without the slightest danger of a spin is a wonderful performance of modern Aerodynamics.

The manufacturers of conventional planes will have to think again if they wish to equal this type of safe flying. The influence which the VariEze will have on general aviation cannot yet be judged, but I have the feeling that it will be a great influence. After the first flights, I was sure that Rutan had not promised too much. The plane which Rudi Kurth had built was exactly according to the specifications which could be found in the handbook.

ENGINEERING TEST FLIGHTS

Engineering test flying differs in some respects from builders' first flights. The prototype is brand-new or a new flight envelope is being explored are usually the reasons for the flights; the flying is usually done by well-qualified test pilots.

Both Dick Rutan and Mike Melvill are members of the Society of Experimental Test Pilots. Of interest is Mike's background, from the initial flying in his own VariViggen through the test-flight program of the Solitaire. We recently saw him in a $2M Beech King Air flying chase on engineering hops with Dick Rutan piloting the new Starship I.

Perhaps the most extensive engineering test flying ever done on a homebuilt was at Mojave by NASA research pilot Philip Brown and researcher Bruce Holmes. They were studying dynamically several experiments on natural laminar flow, stall characteristics, and departure susceptability which had previously been conducted in NASA-Langley's 30×60 wind tunnel.

NASA pilot Brown put the Long-EZ through all types of extreme stall entry, accelerated entries, and vertical entries with all combinations of control inputs. He also alternated left and right rudder inputs at the Dutch roll natural frequencies, combining opposite aileron to add adverse yaw effects, and all this at a maximum attainable angle of attack. Despite all combinations and gross misuse of the controls, Phil could find no way of inducing loss of control in the Long-EZ.

Visitors at RAF in Mojave have been privileged to see videotapes of this flight testing. It's wild and wonderful and should be extremely comforting to nervous builders.

During this test program, it was documented that insects or the thickness of a paint strip will destroy laminar airflow aft of 5 percent chord, while small insect remains on the leading edge forward of 4 percent chord will not trip the boundary layer (Fig. 13-2).

TEST-FLYING TIPS

The "Real" George Scott added a collection of building and flying tips for his newsletter subscribers. He detailed prerequisites and actual test flying of his VariEze this way:

Stop! After all those hard-earned dollars and many, many hours of labor on your VariEze, stop for just a minute and reflect on your flight test procedure. Ask yourself a few questions, such as:

- ☐ Am I current with recent hours in a couple different airplanes such as a Yankee or Grumman American trainer and a Piper or Cessna?
- ☐ Do I have an up-to-date BFR and medical?
- ☐ Has my local EAA Designee inspected the aircraft?
- ☐ Have other VariEze builders inspected the aircraft?
- ☐ FAA inspection and airworthiness certificate?
- ☐ Am I following Rutan's procedures in the owners manual with updates from the "Canard Pusher?"
- ☐ Is the weather perfect?
- ☐ Am I psychologically ready?

A technique that worked well for me was to fly the wife's Skyhawk from the right seat with the seat tilted back to simulate the reclining position of the VariEze seat along with right hand on the stick and left throttle. This forces you to glance out the canopy to the edge of the runway as the nose comes up in the flare just before touchdown. Don't move your head and take a chance of causing vertigo, but just move those eyeballs and look as far forward on the runway as the instrument panel and canopy allow.

On my first flight, I requested our EAA chapter designee to fly along in his PL-I for observation. Don't try any formation flights on that first test flight, but it is comforting to have someone else up

Fig. 13-2. Flight testing in all types of weather to discover how insects, rain or other contaminants can affect the airfoils.

there with you and the good Lord. If you do need to make an emergency landing, the chase plane can do some radio work to clear other air traffic for you. (Remember, you are still over the airport, so a deadstick landing is "VariEze.")

A few months ago I had a checkout ride in the rear seat of a VariEze which ended in a main gear failure. This was at a busy fly-in with about six aircraft in the pattern, and I can still remember that courteous Pitts pilot behind us as he radioed others on the frequency—"Gainesville traffic, we have a VariEze down on Runway 22; go around, go around; the runway is closed." Even though the airframe suffered damage to winglets, prop, belly and air scoop, the craft was back in the air in two weeks!

Those of you that are close to the test-flying stage should arrange two things. First, ask for some rear seat stick time in another VariEze to get used to the sensitivity of the controls. Second, ask another VariEze pilot to check the flight characteristics of your new airframe. This is no doubt one of the most difficult things you'll contemplate and I can argue either side, but look at it this way. That pilot who already has several hours in a VariEze will know instantly as he lifts off whether or not you

have an out-of-trim airplane or possibly something else wrong, where on your first flight you might over-react to a normal rotation or out-of trim condition. What's that you say? "I built that aircraft with my own hands and by golly I'm going to test fly it myself!" Well, okay, I can understand your feelings on that, but at least coax your friend to make some high speed taxi runs up through about 80 mph to test flight controls, trim settings, engine operation, and the like.

After your first takeoff, establish a cruise climb and, staying close to the airport, make some gradual turns to gain altitude to about 6,000 feet. Then try a 500-foot per minute descent to 5,000 feet for a simulated landing. Try two or three of these before your first actual landing and get used to the attitude of the aircraft at touchdown. Of course, you can't simulate the depth perception of the runway at five feet while you are at 5,000 feet, but the practice will help.

Make your approach at 95-100 mph to at least a 3,500′ strip. This airspeed is high but will make you feel more comfortable with the visibility over the nose. A slightly circular approach from downwind to final provides excellent visibility, but don't practice this on your first test flight if you haven't made a practice of it.

The thrill of your first flight in your VariEze simply can't be put into words by this writer, but I can assure you that the euphoria lives and flies on and on!!

I'd sure like to tell you that test flying is difficult; but really it's VariEze.

TRIO OF TEST FLIGHTS

The first three Eze builders to reach 500 hours, Ed Hamlin, Les Faus and Dr. Don Shupe, told of their building experience in Chapter 8. We continue here with some of their test flight experiences.

What problems did you have during test flights?

Les: Everything went beautifully during the test flight. The only problem I had was pilot error—I didn't put the gear down once. I flew 50 hours for certification—right on the money when I got it signed off—in a little over a month. I did all my flying around Mojave; some days I got in eight hours of flying. You have 25 miles for a test area. There were three of us flying the test area. The other two were a BD-4 and a Grumman TR2. The Grumman was a composite aircraft—two wrecked ones that had been glued back together. He had to fly off 15 hours and it took him about four months to get the 15 hours.

Don: I had been practicing so it was lifting off a couple of inches, and I could feel that it was stable. On this one particular day, I used full power toward the middle of the runway and instead of holding the stick down, I let the stick neutralize itself. It centered itself and the plane just came right off and it went up about 20-25 feet. It scared the hell out of me and I didn't know what to do. I was holding the stick forward by that time to keep the plane from flying and I hadn't pulled the power off yet. So here I was cruising along about 25 feet off the ground and the end of the runway was coming up really fast, because I must have been doing 80 or 90. So I jerked the power off, and when I did, with the forward stick, I just ran right down into the runway. Broke the nose gear clear off, spread the gear out—the main gears were spread out so far that the brake discs drug on the ground. And that was the first test flight experience. After I repaired that—it only took five days to repair the nose gear—a friend was at the airport who had flown an Eze, and he flew it around the pattern a couple of times and said it was just fine.

Ed: My first flight was really a super exciting thing for me. I broke ground and the first thing the airplane wanted to do was turn right. So I was busy trying to level off and get some trim into the airplane. It wanted to nose down as I didn't have enough up trim in it. I was holding it from turning right and nosing down with the stick to compensate trying to get trimmed. By the time I got it all trimmed out and looked around, I was climbing 1,000 fpm and I thought to myself, "Holy smokes, I've really got something here!" I brought it around and it took a considerable amount of gumption to try to land it because I thought here I had a dream machine and I didn't want to ding it up. After four or five hours, I got acquainted with the machine and realized I had been flying it too slow for landing.

Les had more than his share of problems that could only happen in a VariEze. As he repaired the minor damage to the nose from a gear-up landing, he put the canard into position to add weight on the nose, but he didn't bolt it. Yes, he started his takeoff and the canard came off at about 65 mph. The canard was attached only by the control rod, which broke, pulling the canard off sideways so that it cleared the canopy and prop. The canard tumbled down the runway without sustaining structural damage, and Les came to a red-faced stop as members of his flying club watched from the sidelines.

When asked what other unusual incidents were recalled, Les told about picking up another VariEze builder at Santa Barbara to accompany him to Watsonville. "To give him room, I put a jacket behind the backseat. We're flying along near King City and the engine quit. I knew I had lots of fuel, so I thought I had a terrible fuel leak. The ground was covered with fog except for a mile strip around Greenfield. I tried to make it back to King City Airport and couldn't get through the fog, so I just pulled up and landed on the street there in Greenfield. I started checking things out. The Highway Patrol, three fire units, and the Sheriff showed up about that time. It turned out that my jacket pinched off one of the fuel lines, so I had one full tank and one empty tank. I took care of that and made it on into Watsonville without any more incidents."

ACCIDENTS DO HAPPEN

Any new program will develop problems. Flight testing of the many VariEzes is no exception, though the non-spinnable canard design has a far better track record than most homebuilts.

The following accident and near-accident situations were reported to builders in Rutan's *Canard Pusher:*

By far the most hazardous situations occurred when new pilots took off with the VariEze canopy unsecured. Pete Krauss took off without his canopy locked and it opened wide at 100 mph during initial climb. He grabbed it, pulled it closed with his fingers and held it while he returned for a good landing.

Not so routine was the experience of Tony Ebel whose canopy latch was adjusted so loose that it allowed the canopy to rise and fall noticeably in flight. His flight was recorded in the newsletter by Burt.

Tony was flying at 6,000-foot altitude and 185 mph true (165 indicated) when the canopy opened. He doesn't remember if he had bumped the latch. When it opened the airplane immediately departed from controlled flight, yawed, pitched down past vertical, did a ¼ turn spin, then pitched up. Tony grabbed the canopy; it was pulled from his hand and the airplane repeated the above maneuvers. This happened about six times until he finally got the canopy closed with fingers outside (Tony did not have the knob installed on the inside). Once recovered to level flight (only 800-foot altitude), he noticed that his prop was stopped and thus he had to make a forced landing. While the prop will windmill down to 60 knots, once stopped you must go above 120 knots to restart. Tony's engine failed due to negative G at a speed below 60 knots during gyrations.

Tony's airplane dug a large hole, cartwheeled once, tore off the right wing and ended up inverted. Tony dug himself out and found that his injuries were minor—cuts and bruises.

Six newsletters and a year and a half later, an unlatched canopy caused this fatal accident just after takeoff from an airport in Texas (Fig. 13-3). Rutan's report on the accident appeared in the *Canard Pusher:*

The takeoff and initial climb to a few hundred feet were observed to be normal; then the aircraft appeared to lose control, descending in a very steep angle and crashed about three miles from the airport. Both occupants died instantly. The aircraft had over 80 hours flying time. It had been tested extensively and had never demonstrated any unusual flight characteristics, according to the previous owner. Working with the FAA investigator, we found no indication of structural failure, control disconnect or engine failure. Examination showed the canopy was not locked at impact. The aircraft was equipped with the canopy safety latch and its damage showed the canopy was open approximately 1½" and engaged in the safety latch at impact. There was no canopy unlatched (light/horn) warning system nor inside canopy closing handle installed. The aircraft was within the allowable gross weight and slightly aft of the aft CG limit.

Since the canopy was unlocked at impact, it would indicate the pilot had failed to complete his takeoff checklist and took off with an unlocked canopy. It appears that the distraction of the canopy opening against the safety latch, combined with a possible panic-stricken passenger (it was the passenger's very first airplane ride) might have caused the pilot to lose control of the aircraft.

Not all mishaps take place on the flight line, as is evident from the following incident.

The engine installation, fuel, mags, exhaust, prop, electrics, induction, instrumentation, etc., was complete. On one freezing cold Saturday afternoon in February, half a dozen friends called in to see the moment when the beast hopefully came to life. Because it was freezing cold, the builder de-

Fig. 13-3. Canopy latches can be seen in this close-up of a VariEze with Mike Melvill in the cockpit. Note full shoulder harness for crash restraint.

cided to see if it wanted to go before pushing it out into the cold. The builder's son got into the cockpit and three friends hung on to the side of the fuselage. "Switches off; master on; throttle primed and set," rang out and then "switches on." What happened in the next few seconds was, to say the least, memorable. The engine caught at the first swing and spun up to a deafening roar. Before the son could hit the switches, the fuselage drove forward and pinned all three friends to the far wall. While this was happening, everything in the workshop appeared to lift into the air and hurtle about the place—wrenches, pliers, pieces of foam, hats and coats—as if a tornado had hit. Within seconds, no one could see a thing because of the dust and debris. When the engine started, another friend, standing in the corner with his camera poised to record the momentous event, had been engulfed by a huge dust cover and was temporarily "lost." When we uncovered him, he had just been trying to figure out whether he was dead or alive as all he rememberd was a deafening roar—then everything went black!

The track record of the EZ designs has been good, however, when compared with other homebuilts. Among the first 193 VariEzes registered, FAA statistics showed that only five were involved in accidents, three of these being fatal. This figures out to 1.98 percent of Rutan designs involved in accidents, compared with an industry average of 3.93 percent for all amateur-built aircraft. As more first-flight information becomes available to EZ builders, there should be an even lower percentage of accidents.

THOSE UNFORGETTABLE FIRST FLIGHTS

Burt lists first flights of all his designs in the quarterly newsletter and encourages builders to share both the joy and the glitches that result. With the worldwide popularity of Rutan's canards, first flight reports pop up from all over the globe. Some reports are very factual and low-key, while others utilize a wide range of adjectives. Regardless of how they are worded, all reflect excitement and great pride. Most contain words of praise for the particular design, the designer, and the building program.

Rich Clark of Hermosa Beach, California, submitted the following account of his first flight in E-Z-GO:

"Liftoff surprised me. Continuing acceleration with the stick slightly back is a lot different from stabilizing my speed with the nose held down. I tried mentally to freeze my hand and succeeded in a series of damped pitch oscillations during initial climb. Roll/yaw okay. I let out a Texas yell, wiggled the wings for the congregation, and settled down to trim out. Descent and approach were smooth. Love those ailerons. Over the numbers at 80 knots, overflared up to 20 feet, and another series of pitch oscillations. Eventually, E-Z-GO got tired of the comedy and sank to the runway. The solid rumbling of gear on runway and straight roll-out were reasuring. Why could I not drive it on? Main factors were pitch sensitivity and Cessna training. Also, confusion with left-hand throttle where up is go and down is slow.

"Later—feeling at home expanding the envelope. Sure enough, won't stall, just nods. Heavy back pressure at low speeds. Easy to locate traffic up here in the bubble. High on final. I ease back to 70 knots to below glide slope. Ease power on to hold it. Good flare and soft rumble and I'm at jogging speed. Had a lot of confidence before I had flown it; now I have much more."

Paul and Kim Prout (father and son) flew their Long-EZ after 23 months of construction time. They advised that "the high-speed taxi testing in preparation for our first flight was conducted at the airport in Chino, California, using Runway 21/3 which is 6,200 feet long. This was about the right length needed to achieve canard flying speed (50 knots), rotate, hold altitude, and lift off (60-65 knots) to 5-10 feet altitude, and then touch back down and stop. This enabled us to get a good feel for the landing flare and develop roll control (which is substantially quicker than most general aviation aircraft)."

Sometimes first flights are not always reported from the cockpit. Mrs. Thelma Hamel described watching her husband Ellsworth's first flight in VariEze N235EH this way: "It was a tremendously scary and exhilarating moment when Ellis started climbing. There is nothing in my life that can compare to the shudder and thrill I felt—not even the birth of our first child!"

FIRST FLIGHT FOR A VIGGEN

When Leonard "Dobby" Dobson completed his VariViggen in Georgetown, Texas, he deliberately kept his first flight a low-key project with no advance publicity as to date or time. As he reported it in the *Pusher*, he had two fellow EAA members to assist him:

They each inspected the aircraft and checked my weight and balance figures. They also made sure that I used my checklist for preflight before they turned me loose and got into the chase plane. At approximately 9:00 A.M., August 1, 1981, three years and one month after the start of construction, Rutan VariViggen N73LD, serial #533, lifted off. Some preliminary pilot induced oscillation and wing rock caused by nervousness and heavy-handed input made the takeoff a little wild. However, I established a rate of climb at about 800 fpm, leveled off at 3,000 feet, and then took a few seconds off to congratulate myself on my achievement so far. I did not retract the gear during this flight and I kept the speed below 120 mph. I spent the next 30 minutes getting acquainted with the airplane and then made two simulated approaches and landings at altitude. Cylinder head temperature had been running on the high side, so I decided to terminate the flight before I had completed my program. The landing was interesting. It is very difficult to break the habit of years of making stall landings; 2,000 or so hours in Cessnas, Pipers, and Beeches doesn't make an expert in a Viggen! Finding the correct pitch attitude is the tough part. I have an angle of attack indicator, but by the time I get it calibrated, I probably won't need it any more.

My second flight was much more enjoyable because I was relaxed. Takeoff and landing were beautiful. Handling in the air was delightful. My wife was a passenger in the chase plane, and she described the flight as that of a graceful yellow butterfly.

After Dobby had completed his flight program, he had some suggestions and comments for Viggen builders:

Program your test flights. My Viggen costs me about $18 per hour to fly just for fuel. That amounts to $720 to fly off the restrictions. I made it a worthwhile expenditure by making up my own flight manual on performance and flying characteristics, instead of just aimlessly flying around in circles.

I have heard and read many stories of homebuilders praising the ability of their creations to fly "hands-off." My Viggen is not a hands-off airplane. I neither wanted it to be nor expected it to be in that category. Either I fly it or it will fly me, but I love it.

Plans for the VariViggen have been available since 1974, but very few airplanes have been completed and flown, and that is too bad. Sure, it's a complex airplane to build and sure, it's not cheap, but it has been a worthwhile project. My Viggen is not a Grand Champion or even close to it, but it sure draws a crowd. Hundreds of people have admired it, both in the air and on the ground. I have approximately 50 requests for rides when the restrictions are flown off. Included in this group are a number of corporate pilots who fly Gulfstreams, Lears, MU-2s, King Airs, and 421s. These are pilots who have to wear neckties when they fly, and generally they don't get overly enthusiastic about any airplane.

I can only hope that this report from an enthusiastic youngster of 68 will get some of you guys back on the stick to finish your Viggens.

Chapter 14

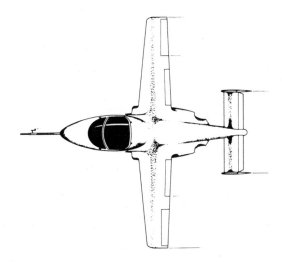

SCALED

It was early in 1983 when SCALED Composites, Inc., was introduced to the aviation community. As reported in the *Canard Pusher*: "SCALED is, in fact, an acronym for Scaled Composites: the Advance Link to Efficient Development. Pat Storch spent several late nights and the better part of a carafe of white wine to come up with that name!"

Burt sent out a simple mimeographed announcement that said, in part: "The invitational Hangar Warming today marks the end of the organizational phase of the new company and is an opportunity for SCALED to show you its new facility, as the building is normally closed due to the proprietary nature of SCALED's projects."

The SCALED concept is to provide aerospace companies with a complete engineering, technical, and flight-test staff to develop and test scaled-down, manned prototypes. Customers are provided the entire picture of static and dynamic flying qualities at a reasonable cost because of the small development team working in a low-overhead environment.

Directing projects at SCALED with Rutan are Vice President Herb Iversen and Corporate Secretary Pat Storch. Iversen and Burt are long-time business associates, dating back to 1976 and the NASA AD-1 skew wing (see Chapter 2) and, more recently, the NGT jet trainer project (Fig. 14-1). Iversen had been with Ames Industrial Corp., Bohemia, New York, for ten years, rising to Vice-President/General Manager.

It proved inconvenient and inefficient for Iversen to work on the East Coast and Rutan on the West, so the pair combined forces and established SCALED. Herb, his wife and daughter now reside in Mojave. He is one of the few team members who is not *yet* a pilot.

Pat Storch came from the midwest, growing up on her grandparents farm in Crete, Illinois. She spent eight years as a veterinary medical technician and paramedic before coming west. She went to work at RAF and took her initial flight training from Dick Rutan in the company's Grumman Tiger. She flew solo in the Long-EZ as a student pilot (Chapter

Fig. 14-1. Herb Inversen and Burt Rutan are shown at the SCALED Open House.

7) and has flown the sleek new Solitaire. She now has a private license and recently purchased a vintage Luscombe.

Pat explained that SCALED is a small enough company that everyone pitches in to do whatever is necessary at the time. Office titles are required to deal with outside business, but are not necessarily job descriptions. "Herb and I screen out data and give the pertinent things to Burt," she explained. "SCALED is different than RAF because we must maintain our secrecy. I even do my own color film processing."

PHOTOS BY PAT STORCH

Pat became an instant photographer on one of those beautiful days when big puffy cumuli were popping over the desert and the Grizzly was flying. It seems as though a full RAF crew climbed aboard the Grumman chase plane and Pat was the only one

Fig. 14-2. Pat Storch uses the open baggage compartment of the Grumman Tiger as a camera platform. This is not the world's greatest place to shoot air-to-air pictures.

carrying a camera. The results were excellent and she's been at it ever since, including turning in more than her share of air-to-air covers on monthly publications. Pat uses a most unconventional technique with the low-winged Grumman Tiger. She climbs into the baggage compartment (Fig. 14-2) with the door off and shoots from there. No, she hasn't dropped a camera yet!

Her favorite photo to date is an early air-to-air shot of the Solitaire that *Soaring* magazine used on the cover.

Almost all the members of the small SCALED staff are homebuilders who have worked on previous Rutan designs. In fact, much of the initial recruitment for the company was done in issues of the *Canard Pusher,* which now has a quarterly mailout circulation of 3,500, including 300 overseas customers. One such early announcement stated, "SCALED is still in need of a few good shop bodies to start after Christmas. Work will include helping with layups, building tooling and jigs, sweeping floors, etc." A more technical opening read, "SCALED has purchased a new computer-assisted drafting package and we are looking for an enthusiastic engineer/draftsman to use it. The system is based on the Apple II + microcomputer."

"SCALED is a company through which we can do research projects," explained Burt. "I had a situation with the Fairchild Republic New Generation Trainer (NGT, Fig. 14-3) program in which part of the developmental work was being done by Rutan Aircraft Factory (RAF). In the same building where we were attempting to conduct proprietary work, including a flight test program of a very sensitive nature, we had the need to bring in our VariEze and Long-EZ customers to service them. It quickly became obvious that we needed a separate facility for SCALED so that both RAF and SCALED customers could be served in an appropriate manner."

The entire SCALED project, including the new 30,000-square foot, fully air-conditioned facility right on the flight line at Mojave, was funded by the principals and two private investors. Included in the building is a Jacuzzi and a racketball court. Conference rooms and offices are completely functional, but when compared with the rather Spartan facilities at RAF next door, the immediate impression was that SCALED was really plush. However, Burt defended the expense, saying, "When you live in Mojave, you're really not downtown. We feel that any amenities we can provide to keep our employees happy and comfortable are well worth the effort. When you live in Mojave, you'd better be really in love with airplanes and with your family. There really isn't much else to do."

Fig. 14-3. Mike Melvill flies the NGT during test flights. The probe on the nose is for precision airspeed and angle of attack data collection. Aircraft is 2/3 scale "flying model" of Fairchild T-46.

Fig. 14-4. Lotus Microlight on the flight line during SCALED's Open House.

More than 350 guests attended the initial open house, including local officials, key Edwards Air Force Base personnel and China Lake NAS staff, writers, and employee families. There were fly-bys just before dusk, including a brief flight by Dick in a brand new European microlight developed for Colin Chapman, former director of the Lotus Company. Chapman had suffered a fatal heart attack within the previous week.

THE LOTUS MICROLIGHT

This two-place, side-by-side canard microlight was in the 300-pound empty weight class to conform with British microlight specifications. During its brief—and only—public appearance, the Chapman microlight was powered with a KFM 109 engine "just to get it off the ground." Later, it was to be powered by a brand new four-cylinder, four-stroke Lotus engine that was subsequently introduced as the Eipper-Lotus engine. Dick made a few passes down the runway in Mojave's notoriously gusty wind that just about equaled the design envelope of the tiny craft. This flight was made on only the third day of test flying (Figs. 14-4, 14-5).

Later the Chapman prototype was shipped to England, where a new company was formed for the express purpose of putting the new ship into production on the Continent. No plans had been made to market the microlight in the United States.

An insight into Burt's expanding business philosophy was obtained during the open house by Jack Cox, Editor of *Sport Aviation* magazine, and his

Fig. 14-5. Dick Rutan makes a low pass with the Lotus Microlight late in the afternoon near the mothballed 707s at Mojave.

ubiquitous tape recorder. Cox recorded:

"Whatever we do will have to be of a low-visibility nature. One of the reasons SCALED is attractive to our customers is this low visibility. The project is not in the customer's facility, it's out here in Mojave and if it's a failure, then it's not really their failure. It's just something they hired out. If it's a success, though, it's *their* success.

"We are staffed for the projects we have under contract now. Our facilities will permit expansion to around 30 or so employees, but I expect that SCALED will stay within the 18 to 30 level indefinitely. There will be . . . already are . . . pressures to grow larger, but we want to hold SCALED to that size.

"We are not in the manufacturing business. We will build one or two prototypes of a particular design concept. . . to prove the concept. Beyond that, the customer will do what manufacturing that may result.

"One reason I don't want to grow too much is that I like to get personally involved in almost every aspect of the business . . . be it helping the tooling man decide just how best to get a good release from a mold, to helping with the details on how to vacuum bag a part, to the selection of materials, to structural design, to assisting with the designing of the smallest bracket to, say, a major landing gear or that sort of thing. I enjoy all this and if we get much bigger, then I'm going to have to fade into the background and just do conceptual things . . . or administrative things, which I *don't* want to do.

"So what I've tried to do is bring people around me who are good at these things. Herb does the administrative things very well and Pat does likewise with the bookkeeping, office management, being sure we have all the supplies, that we get paid, etc.—so I don't have to do all that.

"I do like to stay very personally involved with the aerodynamics, certainly, and with structural design—and the writing of the software for computer programs that do these things.

"I like the personal motivating and helping put together a team that works well together . . . I like that.

"If we get too big, I won't have time to do the things I want to do with RAF . . . and to go to Oshkosh every summer.

"I also like to keep my finger on other research programs—the commuter research NASA is doing, for instance. We've assisted a little bit in that. I like to go back there and help them occasionally, and to learn from what they are doing.

"I also want to be comfortable doing things. We've tried to tailor the building to maximize my time and effort . . . with things like a lunchroom with a microwave so I don't have to go out to eat . . . and a racquetball court and a Jacuzzi so I can get the exercise I should have without leaving the building. We used to drive an hour, round trip, to Lancaster to get in an hour of racquetball.

"Time is so valuable. Time and people are really the greatest resources we have in doing what we are trying to do." (The foregoing reprinted from *Sport Aviation* by permission of the Experimental Aircraft Association.)

STARSHIP I

Following the open house, the doors were shut at SCALED except to employees. Industrial security continues to be maintained at a remarkably high efficiency. While the first large project of SCALED was under development, none of us on the outside had any feeling for what was undertaken. The first inkling of SCALED's new Beechcraft Starship I occurred because pirated photos from the Mojave flightline were published only within two weeks of the craft's formal announcement and public viewing at the NBAA (National Business Aircraft Association) in 1983 at Dallas. Dick Rutan, Mike Melvill, Bud Francis, Beech chief test pilot, and Linden Blue, Beech president, logged a total of more than 50 hours between first flight and the NBAA Convention where the 85 percent scale flying model plus a full-scale mockup were the highlights of the show (Figs. 14-6 through 14-8).

Burt explained that he and Beechcraft had been discussing the project since 1979. In announcing the new plane, Linden Blue stated:

"Many configurations were considered over a five-year period, with the first tandem-wing, pusher layout initially being studied by Beech en-

Fig. 14-6. Beechcraft's Starship in flight. (courtesy Beech Aircraft Corporation)

gineers several years ago.

"Following development of these initial concepts, we invited Burt Rutan of SCALED Composites, Inc. (SCI), to join in the configuration study. This joint study ultimately resulted in the determination that the tandem-wing arrangement would be

the best solution for achieving the objectives we wanted. A full-scale development program was then launched by Beech, with part of that program involving a contract to SCI to develop an 85 percent scale flying prototype.

"SCI was selected for its broad experience

Fig. 14-7. Starship I is pulled into the SCALED hangar after a test flight. Then the doors were shut!

Fig. 14-8. Starship in flight shows a profile for the future. (courtesy Beech Aircraft Corporation)

with composites and this aerodynamic configuration, plus its unique abilities to quickly and economically build and do preliminary testing on a flying scale model based on composites. They did an excellent job for us.

"With the 85 percent scale prototype, we essentially have a flying wind-tunnel model. However, data obtained is much more valuable because the airplane is operating in actual flight conditions, allowing both a shorter development cycle and a more refined product."

Price for Starship I, with standard Super King Air B200-type avionics, is projected to be $2,742,500 in 1983 dollars.

The $2.5M+ Starship I is a far cry from the initial VariEze, but it is certainly a direct descendant.

Rutan explained to us that the 85 percent scale was dictated by the size of the two 1,000-shaft-horsepower Pratt and Whitney PT6A-60 engines. "This was as small as we could go with the same engine size," said Burt. "We've never built anything this size before. It is presently the world's largest composite aircraft."

Starship I has many innovations besides composite structure. The turbines drive "jetfans," a new term indicating the convergence of jetprop, propfan and fanjet technology. Jetfans on the 85 percent Starship I have four blades.

The promotionally minded at Beechcraft call the winglets "tipsails." Fuel is carried in the blended aft "wet wing." The computer-aided tandem wing has a variable-geometry forward wing. Forward wing geometry is linked directly to the two-position flaps, according to the Beech announcement.

The production Starship I will be 5.5 feet wide, nearly a foot wider than the company's Super King Air B200. It is effectively longer by two feet and taller from floor to top of center aisle by nearly nine inches. Pressurization will be at 8.5 psi for a 41,000-foot cruising altitude.

Shortly after the NBAA preview of Starship I, we were at Mojave while the new plane was out on a test flight. After a four-hour flight, testing sawtooth climbs and asymmetric stalls, the new Beechcraft and its accompanying King Air chase plane made an unscheduled landing at Bakersfield, only 50 nautical miles distant for refueling.

"I was down to about fumes," said Mike Melvill, who was flying the King Air.

As the two aircraft returned to Mojave, we could hear Mike's voice on the radio saying, "You've got a gear; you're two miles out." Then the two classy twins came streaking straight-in, away from the hazy afternoon sun.

Our photo (Fig. 14-9) shows that the landing was made with only partial flaps. Yet Dick made the midpoint turnoff without a problem and taxied up to SCALED's 100-foot hangar door. As soon as the

Fig. 14-9. Starship touches down at Mojave.

crew was out, a tug pulled the new ship into the hangar and the doors were closed. No one invited us inside at this particular time, but that's to be expected at SCALED—and you don't take it personally. Because the flying testbed is only 85 percent of the production unit, Beech officials did not want visitors inside because of the slightly smaller cabin interior.

END OF AN ERA

As activity continued at SCALED, Burt Rutan faced a very basic decision: whether to continue his efforts in designing aircraft for homebuilders or to concentrate on complex developments for commercial and military use. The designer chose the latter course for several reasons, most of them economic. He announced this decision, an unpopular one among the many homebuilders, on the eve of Oshkosh 1985. In that issue of the "Canard Pusher," Burt summarized his work with RAF. "From the onset, I have limited RAF's marketing to that of plans and support items. It is easier for me to assure the quality of these items. RAF's decision not to get into the business of manufacturing parts and kits was based mainly on the desire to stay small and avoid the responsibility (and thus liability) of assuring that each bolt, wing spar, or engine, etc., was perfect. The plans business on the VariEze and initially the Long-EZ was excellent, and with a low overhead, RAF was very successful, paid lots of taxes, and built a reasonable cash health.

"This success story worked, however, only on those two designs. The others—VariViggen, Grizzly, Solitaire, and Defiant—have not been viable in the marketplace. Even though developed and flight tested, the Grizzly was never offered because it did not seem that the costs of preparing drawings could be recovered. The Solitaire cost several times as much to develop as the Long-EZ, and the market was dismally small, resulting in a major drain on RAF's financial security.

"The Voyager project was done primarily because I decided that this significant project would be worth more in terms of the feeling of accomplishment by achieving an aviation milestone than the more obvious financial income to be received by introducing a new homebuilt. I had thought that the Defiant would be a tremendous success for RAF, because of the excitement it generated upon its introduction in 1978, and because I had found it to be my favorite transportation for nearly 1000 hours of very enjoyable flying. However, this did not prove to be the case, since now at the end of its first year of introduction, after its direct costs of printing, mailing, and contract support, its income has not even covered the overhead of one of our four RAF people.

"We, as well as others in the homebuilt market arena, are seeing a market that has been declining in the past two years. Long-EZ sales are down to 20 percent of last year's rate. It is possible that this is due to cost increases, but it is also likely that it is due to saturation."

In his announcement, Rutan noted that the continuing business of developing homebuilt aircraft and selling plans can be self-defeating. He continued, "As the number of new builders grows each year, the number that require support continuously grows to significant proportions. Plans sold in 1974 still get attention for building assistance, and the oldest airplanes still need help with operational problems."

Rutan said that he had the problem of expanding RAF in a declining marketplace or curtailing overhead to do only builder support. He then stated, "As of today, July 13, 1985, RAF will no longer market homebuilt aircraft plans. RAF will be open Monday through Friday for sales of everything but plans. Builder support via telephone will be limited to Tuesdays and Fridays only.

"It is a difficult decision, of course, to retreat from the homebuilt business, since it has been a tremendous amount of fun working with people who also are having a lot of fun. It was a decision made necessary by the nature of the business and our success in the last two years. Also, I have been spread so thin on time, conducting other businesses at SCALED Composites that I have been unable to meet the schedule I wanted on the next RAF aircraft."

This basic decision changed the lives of a number of others. Fred Keller, for example, with two years work in the No. 2 Defiant, did continue builder support for the less than 50 builders who had purchased plans before the cut-off date. And undoubtedly, there were a number of bootleg Defiant plans available. Keller is presently developing a composite bush airplane for Alaskan use.

Long-EZ builders had, as promised, a limited support from Mike and Sally Melvill on a two-day-a-week telephone-only basis. This support, while not required, was Burt's way of continuing to assist the homebuilders with whom he had worked closely for a dozen years.

Nat Puffer with his Cozy moved to Mesa, Arizona. He continued to pay Rutan royalties for his portion of the side-by-side design and is devoting

his full-time efforts to selling plans, helping Cozy builders, and developing a four-place version of the Cozy.

Thus ended the most successful homebuilding company that ever existed. One month to a day before Burt's closing of development work with RAF, Beech Aircraft Corp. announced the acquisition of SCALED as a wholly owned subsidiary for an undisclosed cash payment. Burt and the other key personnel remained with the company (Fig. 14-10).

Probably Burt doesn't remember it, but his mother Irene did. She showed us a letter from Beech in 1958, which said, in part, "Since you mention he is planning to build other Beechcraft models now (in addition to his Bonanza) we're enclosing photographs and blueprints of our other commercial models; also the T-34 (Army and Navy trainer) and

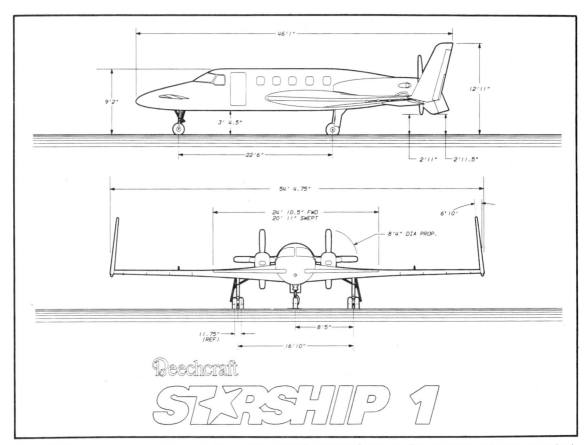

Fig. 14-10. Three-view drawing of the production version of the Beechcraft Starship I. First customer deliveries are scheduled for the second quarter of 1988. (courtesy Beech Aircraft)

Fig. 14-11. Rollout of first full-scale Starship at Beech Field, Wichita, Kansas. More than 1,000 Beechcrafters are working on the new Rutan design.

hope this material will assist him in his future model building.

"I hope, too, since Elbert is so air-minded, he can use this talent—perhaps he will be an aeronautical engineer some day!"

(Signed) L. Winters, Executive Secretary.

SCALED, A DIVISION OF BEECHCRAFT

SCALED has continued to develop a number of hush-hush prototypes for Beech and other companies. At NBBA in October, 1986, Rutan announced that SCALED was building three POC (proof-of-concept) general aviation aircraft. These included a cabin-class piston twin, a turbofan

derivative of the same aircraft, and a five-seat light single with coast-to-coast range. He showed a model of the twin with a piston engine on one wing and a turbofan on the other. The aircraft has a small fixed forward wing with flaps, slightly aft-swept main wing with engine mounting similar to the Starship, and a unique T-tail with a forward-swept stabilizer. Price tag for the proposed piston "son of Starship" was $750,000, with the turboprop $1,000,000. Price tag for the turbofan called "the world's first light-light jet" is $1,200,000.

Base price of the new Beech Starship was listed at $3,667,587 in mid-1987. The price went up 12 percent from the original announcement, while the certified gross weight went from 12,500 to 14,000 pounds.

The five-place piston single will cost less than $200,000 and has less than 2/3 the wetted area of a Mooney. Estimates call for 240-to-245-knot cruise at 25,000 feet on 10 gph.

Mojave flight line scuttlebutt is that the twin has flown, but no announcement has been made as yet (Fig. 14-11). Beech is continuing with an original semiproduction order of six full-sized Starships for the test and certification program. Beechcraft built three as flying articles with one each for static, fatigue, and environmental testing. More than

1,000 Beechcrafters are building the new airplane in a half-million square feet of manufacturing and engineering space in Wichita, Kansas. As of March, 1987, as many as six Beechcraft pre-prototypes are being built at SCALED.

Latest Rutan design to be announced publicly is a Long-EZ look-alike called the CM-44 (Fig. 14-12). Ordered by California Microwave, Inc., for a 1987 U. S. Army drone competition, the CM-44 is powered with a 210-hp turbocharged Lycoming engine, will carry a 400-to-600-pound payload with a top speed of 195 mph and an economy range of 18 hours. The CM-44 can be flown either as a drone

Fig. 14-12. Military drone, CM-44, was developed by SCALED for California Microwave, Inc. The CM-44 can be flown as a drone or as a piloted aircraft. It has an economy duration of 18 hours.

Fig. 14-13. Crowd of potential investors view the debut of Rutan's design, the CM-44 military drone. Note the inward cant of the winglets.

or with a pilot aboard. Financial analysts predict the U. S. Government will spend almost $900 million per year by 1995 (Fig. 14-13).

Although it looks much like the Long-EZ, Rutan assured the crowd attending the official debut of the CM-44 that it was an entirely new aircraft, designed for mass production with proprietary composite structures that do not require an autoclave.

The publication of the Society of Experimental Test Pilotsnoted that SCALED had almost tripled in size in the past one and one-half years, now

having 92 employees. "SCI is now developing (several) aircraft, all of which will have flight tests within the next year (1987). This level of activity in flight test development of new aircraft is probably unsurpassed in the country."

While now not directly involved with homebuilt aircraft—except for Voyager, the biggest and most successful homebuilt of them all—Rutan continues with a seemingly endless list of new and successful designs.

Chapter 15

Voyager: The 23,000-Mile Challenge

What better way to conclude this edition of the Burt Rutan story than to recount the development of Voyager, the "round-the-world-on-one-tank-of-gas airplane." At the successful conclusion of the Voyager project, this trimaran was probably the best known aircraft of the decade.

In a world of aerospace achievements ranging from supersonic flight to the space shuttle, from bicycling across the English Channel to ballooning across the oceans, very few challenges remain. One of these was to fly an airplane around the world nonstop, nonrefueled. There was no Kremer prize for this effort, no pot of gold at the end of the trip, no production aircraft result from the effort—nothing, except that it hadn't been done before.

"It's like Mount Everest still unclimbed," said Dick Rutan. He might have said that he will fly around the world because it is there.

Basic idea for the flight and the initial concept for Voyager actually began in 1981, when the Rutans were eating a Basque burger, if you will, at Reno's Cafe in "downtown Mojave," a mile from the RAF hangar. The discussion got around to what

worthwhile aviation records were yet to be broken. Dick said, "The only suborbital flight that really amounts to anything would be to fly around the world nonstop, nonrefueled." Burt picked up a paper napkin and sketched out what eventually became Voyager (Fig. 15-1). Later Dick said, "He (Burt) got that look in his eye and that became our overwhelming activity for the next six years."

Actually, Voyager probably goes back farther than Mojave—back to the days when Burt was working for Jim Bede in Kansas, where he was somewhat involved with Bede's BD-2, a modified Schweizer 2-32 sailplane built for Dave Blanton of Wichita, Kansas. Blanton planned a LOVE (Low Orbit Very Efficient) flight to circle the earth well north of the equator, at 35 degrees north latitude, where the distance around the globe is only 20,000 miles. Although the round-the-world flight never materialized, the plane did establish some notable nonstop flights.

WHAT IS VOYAGER?

First official announcement of Voyager was

AN EARLY SKETCH OF THE VOYAGER CONFIGURATION

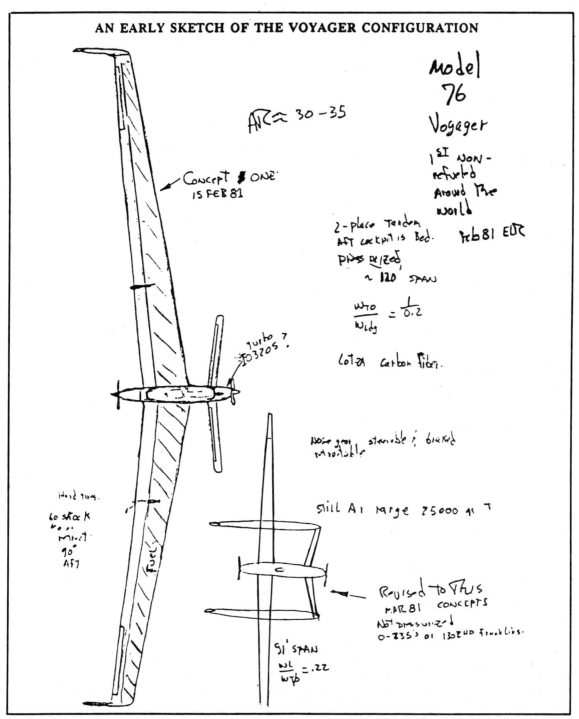

Fig. 15-1. Early sketch of Voyager configuration. Initial sketch, on left, dated February 15, 1981, shows a single small cockpit, no fuel booms, and a wingspan of 120 feet. Smaller sketch at bottom, revised in March, 1981, showed planform that was essentially used. Original span was 91 feet; drawing has the notation, "Lotsa carbon fiber."

made in 1982, when Burt spoke at the annual Charles A. Lindbergh Aeronautics Lecture at the National Air and Space Museum. He outlined the basic design problems in developing Voyager. In part, he said, "The range equation that tells how far an airplane will go is based on four things: one is propeller efficiency; one is fuel efficiency of the engine; one is aerodynamics, or the lift-to-drag ratio of the airplane; the fourth is the ratio of takeoff to landing weight.

"This airplane doesn't ask for improvements in propeller or engine technology. It does use good aerodynamics—very low span loading, very high aspect ratio. It represents some major advances in composites, using carbon fiber structures to allow a large part of the plane to be fuel.

"The airplane is indeed almost all fuel; it is easier to say where the fuel is *not*. It is *not* in the vertical fins; it is *not* where there are engines, and it is *not* where there is just enough room for a reclinable seat and an adjustable bed for the crew of two.

"It has a very small bubble canopy on top so that when the pilot is sitting straight up he will be able to see all around. But most of the time the crew will just look out the portholes on the sides.

"It is going to be both a technical challenge and a very interesting adventure."

The end result was Voyager, a one-of-a-kind push-pull aeronautical trimaran mounted on a wing, the length of which is 34 times its average width. Engines were mounted in tandem. The machine was essentially a flying gas tank with 17 different fuel tanks located in the wings, tail booms, canard, and fuselage.

In his initial announcement, Burt Rutan said, "When the aircraft is heavy, true air speed will be about 130 knots with both engines operating. As fuel is burned off, speed will be gradually reduced to under 70 knots, where less than 25 horsepower will be required with a fuel burn of only a couple of gallons per hour. It is planned to shut down the front engine early in the flight and restart it only in case of a malfunction in the rear engine (which then can be run at fairly high power settings for best efficiency). Propellers are wood and fiber and full feathering; they were developed in West Germany

by MT-Propellers." (These were later changed to metal Hartzell propellers.)

Originally, Voyager incorporated the same kind of a collapsible cabin fuel-bladder tank that the two pilots developed for the Alaska-Caribbean record in their Long-EZ, where a waterbed carried fuel in the rear cockpit (see Chapter 1). As the fuselage tank was exhausted, Dick explained that the space would be used for crew to live in. However, Burt Rutan configured sufficient fuel in conventional tanks so that the bladder tank provision was discarded early in the design stage.

AROUND THE FAT PART

Voyager's record attempt differed materially from older speed dashes that went via Paris, Rome, Calcutta, and Tokyo. "Around-the-world" records were flown in 1931 by Wiley Post and Harold Getty in the Lockheed Vega *Winnie Mae*, and two years later, a solo record of 7 days, 18 hours was set by Wiley Post. Post's records were along a shortcut route over northern Russia and Alaska, a distance of only 15,474 miles (Fig. 15-2).

At least one other serious attempt at the intriguing goal of around-the-world, nonstop, nonrefueled was undertaken at Mojave. Tom Jewett, co-developer of the *Quickie* (see Chapter 6) and Eugene Sheehan developed *Big Bird*, later renamed *Free Enterprise*, for an attempt at this record flight. The aircraft was a single-engine conventional tractor with a fixed tri-gear, powered with a four-cylinder turbocharged Franklin Pezetel 130-hp engine. *Big Bird* had a span of 51 feet 6 inches, empty weight of 1700 pounds, and a calculated maximum range of 24,500 miles at 20,000 to 30,000 feet. The original design called for 365 gallons of fuel, but the modular construction could have permitted up to 550 gallons. An autopilot would have permitted up to an estimated 10 hours of sleep during a 90-hour proposed flight by a single pilot. Jewett was killed when the plane crashed at Mojave some four months after its first flight and the project was cancelled.

Dr. Paul MacCready, developer of the man-powered Gossamer Condor series, looked at the

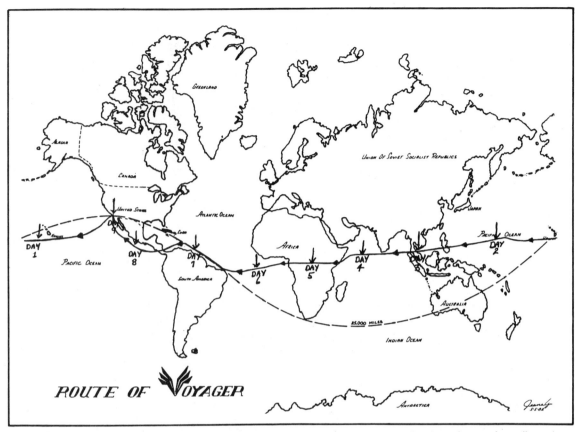

Fig. 15-2. Rough sketch used during world attempt showing proposed route (dashed lines) south over Australia and actual route (solid line with arrows).

project with interest. Shortly after Voyager was initially announced, he asked us about the availability of a Mooney Ranger, a low-production pressurized four-placer that might be adapted for such a mission. However, this effort was not pursued further. Dr. MacCready told us it was because he felt that the Rutan Voyager project was far enough developed and had a reasonably good chance of success—this, over three years before the record flight.

Several other projects have been proposed, but none has surfaced at press time that appears to hold any serious competition for Voyager. Terry Bloodworth of Memphis, Tennessee, is looking at U-2 fuselage with modified variable sweep wings. Jerry Mullins of Oklahoma City, Oklahoma, is reported to be working with the Bede Love One that holds

the piston engine straight-line distance record, and Julian Nott from London is considering a flight around the world in a "Super Pressure Balloon."

COPILOT JEANA YEAGER

On one occasion, long before Voyager was announced, we met up with Jeana Yeager as she came out the back door of the RAF hangar. She wore a half-detached surgical mask and old spotted work clothes. As she carefully cleaned the carbon fiber from under her fingernails, she commented, "I never knew there was so much sanding to do on any airplane." In a biography prepared when Jeana was establishing six closed-course records in the Long-EZ, we find that she had 13 years' experience in design drafting—mechanical, architectural, aero-

233

nautical, electrical, and illustrative. Before coming to Mojave, she was an administrative assistant for a geophysical company and a designer for rocket propulsion systems, fuel/body installations, and development and testing. A petite 98 pounds, she comes from Texas. Her first love was training quarter horses.

THE GAME PLAN

The game plan for Voyager was for Burt to design the machine and build it with a very small team at RAF. After proving the structure by flight test, the aircraft was turned over to Voyager Aircraft, Inc. (Dick and Jeana) for installation of special engines, props, and navigation equipment.

The basic structure of Voyager was built in the 40-by-45-foot workshop area in the back of RAF. A small crew, never more than five people including Dick and Jeana, did the fabrication. Key builder in the project was crew chief Bruce Evans, an early Long-EZ builder who put in over 7,000 hours, sometimes at 20 hours a day, on the machine. After the world flight, he literally disappeared into the back country of Baja California, where he sent back a ghostly tape recording of what fishing sounds like. "Maybe he'll never come back," said Dick Rutan. "If so, he earned it."

There were only 11 engineering drawings made for the entire aircraft, belying the axiom around production aircraft that "when the weight of the drawings equals the weight of the aircraft, it's about ready to fly."

THE COMPOSITE INDUSTRY HELPED

Hercules Aerospace Company, Salt Lake City, Utah, was the first major corporate sponsor. Wing spars were fabricated in the Hercules Bacchus Works southwest of Salt Lake City. The magnamite graphite fiber and graphite components of the C-shaped spars are also used in satellites, missiles, the Space Shuttle, and high performance aircraft. The spars were baked in the autoclave at Hercules and brought home on a sailplane trailer by Dick and Bruce. The autoclave produces higher pressures, up to 200 psi, while normal vacuum bagging does not exceed 14.7 psi. The high pressure autoclave

can squeeze out unnecessary epoxy to cut weight and produce a more consistent part. (Subsequently, a jet black cat that wandered into the Voyager hangar and was adopted by Office Manager Wanda Wolf was appropriately named Magnamite.)

Originally, the wing had balsa wood trailing edges with urethane foam that warped when the mylar covering was applied. Urethane was put between the ribs and then a layer of glass on the covering as a fix.

The Hexcell Corporation, San Francisco, California, provided the structural material, an HRH-10 Aramid honeycomb core and high modulus graphite facings that are lightweight, high strength, stiff, and workable. The core is 1/4-inch thick, and the facings, carbon fiber preimpregnated with epoxy, are bonded to both sides of the core under heat and pressure. When the epoxy is cured, these "skins" are 14/1000 of an inch thick but have the tensile strength of heat-treated aircraft steel at only 1/6 the weight. This sandwich combination weighs 4 ounces per square foot.

The prepreg carbon fiber tape/nomex honeycomb sandwich structure required RAF to build a special, large oven for curing the skins at 250 degrees. One reporter called it "a home-brew oven made of corrugated house siding and the heating element from a home furnace."

"This couldn't have been done a few years ago," said Burt. "It would be impossible for an aluminum airplane. The graphite and honeycomb structure makes the whole difference."

If the airframe had been made of conventional sheet aluminum, the thickness would have had to be .016 to equal the same weight, and metal in this thickness would completely distort out of shape in large structures like the wings.

Hexcell's firewall structure was made of composite prepreg facings and a glass-reinforced polyimid honeycomb core. Each firewall weighed a pound and a half and had better fire resistance than 15/1000 stainless steel.

WINGTIP ADD-ONS

After Voyager was built, it was determined to be somewhat tail heavy, so 3.5-foot wingtip extensions were built to solve the center of gravity problem and improve stability. Because there was adequate fuel capacity in the existing tanks, the tips were made with styrofoam core—just like the Long-EZ—covered with composite glass. The only foam in the entire structure was the wingtips and control surfaces. Had fuel been used here instead of foam, the world record takeoff might have had a different conclusion.

Total design thrust for Voyager was the lightest possible airframe. Everything was designed to be just barely strong enough (Table 15-1). For example, on the first night flight, one landing gear tube buckled, and the gear could not be retracted, but the flight continued uneventfully.

On the heavy takeoff roll, the 600x6 main tires swelled so much that they touched the bolts on the bottom of the tires. The tires were designed for 2300 pounds; takeoff weight per tire was 3400 pounds.

Everything that weighed anything was gauged against six nautical miles per pound of weight in fuel. When Jeana cut her flowing hair, it saved six more nautical miles for fuel, and Dick quipped in the briefing TV tape, "Do you know how hard it is to swim six miles?" Actually, Jeana's haircut was as much for comfort in the tight cabin as for the weight, but it made a good story.

There is a single brake on the nose wheel only; it serves as a parking brake to save weight.

The rudder cables were 1/16-inch aircraft cable. "There wasn't much crosswind component,

and with the single rudder on the left fin, roll rate was faster to the left than the right, so most patterns were made to the left for an easier rollout," Dick advised (Fig. 15-3).

In his original press roll-out on June 2, 1984, Burt commented, "No promises are now being made; it is up to the laws of aerodynamics and a lot of luck."

FIRST FLIGHTS

The story of Voyager has been a cliff-hanger since its first flight. Early on the morning of June 22, 1984, when the air was cool and calm, Voyager began taxi tests on Mojave's broad Runway 30-12. Initial runs were made with no prop on the front engine and skimming flight came soon. Then Dick pulled the ship to a halt, the front prop was installed and Voyager flew.

Mike Melvill was in the chase plane, Rutan's Grizzly, and he moved in close after takeoff to check for any glitches. He called Dick on the company radio frequency and advised, "You have a major oil leak on the front engine."

Dick promptly shut down the front powerplant and continued the 40-minute flight—but he remained in the immediate vicinity of the airport. It should be remembered that the initial flights, even the Oshkosh trip, were made with tired old engines from a Piper Apache and fixed-pitch wooden props furnished by Bruce Tifft (Fig. 15-4).

The game plan was to establish an early closed-course distance flight between Mojave and Osh-

Table 15-1. Voyager Specifications.

Dimensions			Cabin/Cockpit Dimensions		
Wing Span	110.8	ft	Cabin Length	7.5	ft
Canard Span	33.3	ft	Cockpit Length	5.6	ft
Fuselage Length	25.4	ft	Cabin Width	2.0	ft
Boom Tank Length	29.2	ft	Cockpit Width	1.8	ft
Vertical Tail Height	10.3	ft	Maximum Height	3.3	ft
			Weights		
Wing Area	363	sq ft			
Canard Area	61	sq ft	Structural Wt.	939	lbs
Total Area	424	sq ft	Empty Wt.	1858	lbs
			World Flight T/O Wt.	11326	lbs
Wing Aspect Ratio	33.8		World Flight LDG Wt.	2276	lbs
Canard Aspect Ratio	18.1		Fuel Wt. (1489 gal.)	8934	lbs

kosh, but Mother Nature put her foot down. Dick and Jeana got as far as Salina, Kansas, before the afternoon thunderstorms proved too much to handle. Both pilots were banged around badly in the tiny cockpit before landing. It was this experience as much as any single thing that dictated the formation of a full weather forecasting team for the record flights that were to come.

There was a full house of nearly a half-million people watching the popular 1984 Oshkosh EAA fly-in under ideal weather in Wisconsin when Voyager appeared overhead. The airport was closed during the regular air show so Dick and Jeana circled quietly, acting as a background for the aerobatic demonstrations. Conversations between the crew and Burt were broadcast on the public address system. After the air show was over, most of the crowd remained to watch Voyager land and taxi into the review area. Voyager's arrival was the highlight of the show. For those of us who had followed the project thus far, it began to look as though Voyager had some possibility of success (Figs. 15-5, 15-6).

PICKING UP THE TAB

During the remainder of the week, Dick and

Fig. 15-3. Voyager roll-out was attended by only a small number of press and well-wishers. Note size of Voyager from this aerial photo in comparison with the two Long-EZs and the Defiant at the far right.

Fig. 15-4. Voyager during early flight over its home base at Mojave, California. Visibility from the tiny cockpit bubble was extremely limited. Note that the strakes used on the world flight have not yet been installed. "Mothballed" jetliners in the background no longer meet U.S. noise and emission standards.

Fig. 15-5. Voyager on the ground at Oshkosh was surrounded by a huge crowd of aviation enthusiasts. It was by far the hit of the EAA fly-in.

237

Fig. 15-6. Voyager parked at Oshkosh during the week-long program. Note the contrasting size and "boxy" structure of the classic biplanes parked nearby.

Jeana embarked on what was to become their never-ending effort for the next two or three years: collecting funds to complete the project. The final world flight would take well over $700,000. Sponsor money for this monumental effort had been a problem since Voyager's inception. A number of companies, including one in Japan, were interested in underwriting the trip—but with stipulations, including dictating the route of the flight. Dick and Jeana ultimately decided to go it alone, using American know-how and what little American money might be available.

Sponsorship was readily available from the tobacco industry, but Dick Rutan is well known for his aversion to such products. "I could be a millionaire right now, driving a Cadillac rather than my beat-up old car, if I'd taken a cigarette manufacturer for my sponsor," he said. "I've never smoked and neither has Jeana. If people smoke, I don't have a lot to do with them. There are going to be no narcotics on my plane!"

During the arduous times of early test flights and endless public appearances for EAA Chapters, airport association meetings and colleges begging for funds, Dick said, "Our cars are falling apart; we need a van for utility; my Toyota station wagon has 85,000 miles, and Jeana is driving an old Buick with the same mileage. It's a maintenance nightmare!"

Financing continued at the grass roots level, time consuming and very slow. One day, Jeana showed us a file of letters that had come in, most with small checks for the project. When a 10-year-old St. Louis boy asked, "Why?," Jeana wrote back, "Dick and I have become obsessed with the challenge of record setting. The Voyager is the ultimate; but even better, it's a record that has never been done—a first! That's probably what makes it so exciting."

A Chinese pilot, born in 1906, wrote, "My flying days were over long ago, but my heart still soars toward the sky, and my eyes peer toward distant horizons. Against inertia and tradition, you are beating a new path for the advancement of science. Your pioneering spirit commands my profound admiration and respect." He enclosed a check for $100.

Another letter said, "Age prevented me from meeting you at Oshkosh this year as I would have loved to see your craft up close. I admire you young kids and the effort you're putting into your adventure. Count this old coot in; here's $50 to help you along. Good luck and God speed."

There's a VIP (Voyager Impressive People) club with members all over the free world. For a $100 donation, members received a membership number, a VIP card, a newsletter, and had their name carried in the world record flight and will have their names in the Voyager Log Books that will go with the airplane to the Smithsonian National Air and Space Museum.

Additional money was obtained from buttons, posters, patches, ball caps, T-shirts, a color photo poster, record album, a belt buckle, jewelry, and a videocassette. There's a 1:64 scale model for desk top display that sells for $200. Dick says, "Some of these items may seem a little high (in price), but please consider that you are helping the Voyager project."

NEW ENGINES, NEW AVIONICS

One of the full-time employees during the lat-

ter part of the building program was Glen Maben, who first met Dick at a lecture at the University of Buffalo, New York. His specialty was engines, and he advised us that the water-cooled rear engine was a Continental 0-240 and was a spin-off of a drone engine but without the turbocharger. Rated at 130 hp at 2750 rpm, he said that the prop governor was set for 3000 rpm on takeoff for the record flight (Fig. 15-7).

Maben noted that Voyager was the first aircraft that the rear engine had ever flown in, adding to the risk factor. There was no starter on the rear engine, and the normal starter drive actuated the water pump. The rear engine had a smaller bore with a compression ratio of 11.4:1, while the front one had a ratio of 8.5:1. The front engine, with its starter, was run a total of 72 hours. The final rear prop was reversible, while the front was full feathering.

In 1984, Ed King, company founder and then chairman of King Radio Corp., offered not only to supply the avionics, but also to modify and install the equipment if needed. The autopilot, absolutely essential to the flight because of the inherent instability of Voyager, was a highly modified KAP 150 autopilot. The system flew the aircraft by controlling roll with the aircraft's right rudder, unlike the conventional method of using an aircraft's ailerons. Pitch control was conventional from the aircraft's elevator on the forward canard wing.

Long-range navigation was with a King KNS 660 navigation management system that utilizes signals from eight omega and nine VLF ground stations. The unit continually calculated the present position of the aircraft as well as the course and distance to the navigation points in the flight plan, and it computed actual ground speed which, in turn, provided the winds aloft velocity (Fig. 15-8).

High frequency long range communications were with a King KHF 990, a unit designed specifically for helicopters. The 100-inch-long whip antenna was mounted directly behind the left boom. For short-range navigation, the King KS 165 Navcom was used.

A slaved KCS 55A compass system was included. Gyro-stabilized to prevent bouncing in

Fig. 15-7. Cut-away model of Continental rear engine. Note small water cooled chambers only around combustion chamber. This engine was adapted from a drone powerplant specifically for Voyager. It performed flawlessly on both record flights.

rough air, the heading information is both visual and used by the autopilot.

It is interesting to note that airborne radar will be carried. At the time of the rollout, designer Burt Rutan commented that he felt radar was not worth its 18 pounds of weight whereas pilot Dick wanted it for thunderstorm avoidance. Radar went aboard!

KEEPING THE COMPOSITES WARM

During one of our visits, the airplane was virtually cocooned in an envelope of plastic sheets, looking much like a small house during fumigation. The covering was not to protect the plane and its instruments from dust; it was really to direct warm air into the areas of the plane where composite work (Fig. 15-9) was being done. "It gets down to 30°F and colder at night," explained Dick, "and we can't work with composites in those temperatures."

There were no major changes in the airframe after the shakedown flights. Gear doors were add-

ed, and the engine cowlings were rebuilt out of Aramid fiber to house the new engines.

The most significant change as the program developed was a complete rerouting of the course. Originally, the plan was to fly eastward. After a year and a half of meteorological study, Voyager was routed to fly westward from Southern California and take advantage of the trade winds to the international dateline.

The planned route was to Australia, across the Indian Ocean, the tip of South Africa, and then following a narrow band of westward winds, across the Atlantic. "We can follow the trade winds right into Texas," explained Dick a year before the actual flight. "The extra plus for flying westward is that it puts us over land for the final two days of the voyage. Thus, if we're marginal on fuel or have a maintenance problem, we can continue on. Going the other way, we might have been forced to land in Hawaii."

Starting at full gross weight and flying immediately out over the Pacific Ocean eliminated the hazard of thunderstorms that can be expected across the United States during the fall months. One added factor in flying westward is that there will be less jet lag. Physicians working with the flight suggested that the pilots adopt sleep cycles out-of-phase with each other. Thus, when one expects to sleep, the other will expect to be awake. (However, this procedure was not actually used.)

The flying program for Voyager began in the summer of 1985, with local shakedown trips to prove out all the aircraft systems and procedures for the crew. At the conclusion of the last 1.5-hour test hop before the initial engines were changed, Voyager landed with enough fuel remaining on board to have broken the 12,500-mile closed-course record.

COCKPIT SIZE: JUST ENOUGH

Over a year before the record flights, we asked Dick whether or not it was feasible to enlarge the cockpit area—literally cut the cockpit in half and insert a plug—to give the pilots a little more breathing room. At that time, he replied that the structure was intricate and the design so finely tuned that such a major modification was out of the question, both because of time and money. He acknowledged that the idea had been discussed—and discarded.

After the world flight, Burt said, "If the cockpit had been significantly larger, or if the cockpit had been pressurized, the airplane would have landed in Mexico (out of fuel)."

Flight testing continued with endless details to be ironed out. Continental delivered their yet-untried engines. which were mounted in place of the run-out test powerplants. Lightweight full-feathering German propellers were installed. The King Autopilot was beefed up and an intricate program written for its computer that would compensate for Voyager's lack of inherent stability.

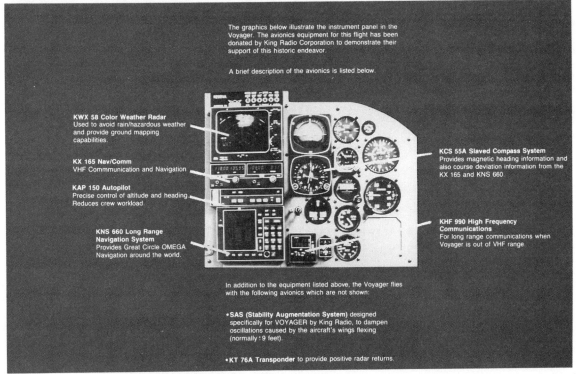

The graphics below illustrate the instrument panel in the Voyager. The avionics equipment for this flight has been donated by King Radio Corporation to demonstrate their support of this historic endeavor.

A brief description of the avionics is listed below.

KWX 58 Color Weather Radar
Used to avoid rain/hazardous weather and provide ground mapping capabilities.

KX 165 Nav/Comm
VHF Commmunication and Navigation

KAP 150 Autopilot
Precise control of altitude and heading. Reduces crew workload.

KNS 660 Long Range Navigation System
Provides Great Circle OMEGA Navigation around the world.

KCS 55A Slaved Compass System
Provides magnetic heading information and also course deviation information from the KX 165 and KNS 660.

KHF 990 High Frequency Communications
For long range communications when Voyager is out of VHF range.

In addition to the equipment listed above, the Voyager flies with the following avionics which are not shown:

• **SAS (Stability Augmentation System)** designed specifically for VOYAGER by King Radio, to dampen oscillations caused by the aircraft's wings flexing (normally : 9 feet).

• **KT 76A Transponder** to provide positive radar returns.

Fig. 15-8. King Avionics were prepared specially for the requirements of Voyager. There was no back-up of navigation, communication or autopilot equipment. It had to work the first time—and it did.

Fig. 15-9. Modification work on Voyager during cold weather in Hangar 77 at Mojave. Plywood and plastic enclosures were fitted to heat the airframe sufficiently for composite repair.

Without the autopilot—and there was no backup— the flight would have had to abort.

THE CLOSED COURSE RECORD

Next on the test schedule was an attack on the world's nonstop, nonrefuel distance record. Dick and Jeana were gunning for the 1962 straight-line record established by a B-52H in 1962 from Okinawa to Madrid, 12,532.28 miles. Here, again, things did not go according to plan. We watched the departure of this flight from Mojave on July 9, 1986 (Figs. 15-10, 15-11).

Original press announcements called for a 7 A.M. briefing with a 9 A.M. takeoff. The short brief-

ing took place on schedule as the notorious wind at Mojave puffed between 15 and 20 knots. Would the attempt go? With 3600 pounds of fuel aboard, Voyager was less susceptible to wind on the ground and was wheeled out of Hangar 77 at Mojave with its wings drooping like a molting chicken from the fuel load. Only once before had Voyager taken off with a heavier load than the 5929 pounds aboard, and that was only a few pounds heavier. Fuel load was 3000 pounds (600 gallons). Takeoff time was pushed up by an hour to keep ahead of the increasing surface winds.

When we talked with designer Burt Rutan, looking tired but clean-shaven as becomes a cor-

Fig. 15-10. As the Voyager story developed, more and more press representatives visited Hangar 77 at the Mojave Airport. Here the crew prepares for the closed-course record.

porate vice president, he said that there would be just one full-gross takeoff, and "that's when it's a go for the record." He said frankly, "I don't know if it will work."

The press corps trooped out to the side of the runway under the watchful eye of Peter Riva, a New Yorker who had accepted the full-time assignment of handling the media for Dick and Jeana. Voyager taxied out slowly and turned around at the end of Runway 30. There was a brief runup and the ship began to roll, very slowly at first and then picking up speed. Somehow we expected more noise from the engines, but remember, they put out less horsepower than most light twins.

Fig. 15-11. Closed-course records were painted on the side of Voyager to go along with names of pilots, designer, and crew chief.

In well under 3500 feet, Voyager was airborne. Volunteer engine specialist Ferg Fry said that Burt's estimate of where the plane would break ground was within a couple of feet of actual liftoff. Voyager headed out toward the Pacific Ocean, well on its way, we all thought, for a new set of records.

The course for the record was a 251.8-nautical-mile leg (503.7 nautical miles to the lap) from a point off San Luis Obispo, California, to Stewarts Point north of San Francisco. Eventually, 20 laps were flown. (On the weekend before the record attempt, Voyager had flown 12 hours, and observers reported that this flight had been the first in which everything worked.)

Things went smoothly for seven hours on the closed-course record flight before the variable speed prop motor on the rear engine developed a problem, and Dick decided to land at Vandenberg Air Force Base to check it out. Being a decorated Air Force Lieutenant Colonel probably helped eliminate any paper work, although the landing could have been termed an emergency.

Crew Chief Bruce Evans was having lunch in Bakersfield after having flown chase plane for five hours when he found out about the Vandenberg landing. He returned to Mojave, spoke with Dick to find out what was needed for repairs, and then he and Glen Maben flew the chase plane to Vandenberg with the necessary tools and parts. The repairs were quickly made, and the team decided to try it again, this time directly from Vandenberg Air Force Base.

Maben commented later, "Dick's takeoff was probably the best I have seen him do. It was nice and level, the way they are supposed to be. Bruce was with him in perfect formation."

Back at Mojave, the complete support team was in operation, not only providing meteorological, operational, and medical data to the crew but also getting their act together for the record attempt. Not enough praise can be given these highly skilled volunteers. In charge of the team was Larry Caskey, ex-Burma Hump pilot and retired Lockheed test pilot. "In the control room, we had a successful training period for the engineering flight which involved 16 full-time and five part-time work-

ers," said Caskey. (There were 45 volunteers in all.) "This was a perfect opportunity to exercise our communications and weather equipment." The support team included Len Snellman, Director of Meteorology; Don Rietzke, Communications Chief; Jack Norris, Aircraft Performance, and George Jutila, M. D., Flight Surgeon.

After riding on one intercept flight, engine technician Ferg Fey commented, "The most satisfying emotion comes when you see Voyager in flight on either the morning or evening chase intercept. After a quick inspection of the belly for traces of oil, checking to make sure the gear doors are closed and just general cleanliness of the craft, the thought comes to mind of 'Hang in there parts and people; keep performing just as you are!' "

The decision was made not to chase Voyager continuously, but to fly out and join them for an hour or two each day at dawn and again before dark. Mike and Sally and photographer Mark Greenberg took off in the Beech Sierra and, with excellent help from Los Angeles Center, were vectored to an intercept with Voyager 20 miles off the Pacific Coast at Big Sur. Some feeling of the enthusiasm generated on this flight was written in the "Canard Pusher" by Mike Melvill:

"The sun was getting low, the ocean was sparkling blue and the Big Sur coastline was beautiful," wrote Mike. "All eyes in the chase were searching the endless blue skies. Center called them at 12 o'clock and six miles. Sally was first to spot them, a thin, curved line in the sky. As we closed in on them, the air was glassy smooth and the sight of the regal shape of Voyager, as it slowly floated back toward us, was breathtaking. Mark, the photographer, was shooting film like mad as we slid into a close trail formation to give Voyager a quick look. She was absolutely clean, except for a tiny trace of oil from the aft engine breather, which is normal. Dick and Jeana were fine and sounded in good spirits.

"We parked off their wing and floated up the coast beyond San Francisco. We chatted and took photos and they took photos of us. We made the north turnpoint at dusk. As the sun sank into the ocean like a ball of fire, the Voyager looked magnificent against the skyline—the photographer was blowing his mind. As it got dark, we moved in very close for a thorough inspection of the machine, reported to the crew that they looked great and said 'good night.' We were low on fuel ourselves and headed toward the coast to refuel at Salinas.

"As we drifted away from Dick and Jeana; the silhouette of the Voyager against the night sky with the evening star and a two-day-old moon just over her—it was a sight we will never forget."

The flight itself was relatively routine until the craft returned over the coastline for a landing at Mojave. Voyager encountered turbulence over the Tehachapi Mountains that ring Mojave to the northwest. The extreme turbulence made the wings flex in a 16-foot arc, according to Dick's estimate. (Design specifications call for a maximum failure-flex of 30 feet.) The crew reported that the "flapping" of the wings was bad enough that they considered landing at Bakersfield. When finally in contact with Mojave, Dick reportedly radioed, "I'm not going to fly this mother one second more than I have to."

During his landing approach to Mojave, the chase plane advised that he was too high for a landing. Dick replied that he would not go around because he and Yeager just did not want to spend any more time in the airplane.

The closed-course record (Table 15-2) was actually flights #46 and #47 for Voyager. The remaining fuel aboard, 140 gallons, would have been sufficient to fly another 3600 miles.

ONE RECORD DOWN; ONE TO GO

Many lessons were learned, as they should have been, from this longest-yet flight. Closer monitoring of food and particularly water was dictated. After landing, Jeana nearly fainted from dehydration. After she put down 24 ounces of fluids and rested a bit, she was right back on her feet.

Special acoustical noise cancelling (ACN) headsets were developed by Bose Corp., an international audio products manufacturer from Farmingham, Massachusetts, with microphones in the earcups that monitor the sound at the user's ear. The measured sound was compared with the sound the user

Table 15-2. Voyager Flight Data.

Provisional Record Dist.			10,074.6 Nautical Miles	18,665.8 km
			11,600.9 Statute Miles	
			+263.98 Miles	102.33%
Previous Record			11,336.92 Statute Miles	18,241.1 km
Actual Distance			10,297.30 Nautical Miles	
			11,857.39 Statute Miles	(+256.49 mi)
				19,078.4 km
Time Off Vandenberg	14:52	PDT	Thursday July 10, 1986	
Start On Course	15:02	PDT	Thursday July 10, 1986	
Completion	05:15	PDT	Tuesday, July 15, 1986	110:13 hrs
Landed	06:36	PDT	Tuesday, July 15, 1986	111:44
Gross Wt. at Takeoff	5929	lbs		2691.8 kg
Gross Wt. at Landing	3234	lbs		1468.2 kg
Fuel Consumption	2695	lbs	460.68 Gal; 25.738 MPG	32.1 MPG
			1743.7 Litres; 10.93 km	(18 th lap)
				(13.65 km)
Hours Fuel Remaining			34.47 Hours	
Range at			90 knots; 3572.3	
			Statute Miles	
			1034 MPH; 5747 km	
			167 km/hr	

wants to hear; a communication signal from a radio or, if no signal is provided, silence. The difference is then processed to create out-of-phase, "anti-noise," a signal that is the mirror image of the undesired noise. This "anti-noise" is reproduced by the speaker in the earcup; there, it cancels most of the noise, leaving communications undisturbed. Dr. George Jutila said that the Bose system was "one of the significant innovations that were part of the Voyager project."

Following the closed course record, the pitch trim control system was improved to better handle turbulence. Iridium spark plugs by Champion were installed. The alternator on the rear engine was replaced. Oil discharge with metal filings was thought to be an engine component failure, but investigation showed the discharge tube was rubbing on the cowling and chafing pieces of metal into the normal oil discharge. (The fix took ten minutes.) The sleeping mattress was replaced with one that didn't have a hole that let the air leak out!

There had been questions about the durability of the composite propellers. The Rutans had said the results of a post-flight inspection "were not very encouraging."

As early as September 15th, the premature rotation problem on takeoff at maximum weight had been recognized. The wings were making the airplane lift off at too low a speed for desirable pitch control. The solution was to reduce the hydraulic extension of the front gear strut from 4 inches to 1 1/2 inch, enabling Voyager to "drive through" the speed at which it had been lifting off, thus achieving a higher speed before rotation. What was either missed or considered no problem was the negative loads on the flexible wings during this nose-down "drive through."

The aircraft had been flown twice as much as it was designed for. The control system was starting to wear. There was not enough grounding near the fuel pumps, and the composite fiber was getting hot enough to melt the epoxy and produce fumes. These fumes showed up at flight #50 after the landing at Edwards Air Force Base to fuel up for a heavyweight flight, and a fix was made.

Shortly before the world record attempt, two

"spades" (auto servo tabs) were fitted on the trailing edge of the canard's elevator, to give both more pitch authority and more feel in the controls. Later, the right spade was removed and the remaining one provided more than enough trim authority over a wider speed range.

Roncz's canard airfoil design was such that bugs were forced to strike an area where they would do the least aerodynamic damage. After the world flight, Roncz and NASA's Dr. Bruce Holmes inspected the surface and counted each bug strike!

At this point, team enthusiasm was at a peak. After completing the closed-course record flight, Dick said, "Other than the failure of a small propeller magnet, the flight was a mechanical and technical success and gave our entire program a big lift. The nights over the Pacific were darker than the inside of a cow. It was great to talk to our people on the ground and there was a warm 'I could stay here forever' relationship that developed with Voyager as the flight progressed."

Jeana said, "Things went very well. There were areas of discomfort where we need to discipline ourselves to—especially myself on eating and drinking. My impression? WE CAN DO IT. It's getting awfully close, and the taxi tests went very well. The foods are almost sorted out, and the noise suppression equipment is very effective. A few more details to take care of, and we're ready for world flight."

Dick added that there are still "a ton of things to do; 9000 + - pound world flight taxi tests, running in new radio gear, engine and instrument modifications, recalibrating the 17 fuel tanks, rehearsing cockpit procedures at Edwards. The weather maps look good and the aircraft is ready; the test person in me says 'let's do it,' so we are going at 0-dark 30' (dawn plus 30 minutes) on the first day that our Mission Director gives us a weather go, hopefully during a full moon so we can have light at night."

PROPELLER FAILURE CAUSES DELAY

Again, it didn't work out that way. On what was to have been the last long flight before the world flight, the airplane was fueled to its heaviest weight yet. On this flight, the front propeller shed one full blade at the hub in flight. The instant vibration threatened to tear the airplane apart and Dick instinctively shut everything down. He had to slow Voyager down almost to a stall to stop the front engine and its damaged prop. The subsequent landing at Edwards Air Force Base was uneventful, but any pilot who has ever shed a part of a propeller blade in flight will confirm that this is a violent, unnerving experience. However, if you're ever going to throw a prop, there are few places more desirable than within range of Edwards Air Force Base and its broad dry lake—rather than in mid-Pacific.

When the prop broke, it produced a leak in the forward fuselage tank and cracked the front motor mount. All accessories were sent back to the manufacturer for a check. Magnafluxing showed that there was a crack in the rear main bearing case and the motor mounts were beat up; however, they magnafluxed fine. There was also some damage to the rear cowl.

After a series of field repairs to get Voyager back in its home hangar for more extensive work, one of the old wooden fixed pitch props was stuck on the front engine, and the plane was ferried carefully back to Mojave. (You don't put a plane this size on a trailer!)

The decision was made to abandon the lightweight composite German props, even at a severe weight penalty. Dick called John Roncz, who was attending the NBBA (National Business Aircraft Association) meeting in Los Angeles, along with key representatives of both Continental and TRW Hartzell. Dick, Jeana, Bruce Evans, and Peter Riva met the next day and charted a super-rush course. The engines had to go back to Continental, so Dick flew them back to Mobile, Alabama, with Glen Maben aboard. Engine expert Maben stayed with the power plants.

Roncz needed to get home to his computers in South Bend and when airline schedules were poor, he hitched a ride with Dr. Sam Williams in his Citation. He had 86 hours until Monday morning to get his redesigned propeller data to Hartzell. At the start of business that week, Roncz's designs for the planform and 16 airfoil designs were transmitted by modem, and the propeller team went to work. Ten days later, Roncz went to the factory to check contours which would require a little hand filing. The blades were put into a rack with heavier blades for anodizing and the rack collapsed. Two Roncz blades were damaged, one from each propeller. Rather than salvage the blades, Hartzell made new ones that were ready when Dick showed up on Saturday to fly them to Continental (Fig. 15-12).

The old props and governors weighed only 26 pounds; the new ones were 75 pounds, including a heavy front spinner that came from a Malibu—or something. The rear prop had a heavy gyrocopter caliper (developed by Ken Brock, who also made the landing gears) that was used as a hydraulic brake to stop propeller rotation in case the rear engine had to be shut down.

The new heavier props could be run at lower rpms with high manifold pressures without vibration. In all, the engineers calculated that the props were 3 percent more efficient in cruise, but not as efficient for acceleration, so Roncz redesigned the trailing edges of the blades, and minor reprofiling was done at Mojave.

The front prop had been optimized for climb and then retuned for efficiency at low power. Roncz called this exercise "the most frustrating of my life."

Everything at Mission Control had come to a halt. Most volunteers returned to their homes but remained "on call" pending overhaul. The "window" for suitable weather was rapidly closing, and the future of the world flight looked grim for that year.

When the engines returned with the new metal props, they were reinstalled in short order and flight testing followed.

OXYGEN AND MEDICINE ABOARD

The oxygen system carried on the world flight was a 40-pound Tri-Tech DOC (demand oxygen control) system that produced three and a half days of available oxygen instead of one day's supply at the same weight. The DOC system dispenses oxygen on inhalation only, not as a constant flow. The

Fig. 15-12. Voyager in front of its hangar following the final heavy-weight flight. Irene Rutan is shown by the drooping right wingtip where some fuel is leaking from the vent. Nose strut has been depressed.

system included an Apena device—a safety alarm that would sound if one of the pilots wasn't breathing.

Although strong emergency drugs were carried, including pain medication, antibiotics, and medication for diarrhea and motion sickness, the only medication used was baby aspirin to help prevent blood clotting. Jeana had a head cold on take-off and used a nasal decongestant spray for the first few days of the flight.

Jeana's fainting spell in front of cameras following the closed course record proved to be a mixed blessing. It convinced all involved that a full allowance of liquid be taken regularly. Jeana had

a minimum of 1.6 liters of water daily; Dick had 2.22 liters, and each was allowed an extra liter of fruit juice. Dr. George Jutila said, "One of my biggest hurdles was to convince Dick of what I thought was a necessary fluid intake. To make certain they were drinking enough fluids, a protometer was on board so that the crew could test their urine."

The flight plan called for Jeana to be responsible for food and water intake for both pilots. The daily water allowance was stowed in plastic bags, and the pilots made sure to drink all of the prescribed amount daily. Food included Eureka foil packs, Shaklee mixes and crackers, vitamin pills, Life Savers, and chewing gum. What turned out to

248

be the most appetizing was a mixture of peanut butter and honey that Jeana had prepared to put on crackers. Actually, the crew ate only about 10 percent of the food they carried.

So, once again it was a race against the weather. The Command Post team reassembled as final heavyweight flights were made. Finally, on flight #66, Voyager was ferried the dozen miles from Mojave to Edwards Air Force Base and readied for a test at near world circling weight—8600 pounds on 83/ of the maximum weight. Liftoff was at 82 knots, and Dick Rutan noted by radio one of his very few statements that later proved to be erroneous. He said, ''Handles perfectly—heavier will be no problem.''

Later that day, Voyager returned to Mojave to make last minute preparations for the maximum effort. One hundred pounds of food and water were to be loaded, and the ship would be fueled again at Edwards the evening before takeoff (Figs. 15-13, 15-14).

We visited Mojave on this particular afternoon, December 4th. When we taxied up the ramp at Mojave, Voyager was parked in front of Hangar 77. Fuel was siphoning slightly from the right vent mounted atop the winglet as a crew of volunteers prepared to push the aircraft into its hangar. On the ground, with near full fuel, the wingtips droop to within 6 inches of the ground, and the fuel vent is higher than the center of the cabin. However, the

Fig. 15-13. Ground support personnel prepare to push Voyager back into the hangar after its last heavyweight flight. Dr. George Rutan, with video camera, records the event.

Fig. 15-14. Voyager passes the 7000-foot mark on the Edwards Air Force Base runway during its takeoff. The aircraft is being held nose down and both wingtips are almost touching the runway. As more speed was built up, the tips did touch just before lift-off.

wings were expected to flex upward as soon as any air loads existed and this venting would cease. (The wings didn't flex upward when the nose was held down.)

Only one more flight was planned; the 10-minute hop from Mojave to Edwards Air Force Base, before the aircraft was fully fueled and the record circumnavigation attempt begun. The engines were bore-scoped and an oil analysis run prior to this short flight.

ON THE GO

So it was that Voyager was ferried back to Ed-

wards on December 13th, and the fueling process began at about 2 P.M.. The filler necks on the 16 auxiliary tanks have only 1/8th-inch pipe plugs for filling and fuel could be pumped in at only ten pounds per minute. The main feed tank had a regular 2-inch filler cap, but it took until 4 A.M. to finally put the tanks at the desired level. The 42-gallon main feed tank was the only one with a fuel gauge, a plastic tube with a styrofoam ball. Six of the wing tanks were not filled to capacity to allow for fuel compression during wing bending. The aft boom tank had only 80 pounds of fuel loaded because of the difference in weight of the final larger front engine and prop. With all tanks full, there would have been an aft-C.G. problem and pitch control was marginal anyhow. Takeoff weight was 9400 pounds, while earlier calculations called for a total of 11,326 pounds.

There was one oil tank in the aft engine compartment with 17 quarts aboard. The rear engine started with 9 quarts and the front had 6 quarts. Oil was pumped to either engine with a hand pump, and the oil reserve tank was empty at the conclusion of the flight.

The night was cold and, unusual in the high desert, there was enough moisture to cause frost. The Voyager's wings had been covered with sheets to keep the frost off, but it reformed as fast as the ground crews wiped it off once the pilots were aboard. The scheduled takeoff of "0-dark 30" did not hold up because of this. It would have been a simple matter to delay the takeoff and let the morning sun melt the frost, but warmer air would increase takeoff roll as well as the chance of turbulence. The Air Force brought in heaters and defrosted the airframe—twice; but by the time Voyager had reached the takeoff point, it was frosted up again.

The flight plan was filed, Edwards AFB to Edwards AFB, estimated time enroute, 11.8 days!

One of the wing walkers at Edwards was actor Cliff Robertson who plugged the fuel vent with his finger to keep fuel from exiting.

With the engines running and their temperatures climbing rapidly, Dick finally said tersely, "Give it a lick and a promise and let's go." Thus started what may well have been the longest takeoff roll in history. As the takeoff roll began, Burt and Mike Melvill followed closely behind with the Duchess. Acceleration was a little slower than had been calculated. There were three radio-equipped check points down the runway, with the final check point, at 7500 feet where the go-no-go speed had been calculated at 82 knots.

We were far to the side of the runway, at the 7000-foot point, watching Voyager as she inched forward, those two small engines tweeked up to 3000 rpm on 2700 rpm designs. As the ship passed us, the wingtips were brushing the runway (Fig. 15-15) and the nose was down, way down!

Over the radio, and patched to the public address system, we could hear Burt say, "Get it up, damnit; get the nose up." It was well past the 10,000-foot mark before the nose did come up. Wingtip damage from dragging on the runway had occurred in the last 1000 feet before takeoff. Immediately after breaking ground, Dick punched his microphone and we heard him comment, "I guess I blew it."

Television viewers the world over saw the chilling takeoff live or on later news broadcasts. Voyager was front-page news for each of the nine succeeding days.

Once free of the runway, acceleration was good and rate of climb much, much better than had been expected. Later, Dick commented that he felt he could have taken off with an extra 800 or 1000 pounds of fuel.

As Voyager circled slowly over the huge dry lake, gaining altitude, Dick and Mike pulled in close with the Duchess to ascertain the damage. It was only then that Dick heard over the radio that in fact there had been wingtip damage.

As Dick recalled it, his brother radioed, "I don't want to concern you or anything—(which was the gross understatement of the year)—but you've scraped the wings and the integrity of the winglets is in question." It was then that Dick could see the damaged winglets (Fig. 15-15) as Voyager continued to climb above "nosebleed altitude" (the height at which the crew could successfully bail out).

Dick began yawing the heavily laden plane from side to side and watched as the right winglet came off. He was hoping that the tips did not cause the top skin to peel off the wing inboard far enough to rupture a fuel tank. The wing structure remained intact, and the left winglet parted company all on its own with the first little bit of turbulence.

Now was the problem of making certain that the fuel vents that vented the three outboard fuel tanks were not damaged and would vent properly. One of the many fortunate things on the flight showed up when the structure remained intact. The last 4 feet of each wing had been built like the VariEze with carbon fiber/epoxy skin over blue

Fig. 15-15. Voyager circles back over Edwards Air Force Base as Burt Rutan and Mike Melvill pull in with the Beech Duchess to assess damage. Right winglet has broken off and the left one still remains with the aircraft. It came off a few minutes later.

foam. The solid core kept the slipstream from getting into the inboard area where fuel was carried. The position lights were gone, but aside from some carbon fiber skin trailing behind, everything seemed to be functioning properly.

Few who watched the takeoff would have been particularly surprised if Voyager had flown offshore into calm air, circled to burn off fuel and returned to Edwards for a complete check and repair job. However, that solution would have been to disavow the driving, almost fanatic urge to succeed that the entire team displayed, particularly Dick with his Air Force combat training. This was a different kind of a war but just as hazardous as Viet Nam. And don't underestimate Jeana, who did everything that had to be done for the next nine days: flying, making in-flight repairs, monitoring food and water intake.

The first day of Voyager's flight was perhaps the calmest of the entire adventure. Except for worry about wingtip damage and proper fuel management, Voyager proceeded on schedule. This gave the Command Post team the opportunity to clear the decks and get smoothly running. The communications team of 12 worked eight-hour shifts. Weak radio signals plagued the entire mission. Dick Blosser, radio communications coordinator, said that only about 5 percent of the transmissions were made available to the public, and these were the clearest and strongest signals. He said that during half of the flight, "communications were so poor that the average individual couldn't understand them." When Mission Control asked Dick about the winds, he misunderstood "wind" for "Jeana" and replied "Jeana's awake and doing fine." Many times the communications team had to patch through a ground controller who was geographically located where he could reach Voyager.

From Hawaii westward, emphasis on our report shifts back to Mission Control and the weather team which, in the final analysis, made the key difference between success and a very unhappy ending.

THE METEOROLOGIST DETAILS THE PROBLEMS

Navigational and weather data was transmitted at least every six hours, usually more frequently. We had the opportunity to interview Len Snellman, Chief Meteorologist and retired Chief of the National Weather Service, Western Region, during the final day of the record flight. His input gives a clear insight into how the world flight actually progressed, undoctored by the needs of the daily news reporter to come up with a headline every day for nine days. It is reprinted from Private Pilot Magazine.

The mystique of Voyager was all around us as we found a relatively quiet corner on the balcony of the hangar. Minutes earlier, a full-blown press conference had jammed the hangar floor as key Voyager team members were on camera for a hungry world to share the last day of the Voyager flight. Our discussion, however, was on the weather and its problems.

"Routing was originally planned to pass through the intertropical convergence across Australia and then the Indian Ocean," Snellman explained. "There was real concern, as the westerly jet stream went so far north that the sea temperatures in the equator were abnormally high and formed organized storms that a few weeks before had 175-knot winds. During the flight, they were only up to 75 knots."

The flight path was moved farther north, which required a flight across the African continent. Snellman said that the weather across Africa was "a sea of thunderstorms. However, Voyager was so slow that you couldn't go through at night because it would take 18 hours to get across. So it happened that we hit Africa at dawn so that Dick and Jeana got bounced around; but by watching the satellite pictures, we were able to keep them in the best of the worst. They still had a rough ride."

After landing, Dick noted, "I never want to see Africa again."

Before we went into more meteorological detail, Snellman pointed out that it was a team effort all the way along. The staff had two "watch chiefs," for lack of a better title. They were Rich Waggoner, NWS Headquarters, Washington, DC, and Larry Burch, FAA, Palmdale, California. Working on the team were Frank Snigielski, retired NWS; Peter

Mueller, Nuclear Support Office, Las Vegas, Nevada; Walt Rogers, Burch's boss from Palmdale FSS who specialized in programming satellite photos; Rick Barrett of the Palmdale FSS; and Mary Waggoner, a graduate meteorologist. Mrs. Lynn Snellman and the flight surgeon's wife, Sylvia Jutila, rounded out the 24-hour-a-day meteorological staff.

"One of the high points of this flight was that Dick told me, 'This is not a flight from A to B. You (and your crew) tell me where to fly and I'll fly it.' And he followed that to a T," advised Snellman. "Early in the flight, west of Hawaii, we kept him in the strong tradewinds headed right for Typhoon Marge. Typhoon Marge was a meteorological hazard that we turned into an asset by having him fly just as close to Marge as he could and right down the good weather slot with tailwinds up to 40 knots. We just shot the curl and edged the bullet. The flight path was within 350 miles of the center of

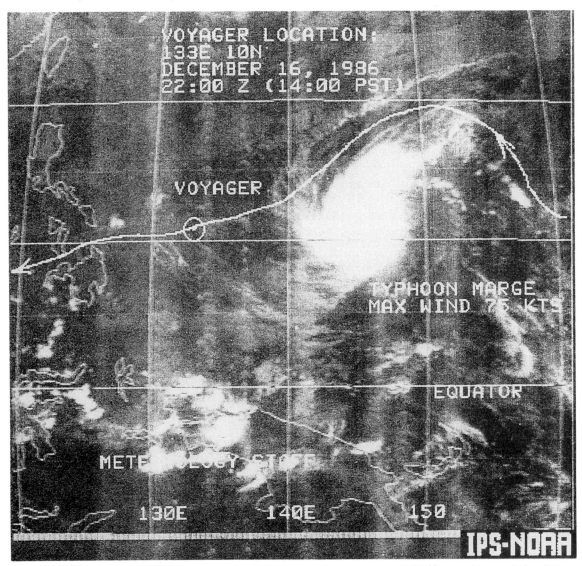

Fig. 15-16. Typhoon Marge as it showed up on the IPS-NOAA weather equipment in the Voyager hangar during flight.

the tropical storm. I think that the satellite picture is absolutely miraculous (Fig. 15-16).

"When I first came down here to work on the project, I said, 'Gee, I hope we have some real good hurricanes in the Pacific.' This was in September, of course. Fortunately, in some of the simulations before the actual flight, there were hurricanes and the people sort of questioned me. We headed the airplane right at these storms with the understanding between Dick and me that we would get as close to the hurricane as we could and get the best winds. During the actual flight, out in the Pacific it turned out that they had a hurricane—an antityphoon with feeder bands where it is very, very rough. It won't tear an airplane to pieces, but it is rough.

"That was miraculous. The very fortunate thing was that if you were to place a typhoon in the most advantageous place, that's where Marge was. There was a great element of luck, but it was Dick's skill and his faith in us as a result of the simulations that we turned a potential hazard into an asset. That's one of the reasons they're coming home early.

"Forecasting that typhoon was absolutely critical," continued Snellman. "If we missed that, we would have had to take them tremendously out of the way. At that stage of the flight, there was considerable concern about how much fuel was going to be available because of the wingtip accident. The forecasting wouldn't have been possible without the I.P.S. satellite recording equipment for animation that Clarence Boyce donated. Also the Siscorps Organization made available weather maps and data."

Snellman said that the team used a Hoverebar geostropic wind technique where you don't take friction into account. It was developed to forecast lakefront breezes in the Chicago area many years ago.

Snellman had been living with Voyager for nearly nine months before the successful record. "We made dry runs in August and early September. What was learned from these simulations cut the estimated time of the flight from 10 to 11 days down to 10 or less," said Snellman. "The pilots watched very closely. The meteorology crew radioed a message to the pilots every six hours outlining the expected weather for the next 24 hours. This would indicate where the major systems were and advise the crew which way to deviate. During the simulations, we developed a mutual understanding between Dick and Jeana and the meteorology team. Dick's faith in us made it very rewarding, and I think that also made us do a really better job.

"I would spend several hours taking current weather maps, and I would make a flight path, and we even filled out some of these messages just for practice—and that's how we developed procedures. Then I would indicate why we were flying the way we were and show Dick and Jeana the weather maps and the satellite pictures. I remember one simulated case very specifically where we had the flight path planned over Texas. Twenty-four hours in advance, I said, 'No way. You're going to reroute over Mexico—you can't possibly fight that weather.' They were kind of reticent about that because there are a lot of mountains in Mexico and Dick wanted to come over Texas. The next day, the weather over Texas was impassable while the weather over Mexico was really excellent with tailwinds; there would be some turbulence but nothing really bad and the Texas route was impossible.

"We did a number of these simulations. Dick was adamant about how many simulations missions we were going to do. The success of the weather support was not by accident. It's not a case of a pilot coming in and flying around the world; it's a case of darned good hard work in preparation spearheaded by Dick."

Low point of the flight, from the weatherman's standpoint, was over the central Atlantic. "After fighting the turbulence across Africa for almost 24 hours, they got out over the Atlantic, and we thought the worst was behind us. But it turned out that one line of thunderstorms developed very rapidly. There was no way we could have him fly around that. It was sort of like arms that developed with Voyager right in the middle, and he tried to go through that. The deviations were so great that the performance people ran into the trailer and said, 'Hey, he's getting headwinds.' Actually, he was still getting 20-knot tradewinds but his forward progress was essentially nil because of the major deviations he had to make. In test pilot language he told his brother over the radio, 'I almost lost it.' Dick's comment after he got out of that was, 'I'd rather turn around and fly over Africa again.'

"This was just a line of thunderstorms. We had him flying very close to the tropical convergence zone. In our six-hour message, we told him about the major weather systems and which way to deviate. There were a lot of cirrus, and we had him fly under them. That air was so unstable, even at night and that was the worst time. I think that the radiation of the tops of those cirrus caused a little convection way up that developed little snow flakes that came down and seeded the lower clouds to the point where very quickly this line of thunderstorms developed. Also, we missed a satellite photo at that time. We didn't see what was developing. It was just a very small scale feature and you'd never find it on the weather map."

There were rough times during the flight when Snellman would talk with Dick by radio. "I think that Dick wanted someone to hold his hand," said the weatherman. "I was reassuring to him and could honestly tell him when the worst was about over. The communicators said that they could notice a difference in Dick's voice after we'd talked.

"We sent them very close to the Brazilian coastline where there were 35-knot tailwinds. We had expected that."

Snellman said that weather over the Caribbean was unexpectedly good. The National Hurricane Center in Miami said that this was the quietest they had seen the Caribbean in December—ever! "We still had to go through the intertropical convergence line," Snellman continued, "and Voyager got bumped around; but it was not dangerous turbulence, just darned fatiguing. Dick wanted very badly to fly over Texas so he could get back over the U. S. as fast as possible, but we told him two days in advance that this was absolutely impossible because of a winter cold front, icing, and extremely dangerous headwinds. So, we sent him through Costa Rica. The only problem there was that there were small tropical disturbances where the weather was usually avoided, but the airplane was pretty light by now."

As the flight was actually proceeding up the west coast of Mexico, Snellman said, "The problem right now is turbulence. We want him to fly low and diminish headwinds. But that's where the turbulence is, and we can't stand any more of this. There were 20-knot headwinds as they came into the Pacific at Costa Rica. Headwinds were 16 to 20 knots farther north, but that's one of the hazards of December weather."

Timing for the December flight was at the very edge of the weather envelope. Snellman said, "The best weather was going to be shut off in September, and we talked about the fact that we'd have to have a lot of luck if we weren't going to make it by the end of December. The local (Southern California) weather would be adverse for takeoff and landing, and you'd have had to knock it off until June."

Prior to Snellman's forecasting group, for Voyager's test flights they would either send a plane up ahead (frequently volunteer Lee Herron in his VariEze) to see if the weather was okay or just get up in the morning and take a look. "On their flight to Oshkosh in 1985, they nearly lost it (Voyager) because of weather. This year they had better weather support," Snellman commented.

"Meteorology can be a great help to pilots," the weatherman advised. "On more than one occasion, our meteorology crew could tell them (Dick and Jeana) that the weather around Mojave would not be acceptable, and they would cancel the test flight right then."

When Voyager and the crew were presented to the international media at the conclusion of their globe-circling flight, Snellman was one of the several dozen beaming volunteers who were present. It was a magnificent team effort.

JUST A FEW HIGHLIGHTS

In a flight so loaded with highlights, we'll touch on only a few. A last minute government approval was given to use the UHF satellite network, but the aircraft was down for so long while the new propellers were installed that a proper antenna had not been installed. To operate the satellite communications, Jeana had to crouch in the "doghouse," aiming the handheld antenna like an old ADF loop. The UHF system proved less than satisfactory, however, because it was a fixed-power-type in which communications would drop out when it was shared by too many users.

What had to be the most frustrating experience for support crews during the world flight was the experience of Bruce Evans, Glen Maben, and Mark Greenberg in Thailand on the third day of the flight. The trio had boarded a Singapore Airlines 747 and were able to talk with Voyager as they passed them 100 miles to the north enroute to Taipei. From Singapore, the trio were met by far-east pilot Bill Ernst, as arranged for in advance by Beechcraft. (He was flying a Piper Navajo.)

A landing was planned for Cota Baru in Malaysia, but the rain and low ceilings forced the group to continue to Hat Yai in Thailand. Because of poor local communications and the change of destination, none of the Thai officials expected them—nor knew what to do with them—so they did nothing.

"It was a weird situation," said Maben. "After flying 24 hours on an airliner, we were in a totally different world, totally. It turned out that there were no people who were in authority. They didn't have the rubber stamps or anything. The big problem was, we had entered the country without visas. They took our passports but allowed the pilot to keep his. We took our little *baak* bus back to the airport and, about 45 minutes later, Dick and Jeana flew over.

"Finally, the local control tower operator pitched in and was able to get to Voyager on the local VHF tower frequency.

"We were pretty disappointed that we didn't get to fly (and make the intercept). We had wired some aircraft landing lights into the electrical system on the Navajo so, if we did get up, we could shine them on the plane and Mark could get good video.

"We could see his strobe lights and actually hear him when he got about two miles away."

Two days later, Doug Shane had better luck. He had gone around the world the other way with a stop in London before arriving in Nairobi. Here he was met by Tim Sarginson with a Beech Baron to use for the rendezvous. Using a base-station HF radio, whose frequency had been relayed to Voyager the day before, Doug was able to talk with Dick, and the meeting point was set for over the Samburu South Buffalo Springs located on a game reserve some 150 miles northeast of Nairobi.

The Baron flew to this isolated strip and refueled from Jerry cans carried in the nose. After takeoff, they were able to find Voyager visually (no radar in the area) in about ten minutes. As Doug described it, "Everyone in the cabin was yelling, cheering, crying . . . it was wonderful. Then I took the helm and started to ease into position and . . . stall warning . . . nose drop . . . left wing drop . . . cameras on the ceiling . . . oh dear! Well, there was my embarrassment for the rest of my life."

Doug recovered from the spin cleanly; Dick speeded up Voyager slightly, and the two planes closed in for a visual inspection. Nothing seemed "leaky" so climb maneuvers were made to verify the gross weight and thus the fuel remaining. The two airplanes began to climb together to clear a heavy line of thunderstorms ahead. At 20,000 feet, the Baron couldn't climb anymore. Dick and Jeana were on their limited supply of oxygen with the engines running flat out. They finally broke out over Lake Victoria.

Dick celebrated his 49th birthday during the flight. Somewhere over the Indian Ocean, Voyager broke the 1962 nonstop, nonrefuel record set by then Major Clyde P. Evely and his Air Force crew in a specially-prepared B-52H. Evely, retired and living in Cary, North Carolina, telephoned his congratulations to Mojave, saying that records were made to be broken and that he'd be saying a few Baptist prayers for them. He told a local newspaper that "People don't believe me—it was the easiest flight I had every flown. Unlike the Voyager, flying around in turbulence and storms, we just flew above everything. Anybody who can stay in that airplane for 11 days (this was at the midpoint of the flight) has earned my respect. I'm elated for them."

HOW MUCH FUEL REMAINS?

During the world flight, much media headline

copy was derived from the possibility that Voyager might be using substantially more fuel than was forecast. The 17-tank fuel system was designed to feed either engine from any tank. When the problem was discovered, Bruce Evans was in Singapore and Mike Melvill, who helped build the fuel system was in Mission Control. The fuel from the fuel-injected, water-cooled engine in the rear had a vapor return line installed from the fuel injector. Rather than going back to the feed tank and risk a leak, this line went into the aluminum tube that went from the pump up the firewall and over the top. When Dick was running at full throttle, there was very little vapor to return, but at reduced power using perhaps 2 1/2 gph, 6 to 7 gallons were coming back down the vapor return line. Instead of going into the feed tank, it went downhill through the fuel counter and back into whichever tank happened to be in use. The fuel counter is a photoelectric cell looking at a turbine wheel and it counted up, not down. It didn't subtract fuel, it added it.

Before the fuel counter dilemma was solved, Dick had radioed, "This sucker is never going to make it." He called Mike and said, "If you don't tell me where the hell that fuel is or tell me that I've got fuel, I'm landing in Africa, and that's going to be horribly embarrassing. How do you recover an airplane from Africa? If you can recover it. I'm going to land and burn it! I mean, I want this nightmare over with." But the problem was finally resolved.

The newly designed liquid-cooled rear engine had been run at the highest possible manifold pressure and the lowest rpm that would maintain altitude all the way around the world. To conserve fuel, the mixture was set at 125 degrees on the lean side of peak with the fuel specific at about .375.

Then there were "little things," though they didn't seem that way at the time—like running low on oil or having the rear engine quit at night or a fuel pump that sheared a coupling shaft. The oil transfer pump was actually a two-way medical pump mounted on the back wall of the sleeping compartment with a line extending to the kidney-shaped oil tank on the rear engine. Procedure was to draw oil out of the tank until the pump was suck-ing air, then reverse it, put back the oil that had been taken out plus 1 quart. This pump was used on schedule, except for the turbulent flight over Africa when it was just plain forgotten. The engine warning light came on and 2 quarts were hastily pumped into the rear engine. The low oil pressure and high temperature persisted for several minutes when the oil aerated (frothed) and finally cured itself, but not before communication with Mojave had taken place and new headlines cropped up in that day's media coverage.

There was a heated discussion between Dick and Mission Control when the right side fuel pump failed over Costa Rica. Jack Norris and his aircraft performance crew went into a hasty huddle with Burt, and it was concluded the best procedure was for Dick to transfer as much fuel as possible from the left side to the feeder tank with its operating fuel pump, then rearrange the plumbing to draw from the right side.

Dick objected strongly, feeling that fuel might be spilled inside the tiny cockpit. The pilot wanted to trust the remaining engine-driven pump to draw fuel from the remaining tanks far out on the wing, and the staff on the ground felt that the small engine-driven pump wouldn't last long under that sort of pressure. This late in the flight, everybody was tired and fuses were short. Finally, one of the unidentified ground crewmen, and from what we've seen over the years, it sounded like Melvill, picked up the mike and said where Dick could hear it, "Just wait, 49 hours after he lands, we're gonna kill him!" (One of the singular requirements to claim a world's record is that the pilot remain alive for 48 hours after landing.) This eased the tension and the flight crew finally replumbed the system.

Any of these failures could have failed the mission, but it seemed at long last that "Murphy" had taken a week off. Murphy, you may remember, is the author of Murphy's Law which states, "If anything can go wrong, it will; and it will take place at the most inopportune time and place."

BACK HOME AGAIN

The cliff hanger that was Voyager had a regular Cinderella ending. It was bitter cold before dawn just one day before Christmas, 1986, when Voyager approached Edwards Air Force Base. A crowd of 15,000 to 20,000 braved the weather to watch. The public address system finally picked up Voyager shortly after the sun crawled its way past a bank of clouds. Eventually, the flying trimaran came into view, escorted by a covey of camera planes and Voyager volunteers who were there to make sure that flying spectators or media aircraft not get too close to the aircraft.

Dick and Jeana chatted with the crowd over the VHF radio as they circled leisurely over the dry lake at Edwards. If Dick had known that only 18.3 gallons of fuel would be found in all the 17 tanks, he might have landed sooner. But eventually, Jeana cranked down the landing gear, and Mike Melvill

pulled into formation just like they did at Oshkosh and counted down the altitude until Voyager touched down on the dry lake (Figs. 15-17, 15-18).

The important statistics: 9 days, 3 minutes, 44 seconds; 25,012 miles at 115.8 mph; 18.3 or 1.8 percent of total fuel remaining. (See Table 15-2.)

Mobil Oil, which supplied both fuel and a new type of synthetic motor oil, was quick to point out that the company had also supplied the oil for Lindbergh's Paris flight in 1927, nearly 60 years earlier.

In presenting the Presidential Citizens Medals, President Reagan called the crew "Heroes exemplifying the voluntarism, the enterprise, the imagination, and just plain courage that make this country great (Fig. 15-19)."

After the record flight, Voyager was ferried

Fig. 15-17. Voyager touches down on the famed Edwards dry lake, landing pad for the Space Shuttle, 9 days, 3 minutes and 44 seconds after its lift off from the nearby runway.

Fig. 15-18. Voyager pulls up in front of the crowd as Air Force ambulances arrive to take the crew in for physical examinations.

Fig. 15-19. President Reagan presents medals to the flight crew and the designer.

back to Mojave as a photo flight with Clay Lacy's Jet Ranger and Lear 24 took just two minutes short of three hours to shoot footage for a documentary film. Then Voyager landed for the last time at Mojave. The airport's fire trucks laid up an arch of streams of water as Voyager taxied underneath. It was the end of Flight 69, the same as the N number on the tail.

Voyager proved a popular attraction in its hangar. Visitors, 2,000 a week or more, came in private cars, private planes, tour busses, and school busses to walk through the hangar, watch a one-hour video and, if they wished, purchase souvenirs. The average Sunday fly-in count of private planes rose from 50 to as high as 324. There was no charge for admission. When Dick or Jeana or Burt were around, they would autograph 16 × 120 lazar-print reproductions of one of Doug Shane's photographs of Voyager in flight. The prints sold for $10 and are worth every penny of it (Fig. 15-20). Dick said that during one electronics show where he and Jeana were speakers, they personally autographed 2,200 of these prints in a 4 1/2-hour

period. No wonder that Lee Herron quipped to Dick as he walked by, "The price of fame is a sore wrist."

"If we sell and sign enough of these, and if we give enough illustrated lectures, we may be able to pay off the $300,000 that we're still in debt for the flight," Dick advised.

Total cost of the Voyager project is next to impossible to figure. Originally, Dick estimated $400,000, then upped it to $700,000 out-of-pocket, and probably $1 million would be a very lowball guess; so much effort was volunteer and so many items were donated, particularly late in the game when some chance of success was foreseen.

The complete Voyager story by Dick and Jeana, along with writer Phil Patton, has been published by Knopf Publishing Co. We recommend it for your aviation library, because it will be devoted solely to the Voyager effort and royalties from this book will help defray some of the expenses of the trip. Titled simply *Voyager,* it can be obtained through Voyager Aircraft, Inc., Hangar 77, Airport, Mojave, CA 93501, on or after September, 1987.

Fig. 15-20. Voyager in its hangar at Mojave before delivery to the Smithsonian Institute in Washington, D.C. In the left background is a VariViggen, Burt's first homebuilt design.

At the many illustrated lectures throughout the country where Dick and Jeana show slides and tapes of Voyager and its record flights, it was not uncommon for Dick to start the presentation by telling the group that he would answer the most commonly asked questions before he got started with the program.

"No, I wouldn't fly that plane around the world again."

"We put it in small plastic bags and dumped it overboard."

"Before the flight the question was, 'Is Jeana related to Chuck Yeager?' Since the successful conclusion of the flight, everyone asks it the other way around."

IT FLIES, BUT MARGINALLY

Voyager was not a good-flying airplane. In design, Burt sacrificed everything to save weight and drag. "If the Voyager was easy to fly, Burt didn't do his job right," explained Dick. These marginal handling characteristics were not discussed in any great detail before the record flights, but Dick did tell us after the record, "It's a dangerous airplane. It will never fly again! It's a terrible flying airplane (with) very poor ailerons, extremely stiff; very heavy stick forces and very ineffectual control.

There's a two-per-second pitching motion that the autopilot had to fight the whole time."

To reinforce his point, Dick said, "I hate flying it. It's the only airplane I've ever been in that scared me to death. (I felt) the airplane is going to kill me."

Voyager is scheduled to go to the Paris Air Show in a military C-5. The tail booms will be disconnected for the flight. After this final cargo flight, the airplane will be delivered to the Smithsonian Air and Space Museum in Washington, DC, to join the original Wright Flyer and Lindbergh's *Spirit of St. Louis* on permanent display. Not bad at all, for the world's biggest homebuilt!

When this book on Burt Rutan was started, little did the authors know that it would point down the road to such a spectacular conclusion. Voyager was a magnificent grassroots effort that showed how dedicated individuals with limited resources could accomplish what massive amounts of government money might not have been able to do.

But to get back to our title, *The Complete Guide to Rutan Aircraft,* don't you ever believe it! Burt Rutan, at 44 years old, is certainly no has-been. If our history indicates anything, we'll see a great deal more innovative Rutan designs in the not-too-distant future.

Index